M·I·S·T·R·E·S·S O·F U·D·O·L·P·H·O

Mistress of Udolpho

T·H·E L·I·F·E O·F
A·N·N R·A·D·C·L·I·F·F·E

———— • ————

RICTOR NORTON

Leicester University Press
London and New York

Leicester University Press
A *Cassell imprint*
Wellington House, 125 Strand, London WC2R 0BB

370 Lexington Avenue, New York, NY 10017–6550

First published 1999

British Library Cataloguing-in-Publication Data

A catalogue record for this book is available from the British Library.

ISBN   0-7185-0201-9 (hardback)
              0-7185-0202-7 (paperback)

Library of Congress Cataloging-in-Publication Data

Norton, Rictor, 1945–
    Mistress of Udolpho : the life of Ann Radcliffe / Rictor Norton.
       p.   cm.
    Includes bibliographical references and index.
    ISBN   0-7185-0201-9. — ISBN   0–7185–0202–7 (pbk.)
       1. Radcliffe, Ann Ward, 1764–1823—Biography. 2. Women novelists, English—
    18th century—Biography. 3. Gothic revival (Literature)—Great Britain.
    4. Horror tales—Authorship. I. Title.
    PR5203.N67 1998
    823'.6—dc21   98–8412
    [b]   CIP

Designed and typeset by Ben Cracknell Studios

Printed and bound in Great Britain by Biddles Ltd, Guildford and King's Lynn

Contents

List of Illustrations

1 Holborn Hill, London. Ann Radcliffe was born in No. 19 and christened in St Andrew's Church.
2 Monument to Thomas Bentley in St Nicholas Church, Chiswick.
3 Carisbrooke Castle, Isle of Wight, a possible model for the Castle of Udolpho.
4 Haddon Hall, Derbyshire, the legendary inspiration for Château-le-Blanc in *The Mysteries of Udolpho*.
5 Adeline flees from a mysterious figure in the ruined cloister. Woodcut from Radcliffe's *The Romance of the Forest*.
6 Sister Olivia is recognized by the old servant Beatrice and reveals herself as Ellena's mother. Woodcut from Radcliffe's *The Italian*.
7 Contract for *The Mysteries of Udolpho*, dated 11 March 1794.
8 Frontispiece to Anne Ker's *Adeline St Julian; or, The Midnight Hour* (1800), an example of 'the Radcliffe school'.
9 Netley Abbey, Hampshire, from John Hassell's *Tour of the Isle of Wight* (1790).
10 Mr and Mrs Radcliffe enter their names in the Knole Visitors' Book, 14 September 1807, for the pleasure of the Duke of Dorset.
11 Ann Radcliffe's last entries in her Commonplace Book, twelve weeks before her death.

Preface

In 1883 Christina Rossetti abandoned her efforts at a biography of Ann
Radcliffe because the material was too meagre to make such a project
feasible. Subsequent biographers have been frightened off by Rossetti's
estimation that the material was insufficient for the purpose, and for the past
fifty years the field has been dominated by interpretation rather than
scholarship. One result has been that many of the rumours about Ann
Radcliffe's madness and death have simply been repeated (and rejected)
without being traced to their sources and placed in context. The 'Tour
through England', in which Mrs Radcliffe is said to have been confined in a
madhouse in Derbyshire, and 'an Ode to Terror published by a clergyman
in 1810', which declared that she died in 'the horrors' – both items referred
to in Talfourd's *Memoir* of 1826 and incorporated into the article in the
Dictionary of National Biography – do not seem to have been systematically
sought out despite the clues offered in the *Memoir*. These sources are
identified for the first time in the following study, and many other facts are
uncovered and rumours evaluated. Many pieces of the puzzle hitherto left
unassembled will be pieced together, to reveal more about Ann Radcliffe's
life and legend than Christina Rossetti thought possible.

Ann Radcliffe's eminence has guaranteed that there would be numerous
critical studies of her novels, and there have been two biographies. Aline
Grant's 153-page *Ann Radcliffe: A Biography* (1951) has not been regarded as
a serious scholarly study because it lacks notes, and because it contains
virtually no analysis of her works; however, Grant's bibliography of items
relating to Ann Radcliffe's childhood has offered invaluable pointers for the
present study, though her idealized and romanticized portrait of the author
cannot be taken too seriously – there is no evidence, for example, that *The
Italian* was written with 'shutters and curtains closed against the outside
world' (p. 78). Pierre Arnaud's *Ann Radcliffe et le fantastique: essai de
psychobiographie* (1976) is narrowly restricted to classic Freudian

psychoanalytic theory; he constructs a crude Oedipal bed upon which every character is laid to rest. Arnaud's speculation upon avuncular incest may be an intriguing line of enquiry, but this standard approach leads him to ignore what modern feminist critics will see as the crucial 'problem' in Ann Radcliffe's life and work: the mother–daughter relationship. Ann Radcliffe does seem to plant clues to her life in her works, but Arnaud's analysis is marred by an injudicious readiness to see hieroglyphs in everything; for example, his view that the title *Athlin and Dunbayne* might be an anagram of 'I Ann haunted Bentley' is not only just plain silly but also fails to match the number of e's and t's and a's in the title (and altogether ignores *The Castles of*).[1]

Robert Donald Spector in *The English Gothic: A Bibliographic Guide to Writers from Horace Walpole to Mary Shelley* (1984) may be unduly severe in his view that 'the standard of full-length studies of Radcliffe in the twentieth century has not been high': in his view Grant's biography is 'a strange production.... Sundry in its information, Grant's work appears tangential to Radcliffe's life and writing'; Clara McIntyre's *Ann Radcliffe in Relation to Her Time* (1920) 'never presented an altogether satisfying account of its subject'; Alida Alberdina Sibbellina Wieten's *Mrs Radcliffe – Her Relation towards Romanticism* (1926) presents 'an old-fashioned thesis' that 'may be dismissed as of little consequence'; Malcolm Ware's *Sublimity in the Novels of Ann Radcliffe* (1963) 'reaches the unsurprising conclusion' that Burke influenced her; E. B. Murray's *Ann Radcliffe* (1972), a short study in the Twayne English Authors series, 'offers no great insight into the author's personality or art'; and the series of Gothic doctoral dissertations published by the Arno Press in 1980 presented more of 'a bright prospect' than a fulfilment of scholarship.

S. Austin Allibone's *A Critical Dictionary of English Literature* (1870) cites more than one hundred sources and is the starting-point for any Radcliffe research; McIntyre's 1920 doctoral dissertation contains a virtually complete list of the reviews of Ann Radcliffe's novels and is unlikely to be superseded. Some of the more important reviews are usefully reprinted in *The Critical Response to Ann Radcliffe* (1994), edited by Deborah D. Rogers. Rogers's own *Ann Radcliffe: A Bio-Bibliography* (1996) is a valuable annotated bibliography of reviews, notices, criticism and imitations, but the biographical chapter consists merely of a disconcertingly cursory summary of Talfourd's 1826 memoir; Rogers adds no new biographical details (and repeats some errors), though she does publish one extant letter and extensive material from the usually ignored (though not unknown) commonplace book of 1823.

Robert Miles's full-length critical study, *Ann Radcliffe: The Great Enchantress* (1995), persuasively demonstrates that Radcliffe's works 'conceal a hard edge, one sharpened by the robust, liberal, critical energies of the dissenting "middling classes" to which she belonged'.[2] Miles employs the standard biography to emphasize the political and social themes of her work; it is not part of his plan to expand our knowledge of Radcliffe's background with first-hand biographical research, but to provide a kind of summing up of the modern approach to her 'transgressive' narratives. My own aim will be to clearly establish the Dissenting – and specifically Unitarian – background to Radcliffe's life and work.

The following study is offered not as a critical literary study, but as a 'cultural history' of a writing woman, and it is organized chronologically rather than thematically. I have preferred not to refer to my subject simply as 'Radcliffe' throughout (as would be usual in a purely literary study), but to occasionally acknowledge her biographical reality as '*Mrs* Radcliffe': for example, when I speak of the woman who visited the seashore with her husband, or when I wish to retain the ambience of propriety attached to her name as a cultural icon. My own overriding project has been to uncover biographical information through traditional research, rather than to exploit the admitted paucity of information as an excuse for unhampered psycho-analytical, sociological or poststructural theory. Some of the best modern readings of the Gothic are by Jacqueline Howard and Robert Miles,[3] both of whom use the theories of Mikhail Bakhtin to view texts as 'dialogues' of contemporary discourses, emphasizing an appreciation for historical context that in some important respects runs counter to the overarching ahistorical theories of Michel Foucault. I have elsewhere written a book-length critique of the dogmas of 'social constructionism',[4] and this present biography may appeal most to those scholars, students and readers who are not altogether seduced by the poststructuralist theory that the author of the text *n'existe pas*. Indeed, part of the pleasure in reading Ann Radcliffe's novels is the recognition of her own delight in constructing an image of 'the author' within their pages. Part of the aim of this biography – by employing scholarship rather than theory as a strategy for knowledge – will be to examine how that image is forged from the resources of the life of the novelist.

Eugenia C. DeLamotte in *Perils of the Night* (1990) rightly insists that 'Radcliffe must be regarded as the center of the Gothic tradition' because she first codified the 'contract' between reader and writer of the Gothic novel, and castigates male critics such as Leslie Fiedler who 'relegated [her] to the periphery of the genre she herself did most to define'.[5] DeLamotte makes the point that a major source of the heroine's anger and anxiety 'is a per-ception that in an important sense, the evil Other the Gothic heroine confronts is not a hidden self at all but is just what it appears to be: an Other that is profoundly alien, and hostile, to women and their concerns'. To interpret the heroine's horror at male tyranny as an expression of masochistic sexual desire – a common technique for casting guilt upon the victims of sexual oppression – is wholly inadequate, and DeLamotte analyses how the profound alienation, claustrophobia and powerlessness in Gothic novels by women demonstrate the circularity of women's real lives trapped in domestic space, and the inescapable victimization of women in general.[6] A consensus is emerging, not only among feminist critics, that Gothic novels by women offer a critique of domestic male tyranny, and that in Ann Radcliffe's heroines we find at least a proto-feminist protest and claim for equality:

> A whole cluster of positive qualities is attributed to feminine consciousness in the course of her fictions, all deducible from the fact of its special degree of sensibility: quickness of perception, self-knowledge, self-control, courage, resilience, foresight, flexibility and, perhaps most daring of all, a certain guarded intellectual freedom. . . . [The self-exploration of heroines] who have been divested of all power except that which they exercise over themselves . . . is not pointless retreat but retreat with a purpose – a vital stage in the coming to consciousness of modern woman.[7]

I hope that current Radcliffe criticism will take up the view of Deborah Ross, who castigates not only male critics who 'distinguish the novel sharply from romance' but also feminists who conclude too easily 'that romance elements are a sign of the crushing effects of patriarchy'.[8] My own view is that Radcliffe not only uses the conventions of romance as a means for realistic female self-expression, as Ross illustrates in *The Italian*, but that she felt conscious of her central position in the history of English literature and the devaluation of romance by the male critical establishment.

Radcliffe was more of a Sibyl than a Pallas Athena, and the ideological and feminist issues in her work can be over-exaggerated – but it would be an even greater mistake to ignore them altogether. Her position in literary history – creator of the female Gothic, best-paid novelist of her generation, most highly praised woman writer of her age – calls for a reading that places her in the context of feminist literary history.[9] Although Radcliffe's three major novels are key feminist texts, feminist critics generally pay greater attention to the more obvious attractions of Mary Wollstonecraft, Mary Shelley and Charlotte Brontë.[10] I find it surprising that Radcliffe has not fared better with the new emphasis on feminist reading. Instead, she has been brought within feminism through the back door, as though she were feminist despite herself, and as though she were naïvely oblivious to the potentially subversive nature of many passages in her novels. The view that writing by such a highly skilled novelist – moreover, one who takes a highly analytical approach to aesthetics and psychology – can somehow have such accidental, 'covert', 'subconscious' meanings should not be allowed to stand unchallenged. As I hope to show, Ann Radcliffe was fully aware of the radical politics of her time and sympathized with them. E. J. Clery is right that 'it

is in the narratives of this for the most part ideologically conservative form
of popular literature [i.e. the Gothic novel] . . . that we must look for signs
of the development of a feminist critical self-consciousness'.[11] But Clery
disappointingly fails to detect more than a merely latent radicalism in
Radcliffe's work:

> Read episodically, the fictions of Radcliffe and her followers yield the
> suggestion that patriarchal right is founded on force, not nature; that the 'right'
> of patriarchy is itself a fiction. But such a reading is against the linear flow of
> the narrative towards resolution and closure. For the significance of the whole
> is subsumed in the final tableau of idealised wedlock.[12]

This is to grant far too much value to the abrupt conclusions of Radcliffe's
novels, which are little more than single brief paragraphs whose conservative
ideology in fact halts and reverses, in an abrupt U-turn, the radical linear
flow of the narratives. As Robert Miles says, 'Gothic romances either resist
closure, or if they opt for it, they do so glibly, so that endings cannot hold in
visionary equipoise the energies roused.'[13]

Eleanor Ty in her study of five 'unsex'd revolutionaries' of the 1790s –
Mary Wollstonecraft, Mary Hays, Helen Maria Williams, Elizabeth Inchbald
and Charlotte Smith – suggests that apparently 'conservative' women writers
such as Amelia Opie, Elizabeth Hamilton, Maria Edgeworth and Ann
Radcliffe occupy a complex position and weave alternately between Burkean
and radical beliefs, and that Radcliffe's romances 'can be read as attempts
to subvert or challenge the notion of the benevolent patriarchy and the
ideological construction of the docile, delicate eighteenth-century woman'.[14]
Contrary to the received image of Ann Radcliffe as a privileged, well-
educated, refined gentlewoman, I hope to make it clear that she emerged
from a radical Unitarian, rather than a conventional Anglican, background,
and that she fully merits consideration as part of that circle of radical
Dissenters that included Anna Laetitia Barbauld, Elizabeth Inchbald, Mary
Hays and Mary Wollstonecraft. She was indeed one of the 'unsex'd
revolutionaries' of her time.

TO THE MEMORY OF BRIAN FOTHERGILL FRSL

The Great Enchantress

———— • ————

'Valancourt, and who was he?' cry the young people. Valancourt, my dears, was the hero of one of the most famous romances which ever was published in this country. The beauty and elegance of Valancourt made your young grandmammas' gentle hearts to beat with respectful sympathy. He and his glory have passed away. Ah, woe is me that the glory of novels should ever decay; that dust should gather round them on the shelves; that the annual cheques from Messieurs the publishers should dwindle, dwindle! Inquire at Mudie's, or the London Library, who asks for the *Mysteries of Udolpho* now?[1]

Such is William Makepeace Thackeray's touchingly nostalgic testimony to the fading memory of the great enchantress: Ann Radcliffe, one of the most celebrated women of the late eighteenth century, yet the least known. She was perhaps the first self-created 'enigma' in the manner of Greta Garbo; her reclusiveness was possibly a strategy for maintaining her reputation as the greatest novelist of the age – the mysterious author of the sensational Gothic novel *The Mysteries of Udolpho*.

Ann Radcliffe kept no diaries, other than some travel journals which contain very few personal details, and her contemporaries left virtually no reminiscences of her. It is clear that no one knew her intimately – or at all. Even in childhood she was shy to an uncommon degree, and she seems to have acquired no friends and few acquaintances. The first biography of her was written three years after her death by a man who never met her, using material supplied solely by her husband and by his own intuition. Her life resembles one of those manuscripts discovered in a Gothic novel: its leaves faded and almost indecipherable, pages torn in half, whole chapters missing, spurious passages interpolated by other hands – all adumbrating a secret hidden at the centre. For the biography of such a woman, whispers and suspicions are as important as the half-heard sighs which carry the essential meanings in her novels. My task has been that of the detective, piecing together the clues which help to explain the disappearance of the central character.

Literary circles at the beginning of the nineteenth century found it intolerable that the most famous writer in England – perhaps even in Europe – should live a completely sequestered life. The result of their unassuaged curiosity is best summed up by a mid-Victorian critic:

> Leading a life of domestic seclusion, . . . Mrs Radcliffe was utterly unknown to the thousands of English who, in London and in the country, were burning to learn something about her. At last, *society*, tired of being kept in such an ignominious state of ignorance, determined no longer to acknowledge herself unacquainted with the person, history, and circumstances of Mrs Radcliffe, but to borrow from imagination the facts which the lady was so impertinent as to keep to herself. The consequence was that soon every coterie in London had its own absurd story about the authoress of 'The Mysteries of Udolpho'. At one time it was generally believed that the awful creations of her imagination haunted her incessantly, and that she was subject to distressing fits of gloom. The requisite improvements to this story were soon made, and it was stated that at length Mrs Radcliffe's reason had given way, and that she was a maniac under confinement in one of the metropolitan asylums. And this picture being as painful, even disgusting, a one as it is well possible to conceive, society in spite of innumerable contradictions cherished it, and clung to it, and extracted from it the most exquisite delight.[2]

The public image of Mrs Radcliffe as a mad genius and the sensational nature of her novels are in sharp contrast to the ordinary preoccupations of her middle-class domestic life. She loved dogs and music, enjoyed excursions to Dover and Worthing, was fond of the sound of Greek though she could not understand a word of it, and felt it was at least as important to be considered a gentlewoman as a genius. To borrow a trope from her most famous novel, what terrible secret will we discover when we draw aside the veil with which Ann Radcliffe has obscured her life? Will it, as in the novel, be only a waxwork figure? Or will we find a madwoman in the attic?

Contemporaries remarked upon her scrupulous sense of propriety, which is borne out by her journals and her novels, and it is clear that she felt constrained by the pressures placed upon women to preserve an unblemished reputation. Eighteenth-century moralists found it difficult to reconcile virtue and ingenuity in women. Women who wrote for publication were often called 'ingenious', but for many critics this was a coded insult: the very act of *publishing* was innately immodest, thus unwomanly.

Ann Radcliffe was a victim of the cultural definition of 'the Proper Lady' which dominated women's lives from the mid-eighteenth century.[3] Female authors felt frustrated by the expectation that self-denial, endurance and self-control were all that women ought to aim for. Middle-class women in particular experienced the conflict between the individualism, so highly valued for men, and the shyness and subordination that remained the feminine ideal. Ann Radcliffe contributed to the debate about female 'sensibility', never quite resolving her own conflict between moderation and 'enthusiasm'.

Although Ann Radcliffe was of her time, she was also *sui generis*. Most of her contemporary female writers – for example, Clara Reeve – claimed to offer moral instruction to their readers, and many wrote specifically for the young. Female literature was almost wholly concerned with ethics. Ann Radcliffe, on the contrary, praised God not so much for His goodness as His grandeur. She was one of the very few women writers to be seriously interested in aesthetic analysis, a transcendental concern of romanticism. While contemporaries such as Charlotte Smith justified their unwomanly writing by arguing the necessity of earning money to support themselves and their children after being abandoned by their husbands,[4] Ann Radcliffe, in sharp contrast, wrote for pleasure rather than profit. Virtually all women novelists from Aphra Behn to Jane Austen 'turned to the novel for money',[5] and pretended to modest accomplishments in comparison with men. Ann Radcliffe, however, wrote for fame: she threw down a challenge with novels that achieved the standards of epic poetry hitherto reserved for men, and claimed for herself the winner's prize.

And yet, at the very height of her fame, having published five novels, the last three of which were dazzling achievements, she ceased writing. For a brilliant young writer to remain silent and sequestered for twenty-six years after publishing a work which demonstrated her to be at the peak of her imaginative powers is, as Julia Kavanagh says, 'singular in literary history'.[6] Fame threatened to soil Reputation; in a tactic to retain both at their highest pitch, 'like an actress in full possession of applauded powers, she chose to retire from the stage in the very blaze of her fame'.[7]

In 1826 a reviewer asserted that 'She was ashamed, (yes, *ashamed*) of her own talents; and was ready to sink in the earth at the bare suspicion of any one taking her for an author; her chief ambition being to be thought a lady!'[8] But the conflict for her was more complex. Most of her biographers follow Thomas Noon Talfourd, the author of the first memoir (1826), in insisting that she valued 'personal character' above 'literary fame', but every instance they cite to prove this – such as her acute distress at being accused of claiming to have written Joanna Baillie's *Plays of the Passions* – demonstrates the paramount importance of specifically *artistic* integrity in her life. Her choice was not simply between being either a Proper Lady or an Authoress, but being a Proper Lady Author.

Ann Radcliffe lost her battle to unite 'desire and decorum'. She withdrew from the world when journalists attacked her as a sorceress responsible for corrupting the minds of her young readers. An American writer in 1852 observed that she had become 'the prey of the lowest journalists of London', for her silence mingled with her competitors' envy, 'and from that moment there was no end to the malicious suppositions and calumnies about Mrs Radcliffe, the blue-stocking, the sorceress, the Eumenide, the harpy who lived upon corpses and drank blood out of brass cups'.[9] As she drew a protective veil across her image, the suppression of her creative urge may have contributed to a decline in health, both mental and physical, and her cloistered existence fostered the growth of that pensive melancholy discernible in her works.

The first opportunity for redressing the balance of Ann Radcliffe's public image came in 1882, when Christina Rossetti was offered the chance to write a biography in John H. Ingram's 'Eminent Women Series'.[10] Radcliffe, whose work Rossetti began reading around 1844,[11] was one of her favourite authors, perhaps because she sympathized with the 'prophetic' and magical strains in her work. On 24 April 1883 Rossetti wrote to Ingram:

> My brother tells me you are kindly thinking of me for 'Mrs Radcliffe'. She takes my fancy more than many, altho' I know next to nothing about her. And I will try my pen upon her, if you please. Are any hopes to be indulged of private papers, journals, what not, becoming accessible to us? or must I depend exclusively on looking up my subject at the British Museum?[12]

In a few days, Ingram had filled out reader's request slips at the British Museum for Rossetti, though she discovered that 'I can get the four books in question at Mudie's'. Presumably these were Thomas Noon Talfourd's 'Memoir of the life and writings of Mrs Radcliffe', prefixed to her posthumously published *Gaston de Blondeville* (1826); Sir Walter Scott's 'Prefatory memoir' to the Ballantyne Novelist's Library collection of *The Novels of Mrs Ann Radcliffe* (1824); the first full-length critical study of Ann Radcliffe in John Dunlop's *The History of Fiction* (1814); and a modern study, probably J. Cordy Jeaffreson's *Novels and Novelists, from Elizabeth to Victoria* (1858), or perhaps David Masson's *British Novelists and Their Styles* (1859). On 28 May she agreed to the £50 fee, which was 'all I wish for, and if I succeed in finding sufficient material I shall be very pleased with my earnings'.[13]

But money was easier to come by than biographical material. She sought help from Professor Masson of Edinburgh, the literary historian J. Cordy Jeaffreson and Dr Richard Garnett of the British Museum (who eventually wrote the entry on Ann Radcliffe in the *Dictionary of National Biography*). In June she wrote to her brother: 'I *Radcliffized* the other day at the Museum, and perceive that the best resource is Talfourd after all, unless it be a *quotation* made by Walter Scott. I doubt if the Memoir is feasible.'[14] In July she sought assistance through a letter in *The Athenaeum*:

> I am scarcely hoping to collect materials for a memoir of Mrs Radcliffe, the novelist. I have, of course, read up my subject in Walter Scott, Talfourd, Dunlop, &c., and I have been greatly obliged by private letters from Prof. Masson, Mr Jeaffreson, and Mr Garnett, addressed either to myself or to others for my benefit. But all the material as yet known to me falls short of the amount I seek for. Is there any hoard of diaries or correspondence hitherto unpublished which yet the owners might be willing to make public? I would do my best to satisfy such generous owners were they to entrust their treasure to me; above all, I should hope to make my selection with scrupulous delicacy. Failing such hidden stores, I fear my proposed task cannot be executed.[15]

Although she promised 'scrupulous delicacy' – perhaps because of the hints of madness in the existing memoirs – only one brief letter and one short journal have been discovered in the one hundred years since then. The article produced a 'meagre contingent' of 'Radcliffeana' from a Mr Sketchley of the South Kensington Museum, and a few useless responses. She confirmed the collapse of the project to Ingram on 17 September: 'Returned from the seaside I can only say that I have done my best to collect Radcliffe material and have failed. Some one else, I daresay, will gladly attempt the memoir, but I despair and withdraw. Pray pardon me for having kept you so long in suspense.'[16] It is unfortunate that Christina Rossetti did not persevere, because she could have produced a valuable critical interpretation of Ann Radcliffe's work. It has to be said, however, that she lacked the scholarly disposition which would have been required for a biography of Ann Radcliffe. Rossetti's life was nearly as sequestered as that of her subject; it is doubtful that she personally visited the British Library to search for any documents on more than two occasions, and then only to look at books that friendly colleagues had pointed out to her.

Who read the works of the world's first 'popular novelist'? Novels were bought initially by people who possessed drawing rooms and even libraries, not by the less well-to-do. Labourers and domestic servants earned around 8 shillings a week; Ann Radcliffe's first novel, *The Castles of Athlin and Dunbayne*, cost 3 shillings, almost half a week's wages; *The Mysteries of Udolpho* was published 'In Four very large Volumes Twelves, Price One Pound in boards', though one review cited the cost as 20 shillings or £1 5s – a year's savings.[17]

Novels were nevertheless handed down to ladies' maids, finding their way to cheap second-hand outlets, and in the 1790s cast-off novels replaced cast-off wigs at Middle Row, Holborn.[18] Eventually cheaper editions made the most popular works more widely available.

Most sentimental and Gothic novels were written by (lower) middle-class gentlewomen for middle-class girls and young women, the primary frequenters of the circulating libraries. Ann Radcliffe wrote for a well-defined market, even for a specific circulating library. Her first three novels were first published by Hookham, proprietor of the famous Literary Assembly on Old Bond Street. In 1793 Hookham and Carpenter refitted their thirty-year-old suite of reading rooms and promoted it as a centre 'where persons of curiosity may find the best company, the best books, the best intelligence, with the best accommodations'.[19] Their library was regularly supplied with all of the British and Continental literary periodicals and the major foreign newspapers. As well, of course, as 'Hookham's Library', which in that year included Radcliffe's *The Castles of Athlin and Dunbayne*, the second edition of her second novel *A Sicilian Romance* and the third edition of her third novel *The Romance of the Forest*; a host of anonymous historical romances by A Young Lady; romantic classics such as *Sorrows of Werter* and the *Beauties of Rousseau*; and some memoirs and history. Clara Reeve – virtually the only Lady identified by name – was represented by several educational works and *The Progress of Romance*. The standard retail price was 3 shillings per volume; books were free to members of the library, but had to be read on the premises. Subscription to the Literary Assembly was 2 guineas per annum; only subscribers were admitted, and members were introduced by other members or known personally to Mr Hookham.

The library was 'under the patronage' of their Royal Highnesses the Prince of Wales and Prince William Frederic, the Duke of York, the Duke of Clarence, the Duke of Gloucester and the principal nobility and gentry. The nobility might possibly visit these rooms for the sake of the reviews and foreign newspapers from as far afield as the East and West Indies, but the nature of the books on offer makes it quite clear that the gentry – particularly its young ladies – were the principal readers, intent upon romance and refinement. Ann Radcliffe's novels were about as high-class as the gentry could reach.

Despite the élitist marketing of the firm, Hookham's came to be associated primarily with lower-class readers of inferior Gothic novels:

> For Novels, should their critick hints succeed,
> The Misses might fare better when they took 'em;
> But it would fare extremely ill, indeed,
> With gentle *Messieurs Bell* and *Hookham*.[20]

Hookham's declining reputation may account for Mrs Radcliffe's switch of allegiance, first to Robinson's and then to Cadell and Davies – the very firm which published Colman's satire upon their competitor.[21]

Nevertheless we do know that Ann Radcliffe's novels were read and enjoyed by a heterogeneous collection that ranged from lower-middle-class to upper-class and even aristocratic readers. The circulating libraries ensured widespread dissemination to provincial centres. Thomas Poole bought a copy of *The Romance of the Forest* for his Nether Stowey Book Society.[22] A copy of the fourth edition of *A Sicilian Romance* (1809) in the British Library has pasted inside its front cover: 'Mrs Nicholson's Circulating Library, Bridlington Quay'. By all accounts Ann Radcliffe's books were devoured by the daughters of tradesmen at these libraries, but the evidence is skewed inevitably towards readers professionally involved with literature, because they were the ones most likely to leave written testimony of their tastes. She was enjoyed by young newspapermen and journalists, critics, politicians and educationalists, romantics like Hazlitt, classicists like Mathias, even Evangelicals like Jonathan Gray, as well as literary women like Mrs Piozzi, Mrs Carter and Maria Edgeworth, and Lady Ossory, one of the few aristocrats who left any sort of record on the matter. The county nobility hunted foxes rather than read novels or poetry, but some aristocratic amateurs were familiar with her romances. George William Frederick Howard, 7th Earl of Carlisle, gently satirized the Gothic taste in his poem 'The Lady and the Novel', which was printed beneath an illustration of a lady reading a novel, in *The Keepsake* for 1827:

> What is the book, abstracted damsel, say:
> The last new novel, or the last new play?
>
> . . .
>
> Is it departed Scott's illumin'd page,
> The wizard of our unenchanted age?
>
> . . .
>
> Art thou in dim Udolpho's grated tower
> Scar'd at the chiming of the midnight hour?[23]

Highly strung young ladies formed a large part of Ann Radcliffe's readership, particularly the lovesick and those prone to reverie. Sir Walter Scott felt that 'the potent charm of this mighty enchantress' had a particularly strong appeal to sequestered invalids, spinsters and bachelors, for it bewitched them away from their indisposition or solitude, and acted as an opiate upon their world of secret sorrow.[24] Fanny Burney, who read *The Italian* at the end of July 1797, told her husband: 'I believe her writings are all best calculated for lonely hours & depressed spirits. I should probably have done more justice to Udolpho if I had read it in one of my solitary intervals. Don't run away again however, to give me the trial!'[25] A significant number of sensitive and artistic young men appreciated Radcliffe's high camp and yearning. Whatever their class or sex, Radcliffe's readers were romantically inclined, and young at least at heart. People often reread her books later in life with a view to reviving the pleasing sensations of their youth, as if it had been trapped in her pages. Her most Romantic novel, *The Mysteries of Udolpho*, has 'a fascination . . . which those who feel in youth will likely remember in old age'.[26] Thomas De Quincey in his *Confessions of an English Opium-Eater* called her 'the great enchantress of that generation'.[27] Her major works were published during those few years, of which Wordsworth remarked:

> Bliss was it in that dawn to be alive,
> But to be young was very heaven! (Preface to *Lyrical Ballads*, 1800)

The novels written by Ann Radcliffe's female colleagues were regarded as 'sofa companions', never destined to find a place on the library shelves. Critical discourse was dominated by men, who easily dismissed such works, barring them entry into the canon of the Great Masters. Whatever ambivalence about the role of the woman writer Ann Radcliffe might have felt, she never took the easy route of adopting or defending the domestic – i.e. womanly – virtues of her work, and instead resolutely claimed for herself a position within the (patriarchal) tradition of romance and epic literature. What Ann Radcliffe achieved was to place her novels within the Great Tradition of High Art – many of her contemporaries joined in one breath the names of Shakespeare, Milton, Ariosto, Radcliffe. She seems to have accomplished this quite self-consciously, deliberately and in a manner that we now call feminist. She asserted the right of a woman's work to be deemed a masterpiece: *The Mysteries of Udolpho* occupied a place on the top shelf in the canon of literature for three generations, and has been continuously in print for two hundred years. Prior to the publication of Ann Radcliffe's novels, good taste was identified with Reason; after them, with Imagination. The modern study of (and challenge to) canon formation will find it illuminating to focus upon the role played by Ann Radcliffe in the debate about the place of women novelists in that canon.

Ann Radcliffe's popularity peaked just at a time when the 'Victorian values' of xenophobia, male chauvinism, sexism, prudery and self-righteous moralism began to transform British culture. Within a period of scarcely ten years she was canonized and then debunked, as misogynistic criteria were consolidated for canonical membership. Sanctimonious critics sniffed that 'although as an artist Mrs Radcliffe deserves high commendation, yet we would blush to praise the purpose or tendency of her works'.[28] Ann Radcliffe was the first major writer to suffer from the anxieties over authorship that were to beset women writers in the nineteenth century, although she had more self-confidence than they, and wielded her phallic magic wand less apologetically.

It was Ann Radcliffe's success in formulating the genre of the Gothic novel that ironically prompted the attack upon women writers and their subsequent insecurity. By the time the new generation of critics had finished with her, Mrs Radcliffe had been turned into a bogey to warn off women novelists. Pompous critics like Samuel Taylor Coleridge led the conspiracy to stake out Literature as a masculine preserve, aided and abetted by Wordsworth, who complained that good literature was being 'driven into neglect by frantic novels' (Preface to *Lyrical Ballads*, 1800), and by Sir Walter Scott, who very subtly set himself up as the authority on prose literature, so that he, the Wizard of the North, could usurp the throne of the Great Enchantress.

The Gothic novel illustrates the internal struggles of many women writers during the late eighteenth century: patterns of anxiety, guilt, repression, frustration, a sense of imprisonment, curiosity, doubt and rebelliousness clearly link such literature with the status of women in society.[29] As Coral Ann Howells points out, Emily in *The Mysteries of Udolpho* experiences the predicament of all women: 'Everything in her make-up is an exaggeration of those negative responses [anxieties related to isolation, dependence and sexual fears] which were often the only ones available to the late eighteenth-century woman who wished to preserve her own individuality.'[30]

Ann Radcliffe's technique has been characterized as a skilful attenuation of tension rather than a resolution of her contradictory bourgeois and bohemian impulses.[31] More recently, critics have focused upon class and social relations in Gothic fiction, mainly the middle-class authors' love-hate relationship with the aristocracy, and their subconscious confirmation of bourgeois values.[32] Ann Radcliffe's politics were democratic; the trappings of feudalism in her romances only lightly disguise the rebellion necessary for a new order free of the tyrants of the *ancien régime*. In her idealized chivalric past, honour is as important as birth – one of the cherished myths of middle-class gentility. It is characteristically bourgeois to rejoice in the fall of despotism while simultaneously holding the mob in contempt. The class from which Ann Radcliffe drew most of her readers experienced the very same contradictions of commitment, the same political muddle of the reactionary and the revolutionary, the republican and the aristocratic. But those few specifically political views that she expressed are invariably in favour of liberty, democracy and reform – all Unitarian principles advocated by her family. Emily in *The Mysteries of Udolpho* openly demands equal property rights. Adeline in *The Romance of the Forest* 'lamented again the effects of an arbitrary government, where the bounties of nature, which were designed for all, are monopolized by a few, and the many are suffered to starve tantalized by surrounding plenty'.[33] This political consciousness may be rudimentary, but the sentiment would not be out of place in a tract by Mary Wollstonecraft.

The concerns and anxieties felt by many at the beginning of the Industrial Revolution in the late eighteenth century were also reflected in the Gothic novels and novels of sensibility. A new urban middle class and new working classes of skilled craftsmen, with a rapidly shifting urban population, led to job insecurity, uncertainties about status in the community and the decreasing effectiveness of the family. Families became isolated units where men sought relief from the pressures of commerce. The double standard allowed men to exercise competitive skills while requiring women to be a subservient civilizing force within the home. Puritan middle-class values, especially notions of chastity and modesty, increasingly dominated women's lives.[34] Mary Wollstonecraft analysed how 'the life of a modest woman [became] a perpetual conflict', because sensibility was nurtured at the same time as self-denial.[35] The strains and breaking-points of this impossibly contradictory task are perfectly mirrored in the Gothic novel.

Many women novelists struggled to be genteel. Ann Radcliffe, daughter of a china merchant and wife of a journalist, managed to purvey an air of gentility more successfully than most. Her rarefied novels, unlike those of her contemporaries, contain no references to death in childbirth, smallpox or duck and green peas set for lunch. Nevertheless, while she employs none of the specificity of the bourgeois, she adopts many of its more metaphysical values: decorum, prudence, fortitude. We sometimes carelessly think of 'sensibility' as if it were simply a patrician ideology, but it was also a Dissenting tactic:

> Sensibility declared a democracy of the heart, an egalitarian world of feelings where all were equal who wept before scenes of tragic benevolence, or who shuddered with delightful terror before sublime manifestations of the divine power. As such, sensibility constituted a language of equal emotional entitlements, a democracy of feeling hearts that greatly assisted women in defending their personal interests.[36]

Moreover, in Ann Radcliffe's novels will be found none of those frivolous trifles by which female minds, according to Mary Wollstonecraft and her disciple Mary Hays, were enchained and systematically weakened. A moderate but sound financial position is the solid base for the heroine's unshakeable dignity.

But neither politics nor conventional morality were as important to Ann Radcliffe as art. Her reviewers perceived a commendable didactic purpose in her novels, but she herself never attempted to justify her writing on any grounds other than its artistic merit. While Charlotte Smith and many other writers of less stature wrote prefatory apologia to disarm criticism, Ann Radcliffe is content to conclude each novel with a perfunctory moral tag. Though the moral/aesthetic dilemma is an important theme in her works, she did not altogether share her imitators' distrust of the imagination.[37]

The distinguishing feature of Ann Radcliffe's characters is their uniquely aesthetic sensibility. They read books, compose poetry, play music, draw pictures and contemplate the landscape – pausing long enough in their flight from banditti to analyse the affecting contrasts of a picturesque cliff, employing the precise terminology derived from contemporary critical analysis of the Sublime, the Beautiful and the Picturesque.[38] Eighteenth-century good taste was a matter of good breeding, and this upper-class framework for aesthetic discourse inevitably colours Ann Radcliffe's work. Her eighteenth-century sensibility, and her upbringing, required restraint as well as freedom. It was important for her that 'enthusiastic passion' and 'romantic enthusiasm' be governed by polite taste, just as Burke defined the Sublime as '*tranquillity* tinged with terror'. But although Ann Radcliffe certainly revered art and 'high culture', her models are the artists of Romantic impulse rather than classical restraint. She clearly subscribed to the Romantic notion that feeling and integrity were more important than birth. One of her subversive revolutionary messages is that the sublime landscape is a liberating force even for peasants. It is noticeable that art has a more democratic basis for her than for her predecessors.[39] The lower classes are far more sympathetically treated in her works than in contemporary domestic novels. Annette, the maid in *The Mysteries of Udolpho*, appreciates and talks about art, music and literature, and her boyfriend Ludovico sings songs by Ariosto and Petrarch. Radcliffe's novels illustrate not so much an *éducation sentimental* as an education in taste; even moral virtues are secondary to the artistic achievements of her primary characters. She succeeded in creating an *aesthetic* out of her personal conflict between order and disorder, propriety and passion, the Augustan and Romantic impulses. This fundamentally *imaginative* achievement is the hallmark of her genius and the secret of her appeal to some seven generations of readers.

The most sublime event of the year in which her first novel *The Castles of Athlin and Dunbayne* was published was the fall of the Bastille, which Fox, a later admirer of the novelist, proclaimed 'the greatest and best event in history'.[40] Mrs Radcliffe's popularity was at its height as Revolutionary Terror swept France. Mrs Piozzi had great forebodings that the political future of Europe would be settled in 1794, the very year that *The Mysteries of Udolpho* was published: 'the rapidity with which this tide of Democracy rolls forward, shows the down-hill of regal and aristocratic days to perfection. I think all Europe is at length in arms.'[41] Robespierre was murdered in July, and by August many people believed that the revelations of Apocalypse were being fulfilled. In this millennial atmosphere, two images come to dominate our picture of Ann Radcliffe: prophetess and sorceress. Her heroines frequently retire to a 'deeply sequestered spot', at the top of a lonely tower, in a dark forest grove or a cave beside the sea, to sink into reverie and compose poetry. Mrs Radcliffe herself frequently climbed to the tops of mountains and cliffs, where she imagined herself as Prospero the Magician, and wandered through Windsor Forest fancying herself a druidess. She fostered the image of herself as a magician, sprinkling hundreds of allusions to magical enchantment throughout her work. Many readers responded to her as if she were the high priestess of Delphi and her books the Sibylline leaves. But as the new century advanced, as revolutionary idealism was replaced by reactionary anxiety, as male writers tried to regain the heights occupied by women, these two images of the novelist were inverted into their opposites: madwoman and witch. The following study attempts to trace that transformation.

Dissent versus Decorum

———— • ————

The future novelist was born on Monday 9 July 1764, the only child of Ann Oates and William Ward, haberdasher, and was christened on 5 August in St Andrew's Church, Holborn, London.[1] In the *Annual Biography* obituary it was emphasized that 'her family and connections were of the most respectable description', but William Radcliffe in his contribution to this obituary is careful to note that her parents, 'though in trade, were nearly the only persons of their two families not living in handsome, or at least easy independence'.[2] Neither the French Revolution nor the Romantic poets had much impact upon the British conviction that pedigree was at least as important as talent. Ann Ward Radcliffe's respectable connections were mostly collateral and maternal – distant maternal cousins included a bishop and a celebrated physician, her maternal grandmother's father was a member of the minor gentry, and her paternal grandmother was the sister of a celebrated surgeon. As her first biographer summed it up in 1826, her parents were 'persons of great respectability, who, though engaged in trade, were allied to families of independent fortune and high character'.[3]

Both sides of her family had their roots in the north of England. Her father William Ward was a Leicestershire man. Her paternal grandmother was the sister of William Cheselden, surgeon to King George II, born in 1688 in Melton Mowbray, northeast of Leicester. Cheselden's reputation as the father of English surgery was established by his books *The Anatomy of the Human Body* (1713) and *Treatise on the High Operation of the Stone* (1723), and for a famous operation in 1728 whereby he restored the sight of a fourteen-year-old boy by removing part of the iris. A Fellow of the Royal Society and the Royal Academy of Sciences at Paris, he was appointed head surgeon to Chelsea Hospital in 1737, where he resided until his death in 1752, and in whose burying ground he was laid to rest.[4] He was a friend of Queen Charlotte and the Pope, and was a widely popular man, with interests which included athletics, especially boxing, as well as literature. William Radcliffe remembers seeing books which Cheselden had given to William Ward, and Ward's grateful recollection of these presents from his uncle.[5] To round out the paternal line, William Radcliffe speculates that Lieutenant-Colonel Cheselden of Somerby in Leicestershire was another nephew of the surgeon.[6] One of the sponsors at Ann Ward's baptism was her father's aunt, Mrs Barwell, first of Leicester and then of Duffield in Derbyshire.[7]

Ann Ward's maternal relations were Derbyshire people, and again the more celebrated connections went through the female line. Her mother Ann Oates Ward was the daughter of James Oates of Chesterfield and Amelia Jebb, eldest daughter of Samuel Jebb of Mansfield (1670–1743) and Elizabeth Gilliver of Yorkshire (c. 1668–1757).[8] Amelia had six brothers. The three oldest were Richard Jebb, who settled in Ireland; Dr Samuel Jebb, of Stratford Bow, a biographer, and father of Sir Richard Jebb; and Avery Jebb, who settled in Manchester. The two youngest brothers were Robert Jebb, who also settled in Manchester; and John Jebb, Dean of Cashell, and father of Dr John Jebb. The middle brother was the most famous: Joshua Jebb, who accumulated a respectable fortune as a hosier, became an alderman of Chesterfield and retired to a handsome property in the nearby manor of Tapton, where he laid out pleasant grounds and devoted himself to the planting of trees.

Amelia's two sisters were Elizabeth Jebb, who married Mr Moseley and had a family, and Hannah Jebb, who married Robert Hallifax, an apothecary in Mansfield. Hannah and Robert had two notable sons: Dr Samuel Hallifax, Bishop of Gloucester for a short while before becoming Bishop of St Asaph; and Dr Robert Hallifax, physician to the Prince of Wales. Chesterfield's Church of St Mary and All Saints – famous for its twisted spire – has several elegant inscriptions composed by Bishop Hallifax, most notably one north of the high altar to his friend Edmund Burton, Attorney at Law, who married his sister,[9] and a Latin inscription in the south transept on a monument erected in 1796 by Robert in memory of his parents Robert and Hannah, who died in 1759 and 1787 respectively, aged sixty-three and seventy-eight.[10] Local legend had it that a vaulted subterranean passage led from this church to one of the ancient mansions in town, or, alternatively, to a nearby monastery at Hady.[11] We do not know if Ann Radcliffe was aware of these associations; the *leitmotif* of a secret tunnel linking a house and monastery church is common to many Gothic novels, but the legend may have been spoken of in the family, perhaps capturing the future novelist's imagination.

The Bishop's generation, the generation of Mrs Radcliffe's mother, had its share of celebrated members of the Jebb family, who were the leading lights of Chesterfield. Dr John Jebb, son of John Jebb of Mansfield (then Dean of Cashell in Ireland), became the Unitarian Rector of Homesfield, but resigned to take up medicine, and became an eminent physician and controversial political writer. He earned his MA from Cambridge, and studied the classics during his vacations; he published a commentary on Newton in 1765, and was familiar with Hebrew and Arabic as well as French and Italian.[12] In 1770 he failed to obtain the professorship of Arabic because he had offended the electors by 'his prophesying protestantism', and pupils were forbidden to attend his lectures.[13] The post was granted instead to his near relation Dr Samuel Hallifax, and the subsequent dispute between the two men proved bitter. In April 1771 Jebb went to London as head of a committee to lay a petition before Parliament seeking repeal of the Toleration Act, specifically relief from subscribing to the Thirty-Nine Articles and the prescribed liturgy. He may have remained in London throughout September, but he resided chiefly at Bungay in Suffolk. By the time the petition was presented in February 1772, Dr Samuel Hallifax was Bishop of Gloucester and he not only argued strongly in favour of the right of the Church of England to require this subscription, but heaped personal abuse on Dr Jebb.[14] The petition failed. The duplicity of this almost entirely Unitarian commission pretending to speak for Trinitarian Dissenters was emphasized by the Anti-Jacobins in the late 1790s.[15] In 1789 Dr Hallifax, now Bishop of St Asaph, was among those on the episcopal bench who joined in the debate in opposition to Lord Stanhope's proposal to repeal the laws and restrictions against Dissenters, and he was believed to be the author of an anti-Dissenting pamphlet in 1791, 'An apology for the liturgy and clergy of the Church of England'.[16]

From June to October 1772 Dr Jebb lived in Bungay, writing for the public papers. In 1773 he resolved privately never again to read the public service, and he finally resigned his preferments in the Church of England in late 1775. During this period he published numerous tracts advocating academic reform, liberty for the American Colonies, abolition of the slave trade and the promotion of a society of Unitarian Christians. He intensely disliked what he called 'Church-of-Englandism', and was a zealot in support of civil and religious liberty.

Having seceded from the Established Church, he decided to study medicine on the advice of his cousin Dr (later Sir) Richard Jebb. So he left Cambridge in 1776 and settled in London in a house in Craven Street, acting as tutor to two private pupils while he studied at St Bartholomew's Hospital. Having received his diploma (from St Andrews, Scotland) in 1777, he commenced practice in 1778 at the age of forty-four. He sought medical appointments but was rebuffed because of his political activism. He was a friend of Dr Joseph Priestley, whose *Doctrine of Philosophical Necessity* had been dedicated to him in 1777.[17] A constant advocate of electoral reform, he published a pamphlet in support of Charles James Fox's famous speech in

Westminster Hall in 1780. His own writings were as revolutionary as anything written during this tumultuous period of European history. For example:

> The constitution of the commons' house of parliament can never be restored gradatim, nor by any other power than that to which it owes its existence; I mean, the power of the people, whose proper weight and authority in the scale of government, is now rising in every part of Europe; and, I trust, will not, in this country, much longer be depressed, either by lust of power in the monarch, or aristocratic jealousy in the peer.[18]

In autumn 1783 he moved from Craven Street to a house in Parliament Street, where he lived until his death on 2 March 1786, aged fifty-one. He was buried in the unconsecrated burying ground of Bunhill Fields, near John Milton, and his funeral was attended by many friends. Two bishops (one presumably being Dr Hallifax) sent their carriages as a mark of respect (an Anglican bishop could not attend a Dissenter's funeral in person).

Ann Ward and her parents probably attended Dr Jebb's funeral, and it is possible that Ann occasionally resided with her activist granduncle at his residences in Bungay, Craven Street and Parliament Street during various periods from 1771–86. If William Radcliffe is correct that 'a great part of her youth had been passed in the residences of her superior relatives' – and taking into account his belief that she went to Derbyshire only upon the deaths of her parents – then Dr Jebb in Bungay and London, Dr Hallifax in St Asaph and Dean Jebb in Egham, Surrey, are the relatives she is most likely to have visited. If she stayed with Dr Jebb in Bungay, she would have visited the local tourist attraction, the romantic ruins of Bungay Castle, which might well be the *locus Gothicus* of her literary imagination. At a later date, Mrs Elizabeth Bonhote, who lived in Bungay Cottage and owned this romantic property, wrote her romance *Bungay Castle* (1796) to celebrate its appeal. Deep groans, decayed tapestries, a trapdoor leading to a labyrinth of damp passages – all reveal that Mrs Bonhote owed more to Mrs Radcliffe than to history.

Dr Jebb was not altogether a zealot in his personal relations, for friends found him to be amiable, pleasant and even gay – 'but of the frivolous, in him there was nothing'.[19] His belief in egalitarian principles and political freedom would have rubbed off upon his niece, and he may have first stirred her interest in the theories of Rousseau. His expertise in Arabic may also have stimulated her interest in the Arabic legends alluded to in *The Mysteries of Udolpho*. It is almost certain that the young lady would have read his published letters and pamphlets, containing such stirring sentiments as this: 'Everything should be now done, which can contribute to spread the sacred flame of freedom through the country.'[20] The list of subscribers to *The*

Works . . . of John Jebb, which was published in April 1787, contains the names of many of his relatives, including Ann's mother 'Mrs Ward, Milsom-street, Bath',[21] her father's brother or uncle 'Rev John Ward, BA Vicar of Mickleover, Derbyshire', the late Dean Jebb (who died on 6 February 1787), Samuel Jebb, Miss Jebb, Mr Avery Jebb and Miss Oates. Other notable friends in the list of subscribers include Miss Reeve (i.e. Clara Reeve the novelist) and William Seward FRS.

The Unitarians were doubly cut off from the mainstream, for they stood apart from both the Established Anglican Church and the mainstream of Nonconformist Dissent. Aggressive Socinians like Priestley felt that the idea that one should be 'born again' was 'a dangerous delusion', and beliefs in the necessity of conversion or fear of hell were quite opposite to the tradition of Rational Dissent; the only political ideal they shared with the Wesleyans was a vigorous opposition to the slave trade.[22] Unitarians drew their membership 'from the commercial and intellectual élite of the manufacturing towns' where the Test Acts were not so rigorously applied:[23]

> The Unitarian enthusiasm for secular knowledge, the rational discourses elegantly enunciated in Unitarian chapels, the undemanding requirements for communion in Unitarian meetings, the Unitarian toleration of social activities such as dances and theatre-going, all appealed to both potential and successful entrepreneurs far more than did the narrow religious preoccupations, the emotional insistence on self-revelation and personal conversion, and the narrow ethical codes and inquisitorial disciplinary procedures of the Evangelical Dissenters. When Presbyterian congregations divided in the eighteenth century, it was usually the wealthy minority who followed the heterodox path to Arianism and Socinianism and the poorer majority who remained loyal to orthodox Calvinism.[24]

A close analysis of the subscribers to Jebb's *Works* has served to establish the paradigm of the Dissenting élite: some thirty-six physicians and surgeons, forty present or future Members of Parliament (mostly Whigs and radicals) and a few radical peers, sixty lawyers, forty-five businessmen and manufacturers, some fifty gentlemen of the new merchant wealth, and 150 clergymen from the Church of England who presumably shared Jebb's Rational Dissent, 'while stopping short, at least openly, of the Unitarianism to which he eventually came'.[25]

Some allegedly 'conservative' attitudes in Ann Radcliffe's novels need to be seen in the historical *liberal* context of this Dissenting culture. It is true that their heroines (and heroes) temporarily lose their ancient patrimony and regain their proper social status at the end of *The Romance of the Forest* and *The Mysteries of Udolpho*, but 'what is installed is not glorified feudalism but an order based on the progressive promises of female sensibility. Here the bourgeois values of individualism and "companionate marriage" triumph over the prejudices and vices of a passing aristocratic, patriarchal regime.'[26] In a similar way the Glorious Revolution of 1688 re-established the proper basis for English society and constitutional monarchy, and the Unitarians re-established a 'primitive' Christianity. The Unitarians supported the Whig government as their best defence against the monarchy, as their best hope for reform and later as their best defence against the French (and papacy). Radcliffe avoided overt political statement by setting most of her works outside of England, and in an exotic past, but they all illustrate the Dissenting valorization of merit over status. The text of even her first novel, *The Castles of Athlin and Dunbayne*, 'is shot through with the language of meritocracy. . . . the language of "equitable" government also anachronistically creeps into the romance'.[27] Valancourt in *The Mysteries of Udolpho* could be a portrait of a liberal Dissenter. He is a younger brother with a modest fortune, diminished by his education, whom Emily resolves to support with her own inheritance. He expresses indignation at criminal or mean acts, and is impetuously compassionate to the unfortunate. All the servants love him, 'for he used to be so courteous to them all' (621), and 'never would command, and call about him, as some of your quality people do' (621). He obviously has egalitarian sympathies. Similarly in *The Italian*, when Ellena and Vivaldi get married, the author emphasizes that 'this entertainment was not given to persons of distinction only, for both Vivaldi and Ellena had wished that all the tenants of the domain should partake of it, and share the abundant happiness which themselves possessed' (413).

According to Talfourd Mrs Radcliffe regularly attended services in the Church of England, and exhibited a cheerful but sincere piety.[28] We do not need to doubt this simple fact – that is, we should not place her among those many devious Unitarians who pretended to be Anglicans – in order to suggest that she was not a rigorously committed Anglican. Her relationship to the Church of England may have been no stronger than the Sister Superior's relationship to the Church of Rome in *The Italian*. Though head of the convent of Our Lady of Pity:

> Her religion was neither gloomy, nor bigotted; it was the sentiment of a grateful heart offering itself up to a Deity, who delights in the happiness of his creatures; and she conformed to the customs of the Roman church, without supposing a faith in all of them to be necessary to salvation. (300)

There is no suggestion in Ann Radcliffe's novels or journals that she believed in the Trinity, or in many of the Thirty-Nine Articles or in the value of atonement. Nor is there any evangelical fervour in her works except when she attacks the dogmas of the Roman Catholic Church. She cannot have disagreed much with the Unitarian view expressed in 'A liturgy on the universal principles of religion and morality', which her uncle Bentley and Revd David Williams co-authored for use in their liberal church, advocating nothing more specific or restrictive than 'the existence of a supreme intelligence, and the universal obligations of morality': that is, generalized piety and virtue, shared by Jews and Gentiles, Christians and Mahometans.[29] Ann Radcliffe never refers in her novels to Jesus Christ, whom many Unitarians believed to be either subordinate to God (Arian) or simply not divine at all (Socinian). Her God is very much a Unitarian deity, which she described as a 'Supreme Being', a 'Great Author': 'that great first cause, whose nature soars beyond the grasp of human comprehension' (*Romance of the Forest*, 275); 'that Great First Cause, which pervades and governs all being' (*Mysteries of Udolpho*, 114). At His most personal He is little more than the Shaftesburian deity of benevolence; as the God of hope and love He is called upon to soothe troubled minds, but one does not feel much sense of conviction that He is an active agent of consolation. Like La Luc in *Romance of the Forest*, St Aubert in *Udolpho* pretends to believe in this kind of personal deity, so as to console Emily who wishes to think of her father as looking down on her from heaven. In this sense God is merely a consoling fiction, in whose presence a doctrine of personal salvation is irrelevant. In *Udolpho* Sister Agnes has lost her reason as a result of unresisted passion; but whether or not her soul can be saved is not an issue about which the author seriously concerns herself.[30]

Unitarian sermons tended to disregard Scripture in favour of ethics and human reason. Ann Radcliffe cites the Bible only once in the whole of her work, in an inaccurate quotation that probably comes from an intermediate poetic source.[31] When her God is not an abstraction of sublimity, He is part of her period detail or local colouring: that is, the Roman Catholic deity, who is often called upon (together with the Holy Virgin or a local saint) by the servant classes; in this respect He is part of the superstitious baggage of 'the Romish church' (*Udolpho*, 662) for which, as for enforced penance, she has no patience. Although Priestley anonymously published a pamphlet urging toleration of Roman Catholics after the Gordon Riots, he confessed he had been brought up in utter abhorrence and contempt of them,[32] and Richard Price was perhaps the only Rational Dissenter 'who was in any way prepared to accept papists as fellow Christians'.[33] Dissenters opposed the *ancien régime* for both its aristocratic privilege and its papism, and the Bastille, in which Huguenots had been imprisoned, symbolized both civil and religious despotism. Most of Ann Radcliffe's awesomely sublime castles and abbeys conjure up an icon of the Bastille and its inevitable fall:

The abbey of St Augustin was a large magnificent mass of Gothic architecture, whose gloomy battlements, and majestic towers arose in proud sublimity from amid the darkness of the surrounding shades. It was founded in the twelfth century, and stood a proud monument of monkish superstition and princely magnificence. . . . The rude manners, the boisterous passions, the daring ambition, and the gross indulgences which formerly characterized the priest, the nobleman, and the sovereign, had [in the seventeenth century] begun to yield to learning – the charms of refined conversation – political intrigue and private artifices. Thus do the scenes of life vary with the predominant passions of mankind, and with the progress of civilization. The dark clouds of prejudice break away before the sun of science, and gradually dissolving, leave the brightening hemisphere to the influence of his beams. (*Sicilian Romance*, vol. 2, 27–8)

Miles emphasizes that the setting in most of her novels is 'the "Gothic cusp", the mid-seventeenth century, where the medieval is on the wane, and the Enlightenment begins to wax'[34] – which forms a parallel to the rupture of the French Revolution in Ann Radcliffe's own day. To be sure, the above quotation does not illustrate a carefully thought-out system of political philosophy, and the young author's sense of historical progress is rather embarrassingly oversimplified. But there is little doubt that Ann Radcliffe's feelings are those commonly shared by her liberal Dissenting culture, and specifically the Unitarian utopian belief in the scientific progress of civilization. Her despotic villains may last longest in our memory, but every novel contains some praiseworthy figure representing scientific liberalism; in *The Romance of the Forest* it is Montalt's murdered half-brother: 'Henry was benevolent, mild, and contemplative. In his heart reigned the love of virtue; in his manners the strictness of justness was tempered, not weakened, by mercy; his mind was enlarged by science, and adorned by elegant literature' (343). Such figures, like many Unitarians, often follow scientific hobbies: St Aubert studies botany, St Foix geology, and Emily is patently a student of arboriculture (in *The Mysteries of Udolpho* three dozen different species of tree are enumerated, far more than in any contemporary novel).

Part of the reason why the Unitarians supported the French Revolution was specifically because it overthrew papist despotism. Victor Sage, who emphasizes Mrs Radcliffe's links with the Protestant Establishment through her relations the Bishop of Gloucester and Dr Hallifax (Sage does not mention her Unitarian connections), goes so far as to characterize Emily in *Udolpho* as 'really a Lutheran mouthpiece'.[35] The passage in which Emily describes the penitential wax figure as illustrating 'that fierce severity which monkish superstition has sometimes inflicted on mankind' plays, according to Sage, a 'sectarian role . . . deliberately designed to titillate the conscience of the Protestant readership'.

Dr Jebb's wife Ann, whom he married in 1764, was the daughter of Revd James Torkington and Lady Dorothy Sherard, daughter of Philip, 2nd Earl of Harborough. Mrs Jebb was a virago. Under the signature of Priscilla, she had written numerous 'petitions' and letters to the newspapers, to politicians and to archbishops, defending personal interpretations of the Scriptures, advocating parliamentary reform and hailing the dawn of the French Revolution. She maintained this zeal for civil and religious liberty until her death in 1812.[36] Rather like some of the physically unwell women in Mrs Radcliffe's fiction, and despite her mental ardour, 'The Frame of Mrs Jebb was extremely feeble, her countenance always languid and wan. She used to recline on a sofa and had not been out of her room above once or twice these 20 years – she seemed the shadow of a shade.'[37]

Unitarians such as Jebb were ideologically opposed to orthodox hierarchy and the Establishment *per se*, and volubly campaigned against political as well as religious despots. It is not hard to understand why the very existence of Dr John Jebb (and his wife) was suppressed in William Radcliffe's memoir of his wife:

> Since Jebb was one of the Unitarians' main publicists, his reputation for being (in Priestley's words [in 1777]) outstanding for his 'ardent zeal for the cause of civil and religious liberty in their full extent' naturally helped to strengthen further in the public mind a strong association between Unitarian theology and agitation for radical political change. But their reputation helped to make the Unitarians an obvious target in the years of reaction that followed the events of 1789 (though Jebb himself died in 1786); the depth of feeling against the Unitarians being evident in the defeat by 142 votes to 63 of Fox's attempt to remove the penal sanctions against anti-Trinitarianism in 1792. In the debate on this bill Burke maintained that the Unitarians were 'not confined to a *theological* sect, but are also a *political* faction', citing a letter of Priestley to Pitt as evidence 'that the designs against the church are concurrent with a design to subvert the state'.[38]

Dr Jebb's cousin Sir Richard Jebb, Bt., son of Dr Samuel Jebb, was also an eminent physician. Dissent was characteristic of most of Ann Radcliffe's relations, and Sir Richard had little respect for religion; he took pleasure in discomfiting those engaged in religious duties, and had no patience for families who were busy at their prayers when he called to attend the sick. He was a rationalist, intolerant of 'all this nonsense'. An anecdote about his rapaciousness was widely circulated. After attending a nobleman, for which he expected a fee of 5 guineas, he received only 3 guineas from the steward. On his next visit he

> contrived to drop the three guineas. They were picked up, and again deposited in his hand; but he still continued to look upon the carpet. His Lordship asked if all the guineas were found. 'There must be two guineas still on the carpet,' replied Sir Richard; 'for I have but three.' The hint was taken as meant.[39]

Richard Jebb was physician to the fashionable in London, and was made a baronet in 1778. One of his patients was Hester Lynch Thrale (later Mrs Piozzi), who noted that he enjoyed translating ribald verses. He attended Mr Thrale during his last illness in 1780–1.[40] When Dr Johnson asked Mrs Thrale why she loved Richard Jebb so much, she answered: 'He is open & confiding . . . & tells me Stories of his Uncles & his Cousins, & I love such Talk.'[41] The Jebb family were loud in each other's praise, and such family pride might have impressed itself upon the young Ann Ward when she visited her relations.

Dr Samuel Jebb had purchased a property in the manor of Walton in 1768, which was inherited by his other son Joshua Jebb (the property included an old medieval and Jacobean mansion, Park Hall). This second-generation Joshua Jebb, Esq. had rebuilt in 1796, at his own expense, the tower of the Chapel of Brimington, and he established a charity providing annual Christmas gifts to five poor old women of good character living in Brimington and Tapton. He was a churchwarden of Chesterfield Church in 1804, and donated the plot of ground on which was built the Chesterfield National School in 1814.[42] The Jebbs and Hallifaxes had a substantial impact upon the region around Chesterfield, whose population was fairly low. In 1811 the chapelry of Brimington had 526 inhabitants, and even the borough of Chesterfield had only 4,591 inhabitants.[43]

Nothing was recorded about the Oates in the first biographies, nor were any Oates family traditions cherished by Ann Ward. No doubt this is because her maternal grandfather James Oates was a plumber or leadmaker, and his relations were plumbers and glaziers. But his relation's children were christened in the Dissenters' chapel, as were the children of Joshua Jebb (though the latter were also baptized a second time by the Vicar of Chesterfield Church).

The earliest biographical notices of Ann Ward Radcliffe recite this illustrious roll-call of individualists who rose to eminence through their talents, but they all give pride of place to a more ancient lineage: the De Witts of Holland. The story of how, in 1672, the courageous merchant Cornelius De Witt was falsely accused of plotting to poison William of Orange, how he was tortured and condemned by prejudiced judges, how his brother Jan voluntarily came to the prison to join him in his banishment and how the mob tore them to pieces is a famous example of patriotism and a classic case of how a would-be despot whips up mob hatred in opposition to bourgeois independence and thereby consolidates his own rule. The story was retold by David Hume in *The History of England*, (1754–62) (Chapter LXV), and many times by others, and was widely known to the Radcliffes' contemporaries. William Radcliffe in his obituary notice claimed to have seen family papers in which it was stated that

> a De Witt, of the family of John and Cornelius, came to England, under the patronage of government, upon some design of draining the fens in Lincolnshire, bringing with him a daughter, Amelia, then an infant. The prosecution of the plan is supposed to have been interrupted by the rebellion, in the time of Charles the first; but De Witt appears to have passed the remainder of his life in a mansion near Hull, and to have left many children, of whom Amelia was the mother of one of Mrs Radcliffe's ancestors.[44]

Ann Ward would have been justifiably proud of her De Witt ancestors, but the draining of the fens was hardly romantic. What Ann Radcliffe's ancient lineage most clearly establishes is the fact that she was bourgeois to her roots.

William Ward lived and worked at the same location on Holborn (now High Holborn) for twenty-one years. His name first appears in the poor rate ledgers for the Christmas quarter 1751, in an entry for Purnell & Ward.[45] He was probably taken in as an apprentice or assistant to the aforementioned Purnell, and would have been little more than fourteen years old at the time.[46] The partnership of Purnell & Ward lasted through the Christmas quarter 1754,[47] but by the quarter ending 24 March 1755 William Ward is listed as the sole incumbent,[48] and he continues to occupy the premises for the next seventeen years. In the early trade directories he is simply listed as 'Ward William, Haberdasher, *Holborn*, near the Bars'.[49] The 'Bars' is the pair of stone obelisks (today topped by silver griffins, formerly adorned by lanterns) marking the boundary of the City of London, where High Holborn joins Gray's Inn Road. The street number varied, though the actual site is always immediately next to 'Dyers Buildings'. From about 1768 the shop is cited in most of the directories as being at No. 19, Holborn.[50] So it remains even today. The building and shop survived unchanged at least through 1840, when it was illustrated in John Tallis's *London Street Views*. The core of the four-storey building with its original fenestration survives beneath a late-Victorian rebuilding; the ground floor today has a single sheet of plate glass fronting a travel agent. Nos. 19 and 18 (which has been completely replaced) formed a pair of lodges flanking the entrance to Dyers Buildings, a long narrow court lined with solicitors' chambers originally built around 1740 (on a site occupied by the house of Sir John Dyer), all of which were rebuilt in the Victorian period with string-coursing uniform with No. 19. Only one other old building survives on High Holborn today: 100 feet west on the same side of the street is the medieval Staple Inn, the oldest timber-framed building still standing in London – a suitably picturesque structure to be seen by the future Gothic novelist during her childhood.

In the poor rate ledger for the Michaelmas quarter (that is the end of September) 1772 the preprepared entry 'Wm Ward' was crossed out and 'Bowyer & Co' written beside it.[51] From the end of the Christmas quarter 1772 onwards, the occupant is Wm Bowyer & Co., and Ward's name no longer appears.[52] The trade directories are not as up to date as the rate books, and continue to list him for up to two years after his departure.[53] By 1774 the premises at No. 19 were occupied by Bower & Mellersh, Haberdashers.[54]

Having occupied the same premises for twenty-one years, William Ward was clearly not an entrepreneur. He may well have been one of the many small tradesmen whose business prospects collapsed while their debts mounted during a period of economic crisis in London, when the price of food was rising and there was political unrest. His departure from London may be echoed in La Motte's flight from his creditors in *The Romance of the Forest*, and Madame La Motte's sorrow at being forced to abandon her acquaintances may reflect the distress of Ann's mother: 'she had abandoned her dearest friends and connections – had relinquished the gaieties, the luxuries and almost the necessaries of life; – fled with her family into exile, an exile the most dreary and comfortless' (46).

Just as La Motte finds assistance from the Marquis de Montalt, so William Ward received help from his wife's sister's husband Thomas Bentley, of the firm Wedgwood & Bentley, who was an entrepreneur and a successful merchant on the rise. Bentley regularly stayed with his brother-in-law William Ward during his visits to London from Liverpool while he was organizing the London warehouse for Wedgwood's china and famous vases, and he would have known his niece from her first year. Josiah Wedgwood wrote to his brother John in February 1765 that

> Mr Bentley will be in Town on Wednesday Even^g. next. I am just to kiss his hand as he passeth thro' Newcastle in the Coach on Monday next & shall direct him where to find you. L^{rs}. to him will be directed – at Mr Wards Haberdasher in Holbourn.[55]

So Bentley would have known Ward for at least eight years before he used his influence to obtain for him the position of managing the new showroom for Wedgwood in Bath.

The Ward family had moved to Bath certainly by the end of September 1772, and most likely before the end of June.[56] It was probably during the last half of 1771 or the first half of 1772 that Ann Ward was sent on a long visit to her Uncle Bentley's new home in Chelsea, possibly to spare her the confusion of preparing for the removal to Bath, or simply to get her out of the way so her parents could concentrate on this upheaval in their life. The Ward family's removal from London to Bath in pursuit of commercial success is a classic example of familial disruption caused by the population shifts during the Industrial Revolution. Certain recurring themes in Ann Radcliffe's novels suggest that she fictionalized this dislocation as rejection by her father, the death of her mother and 'abduction' by her uncle. Adeline in *The Romance of the Forest* recalls how she was abandoned by her supposed father:

> I am the only child, said Adeline, of Louis de St Pierre, a chevalier of reputable family, but of small fortune, who for many years resided at Paris. Of my mother I have a faint remembrance: I lost her when I was only seven years old, and this was my first misfortune. At her death, my father gave up housekeeping, boarded me in a convent, and quitted Paris. Thus was I, at this early period of my life, abandoned to strangers. My father came sometimes to Paris; he then visited me, and I well remember the grief I used to feel when he bade me farewell. On these occasions, which rung my heart with grief, he appeared unmoved; so that I often thought he had little tenderness for me. But he was my father, and the only person to whom I could look up for protection and love. In this convent I continued till I was twelve years old. (35–6)

Surely it is no coincidence that Nancy Ward was seven years old when her parents left London and she was sent to her uncle Bentley's house; or that she was twelve years old when Bentley moved from Chelsea to Turnham Green (discussed in the following chapter). It seems possible that St Pierre is a portrait of William Ward, a man of reputable family and small fortune, who leaves London after boarding his seven-year-old daughter at a strange place in Chelsea. If the fiction is not over-exaggerated, then it suggests that she resided with Bentley until the age of twelve, and was occasionally visited by her father, but neither returned to Bath nor saw her mother during that period.

Taste versus Trade

———— • ————

Thomas Bentley, born in Scropton in 1730, was a Derbyshire man like the Oates family. At the end of his apprenticeship he visited the Continent, where he learned French and Italian, and upon his return home in 1754, at the age of twenty-four, married Hannah Oates of Chesterfield (his monument in Chiswick Church incorrectly says 'of Sheffield'). He had probably met her father James Oates through their mutual interest in the wool trade. He and Hannah settled in Liverpool, in a good house in the fashionable locality of Paradise Street. Hannah may have given birth to one infant, who died in its first year, and she herself died in childbirth in the second year of their marriage, in July 1759, and was buried in the Church of St Mary and All Saints in Chesterfield.[1] According to Wedgwood's niece Eliza Meteyard, Hannah's elder sister Elizabeth 'took charge of Mr Bentley's household and received his guests. A niece seems also to have occasionally resided with them.'[2] This niece was the young Ann Ward, though she could not have visited them in Liverpool for she had not yet been born.

From 1762 Bentley acted as a general merchant, importing fabrics and exporting woven goods, and was listed as a 'Manchester Warehouseman' in a 1766 business directory; his partner Samuel Boardman, then a bachelor, lived together with him on Paradise Street.[3] Bentley was a 'natural gentleman', a man of taste and intellect, with rational Dissenting religious views. He was one of the founders and a trustee of the Presbyterian Academy at Warrington in 1757, the Liverpool Library in 1758, and most notably the Dissenter's Octagon Chapel in 1763. The Octagonians had scruples about the Athanasian Creed and its damnatory clauses, and parts of the Common Prayer which savoured of Catholicism or allowed insufficient latitude of opinion.[4] The Warrington Academy occupies a central place in Dissenting history. It was not, strictly speaking, Unitarian, but Arian (affirming the subordination of Christ) with a Socinian drift (denying the divinity of Christ altogether). During the 1770s and 1780s 'the success of the Unitarian academy at Warrington shifted the intellectual, if not the imaginative, centre of the kingdom from London to an area bounded by Manchester to the east and Liverpool to the west.'[5] Warrington was not simply the best of the Nonconformist academies, but 'one of the leading educational establishments of the eighteenth century'.[6] It had a secular bias and a higher proportion of lay students than any other Dissenting academy: 'the academy was never intended as a seminary for the training of Dissenting ministers, but rather as a rival to Oxford and Cambridge free from religious subscription'.[7] The pioneering chemist Joseph Priestley (1733–1804) began as a tutor at Warrington Academy, long before he emigrated to America and became a leader in the Revolutionary movement. He followed John Aikin as tutor, being appointed specifically in the language and literature department (grammar, oratory, criticism, *belles lettres*), though during the course of his six years there he introduced history and his hobby, science. He used to discuss religion and politics with Bentley at the latter's home in Liverpool, and he described Bentley as 'a man of excellent taste, improved understanding, and good disposition, but an unbeliever in Christianity, which was therefore often the subject of our conversation. He was then a widower, and we generally, and contrary to my usual custom, sat up late.'[8] It was probably through Bentley that John Jebb first became acquainted with Priestley.

By the time Ann Ward began visiting her uncle, Bentley's friends would also include Joseph Cooper, an inventive printer; James 'Athenian' Stuart, the architect and designer; Sir Joseph Banks; and Dr Solander. Later friendships were formed with many authors, scientists and political figures; Dr George Fordyce; Dr Ralph Griffiths, editor of the *Monthly Review* to which Bentley occasionally contributed; and Benjamin Franklin. Bentley sympathized with the American Colonies' wish for independence and was an opponent of the slave trade, which was at its zenith in Liverpool. Bentley's philanthropic schemes were ridiculed in many quarters, but he 'was indefatigable in his endeavours to persuade the merchants and masters of vessels trading to Africa to promote a trade in ivory, palm oil, woods, and other produce of the country; but all his exertions were fruitless, "sinews bought and sold" afforded a better profit'.[9] He was just as actively interested in poetry and the fine arts as economy, industry, scientific inventions and canal navigation, and he contributed essays to political journals. He wore his own (balding) hair, rather than a wig, which was considered eccentric for his time.[10]

Bentley met Josiah Wedgwood – a fellow Unitarian – in 1764, and became his partner in 1768; for the next ten years the mark of 'Wedgwood & Bentley' was stamped on the black basalts, busts of white jasper and terracotta for which the firm became celebrated. Bentley opened the Etruria works in 1769, and the production of its famous Etruscan vases began in June that year: he was the man who turned the wheel upon which the first vases were modelled. Wedgwood supplied the science, while Bentley provided the taste; both had a good sense of commerce. Bentley gathered together the artistic talent, such as the sculptor John Flaxman, and collected the intaglios, bas-reliefs and ancient art on which the taste for the antique was based. He presented their wares at an audience with the King and Queen in December 1770, and received royal patronage.[11]

Though the name 'Wedgwood' has come to symbolize upper-class elegance, Wedgwood never mixed with his superiors. Eliza Meteyard recalls that according to members of the family still living in 1871 he

> was never very cordially accepted by the proud old local gentry, full of obsolete notions concerning birth and pedigree. . . . To be in trade, or to possess wealth derived from trade, was then a sufficient blot on any man's escutcheon to weigh heavily against the worthiest qualities; particularly in counties so far removed from metropolitan influence as those of northern England. It was enough that Mr Wedgwood was a Staffordshire potter to insure the cold reception of a narrow-minded squirearchy.[12]

Bentley on the other hand, as the son of a gentleman farmer, occupied a higher class than Wedgwood. He was very popular and gregarious, and perhaps a bit of a ladies' man – the perfect marketing manager:

> His handsome person, and polished manners, were irresistible to otherwise haughty duchesses and ladies; and whilst he poised a vase, or showed bas-relief or cameo, and related the antique stories its designs sought to express, the ladies listened, smiled, bowed, and what was more to the purpose bought.[13]

Bentley eventually moved to London, where the new warehouse and showroom at the Queen's Arms, on the corner of Great Newport Street and Long Acre, were opened in February 1769.[14] Later that year he and Miss Oates resided briefly at the business premises near St Martin's Lane where, at Slaughter's coffee house, he socialized with a host of celebrated artists, writers and scientists; later on his second wife acted as hostess during the regular Wednesday meetings held there, when supper was served on a special service of Wedgwood creamware.[15] In November 1769 he and Elizabeth Oates 'settled down handsomely' at Chelsea, in Little Cheyne Row, close to the workshops where the ceramics were painted and enamelled. Elizabeth assisted in preparing designs for the potters, by cutting out shapes in paper, notably the sphinxes – an interesting precursor to her niece's love of mysteries.[16] Wedgwood called her the 'President of the Council' who had to be consulted by Bentley over the pricing of the Etruscan vases.[17] At

Chelsea they kept 'a chariot and pair, had a horse for an occasional ride, and kept up, as in Liverpool, a generous and yet not wasteful hospitality'. The house faced south and was surrounded by a large garden; a field of ripening barley went with the house, together with stabling for three horses; behind all this lay a verdant meadow, and in front was the wide-flowing Thames.[18] It was made for childhood pleasure, and 'a little niece of either Miss Oates or Mr Bentley passed much of her time at Chelsea, and neighbours were accessible and friendly'.[19] That characteristic vision of the flashing white sail of a boat glimpsed through the mist or at twilight, found so frequently in Ann Radcliffe's novels, could have been experienced at nearby Chelsea Reach, an area full of picturesque boats. Ann Ward grew up to be an outdoor girl: she always chose to live in airy situations surrounded by open fields, and she exerted herself on lengthy rambles during most of her holidays.

According to Julia Wedgwood, 'for some years Wedgwood's eldest daughter was their guest' in Chelsea.[20] This was Wedgwood's invalid daughter 'Sukey', who was personally instructed by Bentley, and stayed with him while she attended Blackland's school in Chelsea as a day pupil. Sukey would have been Ann Ward's only known childhood companion. She eventually married Dr Robert Darwin, and her son was the naturalist Charles Darwin.

William Radcliffe affirmed that his wife's two 'chief delights' were the contemplation of the grander scenes in nature and listening to fine music.[21] In February 1772 Wedgwood was negotiating for the purchase of a barrel organ, but Bentley, acting as his factotum, felt the machine was faulty and intended to examine others before concluding a deal on behalf of Wedgwood; in March the organ was bought and sent to Etruria:

> The Organ arrived safe & a most joyful opening of it we have had. About twenty young sprigs were made as happy as mortals could be, & danced, & lilted away, It would have done your heart good to have seen them. I wish we had your little Sprightly Neece with us, but give my love to her & tell her that when the Organ is sent to Town again which It will be soon it shall be sent to Chelsea for her amusement a week or two.[22]

This is Wedgwood's first reference to the young Ann Ward. He had seen Bentley at the end of January, though it is not clear if he came to London; it is possible that she accompanied Bentley and Miss Oates when they visited Etruria in October 1771, and that they had stayed there through Christmas, returning only in late January.[23] Wedgwood had no other opportunity for a recent meeting with her. This date suggests that she resided with Bentley many months *before* her parents removed to Bath.

On 22 June 1772 Bentley got married once again, to Mary Stamford, at All Saints' Church, Derby.[24] She was the daughter of one of Wedgwood's business associates in Liverpool, and Bentley began courting her in 1770; she spent Christmas with him and Miss Oates at Chelsea that year.[25] In March 1772 Elizabeth Oates had resettled in Chesterfield, 'on an annuity secured by deed for her life, by the provident hands of her good brother-in-law and Mr Wedgwood'.[26] One can imagine the confusion of the young Ann Ward at this critical juncture in her life: seemingly abandoned by her parents, only to have her aunt leave her some four months later, and then to be supplanted by a step-aunt several months after that. This may explain why most of Ann Radcliffe's heroines are portrayed as being *doubly* orphaned.

Elizabeth Oates survived another 25 years, to be buried in the church of St Mary and All Saints in Chesterfield on 14 May 1797, beside her mother Amelia and her sisters Amelia and Hannah.[27] In her will she bequeathed £50 'with my Books & plate' to her niece Ann Radcliffe, an indication that books were special treasures for her just as they were for Ann; perhaps Ann Ward Radcliffe's early literary tastes were formed as much by her aunt Elizabeth as by her uncle Bentley or the circulating libraries. Other £50 bequests were left to her cousins Joseph Oates, Richard and Mary Jebb, Avery Jebb and his daughter, the daughter of Joshua Jebb and her friend Sarah Girolor; her sister Ann Oates Ward was appointed her sole executrix.[28]

In the summer of 1774 the Bentleys moved to No. 13 Greek Street, Soho, a small but elegant home which was connected by a chamber above an archway to No. 12 where the business was conducted. But it was a bad situation, and Bentley's health suffered. A surviving letter from the future novelist's grandmother Amelia Jebb Oates, dated 'Chesterfield 1st August 76', is addressed 'To Miss Ward at Mr Stamfords at Derby'. It would seem that Ann had been staying with Bentley, more or less permanently as his ward, and when Bentley visited Paris in August 1776 he sent her to stay with his wife's father rather than her parents in Bath:

Dear Nancy

I am concerned your Box was not sent sooner. your aunt went to Berisford last Wednesday & left no orders about it as she intended to return on Friday; now I can neither see to write nor hold a pen as I used to doe you must excuse me saying more then [sic] that I intend to send ym by Wednesday carryer & hope you will [?] get them safe. . . . Best respects to Mr and Mrs Stamford & yr young Ladyes & am wishing you health & every injoyment that may contribute to y^r improvement of mind or person so as to make you amiabale or usefull in life

yours effectionately
A Oates

I have sent your Box directed for you at Mr Stamfords cariage [sic] paid. . . . May God Bless you my Dear child. Your Box will be at Derby on Thursday . . .[29]

Bentley's niece continued to visit him when he and his wife moved to a house in Turnham Green in the summer of 1777,[30] a large property with stables and extensive gardens.[31] Ann Ward was 'a delicate child needing country air', and 'she stayed often for weeks at a time with Mr & Mrs Bentley at Chelsea, or later at Turnham Green, and enjoyed and benefited by the outdoor life of their garden and the country food'.[32] While staying with the Bentleys in the spring of 1778 Sukey Wedgwood became very ill, and was attended by Ann Ward's relation Sir Richard Jebb.[33] Bentley continued to suffer from the gout, and grew portly; he died at the young age of forty-nine on 26 November 1780, from unknown causes. In his will he left £800 to Elizabeth Oates 'for her entire use and disposal', and £200 to his partner Samuel Boardman of Liverpool. To Wedgwood he left his share of the prints and books of antiquities that they had owned jointly, and to his wife, who was made sole executrix, he left his house and garden at Turnham Green and the remainder of his estate, in testimony of 'her good understanding and fraternity'.[34] He was buried in a new family vault in the church of St Nicholas, Chiswick, on 2 December 1780, and the tablet erected to his memory – designed by Athenian Stuart and sculpted by Scheemakers – records the achievements of his life.[35] Erasmus Darwin declared his loss a public calamity.[36]

Bentley's wife was frail and frequently ill. From mid-1773 she suffered from headaches, insomnia and fainting spells, experienced a bad attack of influenza in December 1775 and an alarming fainting spell in January 1776.[37] Her friends often feared for her life, though in fact she survived her husband by seventeen years. After Bentley's death she removed to Gower Street, where she died on 19 February 1797, and was buried in Chiswick beside her husband on 25 February.[38] She and Bentley had no children of their own, which may partly account for the long visits made by Ann Ward, Sukey Wedgwood and Miss Stamford. It is doubtful that Ann Ward Radcliffe maintained contact with her.

William Radcliffe had to express some surprise at his wife's lack of social confidence in view of the opportunities of her childhood. Though quick-witted and imaginative, and therefore qualified for conversation by her own talents as well as by 'some good examples of what must have been ready conversation, in more extensive circles', she nevertheless 'had not the confidence and presence of mind without which a person conscious of being observed can scarcely be at ease, except in long-tried society'.[39] Though she 'had the advantage of being much loved, when a child, by the late Mr Bentley', a man whom David Williams, founder of the Royal Literary Fund, ranked together with Benjamin Franklin and Athenian Stuart as the three most accomplished men of conversation he knew[40] – she never acquired the social graces of easy conversation.

William conflates the two Oates sisters and the second Mrs Bentley into a single personage,[41] seemingly unaware that Hannah died before Ann was born, and was replaced as mistress of the house by her sister Elizabeth, who in turn was replaced by Mary Stamford in 1772:

> One of her mother's sisters was married to Mr Bentley; and, during the life of her aunt, who was accomplished 'according to the moderation,' – may I say, the *wise* moderation? – of that day, the little niece was a favourite guest at Chelsea, and afterwards at Turnham Green, where Mr and Mrs Bentley resided.[42]

Of course, all three women were 'her aunt' in one sense or another, and this mother/aunt/stepmother ambiguity is reflected in every one of her novels.

At the house in Turnham Green,[43] according to William Radcliffe, his future wife saw several persons of distinction, particularly in literature, including Mrs Montagu, Mrs Ord, Athenian Stuart 'and once, I think, Mrs Piozzi'.[44] Mrs Elizabeth Montagu (1720–1800), 'the female Maecenas', was the first of the Bluestockings, at whose Mayfair salon this celebrated group of intellectual women shone. Bentley and his second wife were guests of Mrs Montagu at her country home in Deal in the summer of 1776, and it is reasonable to assume that she was a visitor to Turnham Green.[45] Ann Radcliffe frequently quotes the poems of James Beattie, who was Mrs Montagu's literary confidant and often attended her assemblies.[46] Beattie's second son was named Montague after his patroness. Wedgwood first met James Stuart during Christmas 1770, to discuss Stuart's design for a building at the Adelphi which was to be topped by a tripod by Boulton to hold a Lantern of Demosthenes, and it was soon after this that Bentley made his acquaintance.[47] Mrs Montagu, Mrs Vesey, Mrs Carter, Hannah More and other Bluestockings frequently met at the home of Mrs Anne Ord, who is little known today because she published nothing and left no letters.[48] Mrs Ord was noted for her fine taste in music and a clear and powerful singing voice. She moved from Newcastle to London after the death of her husband in 1768, which supports the possibility that Ann Radcliffe met her during visits to Bentley in 1771 and later. Fanny Burney found Mrs Ord a bit of a strain when, together, they toured the Western Counties in 1791: she was 'so ungenial, so nipping, so blighting' in her judgements on people.[49] She was one of the subscribers to James Beattie's *Essays* (1776), together with the Lord Bishop of St Asaph, Thomas Bowdler, Mrs Elizabeth Carter, Revd Dr Samuel Hallifax, Mrs Jackson and the Duke of Leeds – all of whom would play a role in Ann Radcliffe's life.

Unfortunately the young girl made no impression upon these celebrities, for none of them have left any record of being aware that they had ever met the famous novelist. On visits to Warrington, Bentley stayed with his friend

Dr John Aikin – a teacher at the Warrington Academy in the second year of its establishment – and his daughter Anna Laetitia, who married Rochemont Barbauld, a former student at the Warrington Academy. Mrs Barbauld moved in Unitarian circles, advocated the abolition of the slave trade, freedom of speech and religion, and defended liberty and Dissenters in general. She was informally tutored by Priestley and became his friend; her earliest datable poem (autumn 1767) is 'On Mrs P[riestley]'s Leaving Warrington',[50] praising the Priestleys' hearth for its 'social genius of gay liberal mirth'. She wrote many poems on Priestley – on losing a game of chess to him, on his family's coat of arms, on his character ('Champion of Truth!') and 'An Inventory of the Furniture in Dr Priestley's Study' and its maps, copies of Juvenal and Ovid, a Leyden jar storing electricity, a thermometer and innumerable books and pamphlets. But when she wrote a brief memoir of Mrs Radcliffe to prefix an edition of her novels, she seemed to be entirely unaware of the tenuous link between herself and the novelist's Dissenting background.

In one of his letters Wedgwood refers to 'Bentley's shy little niece',[51] and she might well have been so overwhelmed by the extroverted characters who associated with her uncle that she fled dumbfounded from their overpowering presence. Indeed, most of Ann's relations were very forceful personalities; she made up in bashfulness for what these ardent behemoths lacked.

Bentley wrote a pamphlet on female education which he read to friends, including Wedgwood, though it was never published,[52] so presumably he took an active interest in his niece's education. But the effect of his effort was the reverse of what he might have intended. It is extraordinary that Ann Radcliffe's writings demonstrate so little sympathy with the Grecian taste of the man whom Wedgwood dubbed 'Vase-maker-General to the Universe', and yet she would have been familiar with the intaglios, bas-reliefs, medallions, busts and statues that it took twelve days to disburse at the public auction following her uncle's death.[53] Instead, she developed a marked taste for the medieval rather than the antique, the mystery of Sicily rather than the grandeur of Rome.

But we should not overlook Bentley's interest in Gothic architecture and the picturesque. Wedgwood was rather taken aback when Bentley sent him a sketch for the proposed new works and house at Burslem: 'Will not the Gothic Battlements to buildings in every other respect in the modern taste be a little heterogeneous?'[54] One of Bentley's chief activities during 1773–4 was the creation of the Imperial Russian dinner service, a 50-place setting for Catherine the Great. As Bentley noted in the catalogue accompanying the exhibition of almost a thousand pieces in 1774, the principal subjects were 'the ruins, the most remarkable buildings, parks, gardens, and other natural curiosities which distinguish Great Britain, and mostly attract the attention of tourists. . . . we have purposely omitted to represent the most modern [i.e. neoclassical] buildings, considering them unpicturesque.'[55] In order to assemble the source material for this great undertaking, Bentley purchased virtually all available published landscapes, as well as commissioning artists to make original sketches. He and his niece would have been surrounded by countless images of castles, abbeys, ruined towers and sublime and picturesque scenery. For massive ruins the future novelist had only to conjure up memories of the vases, plates and gravy boats illustrating the castles of Richmond, Tattershall, Wardour, Bolton, Sudeley, Barry Pomery, Alnwick and Kenilworth; for evocative ruined cloisters she had only to recall the prints of Furness Abbey, the chapel of St Joseph of Arimathaea at Glastonbury and Milton Abbey; and for picturesque waterfalls and forbidding cliffs she had only to remember the views of the Petrifying Well at Knaresborough and numerous views of her family's native Derbyshire, particularly Dovedale and the famous 'wonders' of the Peak District. These illustrated volumes could have provided a rich and delightful field for her young imagination, and any number of these images may well have inspired the lofty towers and ivy-clad ruins of her fiction. She would have had the opportunity to examine the entire stock of books owned by the firm of Wedgwood & Bentley – W. 'gwood complained in 1771 that their library was unequally divided, and Bentley had all the fine books they possessed illustrating the antique.[56]

The Marquis de Montalt's Grecian drawing room in *The Romance of the Forest* has a literary source in the description of the temple in Chaucer's *House of Fame*, the walls of which are decorated with pictures from Virgil and Ovid, in turn derived from one of Marie de France's *Lais*, in which the walls of a chamber are painted with images of Venus and scenes from Ovid's *Art of Love*.[57] But there can be little doubt that Ann Radcliffe's familiarity with Thomas Bentley's large and substantial villa at Turnham Green, which he had ornamented with bas-reliefs on the external walls,[58] was also drawn upon for describing Montalt's 'gay and splendid villa' (160):

> The walls were painted in fresco, representing scenes from Ovid, and hung above with silk drawn up in festoons and richly fringed. The sofas were of a silk to suit the hangings. From the centre of the ceiling, which exhibited a scene from the Armida of Tasso, descended a silver lamp of Etruscan form: it diffused a blaze of light, that, reflected from large pier glasses, completely illuminated the saloon. Busts of Horace, Ovid, Anacreon, Tibullus, and Petronius Arbiter, adorned the recesses, and stands of flowers, placed in Etruscan vases, breathed the most delicious perfume. In the middle of the apartment stood a small table, spread with a collation of fruits, ices, and liquors. No person appeared. The whole seemed the works of enchantment, and rather resembled the palace of a fairy than any thing of human conformation. (156)

The Marquis's tastefully decorated villa is entirely appropriate for a manufacturer of Etruscan ware. Bentley helped to originate the Etruscan taste in interior decoration; we can be certain that Etruscan vases – made by his own hands – were to be found in his home. From 1769 onwards every other letter from Wedgwood to Bentley reports on the production of yet another ovenful of vases, and during Ann Ward's first visits to her uncle she would have been more aware of 'Vase madness' than most of her contemporaries.[59] Illustrated editions of the poets mentioned in the above quotation would have served to inspire his designs for the firm.[60]

From the locked French windows on the balcony Adeline looks out over an extensive garden with groves and lawns, running down to water glittering in the moonlight, 'resembling more an English pleasure ground, than a series of French parterres' (164) – that is because this is almost certainly Bentley's large garden at Turnham Green, which according to the Ordnance Survey 1865 25-inch map extended some 150 yards along Chiswick Field Lane (now Devonshire Road). Adeline's chamber is no less seductive:

> The airy elegance with which it was fitted up, and the luxurious accommodations with which it abounded, seemed designed to fascinate the imagination, and to seduce the heart. The hangings were of straw-coloured silk adorned with a variety of landscapes and historical paintings, the subjects of which partook of the voluptuous character of the owner; the chimney-piece, of Parian marble, was ornamented with several reposing figures from the antique. The bed was of silk the colour of the hangings, richly fringed with purple and silver, and the head made in form of a canopy. The steps, which were placed near the bed to assist in ascending it, were supported by Cupids, apparently of solid silver. China vases, filled with perfume, stood in several of the recesses, upon stands of the same structure as the toilet, which was magnificent, and ornamented with a variety of trinkets. (164)

Except perhaps for the solid-silver Cupids, Ann Ward would have seen the originals of such Etrurian elegance even before they were offered to the public. In late 1775 and early 1776 Wedgwood and Bentley were working on a Birth of Bacchus and a large jasper Triumph of Bacchus, which consisted of at least six separate figures.[61] In March 1776 Wedgwood sent Bentley a box containing Cupid and Hymen,[62] and throughout that year the firm was especially active creating their famous bas-reliefs for chimney-pieces, as well as tripod lamps and a large head of the Medusa for Warwick Castle.[63] In 1777 one of their chimney-piece tablets of the Marriage of Cupid and Psyche cost 5 guineas.[64] (Sir Roger Newdigate, of more refined tastes, was sent an Eagle and Ganymede.[65]) Wedgwood had some difficulty meeting the objections to the nakedness of their figures from the antique; he would have liked to clothe them, but that increased the difficulty and cost of their manufacture. Sometimes they avoided offence by making a simple sea change, as this extract from a letter Wedgwood wrote to Bentley in March 1772 reveals: 'I am glad you have changed the name of our large Bacchante to Cassandra, I like it much better & hope it will sell, now it is regenerated.'[66] And as for flowerpots, Ann Ward knew all about flowerpots from her father's successful marketing of them, as Wedgwood observed: 'Mr Ward orders Devonshire flowerpots by doz[ns]. of a size & what is more extraordinary they sell these without the advantage of the Duchess's patronage or name. What will they do when Mr Ward is instructed to call them Devonshire flowerpots!'[67]

Bentley, far from being a 'votary of vice' like Montalt (*Romance of the Forest*, 163), was a gentleman of the most admirable and attractive character. His most abiding influences upon his young niece were his sensitivity to beauty, his familiarity with paintings and drawings and his love of poetry. Bentley's favourite author was James Thomson, particularly his great poem on 'Liberty', which he sent to Wedgwood, urging him to read it.[68] Ann Radcliffe frequently quoted Thomson's poetry in her own novels, though her own favourite was 'The Seasons'. Bentley also raptured over Rousseau's *Discours sur l'origine et les fondements de l'inégalité permi les hommes* (1754);[69] and presumably he shared the views of *Du contrat social* and *Émile, ou traité de l'éducation* (both 1762), on which Wedgwood asked his opinion;[70] Bentley made a point of visiting Rousseau when he visited Paris in 1776. It is clear that Ann Radcliffe was heavily influenced by Rousseau's novel *Émile*, particularly in *Romance of the Forest*.[71] Bentley's political beliefs would have consolidated the radical views long held by the novelist's family going back through the Jebbs. He never missed a speech by Pitt; indeed, he stood for nine hours in the House of Lords while Pitt (Lord Chatham) arraigned the government in his famous comeback speech in January 1770 – he reported to Boardman that 'His abilities are certainly transcendent, and his knowledge is almost boundless' – and succeeded in meeting him in 1776.[72]

Bentley was strongly opposed to the Athanasian Creed, and he firmly supported the Unitarian cause, though he seems to have been an agnostic privately. The Rousseauesque philosopher La Luc probably reflects the character of Bentley uncoloured by childhood nightmare or Gothic convention. La Luc's religious convictions are those of a sensible Unitarian: he believes in the sublimity of the Deity and in the afterlife, because 'whether they are illusions or not, a faith in them ought to be cherished for the comfort it brings to the heart, and reverenced for the dignity it imparts to the mind' (*Romance of the Forest*, 275). 'In early youth La Luc lost a wife, whom he tenderly loved' (245), as had Bentley, and philosophy 'enabled him to resist the pressure of affliction' (245). 'On the death of his wife he received into his house a maiden sister, a sensible, worthy woman, who was

deeply interested in the happiness of her brother' (246) – this is manifestly
Bentley's sister-in-law Elizabeth Oates. La Luc frequently visits relations of
his late wife in Geneva, just as Bentley often travelled to the north of England
(where he and his wife had relations) to conduct his business. La Luc's home
comprises a small entrance hall, a glass door (French windows) leading into
the garden, his study, a small adjoining room 'fitted up with chymical
apparatus, astronomical instruments, and other implements of science' (248),
the family parlour, and a room used exclusively by Madame La Luc for
preparing botanical distillations and medicines. This is not a small château
in the Alps, but yet another recollection of Thomas Bentley's home in
Turnham Green, with rooms reflecting the experimental science for which
Joseph Priestley was noted, including perhaps apparatus related to the glaze
and manufacture of ceramics.

Though it seems obvious that Ann Radcliffe's recollection of her
residence at Bentley's home in Turnham Green was an important resource
for her novel, it does not therefore follow that Bentley himself is necessarily
reflected, or even refracted, in the character of the villain Montalt. While
Bentley was directly responsible for the cultural fashions exploited in the
novel, the wicked Marquis can more easily be located within purely literary
conventions. The known facts about Ann Radcliffe's life are so meagre that
any speculation about the relevance of the (infrequent) incest themes in her
novels is perhaps unwarranted. Wicked uncles (usually maternal) and incest
are staple fare of Gothic novels and melodramas such as Walpole's *The
Mysterious Mother*, from which she quotes in *The Italian*. What we know about
Thomas Bentley, which is a great deal, does not match the psychological
profile of a habitual child molester. He is known to have been 'especially
fond of children',[73] but there is no evidence whatsoever that this was ever
sexually expressed. I feel that any speculation about the meaning of incest
in Ann Radcliffe's novels should begin with the working hypothesis that the
maternal uncle figure is really a projection of her father. It is not entirely
beyond the realm of possibility that she was sexually abused by her father,
and that she was sent by her mother to live with her uncle Bentley for her
own protection; faced with such a traumatic upheaval, the seven-year-old
girl might well have projected her continued fear of sexual abuse upon her
uncle while endeavouring to reinstate the propriety and virtue of the father.
The Romance of the Forest, for example, suggests that there was little love
between Nancy Ward and her father. She may have felt that he had
abandoned her and had no tenderness for her, just as Adeline felt abandoned
by her supposed father, Louis de St Pierre:

> Sometimes she looked back to her father; but in him she only saw an enemy,
> from whom she must fly: this remembrance heightened her sorrow; yet it was

not the recollection of the suffering he had occasioned her, by which she was so much afflicted, as by the sense of his unkindness. (58)

Later, another apparent father, La Motte, also abandons Adeline, this time to the Marquis de Montalt, and she struggles against the inevitable conclusion: 'To discover depravity in those whom we have loved, is one of the most exquisite tortures to a virtuous mind, and the conviction is often rejected before it is finally admitted' (118). When she concludes that Madame La Motte has similarly united against her, her trust is broken altogether. There are many clues, in biographical facts as well as in the novels, that the relationship between Ann's parents was uneasy, and that her relationship with them was painful.

Ann Ward's parents had been married for five years before Ann was born, and she was their only child. Her mother was almost thirty-eight years old when she was born,[74] though her father was probably about twenty-seven. (One recalls that a nun in *The Italian* sarcastically observes that Sister Olivia, Ellena's real mother, is distinctly middle-aged.) It may fairly be deduced that she was an unwanted child. The heroines in her novels are orphans in search of their 'real' parents, who cannot otherwise account for their 'adopted' parents' coldness towards them and remember their childhood with distress. They marry abruptly in the concluding paragraphs of each novel and allegedly will have children, but only as a matter of literary convention. Mrs Radcliffe herself was to have no children – and would express no interest in them – and there are virtually no children in her novels, other than the happy peasant youth who symbolize the natural life. Images of death in childbirth will occur in *The Mysteries of Udolpho*.

Children of elderly parents often feel themselves to be a generation older than their contemporaries, leaving them set apart, as self-contained and aloof as Ann Radcliffe's heroines. This gap would have been exacerbated by 'the feeling of old gentility, which most of her relatives cherished'. According to Talfourd:

> She had been educated among members of the old school, in manners and morals, whose notions, while they prompted the most considerate kindness towards their young charge, did not perhaps tend to excite precocious intellect, especially in a female of diffidence, approaching to shyness. Something of the formality derived from education may be traced in her works, supplying a massive but noble and definite frame-work for her sombre and heroic pictures.[75]

Talfourd is no doubt thinking, for example, of the pathetic portrait of Adeline in *Romance of the Forest*, who possesses 'symptoms of genius' but who is nevertheless too shy to endure the tumult of mixing in society:

Company, by compelling her to withdraw her attention from the subject of
her sorrow, afforded her a transient relief, but the violence of the exertion
generally left her more depressed. It was in the stillness of solitude, in the
tranquil observance of beautiful nature, that her mind recovered its tone, and
indulging the pensive inclination now become habitual to it, was soothed and
fortified. (288)

Lucy Aikin – herself an active Unitarian – remembers the 'barbarous
ceremonial' that characterized the 'Old Times':

> From the retired life that they led, and the awe and subjection in which they
> were kept by their elders, damsels had then a degree of bashfulness, or
> awkwardness if you please, of which . . . the accomplished young ladies of
> these days cannot even form an idea.[76]

Well-bred ease was scarcely known except in the highest social circles;
certainly Mrs Radcliffe found the familiarity of modern manners distasteful,
'and, though remarkably free and cheerful with her relatives and intimate
friends, she preferred the more formal politeness of the old school among
strangers'.[77] Ann Radcliffe's heroines, passionate about the landscape, are
curiously cold in their social intercourse. Talfourd felt this was because her
own manners were 'peculiarly straight-laced and timorous'. Certainly he is
correct that her 'scrupulous sense of propriety' prevented her from handling
the broad strokes of the pen necessary for the successful portrayal of comic
characters. 'Her old-fashioned primness of thought, which with her was a
part of conscience' is one of the keys to her personality.[78] It may be due, in
part, to an absence of parental love during her childhood.

The relationship between her parents seems to have been formal,
unromantic and distant. Although Ann Oates Ward would live to 1800, she
drafted her first will in 1783, perhaps at a time of illness, which illustrates a
pious coldness between herself and her husband, and hints at an even more
remote relationship between father and daughter:

> As Life is very uncertain, & it may Please God, to take me out of ye World
> with a Short Notice it is my wish if that Event should Happen that as soon as
> it is proper my Body may be sew'd up in flannel, before ye Shround is put on
> & that I may be interd in a plain, Decent, manner, at Weston, [large space left
> blank, perhaps for the name of a church in this Derbyshire town]. I also wish
> to have my Brideing Coat, my new Cotton Gown & Coat, my Black Crape
> gown & Coat, with ye Buff & purple Silk gown & a Black Sattin Coat that is
> unmade, with a narrow Lace, sent to my Sister Raynes with my best wishes,
> for her Happyness. I also Return my best thanks to my Dear Sister Oates for

all her Affectinate kindness to me, & beg it may be Extended to my Daughter who I hope will be deserving of every affectn her friend may shew her, & that she will Remember yᵉ only Road too [*sic*] Happyness, is by Truth, & Virtue, & a strict adherance to her Duty, in what ever Station of Life, she may be placed, & that it will be her Duty to promote her Fathers wellfair & Happyness as much as Lays in her power. I also hope he, will treat her, with Affection, & kindness, for my Sake, who have done yᵉ utmost in my power, from yᵉ first, of [word unclear] and to promote his wellfair, & Happyness, in every Respect.

    Bath Augˢᵗ 14 1782.[79]

Talfourd must also be identifying Ann Radcliffe with Emily, her heroine in *The Mysteries of Udolpho*, as have many readers since. The 'retiring diffidence' (121) of Emily's manner, her 'cold civility' (197) and 'air of timidity' (121) match what little we know of Mrs Radcliffe. It is difficult not to feel that Ann Radcliffe, like Emily, 'had discovered in her early years uncommon delicacy of mind, warm affections, and ready benevolence; but with these was observable a degree of susceptibility too exquisite to admit of lasting peace' (5).

Miss Nancy

—— • ——

Bath, 'the queen of provincial cities',[1] was chosen by Wedgwood and Bentley as the ideal location for a showroom that would attract the attention of the fashionable aristocracy for whom their product was designed. In 1770 Bentley had secured premises in Westgate Buildings, on a curving street in the older southwestern district of the city, and William Ward is listed as the tenant in the rate books as early as December 1771, though he was not yet in occupation.[2] Many preparations had to be made before the Wards could move to Bath at the beginning of 1772, and William Ward was still listed as a haberdasher at No. 19, Holborn, in *The London Directory* for 1772. In late March Wedgwood warned Bentley that 'it will require six weeks or two months to prepare a sortment of usefull ware here, services &c., &c., & to get them to Bath by water'.[3] Mrs Wedgwood had gone to Bath to recuperate from a serious illness in May, and her niece Eliza Meteyard notes that she had received 'the kind attention of a respectable couple named Ward who were to manage the show-rooms'.[4]

Wedgwood went down to help with the opening, planned for June. The showrooms over which William Ward was to preside were decorated with a background of yellow wallpaper to show up the black basalt vases, which were placed on shelves against the walls, and on tables covered with green baize. The first packages to arrive from Etruria were unpacked to reveal mostly pebble vases and painted desserts. Wedgwood realized that they needed a wider range if they were not to be outshone by their competitors, and frantically urged Bentley to send more:

> We are now loseing time & *opportunity* sadly in Westgate Buildings for want of something to open, you had better take the men from Chelsea to pack a day or two than let us want a few crates to complete our assortment. I hope you will send us some enam^d. Tea ware, & in short everything to make a complete

show of it, or we had better do nothing for I think the Toy, & China shops are richer & more extravagant in their shew here than in London.[5]

Wedgwood was dissatisfied with the site, which he felt had been badly chosen: 'The street is full of Coal Carts, Coal horses & Asses – & great way from the Town & Parades & not very near principal Pump Room. It might do perhaps for the seasons, but it will have little Town business the rest of the year.' Though close to the cathedral, the area is decidedly downmarket even today. By the time they were ready, 'the Season' was completely over, so the opening was postponed until the autumn when they had a better chance of attracting the attention of the fashionable, who always returned to Bath in September.[6] The young Ann Ward, who was with her uncle Bentley early in the year, may have rejoined her parents in Bath for the first time in the middle of June 1772, shortly before Bentley married Mary Stamford, but it is also possible that she went back to Chelsea soon after the Bentleys returned from their one-week honeymoon in Derbyshire. Either she or Miss Stamford was in Chelsea for Christmas, for on 26 December Wedgwood wrote to Bentley: 'My best respects wait on your good Lady and Niece.'[7]

The Bath venture, frankly, was never intended to be a jewel in the crown of Wedgwood & Bentley. From the very beginning, it was to be used as an outlet for their poorer quality ware. In a provincial city like Bath they could safely exhibit the pebble vases with the flashy gilding which Sir William Hamilton found so vulgar. Followers of fashion rather than men of taste were the anticipated customers. The shop even had a range of shelves especially devoted to 'cheap Vases'. Wedgwood made his plans clear to Bentley:

> If you had an assortment of these, a number of your customers, who have more taste than money, or want to place them at a great distance from the Eye, or collect odd things, of *fine forms* for their Cabinets, or those of your Customers who are fond *in the extreme* of his Majestys picture *in gold* & yet wo[d]. wish to have some of the fine things in vogue, in their houses or Cabinets – These Gentry altogether make up a numerous class, & may buy up a large qu[ty]. of our odd, & second rate things, which at present are a dead stock.[8]

Eventually the shop in Bath opened, but Wedgwood was shocked by the vulgarity with which William Ward promoted his goods. Wedgwood's attitude to class *vis à vis* his own status in society was perhaps unresolved, and he complained to Bentley about Ward's mass-market advertising techniques in the lead-up to Christmas 1772:

> I have a letter from Mr Ward wherein he tells he has advertised in the papers, & is now going to deliver *hand bills* at the Pump Room every morning, as the

China-men &c do, which I am very sorry to hear. – We have hitherto appeared
in a very different light to common shopkeepers, but this step, in my opinion,
will sink us exceedingly. I suppose these hand bills are publish'd in our names,
as coming immediately from us. – Do you know what they are? I own myself
alarmed at this step, & have wrote to Mr Ward to desire he would not deliver
any more hand bills as coming from us, it being a mode of advertiseing I never
approv'd of, & if they are printed in our names I think either you or I should
have seen the advertisement before it was thus deliver'd.[9]

Presumably Ward was castigated by Bentley as well as by Wedgwood for
lowering the tone.

Their ornamental ware was selling well in early 1773, and Wedgwood was
'glad to hear too that Mrs Ward has some hopes of the business answering
to them at Bath. Pray make my best respects to her, and my love to Miss
Nancy and believe me ever yours most affectionately.'[10] We need not
necessarily infer from this that Ann – affectionately nicknamed Miss Nancy –
has returned to Bath with her parents; Wedgwood could just as easily be
passing his love to her as a resident with Bentley.

Eventually it was appreciated that Westgate Buildings were located in
too old a section of the city to attract the *beau monde*, so at the end of 1774
the showrooms were relocated to fashionable Milsom Street, at a house near
the bottom of the street.[11] In June 1779 it was relocated once more, to No.
22, one door from the top of Milsom Street.[12] This was (and is) the central
shopping spine of Bath, lined with elegant shops, banks and several noted
circulating libraries. It was very modern, having been laid out only in 1762,
though it did not develop into an élite residential district as originally
planned. Most of the houses let out lodgings in the three floors above the
ground-floor shop. The directories listed Ward's house as one of the 'Lodging
and Boarding-Houses', so he obviously supplemented his earnings as a store
manager by taking in lodgers. The general price for the best rooms was 10
shillings a week from September to May, or 7 shillings a week for June until
August, and 5 shillings a week for servants' rooms.[13] The Bath showroom
was largely a failure in Wedgwood's eyes, and he very seldom refers to its
activities in the remainder of his correspondence – as if he wished to push
this distasteful venture out of his mind.

Any record of Ann Ward's life in Bath was almost totally suppressed, as
if she were ashamed of it. The possibility that she might have spent more
than fifteen of her most formative years in the city is nowhere acknowledged.
Talfourd's memoir refers only twice to Bath, to her remembrance of a
performance by Mrs Siddons in its theatre, and to her marriage. It is never
divulged that her father managed the Bath showrooms for Wedgwood &
Bentley, a sure sign that she herself was conscious that it was a second-rate

shop. Her father was not even a member of the 'Middling classes', but a common tradesman. La Motte in *Romance of the Forest* seems to portray just such a tradesman, a man in whose character 'selfish prudence was more conspicuous than tender anxiety for his wife' (55). La Motte is one of the most realistic character studies in Ann Radcliffe's novels, which could easily have found a place in any contemporary novel of manners; the finely observed details are manifestly based upon a real person rather than literary conventions, the most obvious candidate being her father William Ward: 'not a man of very vigorous resolution, . . . rather more willing to suffer in company than alone' (52); a bull-headed man with whom 'opposition had always an effect contrary to the one designed' (143); a man who often speaks 'peevishly' (57), and is sullen and despondent (94). William Ward may have fled his creditors and received financial help from Thomas Bentley, just as La Motte was dependent upon the Marquis de Montalt.

The Italian – which has several teasing autobiographical markers, such as framing the story with an Englishman's visit to the scene in the year 1764, the year of Ann Radcliffe's birth – may reflect some of the feelings experienced by the daughter of a tradesman. Ellena and her aunt Signora Bianchi live in circumstances similar to those of the Ward family: 'they were persons of honourable, but moderate independence. The house was small, but exhibited an air of comfort, and even of taste' (6).[14] When Ann Radcliffe was eighteen years old, her mother was 55; a similarly wide difference exists between the eighteen-year-old Ellena and her mother: her aunt and surrogate mother Signora Bianchi is 'an aged lady, who leaned upon her arm' (5), and a 50-year-old nun ridicules the fact that Sister Olivia (her real mother) is obviously middle-aged. Ellena has the talents of Ann's aunt Elizabeth who copied designs for Wedgwood & Bentley: she earns a little money by drawing 'copies from the antique', such as a dancing nymph from Herculaneum which ornaments a cabinet in the Vivaldi palace (9, 24). Ellena and her aunt busily produce drawings and embroidery, the nuns of the Santa della Pieta acting as their secret distributors so as to maintain the manufacturers' air of gentility. The author goes to some length to defend 'the means of making this industry profitable without being dishonourable' (383). Ellena has mixed feelings about her status, as probably did the young Ann Ward, daughter of a tradesman: 'She was not ashamed of poverty, or of the industry which overcame it, but her spirit shrunk from the senseless smile and humiliating condescension, which prosperity sometimes gives to indigence' (9). Pastoral poverty, as in *Udolpho*, is of course a literary convention, but here the description shows a non-literary knowledge of straitened circumstances. It is worth remembering William Radcliffe's acknowledgement that her parents, 'though in trade, were nearly the only persons of their two families not living in handsome, or at least easy independence'. The strong impression emerges – from both the work and the life – that Ann Radcliffe was embarrassed by her real father; that she yearned after the financial success and the artistic and class respectability of her uncle Bentley, who was in effect her stepfather, but that at the same time she was uneasy about Bentley's liberal (and in a sense 'libertine') views.

Ann Radcliffe has been romantically portrayed as a child of candid eyes, expressive features and marked sensibility, to accord with her later fame. It has been suggested that she 'delighted as a child in daydreams and things supernatural', but this is unfounded speculation, and quite recent.[15] The only visual representation of her is an imaginary portrait prefixed to J. S. Pratt's 1853 edition of *The Romance of the Forest*, thirty years after her death. We do know that both she and her father were uncommonly short. According to her husband, who remembered her from about the age of nineteen, she 'was, in her youth, of a figure exquisitely proportioned; while she resembled her father, and his brother and sister, in being low of stature. Her complexion was beautiful, as was her whole countenance, especially her eyes, eyebrows, and mouth. Of the faculties of her mind, let her works speak.'[16] The portrait of the young Marchioness in *The Mysteries of Udolpho* may be a self-portrait of Ann Radcliffe:

> Dark brown hair played carelessly along the open forehead; the nose was rather inclined to aquiline; the lips spoke in a smile, but it was a melancholy one; the eyes were blue, and were directed upwards with an expression of peculiar meekness, while the soft cloud of the brow spoke of the fine sensibility of the temper. (104)

An 1824 memoir notes that 'Her parents gave her a good, though not a classical, education; and early in life she discovered much taste for literature, and for contemplating the beauties of nature.'[17] Talfourd comments that as a child she was intelligent but docile, diffident and shy; that she exhibited no evidence of her future genius, except for her powers of observation; that she was instructed in the usual womanly accomplishments, but not the classics.[18] Her eagerness for knowledge in this area was satisfied by her husband rather than by any early instructors. William Radcliffe testified that she had

> a gratification in listening to any good verbal sounds: and would desire to hear passages repeated from the Latin and Greek classics; requiring, at intervals, the most literal translations that could be given, with all that was possible of their idiom, howmuchsoever the version might be embarrassed by that aim at exactness.[19]

Quotations from Lucretius and Tacitus in her *Journey* to Holland and Germany have been taken as implying that Mrs Radcliffe had some familiarity with these classics.[20] But in fact the quotation from Lucretius is not ascribed to him, and is introduced as if it were by Juvenal:

> We returned to our low-roofed habitation, where, as the wind swept in hollow gusts along the mountains and strove against our casement, the crackling blaze of a wood fire lighted up the cheerfulness, which, so long since as Juvenal's time, has been allowed to arise from the contrast of ease against difficulty. *Suave mari magno, turbantibus æquora ventis.*[21]

Juvenal and Lucretius are separated by more than a hundred years, so surely this is a misattribution which demonstrates a deficiency in classical learning. In any case William Radcliffe probably supplied the quotations, just as he had supplied the political notes. Her references to mythology are limited to Bacchus, Hebe, the waters of Lethe, the three Graces and the court of Neptune.

A modern argument that she knew German is based upon the mistaken assumption that her trip to Germany preceded *The Mysteries of Udolpho*, but irrespective of this it was her husband who was more likely to get by in German than she.[22] Several French sources have been unconvincingly suggested for her novels. The only reason Maurice Lévy offers to support the view that she was influenced directly by *Les Mémoires du Comte de Comminge* rather than by its English translation in the *Lady's Museum* is his Gallic prejudice: 'Mais sans doute est-ce fair offense à la culture de notre romancière que de supposer qu'elle aît eu besoin d'une traduction anglaise pour lire les *Mémoires*.'[23] But it is possible that her husband, a linguist, taught her a smattering of French more successfully than he taught her Greek and Latin.

It is often assumed that the young Ann Ward attended the school run by Sophia, Harriet and Ann Lee at Bath,[24] and the received opinion is that she personally knew the Lee sisters. Sophia Lee's obituary in the *Gentleman's Magazine* remarked (perhaps speculatively) that 'Mrs Ratcliffe [*sic*] (then Miss Ward), resident at Bath, and acquainted in Miss Lee's family, though too young to have appeared herself as a writer, was among the warmest admirers of "The Recess".'[25] Her own novels certainly establish her admiration for *The Recess* (1783–5), but there is no substantive evidence that she personally knew the Lee sisters. The comprehensive obituary of Sophia which appeared in the *Annual Biography and Obituary* for 1825 makes no reference to Mrs Radcliffe whatsoever.[26]

Sophia Lee and her sisters opened their school soon after their father's death in 1781. They enjoyed the friendship of the Linleys and the Sheridans, and thus obtained 'the patronage of a very wide and respectable circle'.[27]

Other intimate friends included Mrs Siddons (whose daughter Cecilia was a pupil), Miss Piozzi, Mrs Pennington and Sir Thomas Lawrence.[28] A charming picture of their school at Belvedere House has been left by Susan Sibbald, daughter of a wealthy family, who entered the school as Miss Mein in 1797. It was praised as 'the best school' by the widowed Mrs Gambier, a friend who told the Meins that 'the Misses Lee (there were three of them) were so well known, and respected, and their School so highly thought of, that application had to be made some time before for the admission of pupils'.[29] Another pupil was Sophia Anne Templar, daughter of George Templar, Esq., of Shapwick House, Somerset, who married a baronet. When the girls made visits to town, it was common for them to be accompanied by liveried footmen.

The school was attended by fifty-two boarders and some twenty day scholars, ranging in age from eight or nine years old to nineteen, who were taught by two governesses and three regular teachers, plus a visiting drawing master, dancing master and music mistress. The pupils were taught French, grammar, geography, writing and arithmetic. 'Purity of manners and self-respect were taught by example.'[30] Music lessons were given three times a week, with dancing lessons once a week, so the ladies would 'do credit to Bath'.[31] Once every three years the ladies, calling themselves 'the Leevites', would dance in a public performance at the Upper Assembly Rooms: 'We were all to be dressed in book-muslin frocks, with primrose color'd sashes wide and long, and wreaths of roses of the same color on our heads, which might be had at Mrs Somebody's on Milsom Street.'[32]

Now Ann Ward *was precisely* the daughter of Mr and Mrs Ward on Milsom Street, and we must seriously doubt that this daughter of a ceramic trades-man – a dealer in *ware* – was of sufficient social standing to have been welcomed into this polite academy. Furthermore, Ann Ward was already seventeen years old before this education would have become even a possibility for her, as the school did not open until 1781, when she had already attained that age at which most girls would leave school. If Ann Ward did attend the school from, say, 1781 to 1783, it seems likely that the Misses Lee would have taken note of their pupil's marriage in Bath in 1787 to a graduate from Oriel College. The girls and their teachers usually kept track of the marital progress of their colleagues and pupils. The authoress of *The Recess* would certainly have had a sympathetic interest in the authoress of *The Romance of the Forest* and *The Mysteries of Udolpho*, and a little enquiry would have revealed that Mrs Radcliffe had been married in Bath, née Ward. This is precisely the kind of information that would have been ferreted out by Susan Sibbald, who had devoured both *The Recess* and *The Mysteries of Udolpho*, but it is absent from her memoirs. It cannot be merely an oversight that Belvedere House is not mentioned in the first memoirs of Mrs Radcliffe. If she had attended Sophia Lee's school, then surely Talfourd – friend of Mary Russell Mitford who resided for a few weeks in Milsom Street to recapture her spirits,[33] the very same street where Ann Ward once lived – would have discovered this information. It is also the kind of detail which William Radcliffe would have wished to publicize for the sake of enhancing his wife's respectability. But in fact her life in Bath is virtually ignored in all the early biographies. We have to conclude that Ann Ward was not taught at Belvedere House.

Jerom Murch, one-time Mayor of Bath, and President of the Bath Literary and Philosophical Association, claimed in the 1870s that Mrs Radcliffe 'resided at Bath and knew the Miss Lees intimately, [and] was a great admirer of "The Recess"'.[34] This is based on wishful thinking rather than personal knowledge. There is no evidence that Mrs Radcliffe ever visited Bath for any extended stay after she became famous, except possibly to return briefly with her mother after her father's death, and just preceding her mother's own death.

The view that Ann Radcliffe was well educated is really an indication of how successfully she managed to create that impression through the cultural allusions in her novels. But this was a superficial gloss, and some critics (sympathetic women as well as men) have recognized an unhappy ignorance in her novels. For Bridget MacCarthy, writing in 1947, she is 'the extreme example of genuine literary power misdirected for want of education. Any one of her novels contains a thousand testimonies of this fact. All her novels constitute a depressing avalanche of proof. Her style is the style of a poet gone astray.'[35] Her undisciplined emotionalism was confirmed by the period's fondness for excessive sentiment. Julia Kavanagh in 1862 was harsh but perceptive in her judgement:

> There are in Mrs Radcliffe's writings passages of great beauty, told in beautiful language, but these productions, one and all, betray a mind which had long lain dormant, and that wakened too late to the consciousness of great gifts. . . . In character, in penetration, in historical knowledge, in all the minutiae that prove reading, skill, and a cultivated taste, she failed. She was never vulgar, because her nature was delicate and refined, but she was awkward and ignorant.[36]

The cultural attributes with which the novelist invests her characters suggest that she herself had to strive for culture, that it had not been part of her early education. She was almost certainly aware of her lack of learning, 'for she is continually straining after cultural effects. She is everlastingly enumerating statuary and paintings.'[37] Her culture was self-consciously exhibited as conspicuously as the acquisitions of the *nouveau riche*: the excess of the insecure. The cultural signifiers are carefully assembled and displayed as banners of good taste. I do not mean to say that Ann Radcliffe's cultured façade was fake or that she was just a *poseur*: rather, she was sincerely devoted to the *idea* of culture, but unsophisticated at handling its accoutrements.

Her sense of history is superficial, perfunctory and unreliable, certainly not the kind of knowledge one would expect from someone who had been taught by Sophia Lee, the creator of the historical novel. Ann Radcliffe accumulated her culture from an unsystematic reading of imaginative literature, rather than from a disciplined study of history, philosophy or any of the sciences.

Ann Radcliffe had little guidance during her formative years, and her reading lacks breadth, consisting mostly of the 'pre-Romantic' English poets and Shakespeare. She mined a narrow vein deeply. To judge by the evidence of her reading, she needed a world that was more elegant as well as more adventurous than that of her parents, a world to which she could escape from the vulgarity and sordid meanness that coloured the life of a small tradesman. For Ann Radcliffe a proper lady is a cultured lady – the aesthetic equivalent of a moral lady. Men were educated in the classics, and knowingly peppered their 'serious literature' with classical allusions. Women, excluded from a classical education, were restricted to a second-class literature of merely domestic reference. Ann Radcliffe overcame this cultural handicap by incorporating English and Italian literary allusions in superabundance, thus neatly sidestepping one of the impediments to joining the canon of Literature.

Ann Ward could have become familiar with the works of Shakespeare, Ariosto and Tasso (her favourite poets, and of special importance to her novels) at quite an early age. Young persons sensitive to the beauties of the written word could find ample opportunity to indulge their taste in the circulating libraries of either London or Bath: the *New Bath Guide* for 1778 lists five circulating libraries, two of them located in Milsom Street where the Wards lived;[38] the advertising painted across the upper façade of one circulating library is still visible today. The breadth of her literary knowledge and taste were largely formed by the age of sixteen or seventeen, to judge by the fact that she rarely alludes to anything written later than 1782 in her novels. Those writers who were most popular during Ann Ward's girlhood remained the favourite writers of the adult novelist. From a reading of nineteen Gothic novels containing 561 poetical quotations, Warren Hunting Smith has compiled the following league table:[39] Shakespeare 157 quotations (mostly from *Hamlet* and *Macbeth*), Thomson 37, Milton 30, Collins 19, Ariosto 9, Spenser 7, Tasso 5. The league table for Ann Radcliffe's novels is virtually identical (partly because her novels are included in the first list): Shakespeare 51, Thomson 18, Milton 14, Collins 14, Beattie 12, Mason 10 and a scattering from Pope's *Eloisa to Abelard*, *Essay on Man* and *The Rape of the Lock*, Macpherson's *Fingal*, Dryden, Goldsmith, Gray, Young, James

Cawthorne's *Poems* (1771), Walpole's *The Mysterious Mother*, Warton's *The Suicide* and others. She refers to Tasso, Petrarch and Ariosto, but never quotes from their works. Gilpin, Burke and Reynolds are mentioned in her travel journals. Fewer than half a dozen works by writers of nearly her own generation are quoted, most of them by feminists: Hannah More's *David and Goliath* (*Sacred Dramas*, 1782); Mrs Barbauld's *Poems* (1773); Anna Seward's 'Monody on Major André' (1781); Frank Sayers's *Moina* (1789–92); and Charlotte Smith's *The Emigrants* (1793).[40] Charlotte Smith never returned the compliment by quoting her rival.

The revival of interest in Shakespeare during Ann Radcliffe's childhood had a profound impact upon her romances, and a visit to Bath could have provided this first stimulus to her imagination. On Wednesday 27 June 1781 Mrs Siddons performed Hamlet at the Bath–Bristol Theatre Royal, for one night only, though this was her sixth appearance in that character.[41] Ann Ward, almost seventeen years old, may have been in the audience that evening, for Mrs Siddons made an indelible impression upon the future novelist. In her posthumous essay 'On the supernatural in poetry', which was written as an introduction to her novel *Gaston de Blondeville*, she pictures Mrs Siddons as Hamlet:

> I should suppose she would be the finest Hamlet that ever appeared, excelling even her own brother [John Kemble] in that character; she would more fully preserve the tender and refined melancholy, the deep sensibility, which are the peculiar charm of Hamlet, and which appear not only in the ardour, but in the occasional irresolution and weakness of his character – the secret spring that reconciles all his inconsistencies. . . . Her brother's firmness, incapable of being always subdued, does not so fully enhance, as her tenderness would, this part of the character.[42]

It was not widely known that Mrs Siddons *had* taken the role of the Prince of Denmark in the early part of her career – except to those who had seen her perform it.[43] Mrs Siddons also first appeared in Bath in the character of Lady Macbeth, which she made her exclusive property after the triumph of the 1784–5 season at Drury Lane Theatre in London. Mrs Radcliffe was among the many novelists and playwrights who had in mind Mrs Siddons's sublime look and utterance when they created their most imperious female characters. She certainly saw her perform the role of Lady Macbeth, whether it was in Bath or London:

> Whenever the poet's witch condescends, according to the vulgar notion, to mingle mere ordinary mischief with her malignity, and to become familiar, she is ludicrous, and loses her power over the imagination; the illusion vanishes.

So vexatious is the effect of the stage-witches upon my mind, that I should probably have left the theatre when they appeared, had not the fascination of Mrs Siddons's influence so spread itself over the whole play, as to overcome my disgust, and to make me forget even Shakspeare himself; while all consciousness of fiction was lost, and his thoughts lived and breathed before me in the very form of truth. Mrs Siddons, like Shakspeare, always disappears in the character she represents, and throws an illusion over the whole scene around her, that conceals many defects in the arrangements of the theatre.[44]

The neoclassical splendour for which Bath is famous made remarkably little impression upon Ann Ward. Its elegant promenades feature in dozens of novels by her contemporaries, but only in *The Mysteries of Udolpho* do we find a positive appreciation of the porticos and colonnades of Palladian architecture, where the descriptions seem borrowed from travel literature rather than remembered from childhood. One feels that Ann Ward would have agreed with William Gilpin in the late eighteenth century: 'At Bath the buildings are strikingly splendid: but the picturesque eye finds little amusement among such objects.'[45] The architecture within the city of Bath that might have had a greater influence upon her was Bath Abbey itself and Abbey Church House. This latter building was one of the oldest houses in Bath, a Tudor mansion with quaint windows and gables which was sited at the end of Westgate Buildings and thus very near to where she lived. It was at one time owned by Sir E. Hungerford of Farley (Hungerford) Castle, a building about which there circulated rumours of a mysterious death, and whose tower was used for strange imprisonments. During Ann Ward's residence (or visits) nearby, it was known as Hetling House after the wine merchant who carried on his business from these Gothic premises.[46] The legends of cruelty, oppression and murder which circulated about its previous owners bear some resemblance to the villainies of the Marquis of Mazzini in *A Sicilian Romance* and the interrupted story told by the servant in *The Italian*.[47]

It is likely that Ann Radcliffe was as enthusiastic about country walks as a young girl as she certainly was in later life, and the surroundings of Bath would have been more attractive to her than the city itself. Farley Castle, only six miles from Bath, was a very romantic ruin on a rocky hill, whose southwest tower, veiled with ivy, was entire, though lacking its staircase, perhaps an inspiration for the broken staircase in *A Sicilian Romance*.[48] The landscape surrounding Midford Castle and its priory, as described in a contemporary guidebook, resembled 'that about Tivoli; the rocks are no bad substitutes for ruins, and a contemplative eye may wander from the terrace at Midford castle, till the imagination is transported into Italy. The solemn gloom of this enchanting spot, is accompanied by a repose and silence in perfect harmony with it.'[49] Twenty miles from Bath, near Wells, features of Radcliffe's Gothic landscape could have been inspired by Wookey Hole cavern (mentioned in her *Journey*) and the Cheddar cliffs gorge. Glastonbury Abbey, six miles from Wells, would have held a powerful attraction for her imagination; the legend about the mausoleum of black marble containing the bones of King Arthur could well have inspired the black marble halls in her castles. Many Gothic ruins could be reached by an easy day trip from Bath. *Buck's Antiquities* (1774) illustrates many romantic castles and abbeys in the region of Bath and Wells which were popular with antiquarian and picturesque travellers: Farley Castle, Lacock Abbey, Bradenstoke Priory, Malmsbury Abbey, Nunny Castle, Stokecourt Castle and Glastonbury Abbey; even if Ann Radcliffe had never visited any of these, she would have seen views of them in the print shops of Bath. In any case *Buck's Antiquities* would have been one of the books that provided the sources from which Wedgwood & Bentley drew inspiration for the Imperial Russian dinner service, and a copy would have been kept in her uncle Bentley's library.[50]

It is my view that Ann Ward had few memories of Bath because she spent very little time in that city. She might more properly be said to have lived in Chelsea and Turnham Green and visited Bath, rather than vice versa. She recollected seeing Mrs Siddons in Bath, and spoke with pleasure at seeing the actress and her son Henry going to church, presumably in Bath, but this could have been during an infrequent visit to the city, perhaps for her birthday in 1781. It should be remarked that Talfourd (via William Radcliffe) says that she got married in Bath where her parents lived, not that she lived there with her parents: 'The ceremony was performed at Bath, where her parents then resided, and she afterwards proceeded with her husband to live in the neighbourhood of London.'[51] Eliza Meteyard had also noted that she 'occasionally resided' with the Bentleys, not that she occasionally visited them. The early memoirs make a point of saying that she *resided for long periods* with her uncle, and I believe this means years rather than months at a time. A less circumspect biographer in 1849 made this a bald statement of fact: 'her parents were so poor that she chiefly lived with her uncle, Mr Bentley'.[52] Ann does indeed seem to have been hived off by her parents for lengthy periods. She might have effectively lived with Bentley until his death, and then resided with other relatives, such as Dr Jebb in Craven Street, until her marriage. From the evidence of a surviving letter from her mother, dated 12 March 1783, this would seem to be the case:

Dear Nancy

I find Miss Rowlands is not come home yet, & that Mr Poole has been very ill & intends coming to Bath as soon as he is better, he Lodged at a Coffee house upon

Ludgate Hill near ye Church that perhaps Miss R^{ds} & you, might all come together. I hope to see you ye begining [sic] of next week. I have been very indifferent Lately with ye Gout flying about me. I expect a Letter soon, your Father joined in Love to you.

March 12th 1783   Your Affecinate Mother
                                                    A Ward[53]

If Nancy Ward received any formal education at all, she is far more likely to have attended Blacklands School in Chelsea during her residence with Bentley, the same school which Sukey Wedgwood attended while staying with him. Wedgwood sent Sukey, who was less than one year older than Ann Ward, to live with the Bentleys for very long periods while she went to Blacklands as a day student, and it is not impossible that Ann Ward lived with the Bentleys during the same period, and for the same reason. Bentley went to fetch Sukey from Etruria in October 1775,[54] and she lived with him and his wife continuously until she returned to Etruria for the holidays in August 1776 (the month when Bentley made his trip to Paris); she returned to London in September, when Bentley returned from Paris, and remained with them until the summer holidays in August 1777, returning in September or October 1777, this time to their new home in Turnham Green, where she remained until April 1778, when she finally left Blacklands School. Thus Sukey effectively lived with Bentley for two and a half years. During the early part of this stay she was despondent and homesick, and discouraged by her progress at school, where she acquired little more than the standard female achievements in music, drawing and deportment (the school records do not survive).

Sukey continued to visit Bentley afterwards. During one notable seaside holiday to Margate in August–September 1778 when they were joined by Mrs Bentley's niece Miss Stamford, while Bentley and Mary were hunting for shells and fossils, Miss Stamford fell over a high chalk cliff and narrowly escaped death by being caught on a projecting ledge lower down.[55] Ann Ward was not a member of this party, but she could well have accompanied the Bentleys on other visits to the seaside. Mrs Radcliffe's fascination with the sea is extraordinarily powerful, not something she acquired only after her marriage. She undoubtedly shared the response of Adeline in *The Romance of the Forest*:

Of all the grand objects which nature had exhibited, the ocean inspired her with the most sublime admiration. She loved to wander alone on its shores, and, when she could escape so long from the duties or the forms of society, she would sit for hours on the beach watching the rolling waves, and listening to their dying murmur, till her softened fancy recalled long lost scenes.[56]

A Literary Establishment

Almost as much mystery surrounds the life of William Radcliffe as that of his celebrated wife. The brief information which he supplied about himself for the 1824 obituary of his wife hides more details than it reveals:

> In her twenty-third year she married at Bath (where her parents then resided), William Radcliffe, Esq., a graduate of Oxford; and who, intending to pursue the profession of the law, kept several terms at one of the Inns of Court; but, changing his resolution, was never called to the bar. Mr Radcliffe subsequently became the proprietor and editor of the English Chronicle.[1]

The facts of the matter seem to be that, far from renouncing his legal studies, as Sir Walter Scott was to suggest, he was for some reason rejected; and that long before becoming proprietor of the *English Chronicle*, he had worked for, and eventually had a falling out with the editors of, the more radical *Gazetteer*. Eight years of his life have been suppressed.

William Radcliffe, son of William and Deborah Radcliffe, was christened on 11 December 1763 in St Andrews Church, Holborn – the same church in which his future wife would be christened only eight months later. He attended both Cambridge and Oxford, though he acknowledged only the latter. He was admitted as a pensioner to Trinity College, Cambridge, on 23 August 1780, aged sixteen, as the son of William Radcliffe, a haberdasher in London. But his stay was fleeting, and he left St Paul's School, London, in the Michaelmas quarter of the following year. We do not know why William left Cambridge and switched to Oxford. He was admitted as a commoner to

Oriel College, Oxford, on 25 March 1783, and almost immediately committed an offence: 'Caution received, £15.' He matriculated at Oriel on 26 March 1783 at the age of nineteen. Talfourd says that he 'kept several terms at one of the Inns of Court, but . . . afterwards changed his purpose';[2] in fact he entered the Middle Temple, in 1783, as the son 'of William, of Maidstone, Kent'. He received his BA from the University of Oxford on 3 February 1785.[3]

While examining the rate books for Holborn it is difficult not to remark upon the coincidence that in 1773 a haberdasher named James Radcliffe first occupies the premises at No. 52 (confirmed by Lowndes's *London Directory* for that year), and continues there until he is replaced by a haberdasher named William Radcliffe in 1776 at least until 1780 (the rate books for 1781–3 are missing). Pierre Arnaud suggests that these are respectively William Radcliffe's grandfather and father, and the fact that William Ward, William Radcliffe *père* and Thomas Bentley were all merchants in London provides the link between the young William Radcliffe and the young Ann Ward.[4] But William Ward was in Bath by 1772, and the existence of a haberdasher named Radcliffe some distance from his former premises in Holborn in 1773 is no more than an intriguing coincidence.

The possible link between Radcliffe and Bentley is tenuous. It has been asserted – in 1927, without documentation – that William Radcliffe met Ann Ward at Thomas Bentley's home in Turnham Green.[5] It is not clear how this could be possible. Thomas Bentley died in November 1780, three or four years before William Radcliffe says he met Ann Ward, according to the notes which he himself wrote for the 1824 obituary: 'whom I remember from about the time of her twentieth year',[6] i.e. 1784. Arnaud believes that this passage should not be treated with exactitude – but putting it back four years is allowing too much latitude. It is difficult to believe that William and Ann had met by the age of sixteen and had known one another for at least seven years before they got married in 1787. Nor is it clear why a schoolboy should be invited to Turnham Green. The essential link is missing from Arnaud's theory. (In 1773 an Edmund Radcliff or Radcliffe, a Manchester merchant, assisted Wedgwood & Bentley in exporting their ornamental ware,[7] but we do not know how long he was associated with the firm, or if he was any relation to William Radcliffe.)

My own view – a line of speculation that has not previously been pursued – is that William's father was the older brother of Revd Ebenezer Radcliffe, the Dissenting minister who lived in Walthamstow, and who was one of the group of men, including Wedgwood and Mr Moseley (whom I assume is the Moseley Elizabeth Jebb married), who regularly contributed money towards supporting Joseph Priestley.[8] It is not necessary to establish a link via Bentley for the introduction of the young couple. Ann and William are more likely to have met through Ann's Dissenting uncle John Jebb: in the list of subscribers to *The Works . . . of John Jebb* (1787), among all the entries for the Jebbs, the Oates and the Wards, there appears the name of 'Mr Radcliffe Walthamstow Essex', i.e. Ebenezer Radcliffe.

Ebenezer Radcliffe was christened at the Upper Independent Presbyterian Chapel in Sheffield, Yorkshire, on 14 January 1732, the second son of William and Hannah Radcliffe. His brother William, who was christened at the chapel on 4 September 1736, may be the father of the novelist's husband. Ebenezer received some schooling from the famous Dissenter Dr Philip Doddridge in Northampton and Edinburgh, and in 1758 or 1759 he settled briefly in Boston, Lincolnshire, before moving to London in late 1759. He lived for several years in the Temple, together with Sir Wadsworth Busk, a fellow student of Doddridge at Northampton, while preaching to the Congregationalist Dissenters at Walthamstow, where he was the afternoon preacher and assistant minister until 1779. (Incidentally, 'After Doddridge's death in 1751, his [Unitarian] academy was moved to Daventry, where the first student to enrol was Joseph Priestley.'[9]) In 1761 Ebenezer Radcliffe succeeded to the pastoral charge of the Jewry Street congregation. He married a Miss Parish in 1769 and had one child, a daughter. In 1773 he wrote the celebrated *Letters to the Prelates* in support of the repeal of the laws against Dissenters. Ebenezer Radcliffe was an outspoken advocate of religious liberty and liberty of conscience, who castigated Parliament for failing to pass the Dissenters' Bill: 'Though you have denied us redress, you have not taken away the liberty of complaining, nor destroyed the force of any of those principles upon which our bill was grounded. . . . You have convinced us, that bigotry and spiritual despotism are not totally annihilated.'[10] He retired in 1777 at the age of forty-six, because his Sunday exertions left him indisposed for two or three days each week, though he frequently contributed to the *Gentleman's Magazine*, and died in Walthamstow on 17 October 1809 in his seventy-eighth year.

Ebenezer Radcliffe's roots in Yorkshire and Lincolnshire might help to account for Ann and William Radcliffe's visit 'to Relations' in those counties in 1794. If Ebenezer is William's Dissenting uncle, this would help to explain William's liberal/radical sympathies, and would also establish a common link with his wife's Dissenting background. William resided briefly at the Temple – perhaps because his uncle Ebenezer had done so.

William and Ann were married in the parish church of St Michael in Bath on 15 January 1787; their signatures to the marriage register were witnessed by William Ward and Rose Forbes. Rose Forbes might have been a relation of Mrs Mary Forbes, a china dealer who was Bentley's 'very agreeable neighbour' in 1764.[11] The announcement was made in the *Bath Chronicle* for

Thursday 18 January: 'Monday, was married at St Michael's Church, the Rev William Radcliffe, A.B. of Oriel College, Oxford, to Miss Ward, daughter of Mr Ward, in Milsom Street.'

They returned to London to live, where William quickly began to supplement his income by editing and translating. Several weeks before their marriage, he had finished a new edition of *An Introduction to Universal History*, in which he had the temerity to revise, correct and improve upon Gregory Sharpe's translation from the Latin of Baron Holberg.[12] This textbook for the use of young students was published shortly after their marriage. Two more books bear William Radcliffe's name, both translations from the French: *The Natural History of East Tartary*, which appeared in 1789,[13] and *A Journey through Sweden*, which was published in 1790 in both London and Dublin.[14] The Russian natural history was published in the very same year that his wife gave her first literary effort to the world.

Ann Radcliffe's first novel *The Castles of Athlin and Dunbayne*, published during the first half of 1789,[15] was not widely reviewed. One critic, who perceived more action than sentiment in its pages, assumed the author was a man. The Scottish manners and costume had not been carefully observed by the author: 'He [*sic*] seems to be unacquainted with both.'[16] Another critic felt it would afford considerable amusement at least to 'the young and unformed mind' and 'to those who are delighted with the *marvellous*, whom wonders, and wonders only, can charm'. The principle behind the work was perceived as a desire 'to *elevate and surprise*' by means of trapdoors, false panels, subterranean passages and romantic imagery.[17]

The novel is essentially a late flowering of the traditional novel of sentiment, but in which the one-sided emphasis upon Pity was compounded with Terror. The moods of Ann Radcliffe's characters – from pensive melancholy through delicious shudders to suspense and curiosity – are said to be mirrored by their environment. Osbert, like the female protagonists of Radcliffe's subsequent novels, fears that his visions are 'the phantoms of a sick imagination' (161). The murder of his father 'exasperated his brain almost to madness' (39); the identical phrase will be reused to describe Julia in *A Sicilian Romance*: 'her brain was at length exasperated almost to madness' (vol. 1, 100). Osbert's enthusiasms are those of the typical Radcliffean *heroine*:

> His warm imagination directed him to poetry, and he followed where she led. He loved to wander among the romantic scenes of the Highlands, where the wild variety of nature inspired him with all the enthusiasm of his favourite art. He delighted in the terrible and in the grand, more than in the softer landscape; and wrapt in the bright visions of fancy, would often lose himself in awful solitudes. (8–9)

Losing his way in the mountains, Osbert remains 'in a silent dread not wholly unpleasing' (9) – no doubt derived from Thomson's description of the majestic works of Nature: 'With what a pleasing dread they swell the soul' (*Winter*, ll. 106–10). Before it is discovered that the Highland peasant Alleyn is really the long-lost son of the Baroness Louisa, there is much anguished debate over whether or not one of ignoble birth can unite with an aristocrat. Matilda wants an alliance between Mary and the Count de Santmorin to support 'the ancient consequence of her house' (206), but Ann Radcliffe clearly intends the reader to sympathize with Mary and Alleyn that true love is more important than class. Robert Miles detects a 'coded anti-aristocratic animus' in the narrative,[18] but this subplot is borrowed almost whole from Clara Reeve's *The Old English Baron* (1778; originally published as *The Champion of Virtue* in 1777): when Alleyn's real name turns out to be Philip, we recognize a gracious salute from Ann Radcliffe to Sir Philip, the old English baron of Clara Reeve's novel.

The Castles of Athlin and Dunbayne became more popular as the taste for the Gothic grew, though it did not bear Ann Radcliffe's name on the title page until the third edition in 1799.[19] Ann Radcliffe lost no time in writing her second and more interesting novel, *A Sicilian Romance*, which appeared by early autumn 1790 and was reissued that winter.[20] Two volumes (instead of the single volume of her first novel) enabled her to develop a more believable plot and greater suspense and atmosphere; a marked increase in writing skill is also apparent. *A Sicilian Romance* was somewhat more widely reviewed than the first novel. One critic even declared the work to be 'of the first class' after reading it through twice, something reviewers did not often do.[21] All critics agreed that the still anonymous author (though her sex was known) possessed a happy invention as well as correct taste, and 'elegant and animated language'.[22]

Clara Reeve's *The Old English Baron* influenced the suite of lofty ruined apartments with a chapel-like recess. Ann Radcliffe picked the cherries from Clara Reeve's novel but left the naturalistic dross behind, as well as the moral didacticism. What she might allude to vaguely as a simple peasant meal, Clara Reeve would spell out as new-laid eggs and rashers of bacon. The peasant woman in Reeve's novel is glad to adopt the foundling Edmund, because her infant has just died and her excess milk is troublesome, so she is glad to be eased of it (58). Mrs Radcliffe would never indulge in such coarse realism. Both novels nevertheless conclude with the identical moral, in almost identical language: Clara Reeve's story 'furnish[es] a striking lesson to posterity, of the over-ruling hand of Providence, and the certainty of RETRIBUTION' (*Old English Baron*, 153), while Ann Radcliffe's story demonstrates 'a singular and striking instance of moral retribution (*Sicilian Romance*, vol. 2, 216)'.

The 'low hollow sound' that echoes throughout the novel is borrowed from several sources – the 'deep and hollow groan' that issues from Alfonso's ghost in Walpole's *The Castle of Otranto*; the 'deep hollow groan' that emanates from the ghostly knight in Aikin's *Sir Bertrand* (1773); the noise from the unquiet ghost buried beneath the floor of the haunted chamber in Reeve's *English Baron*. In all these works it symbolizes the demand for vengeance or retribution. The difference is that the 'low hollow sound' in *A Sicilian Romance* originates not from the dead, but from the buried alive: the origin of this groan is finally unearthed by Julia, who enters a cavern in the forest and makes her way into a vault where she discovers a pale and emaciated woman seated 'in a kind of elbow chair', who utters 'My daughter!' and faints away (vol. 2, 159). The horror of the ghostly cry of anguish is not so much explained away as *intensified* when we realize that it issues not from a supernatural being after all, but from the sighing of the Marquise who has been *imprisoned for fifteen years*, virtually in solitary confinement, in a cell beneath the castle. This natural explanation surpasses in horror the supernatural terrors it has given rise to. The use of 'the explained supernatural' for which Ann Radcliffe became so well known can be seen as the flower of the discourse in Unitarian thought about the place of the supernatural in a Rational view of the world (see Chapter 6).

A Sicilian Romance, according to the first obituary of Mrs Radcliffe, 'established her fame as an elegant and original writer'.[23] When it appeared, 'as we ourselves well recollect', wrote Sir Walter Scott a year after her death, it 'attracted in no ordinary degree the attention of the public'. The imagery and scenery were 'like those of a splendid oriental tale', and the novel 'attracted much notice among the novel-readers of the day, as far excelling the ordinary meagreness of stale and uninteresting incident with which they were at the time regaled from the Leadenhall press'. It was on the basis of this novel, and her introduction of a tone and imagery hitherto reserved for poetry, that Scott awarded her the title of 'the first poetess of romantic fiction'.[24]

It remained in people's memories for many years: one day in 1817, for example, Henry Crabb Robinson called at the library and, though he was a Unitarian, stole a copy of *A Sicilian Romance* and returned with it to his inn, where he settled down to enjoy himself, and read it 'with interest and curiosity, though I read it some twenty years ago'.[25] The novel had an immediate impact even in France, where it influenced Marsollier's *Camille, ou le souterrain*, an opera which Matthew Gregory Lewis saw in September 1791, and which was to influence the scene of Antonia in the crypt in his novel *The Monk* five years later.[26] Robert Princeton Reno makes the important point that there were very few Gothic novels between *The Castle of Otranto* and *A Sicilian Romance* but a flood of them afterwards; he suggests that this is accounted for by Ann Radcliffe's rejection of the medieval trappings which Walpole had used to justify the blending of the ancient and the modern romance, thereby freeing novelists to develop the more modern European and Renaissance Gothic which dominated the genre.[27]

William Radcliffe meanwhile was distinguishing himself as a parliamentary reporter. It was said that

> he would carry the substance of the debates in his head direct to the compositors' room, and there dictate to them two distinct articles, embracing the principal points of what he had heard, without referring to any notes, or committing any portion of his articles to paper; so that while a sentence in one article was being set up, he had resumed the other, and was dictating it without hesitation or confusion.[28]

The publisher Dr Thomas Rees recalled that the middle of the Strand was full of newspaper offices, like a hive of bees swarming during the sitting of Parliament, their business conducted during the night.[29] It was William's work as a parliamentary reporter very soon after their marriage that compelled him to stay out late at night. This part of his career was suppressed in Talfourd's memoir, which mentions only his work for the *English Chronicle*, which did not begin until 1796. Through the discovery of papers in the Public Record Office relating to a chancery suit brought in 1799, we now know that William Radcliffe began his career as a journalist not for the *English Chronicle*, but for the *Gazetteer, and New Daily Advertiser*, a celebrated journal referred to by Fielding in *Joseph Andrews* and by Goldsmith in *The Vicar of Wakefield*.[30] His association with the *Gazetteer* was not altogether successful, and he preferred for it to be buried in oblivion.

Early in December 1790 the proprietors planned to offer William Radcliffe the position of editor-in-chief, to replace James Perry, the Charles James Fox sympathizer, who was negotiating for the purchase of the *Morning Chronicle*.[31] Perry had revolutionized newspaper reporting (all newspaper reporters were essentially 'debate writers' at this period) by employing relays of reporters so that the previous evening's parliamentary debates, which might continue past midnight, could be reported the following morning, up to twelve hours before the other newspapers printed their reports.[32] It is likely that William had been serving as one such reporter for some eighteen months previous to his appointment as editor, and had so distinguished himself that he seemed a natural replacement for Perry. William's early association with the *Gazetteer* is proven by the fact, not previously noticed, that its printer, Mary Vint, was also the printer of his translation of *The Natural History of East Tartary* in 1789. (Mrs Mary Vint published the *Craftsman: or*

Say's Weekly Journal, the *General Evening Post*, the *Gazetteer* and, after 1795, the *Selector*, from the same address at No. 10, Ave Maria Lane, Ludgate Street; it was she who brought the 1799 chancery case, for money owed to her for printing the then-insolvent newspaper.[33])

The *Gazetteer* demonstrated strong republican sympathies. Perry had accepted the editorship on condition that he could express his Foxite political opinions, and after he moved to the *Chronicle* he was once imprisoned for calling the House of Lords a 'hospital of incurables'; in 1781 Mary Vint had also been imprisoned for a libel against the Russian ambassador.[34] Each year, including the period of Radcliffe's editorship, the *Gazetteer* printed a poem celebrating the anniversary of the French Revolution. On 10 November 1790 it published long extracts from a poem on 'The Laurel of Liberty', and several revolutionary songs appeared in its pages up to the end of the year. The editorial of 14 January 1791 makes it clear that the paper under the direction of its new editor

> shall continue to be a paper permanently devoted to the CONSTITUTION, not to PARTY; to WHIGGISM, rather than to OPPOSITION; to the PEOPLE, not to any set of political LEADERS. . . . [The editors] believe Mr Fox to possess a greater degree of EXPERIENCE, of INTELLECTUAL POWER, of the NOBLE SPIRIT . . . than has ever been united in any person.

The group of Protestant Dissenters known as the Revolution Society was given space to publish long reports of its meetings in the issues of 12 November 1790 and 27 August 1791. The Revolution Society was formed in 1789 ostensibly to celebrate the Glorious Revolution of 1688, but used the ambiguous name to emphasize the continuity between that and the French Revolution. It was from the immediate aftermath of the Glorious Revolution – the passing of the Act of Toleration in 1689 that granted freedom of worship to all Protestants *excluding* Unitarians – that Unitarians ironically dated their oppression. The Revolution Society commissioned an address from Richard Price to celebrate the centenary of the Glorious Revolution:

> We are met to thank God for that event in this country to which the name of the Revolution has been given; and which, for more than a century, it has been usual for the friends of freedom, and more especially Protestant Dissenters, under the title of the Revolution Society, to celebrate with expressions of joy and exultation.

Price was an original member of the Unitarian Society at Newington Green. When he delivered this famous 'Discourse on the Love of Our Country' to the Revolution Society on 4 November 1789 he directly linked the Glorious Revolution of 1688 with both the French and American revolutions, and at their supper that evening the Revolution Society sent 'their congratulations on the Revolution' to the French National Assembly. It was specifically this address that provoked Edmund Burke's scathing attack, *Reflections on the Revolution in France* (1790). (This in turn occasioned famous replies by Thomas Paine, Mary Wollstonecraft and Joseph Priestley, all attacking the despotism of the few over the many.) To the anathemas in Burke's *Reflections* can be attributed the anti-Dissenting reaction that swept the nation. 'The enemies of the French revolution were roused to the highest pitch of wrath; became loud in their execration of it, and of all who were concerned in any of its scenes, or who stood up in its defence.'[35] The Dissenters' advocacy of religious freedom aligned treasonably with the French Revolution in the eyes of the British government and the Anglican clergy. 'In addition to the common share of odium which was liberally poured on the friends of the French revolution, the dissenters had a peculiar portion thrown upon their heads, because they were seperatists from the church.'[36] The Rational Dissenters in particular – that is the Unitarians – came to be construed as the head of the English Jacobins, because of the extreme radicalism of Price and Priestley. When Price died in 1791, it was Joseph Priestley who related his funeral sermon.

One of the primary responsibilities of the editor, especially as the revolution in France was following its course, was to translate from the French newspapers and pamphlets, and William's linguistic skills may have been the most important factor affecting his appointment. On 19 January 1791 the proprietors offered William the editorship at a salary of 3 guineas per week.[37] Although this was 1 guinea a week less than his predecessor had received, William accepted, and commenced his new position from Sunday 23 January.

If Ann Ward had accompanied William Radcliffe to the Drury Lane Theatre during their courtship from about 1784, and shortly after their marriage in 1787, she could well have seen Mrs Siddons (and often her brother John Kemble as well) perform in *The Orphan* (based upon Charlotte Smith's *Emmeline*), *Hamlet* (as Ophelia), *The Tempest*, an adaptation of Milton's *Comus*, *Cymbeline*, Sedaine's *Richard Coeur de Lion* (as Matilda), Jephson's Gothic *Count of Narbonne*, Jephson's *Julia* (in which Kemble was 'the dark designing Italian') and *Macbeth* – from all of which we can trace some influence in her novels.[38] But I believe that it was especially during the first few years of Mrs Radcliffe's marriage, and specifically during 1790–1 while her husband worked for the *Gazetteer*, that she most frequently attended the opera and the theatre. In his memoir Talfourd sums up Mrs Radcliffe's cultured graces by saying that she loved music and sang with exquisite taste though a limited compass; she frequently went to the opera, and would sit up singing the airs on her return home, until a late hour; she especially liked sacred music, and occasionally went to the oratorios by Handel; she sometimes, but more rarely, accompanied her husband to the theatre. Later in life as her health declined and her hypersensitivity increased, she generally sat in the pit, 'partly because her health required warm clothing', and partly to avoid being observed.[39] We know that she went to the Little Theatre in the Haymarket and to Covent Garden before she became famous, because on her visit to Germany in 1794 she compared them to the theatre in Frankfurt.[40] She refers in her writings to Paesiello and Handel, and her love of opera may be traced to the productions of 1791, which can be followed through the pages of the *Gazetteer*. Much of the advertising revenue of the *Gazetteer* came from the theatres, and it is quite possible that William composed opera reviews (such as they were) as part of his official duties. He and his wife may well have been in the audience for the private rehearsal of *Armida*, with music by Sacchini, at the new opera at the Pantheon, the King's Theatre, whose rehearsals, postponements and performances were frequently reported in the paper between 29 January and 17 February. At the Theatre Royal, Drury Lane, on 14 January *The Siege of Belgrade* was performed, with music by Paesiello; an evening of music and dancing at the King's Theatre, Pantheon, on 26 March consisted mostly of songs by Paesiello; and his opera *La Locanda* was performed at the Pantheon on 28 June. At the Theatre Royal, Covent Garden, on 11 February, there was a revival of *Isabella, or The Fatal Revenge*, from which Mrs Radcliffe borrowed the name of Villeroy for use in *The Mysteries of Udolpho*.

For many years afterwards people remembered the highlight of 1791: the Handel season. Handel's oratorios and selections from his sacred music were performed on Wednesdays and Fridays during the week of Lent, commencing on 11 March at the Theatre Royal, Covent Garden. On that one day alone, the Grand Selection included a coronation anthem, the overture to *Esther*, pieces from *Jephtha*, *Israel in Egypt*, *Samson*, *Athalia*, *Saul* and *Joshua*. The entire *Redemption Oratorio* was performed on 21 March together with other pieces, including *Semele*. Milton's *L'Allegro ed il Penseroso*, as set to music by Handel, was performed on 30 March, followed by the masque of *Comus* on 27 May. *Acis and Galatea* was performed at Drury Lane on 1 April, *Israel in Egypt* on 23 May in Westminster Abbey and the last performance of *The Messiah* was given on 1 June in the presence of His Majesty. Mrs Radcliffe was almost certainly present at some of these performances.

The great Handel season, which continued until the end of May, was organized by the Royal Society of Musicians; at the head of its list of Honorary Vice-Presidents was the Duke of Leeds. The *Gazetteer* frequently refers to him in its gossip column, almost as if someone on the newspaper has direct knowledge of his activities: 'His Grace the Duke of Leeds continues confined to his room with the gout' (19 May). He was 'much recovered' by 24 May and had been able to attend the Grand Selection of Handel's music in Westminster Abbey on 23 May, though he was again lame in the right foot on 26 May and unable to attend the Levee. It may have been after one of the Handel performances organized by the Duke of Leeds that Mrs Radcliffe made the acquaintance of the Duchess of Leeds, to whom she was to dedicate the fourth edition of *The Romance of the Forest* several years later.

To the season of 1791 we can trace Ann Radcliffe's transformation of Handel's reworking of themes of romance and sorcery from Ariosto's *Orlando Furioso* and Tasso's *Jerusalem Delivered* for *The Mysteries of Udolpho*. Even a hotch-potch such as *The Tempest; or, The Enchanted Island*, which was coupled with the *Masque of Neptune and Amphitrite* at Drury Lane on 5 May, probably contributed to Emily's remarkable personification of herself as a sea nymph in *The Mysteries of Udolpho*. With music by Purcell and Arne, *The Tempest* was performed again on 30 May and on 25 November. Other works regularly performed during this season which may have had an influence were James Cobb's comic opera *The Haunted Tower* at Drury Lane and the opera of chivalry *Richard Coeur de Lion* at the Haymarket. The scene in which Emily wanders on the terrace of the castle of Udolpho and hears a man singing whom she assumes to be her imprisoned lover Valancourt is ultimately derived from the story of Blondel's attempts to rescue Richard I by such singing. More specifically, however, it can be traced to two English translations of Sedaine's *Richard Coeur de Lion*: the Drury Lane 1786 production in the translation by General John Burgoyne and the 1786 Covent Garden comic opera production in the translation by Leonard Macnally; in both of these productions the discovery of Richard's confinement is assigned to Matilda rather than Blondel, an important gender change mirrored by Radcliffe. In both productions an Udolpho-ish castle, though in a wild and sequestered spot, has a terrace.

Evenings at the opera, however stimulating, were limited to one short season each year, and Ann Radcliffe probably began writing through sheer boredom as much as anything – boredom and escape, the twin motivations of many women novelists. It is clear from Talfourd's account that William was obliged 'to be frequently absent from home till a late hour in the evenings' at the time when his wife first began writing her novels. (What Talfourd says about William Radcliffe's work for the *English Chronicle* can be confidently backdated to the period when he worked for the *Gazetteer*.) 'On these occasions, Mrs Radcliffe usually beguiled the else weary hours by her pen, and often astonished her husband, on his return, not only by the quality, but the extent of the matter she had produced, since he left her.' She preferred writing during the evening, secure from interruption; she 'composed with great rapidity; especially the passages of her various productions in which she felt the most deeply interested. It generally proved that those were the passages which made the most powerful impression upon the public.'[41] But although she was deeply absorbed in her writing, and perhaps drew her most compelling visions from the subconscious, she was fascinated by the literary skills of constructing scenes of horror, and was not merely a transmitter of inner unease. 'So far was she from being subjected to her own terrors, that she often laughingly presented to Mr Radcliffe chapters, which he could not read alone without shuddering.'[42]

Fortunately Ann Radcliffe was nurtured by a literary husband, who encouraged her to employ her leisure time in writing.[43] No doubt they saw themselves as a literary establishment. William's two translations were published in the same years as his wife's first two novels. During these years his wife was obviously discovering her true *métier*, while his rather dull natural history and travel history were only coolly received. There could be no greater contrast than that illustrated by two reviews in the very same issue of the *Monthly Review*: the reviewer of *The Natural History of East Tartary* briefly noted that 'Mr Radcliffe seems to have executed his part with ease and precision', while two pages later the reviewer of *A Sicilian Romance* declared that Mrs Radcliffe 'possesses a happy vein of invention, and . . . elegant and animated language'.[44] The reviewer of the *Journey through Sweden* pointed out some inaccuracies and Gallicisms in the translation, which he impertinently advised William to avoid in future, though he concluded that the work was interesting and 'clearly, if not elegantly, written'.[45] Mrs Radcliffe achieved national – and international – fame in 1791 with *The Romance of the Forest*, and went on to create a novel which became the hallmark of literary genius, while her husband devoted himself to journalism, and even took a self-effacing role when he contributed to her *Journey Made in the Summer of 1794*.

The Aesthetics of Terror

———— • ————

The project of placing Ann Radcliffe in the context of Dissenting culture should not be curtailed by the mistaken assumption that Dissenters can be understood only in terms of politics and socio-economics. That enthusiasm for 'high culture' which persuades modern readers to situate Radcliffe as a conservative, even a reactionary, is a characteristic for which Unitarians were particularly noted. In modern literary history it is usual to speak of 'the Dissenters' as if they comprise a culturally homogeneous Nonconformist unity, but it should be borne in mind that the Unitarians were the Dissenting élite. They should not be linked to the Puritanism that had a bias against literature and artistic culture, and their culture was quite different from orthodox Calvinist and Baptist and Methodist evangelical traditions: Unitarian beliefs lay 'outside the field of revealed religion altogether, and certainly to a point as far as possible from John Knox'.[1] The Unitarians self-consciously regarded themselves, sometimes haughtily and exclusively, as the rational, intellectual élite of 'the elect':

> a Unitarian Evangelical is unthinkable, a sort of *lusus naturae*, for the Unitarians were, and always had been since the days of Joseph Priestley and Richard Price and Mrs Barbauld of the Warrington Academy, an enlightened intellectual minority, particularly strong in those North West Midlands where the Gaskells were in touch with such Unitarian dynasties as the Wedgwoods and later the Darwins.[2]

The Wedgwoods felt no contradiction between manufacturing the very symbols that we have come to associate with Georgian good taste and simultaneously campaigning for political and religious reform. They produced famous statuettes of enchained black men pleading for the abolition of the slave trade. The Unitarian Josiah Wedgwood II would lead

the protest in the Potteries in 1812 that finally led to public pressure to repeal
the Five Mile and Conventical Acts that still penalized Unitarians, and the
passing in 1813 of the Act which absolved Unitarians from blasphemy and
at long last made their sect legal.[3] Similarly, Bentley could turn an exquisite
Etruscan vase and write political songs.

Although Unitarian Dissenting culture aimed to be wholly rational, it was
never either Puritan or philistine as were most other branches of Dissent.
Unlike the Baptists, and later the Methodists, Unitarians did not look upon
the amusements of the world with disapprobation, as Lucy Aikin recalls:

> Long before my time, my kindred the Jennings, the Belshams, my excellent
> grandfather Aikin . . . had begun to break forth out of the chains and darkness
> of Calvinism, and their manners softened with their system. My youth was
> spent among the disciples or fellow-labourers of Price and Priestley, the
> descendants of Dr John Taylor, the arian, or the society of that most amiable
> of men, Dr Enfield. Amongst these there was no rigorism. Dancing, cards, the
> theatre, were all held lawful in moderation.[4]

The Unitarian John Aikin wrote the introduction to an illustrated luxury
edition of Thomson's *The Seasons* in 1794; the Unitarian Gilbert Wakefield
(author of *The Spirit of Christianity*) edited the *Works of Alexander Pope* in 1794;
the Unitarian William Enfield not only wrote hymns and sermons on Christ,
but collected specimens of the best writers for his elocution students at
Warrington (*The Speaker*, numerous editions from 1774, with an essay on
Taste); and the Unitarian Joseph Priestley analysed the concept of the
sublime as much as did any philosopher of opposing Burkean politics.

Ann Radcliffe may have derived an important part of her aesthetic
programme from Joseph Priestley's *A Course of Lectures on Oratory and Criticism*
(1777). Priestley would certainly have presented a copy of this book to his
friend Thomas Bentley, in whose home in Turnham Green Nancy Ward
could have read it. This series of lectures, which Priestley had given while
a tutor at the Warrington Academy, illustrates and explains the doctrine of
the association of ideas advanced by his friend David Hartley, whose *Theory
of the Human Mind* he had edited in 1775. Priestley positively celebrates the
pleasures of the imagination: 'no person of reading and observation can doubt
of the fact, that more tears have been shed, and more intense joy hath been
expressed in the perusal of novels, romances, and feigned tragedies, than in
reading all the true histories in the world' (81). Unlike most historians of the
novel, Priestley does not set up realism and romance at opposite poles: vivid
ideas and strong emotions are associated specifically with reality. As in
Shakespeare, as long as vivid impressions are narrated with rich circumstantial
detail, the idea of reality will *necessarily* arise, even in the most 'unreal' scenes

describing 'such beings and powers as far exceed every thing human, and which never could have had any existence; as of *fairies* in European countries, . . . and *knights-errant* and *necromancers* in modern story' (89–90). His praise of Shakespeare, Akenside and Ossian would accord well with the taste of his friend's niece, and well as most Unitarian – as opposed to Evangelical – Dissenters:

> If, however, the fiction be consistent with itself, and be natural upon any uniform principles, or suppositions, so that it shall require only one single effort of the imagination to conceive the existence of the imaginary beings and powers, and the ideas of inconsistency and contradiction do not frequently occur through the course of the narration, to destroy the illusion; a reader of a lively turn of mind though of good discernment, may enter into the scene, and receive great pleasure from the performance. (90)

Here indeed is a Rational recipe for the explained supernatural.

In 'Lecture XX. Of the Sublime' Priestley emphasizes that the sublime is not limited to '*corporal* magnitude, extension and elevation', but that '*Sentiments* and *passions* are equally capable of it. . . . Fortitude, magnanimity, generosity, patriotism, and universal benevolence, strike the mind with the idea of the sublime' (15, 156). All of these, except for patriotism, are notable in Radcliffean heroes and heroines. The heroine is not simply a beautiful contrast to the sublime villain, but is herself a sublime foil to the villain because of what Priestley defines as 'a species of *transferred sublimity*', a concept seldom noticed by other theorists: 'The *contempt* of power, wealth, and grandeur, is more sublime than the *possession* of them; because, after a view of those great objects, it presents us with the view of a *mind* above them' (158).

More importantly, Priestley emphasizes more than other theorists the pleasure of creating, *as a professional writer*, the sublime: great objects expand our faculties and give us a pleasing 'consciousness of the strength and extent of our own powers' (151). Much of Priestley's analysis of the sublime is from the point of view of the writer employing his or her skill to create such sensations. For example, 'a well conducted *climax* is extremely favourable to the sublime. In this form of a sentence, each subsequent idea is compared with the preceding; so that if the former have been represented as large, the latter, which exceeds it, must appear exceedingly large' (152). He gives detailed notes concerning the construction of sentences so as to emphasize their climax; the avoidance of terms 'that hath ever had the least connexion with *mean subjects*, or even which hath been chiefly used by persons of a low and illiberal class of life' (160); and periphrasis. Such techniques are certainly used by Ann Radcliffe, and the reader often senses her leaning over our shoulder to judge our reactions. It is manifest that she relished the exercise of her powers of enchantment.

Lastly, one cannot help but feel that she took to heart one of Priestley's final admonitions when mapping out her own career: 'Next to the *pathetic*, of all the excellencies of good composition, the *sublime* promises the most lasting reputation to an author. Compositions which are calculated only to *please* and to *divert*, are beings of a day' (162).

Ann Radcliffe was already familiar with the aesthetics of terror when she wrote her very first novel. The 'cold hand of a dead person' that Alleyn stumbles upon in *The Castles of Athlin and Dunbayne* and the subterranean 'intricate winding passage, just large enough to admit a person upon his hands and knees' in *A Sicilian Romance* are both derived from the fragmentary *Sir Bertrand* (1773) by John Aikin.[5] She therefore must have read the essay which prefaced *Sir Bertrand*, by Anna Laetitia Aikin (later Mrs Barbauld), 'On the Pleasure Derived from Objects of Terror'.[6] In this analysis of 'the apparent delight with which we dwell upon objects of pure terror', Mrs Barbauld focuses upon 'well-wrought scenes of artificial terror . . . formed by a sublime and vigorous imagination' and defines terror as a complex aesthetic emotion rather than a simple psychological fear. This essay would have directed Ann Radcliffe to the literary sources of sublime terror which she was to exploit in her own novels: the ghost in *Hamlet*, the witches' cave in *Macbeth*; the ghosts in the tent scene in *Richard III*; Collins's *Ode to Fear*; Milton's *Il Penseroso*; Walpole's *The Castle of Otranto*; Smollett's *Ferdinand Count Fathom*. The aesthetic value of terror is demonstrated by the most highly cultured English poets who set the standards for Radcliffe's generation. That this terror is analysed by none other than Mrs Barbauld suggests that it was fully in accord with Unitarian – rather than superstitious – principles. William Enfield, Lecturer in *Belles-Lettres* at the Warrington Academy, calls Mrs Barbauld 'OUR POETESS', and quotes lines from her poem 'Warrington Academy'.[7]

Talfourd noted that, though no slave to superstitious fear, Ann Radcliffe was 'completely absorbed' in her stories while composing them,[8] and her journals occasionally show her to be overwhelmed by a sense of mystery: 'Why is it so sublime to stand at the foot of a dark tower, and look up its height to the sky and the stars?' I believe that the debate between rationalism and enthusiasm that occurs in her major novels should be understood within the context of the Dissenting debate between the Rational Dissenters (that is Unitarians) and the Evangelical Dissenters, and, more complexly, in the context of the internal debate within Rational Dissent itself, notably the tension between faith and the inevitable trends of Unitarianism towards materialism, determinism and agnosticism. 'Unitarianism' itself is not a homogeneous unity; individual religious conscience led to many specialized congregations growing up around specific ministers, over small details of faith and practice whose importance we no longer appreciate. The Unitarian belief in God necessarily entailed a rational sanction for the supernatural. Nevertheless, hell, purgatory and damnation were not part of Unitarian discourse; sinners were believed either to join in a universal salvation, or simply to remain dead eternally as their only 'punishment'. More radical Unitarians, such as Priestley, did not believe in the personal immortality of the soul, but nevertheless believed in the literal resurrection of the physical body, which was not perceived as a 'rational' contradiction.

In order to justify use of the supernatural in an age which had witnessed the French Revolution and the rise of Evangelicalism – and the antipathy of Protestant Dissent to (superstitious) Roman Catholicism – Ann Radcliffe reached back to Mrs Barbauld's *Rational* analysis of the relationship between the sublime and the imaginative non-superstitious apprehension of the supernatural. This not only informs Mrs Radcliffe's novels, but was even paraphrased by her, as the following two extracts illustrate. The first comes from Barbauld's essay:

> A strange and unexpected event awakens the mind, and keeps it on the stretch; and where the agency of invisible beings is introduced, of 'forms unseen and mightier far than we', our imagination, darting forth, explores with rapture the new world which is laid open to its view, and rejoices in the expansion of its powers. Passion and fancy co-operating elevate the soul to its highest pitch; and pain of terror is lost in amazement. Hence the more wild, fanciful and extraordinary are the circumstances of a scene of horror, the more pleasure we receive from it.

This passage is echoed when Schedoni in *The Italian*, displaying the deviousness of the Jesuits despite being a Dominican, plays the rationalist in his debate with Vivaldi over enthusiasm:

> 'The opinions you avowed were rational,' said Schedoni, 'but the ardour of your imagination was apparent, and what ardent imagination ever was contented to trust to plain reasoning, or to the evidence of the senses? It may not willingly confine itself to the dull truths of this earth but, eager to expand its facilities, to feel its capacity, and to experience its own peculiar delights, soars after new wonders into a world of its own!'[9] (125)

Victor Sage is right to focus upon this brilliant reversal, but whereas Sage calls it 'an Anglican reproof',[10] I see it as a Rational Dissenter's reproof: we should recall that one of Wesley's hymns advises us to beware 'The Unitarian fiend'.[11] Vivaldi's 'susceptibility which renders [him] especially liable to superstition' is the 'prevailing weakness' of Ann Radcliffe's heroines, and the disapproval of this weakness by what I construe as Rational Dissent is a major theme that runs throughout her work, from La Luc's education of Adeline in *Romance of the Forest* (1791) to the last thing she ever wrote, the debate between Willoughton and Simpson in the posthumously published excerpt from *Gaston de Blondeville*. This 'conversation on illusions of the imagination and on the various powers of exciting them, shown by English poets, especially by Shakespeare and Milton',[12] continues the discourse initiated by Barbauld. Willoughton approaches Kenilworth 'in reverie, . . . no longer in the living scene, but ranging over worlds of his own' (*Gaston*, vol. 1, 8). While Simpson merely looks forward to a good dinner, Willoughton 'was following Shakspeare into unknown regions':

> 'Where is now the undying spirit,' said he, 'that could so exquisitely perceive and feel? – that could inspire itself with the various characters of this world, and create worlds of its own; to which the grand and the beautiful, the gloomy and the sublime of visible Nature, up-called not only corresponding feelings, but passions; which seemed to perceive a soul in every thing: and thus, in the secret workings of its own characters, and in the combinations of its incidents, kept the elements and local scenery always in unison with them, heightening their effect.'[13]

Willoughton's – that is, Ann Radcliffe's – full and impassioned analysis of the ghost scene in *Hamlet* provokes a discussion between Simpson and Willoughton that I read as the discussion between two Rational Dissenters concerning the place of superstition in their faith:

> *'Certainly you must be very superstitious,' said Mr S—, 'or such things could not interest you thus.'*

> *'There are few people less so than I am,' replied W—, 'or I understand myself and the meaning of superstition very ill.'*

> *'That is quite paradoxical.'*

> *'It appears so, but so it is not. If I cannot explain this, take it as a mystery of the human mind.'*

> *'If it were possible for me to believe the appearance of ghosts at all,' replied Mr S—, 'it would certainly be the ghost of Hamlet; but I never can suppose such things; they are out of all reason and probability.'*

> *'You would believe the immortality of the soul,' said W—, with solemnity, 'even without the aid of revelation; yet our confined faculties cannot comprehend how the soul may exist after separation from the body. I do not absolutely know that spirits*

are permitted to become visible to us on earth; yet that they may be permitted to
appear for very rare and important purposes, such as could scarcely have been
accomplished without an equal suspension, or a momentary change, of the laws
prescribed to what we call Nature – that is, without one more exercise of the same
CREATIVE POWER of which we must acknowledge so many millions of existing
instances, and by which alone we ourselves at this moment breathe, think, or
disquisite at all, cannot be impossible, and, I think, is probable. Now, probability is
enough for the poet's justification, the ghost being supposed to have come for an
important purpose. Oh, I should never be weary of dwelling on the perfection of
Shakspeare, in his management of every scene connected with that most solemn and
mysterious being, which takes such entire possession of the imagination, that we
hardly seem conscious we are beings of this world while we contemplate 'the
extravagant and erring spirit.'[14]

The crux of the paradox is that one can act in most respects in accordance
with the most Rational and materialist laws of nature, but at the same time
possess an imagination that perceives in accordance with the irrational laws
of poetry.

History held relatively little importance for Ann Radcliffe. Whatever she
learned from Sophia Lee's *The Recess*, it was not an appreciation for historical
authenticity. Her heroines' Protestant distaste for convents is distinctly odd
coming from supposed Italian or French Roman Catholics. *A Sicilian Romance*,
supposedly contemporary with the poetry of Tasso (vol. 1, 15), contains some
delicious anachronisms, as when a sumptuous Renaissance ball is followed
by a private musical trio, in which Ferdinand plays the violoncello, Verezzi
plays the German flute and Julia accompanies her singing on the pianoforte
(vol. 2, 49–50). This detail is borrowed from Patrick Brydone, who in his
deservedly popular *A Tour through Sicily and Malta* (1773) describes how his
party assembled for coffee, ices and sweetmeats after a fireworks illumina-
tion.[15] Louisa de Bernini in *A Sicilian Romance* is said to come from the Val
di Demona, whose 'numberless caverns and subterraneous passages' filled
with banditti are fully described by Brydone.[16]

Ann Radcliffe valued primarily the splendour and mystery of an idealized
late-medieval transitional period when she could commingle high passions
with exquisite taste, and at the same time find justification for portraying
the shift from feudal to modern more egalitarian manners. In her ideal world
reason sits rather unsteadily on the shoulders of passion and imagination.
Medieval and Renaissance history were sufficiently exotic for her to re-create
the fairy-tale setting that accounted for much of her popularity. The mere
use of the iconic words 'splendour', 'gaiety and gladness', 'banquet', 'soft
music' and 'grand ball' was enough to make it seem 'as if the hand of a
magician had suddenly metamorphosed this once gloomy fabric into the

palace of a fairy' (vol. 1, 37). This is the central romantic metonym of all of
her novels.

During Ann Radcliffe's lifetime the highly respected French critic
Chénier praised her energetic *tableaux* and *coups de théâtre* as
Shakespearean,[17] and in 1798 Nathan Drake called her 'the Shakespeare of
Romance Writers'.[18] She seems to have memorized *Hamlet*, *Macbeth* and
The Tempest from beginning to end, and quotes plentifully from Shakespeare
in her later novels.[19] But his influence is powerful even in her first novel,
as when Osbert's mother 'sunk lifeless in her chair' (*Athlin and Dunbayne*,
20) when told of his determination to avenge the death of his father, just
as did Gertrude when confronted by Hamlet with an identical resolve.
Prospero's magic island is alluded to when Osbert 'found himself as a
traveller on enchanted ground, when the wand of the magician suddenly
dissolves the airy scene, and leaves him environed within the horrors of
solitude and of darkness' (160). Many of her poems (including the
posthumous ones) echo 'Ariel's Song' in *A Midsummer Night's Dream*. The
most compelling Shakespearean images for Ann Radcliffe were the same
as those painted by Fuseli for the Shakespeare Gallery which opened in
Pall Mall in 1789: Macbeth confronting the witches on the blasted heath;
Lear renouncing Cordelia; Titania and her sweet love Bottom in *A
Midsummer Night's Dream*; and Hamlet and Horatio questioning the ghost
on the battlements of Elsinore.[20] Some sixty-five paintings were on display
by 1791, and we cannot doubt that Mrs Radcliffe visited this popular
exhibition.

Travel books, particularly descriptions of Italy, made an important
contribution to Ann Radcliffe's evocation of the exotic past. *The Mysteries of
Udolpho* may have been influenced by Ramond de Carbonnières' *Observations
faites dans les Pyrénées* (1789), though none of the 'resemblances' seem close
enough to be called 'borrowings'.[21] Swinburne's *Travels in the Two Sicilies*
(1783, 1785) is cited in a footnote to her posthumous poem 'A Sea-View',
alluding to the optical illusion raised by the 'enchantress' Morgan le Fay.[22]
Tompkins has established the definite influence of Pierre Jean Grosley's
New Observations on Italy and Its Inhabitants[23] (1769, the English translation
of the French original which appeared in 1764); the famous wax figure behind
the veiled portrait is derived from Grosley's description of a tomb in the
Benedictine church of San Vitale in Ravenna:

> the waxen image of a woman, made by her lover who had found her dead and
> buried upon his return: . . . a lizard is sucking her mouth, a worm is creeping
> out of one of her cheeks, a mouse is gnawing one of her ears, and a huge swolen
> [*sic*] toad on her forehead is preying on one of her eyes.

Mary Robinson, in her popular Gothic romance *Hubert de Sevrac*, paints her landscape by quoting directly from John Smith's *Select Views of Italy* (1792) and William Coxe's *Travels in Switzerland* (1789), and in a footnote she suggests that others have made similar borrowings: 'For those beautiful and romantic descriptions, of which so many novelists have availed themselves, read Coxe's Travels in Switzerland, published in the year 1789.'[24] It seems likely that the Alpine landscape in *The Mysteries of Udolpho* owes some of its inspiration to Coxe's description of the 'singularly wild and romantic' passage over the Alps.[25] The first view of the Castle of Udolpho owes something to the eleventh-century castle of Hapsburgh, which became the property of the Emperor Rhodolph (whose very name is suggestive of Udolpho):

> Near Schintznach stands, on a lofty eminence, the ruins of the castle of Hapsburgh, to which we ascended through a wood of beech, that seemed almost coeval with the date of the castle itself. These ruins consist of an antient tower constructed with massy stones, in a rude style of architecture, and a part of a small building of much later date.[26]

And the Abbey of St Clair, and Sister Agnes, may also have been suggested by Coxe's description of the convent of Königsfelden for the nuns of St Clare and its inhabitant 'Agnes queen of Hungary, who assumed the habit of a nun, and here passed the remainder of her days'.[27] Chloe Chard, in her edition of *The Romance of the Forest*, has pointed out the influence (including nearly direct quotations) of Tobias Smollett's *Travels through France and Italy* (1766) and Thomas Gray's letters. *The Mysteries of Udolpho* also borrowed from Hester Lynch Piozzi's *Observations and Reflections Made in the Course of a Journey through France, Italy, and Germany* (1789),[28] especially her description of the approach to Venice along the Brenta to the Grand Canal, a route lined by 'Palladio's palaces': 'The general effect produced by such architecture, such painting, such pillars; illuminated as I saw them last night by the moon at full, rising out of the sea, produced an effect like enchantment.'[29] Ann Radcliffe's most romantic Venetian episode – when Emily hears the gondoliers singing verses from Ariosto and Petrarch – she owes to Mrs Piozzi, who had

> asked several friends about the truth of what one has been always hearing in England, that the Venetian gondoliers sing Tasso and Ariosto's verses in the streets at night . . . [and one night she *does* hear a gondolier] singing to an odd sort of tune, but in no unmusical manner, the flight of Erminia from Tasso's Jerusalem. Oh, how pretty! how pleasing. This wonderful city realizes the most romantic ideas ever formed of it, and defies imagination to escape her various powers of enslaving it.[30]

The obvious borrowing was noted by Thomas Green in his diary for 25 November 1800: 'Read the first volume of Mrs *Piozzi*'s Travels in Italy. Tolerably amusing, but for a pert flippancy, and ostentation of learning. Mrs *Radcliffe* has taken from this work her vivid description of Venice, and of the Brenta, but oh! how improved in the transcript.'[31] (Incidentally, Mrs Piozzi's book contained an anecdote about Mrs Radcliffe's relation Sir Richard Jebb being besieged for cures for blindness as he passed through Savoy.[32])

In the absence of concrete evidence, scholars have refused to speculate about Mrs Radcliffe's own travels before she wrote her major novels. I believe that she – drawn by the spirit of Gray – visited Netley Abbey at a very early date and that it is the model for the ruined cloisters in her novels. We do know that she visited the abbey, though we are not sure when. Although she does not mention it during her first recorded visit to the Isle of Wight in 1798 or in her visit to Southampton in 1801, she does refer to its fretted arches in her undated posthumous poem 'Written in the Isle of Wight':

Here pensive Gray some sad sweet moments passed,
And breathed a spell that saved these falling walls.[33]

Situated three miles south of Southampton, Netley Abbey was visited by Horace Walpole, Thomas Gray, William Gilpin and Charlotte Smith, among many others.[34] The ruins inspired many works, from George Keate's very popular poem *The Ruins of Netley Abbey* (1764) to Richard Warner's novel *Netley Abbey* (1795) and Pearce's comic opera *Netley Abbey* (1795). Keate's picture of the abbey 'forlorn in melancholy Greatness' on the edge of the sea was part of the cultural baggage carried by every subsequent picturesque traveller.[35] Aquatint 'views' of Netley Abbey were published throughout the 1790s, and its picturesque ruins are illustrated in Gilpin's *Observations on the Western Parts of England* (1798), and described in J. Hassell's description in *Tour of the Isle of Wight* (1790). Ann Radcliffe's castles and ruined abbeys could well owe something to Hassell's *Tour*, from the press of her own publisher, T. Hookham. Several passages describing the romantic retirement of the abbey could have come straight from her own pen: 'A thousand agreeable ideas rush into the mind, and we are lost in wonder and contemplation. By such a scene as this, the youthful imagination is expanded, and the genius directed to some useful pursuit' (vol. 1, 29–30). The associative power of ruins, the sensibility of genius and the 'expanded imagination' are important and recurrent themes in Ann Radcliffe's fiction: 'young imagination heightens every scene, and the warm heart expands to all around it' (*Athlin and Dunbayne*, 4). She visited the Isle of Wight on several occasions, and almost certainly consulted Hassell's guide, possibly very soon after its publication in 1790.

Landscapes and images drawn from the discipline of pictorial art inform much of Ann Radcliffe's work.[36] Her novels abound in words such as 'painting', 'picture', 'portrait', 'contour', 'draw', 'delineate', 'lines' and 'images'; a subgroup refers to 'colour', 'contrast', 'tint' and 'glow'; while another important image cluster (unique to her novels) relates to printing: 'a die on wax', 'impress', 'imprint' and 'stamp'.[37] The technical knowledge of landscape, drawing and colouring may have been acquired from observing the techniques practised by her aunt Elizabeth Oates while decorating vases and assisting with the designs for Wedgwood & Bentley, a knowledge possibly reinforced later by some familiarity with the printing techniques used at William Radcliffe's newspaper.

Ann Radcliffe refers in her novels to the works of Claude Gelée (Lorrain), Salvator Rosa and Nicholas Poussin – whose works represented respectively the Beautiful, the Sublime and the Grand – plus Domenichino and Guido Reni. Ever intuitive to the taste of popular culture, she may simply have exploited this triumvirate as an artistic cliché, derived from James Thomson's characterization of 'softening Lorrain', 'savage Rosa' and 'learnèd Poussin' (*The Castle of Indolence*, canto I, stanza xxxviii). The grouping was recognized as trite by 1825: 'It is not uncommon for tourists, in describing some one favourite spot, to say, it possesses all the wildness of Salvator, the majesty of Poussin, and the softness of Claude; words that evince a total incapacity to judge.'[38] Her own scenes are 'framed' by windows, arches or overhanging trees, and their 'perspective' is called to our attention; each of her sketches conscientiously includes the five elements of a proper 'landskip': foreground, middle ground, background, flanking sides and the obscure distant view. Occasionally she speaks of the 'coup d'oeil' or the 'camera obscura', a device for composing picturesque views which she undoubtedly used on her own travels. Mrs Radcliffe carried a telescope with her on her trips, not always to see things close up, but often to judge the effect of a scene 'as through a telescope reversed'. Her novels in due course provided the subjects for ten paintings and drawings exhibited at the Royal Academy.[39]

Even before writing her first novel, Ann Radcliffe seems to have read William Gilpin's most popular book *Observations on the River Wye, and Several Parts of South Wales, &c. Relative Chiefly to Picturesque Beauty* (dated 1782 but published in 1783). Her description of 'the ruins of an abbey, whose broken arches and lonely towers arose in gloomy grandeur through the obscurity of evening' (*Athlin and Dunbayne*, 252) pays heed to Gilpin's consideration of the nature of obscurity: 'Even the rain gave a gloomy grandeur to many of the scenes; and by throwing a veil of obscurity over the removed banks of the river, introduced, now and then, something like a pleasing distance.'[40] Throughout Gilpin's seminal work we find phrases such as 'the grandeur of the landscape' (26), 'a vast amphitheatre' (65) and 'the feathering foliage' (52) – all of which became part of Radcliffe's rhetoric.

Throughout Mrs Radcliffe's journals as well as her novels, 'grand' and 'grandeur' are nearly as important as the sublime. She may have read Lord Kames's *Elements of Criticism* (1762) which gave special emphasis to great magnitude, grandeur and elevation as contributing to sublime emotions. He noted how the internal feeling manifests itself externally by a 'dilated breast' and sense of 'elevated height', a view that accords well with Ann Radcliffe's usual choice of astonishing scenery of 'grandeur and sublimity [which] dilated her mind, and elevated the affections of her heart' (*Udolpho*, 163); 'the magnificence of the scenery inspired Julia with delight; and her heart dilating with high enthusiasm, she forgot the sorrows which had oppressed her' (*Sicilian Romance*, vol. 2, 107). Her critical vocabulary and aesthetic techniques suggest that she carefully studied contemporary discourse concerning 'the Sublime' and 'the Beautiful' during the course of writing her second novel. The word 'sublime' is used only twice in *The Castles of Athlin and Dunbayne*, but half a dozen times in *A Sicilian Romance*; similarly, the terms 'terrible', 'terrific', 'grand', 'awful', 'gloomy' and 'obscurity' occur much more frequently in the second novel.

The seminal work which she no doubt read was Edmund Burke's *A Philosophical Enquiry into the Origin of our Ideas of the Sublime and Beautiful* (1756). She first refers to Burke by name in *A Journey Made in the Summer of 1794*, but she may have first read him in 1790, perhaps made curious by the heated exchange between Burke and Priestley in 1790 over Price's 1789 Glorious Revolution sermon. The fundamental premise of Burke's essay is that 'whatever is in any sort terrible, or is conversant about terrible objects, or operates in a manner analogous to terror, is a source of the *sublime*; that is, it is productive of the strongest emotion which the mind is capable of feeling' (part 1, section 7). Ann Radcliffe certainly agreed with this. All of the characteristics which Burke ascribes to the sublime can be found in abundance in her work: solitude, power, terror, even 'a low, tremulous, intermitting sound' (II, xix), together with a host of visual images: greatness or vastness of dimension (as in mountain ranges and the sea and towers), infinity, grandeur, magnificence, darkness and obscurity. For Burke the highest state of sublimity was created by the juxtaposition of opposite extremes, and there are many illustrations of melodramatic chiaroscuro in Ann Radcliffe's novels, as in her description of Schedoni's cowl, which, 'as it threw a shade over the livid paleness of his face, increased its severe character, and gave an effect to his large melancholy eye, which approached to horror' (*The Italian*, 35).

But the key feature of her work is the exploitation of obscurity to heighten terror. Mrs Barbauld in 1810 observed that Mrs Radcliffe 'seems perfectly to understand that obscurity, as Burke has asserted, is a strong ingredient in the sublime'.[41] By suggesting rather than elucidating, she was able to create 'the world of terrible shadows' that became her trademark. She was indebted more to Gilpin than to Burke for her creative use of obscurity. Gilpin, in *Remarks on Forest Scenery* (1791), explains the process of 'sublimication', by which the skilful writer throws out vague hints that are taken up by the readers and worked up into sublime images in their own minds, thereby becoming all the more powerful for being the joint creation of writer and reader:

> All writers on sublime subjects deal in shadows, and obscurity. . . . Many images owe much of their sublimity to their *indistinctness*; and frequently what we call sublime is the effect of that heat and fermentation, which ensues in the imagination from it's ineffectual efforts to conceive some dark, obscure idea beyond it's grasp.[42]

A Sicilian Romance is almost a handbook of contemporary critical theory. At the conclusion of Volume 1, Madame de Menon's reflections comprise in a nutshell Ann Radcliffe's aesthetic programme: 'Wild and terrific images arose to her imagination. Fancy drew the scene; – she deepened the shades; and the terrific aspect of the objects she presented was heightened by the obscurity which involved them' (239).

By the time Ann Radcliffe wrote *The Mysteries of Udolpho* she had studied Gilpin's *Observations, Relative Chiefly to Picturesque Beauty, Made in the Year 1772, On Several Parts of England; Particularly the Mountains, and Lakes of Cumberland, and Westmorland* (1786). Her use of the terms 'Saxon', 'Saracenic' and 'Gothic' comes directly from Gilpin's history of architecture, as Saxon 'heaviness' was replaced by 'fantastic' and 'ornamented' Saracenic composite or transitional style, which was in turn followed by Gothic 'lightness' and 'enriched' Gothic. Today these are referred to, respectively, as Romanesque, Early English, Decorated and Perpendicular.[43] Her Apennines can be found in the 'amphitheatre of craggy mountains' in Gilpin's Valley of Rydal Mount.[44] Ann Radcliffe uses the word 'amphitheatre' perhaps a dozen times, and characteristically Radcliffean phrases such as 'tremblingly alive', 'power over the imagination' and 'the soul involuntarily shuddered' can be found in Gilpin.[45] Her Sublime, like Gilpin's, 'distend[s] the mind' rather than merely expands it.[46] One of the most evocative phrases in *The Mysteries of Udolpho* – 'The landscape, with the surrounding Alps, did indeed present a perfect picture of the lovely and the sublime, of "beauty sleeping in the lap of horror"' (55) – is a quotation not from Milton, nor from Shakespeare, but from Mr Charles Avison, organist of St Nicolas in Newcastle upon Tyne, regarding Derwentwater, as reported by Revd Gilpin: 'It was once admirably characterized by an ingenious person, who, on his first seeing it, cryed out, *Here is beauty indeed – Beauty lying in the lap of Horrour!* We do not often find a happier illustration.'[47] Ann Radcliffe made it even happier by changing 'lying' to 'sleeping'. (Avison, in his famous *Essay on Musical Expression* (1752), makes some important points about the associations of sounds such as thunder and tempest which strike us with terror, especially when we have a sense of our own security.[48])

Ann Radcliffe is most indebted to Gilpin for his belief in the mutually enhancing contrast of the sublime and the beautiful – in marked contrast to Burke, who felt that the juxtaposition of these two aesthetic categories cancelled one another out. Later theorists, and Ann Radcliffe in particular, elevated this paradoxical marriage into a kind of *supra*-sublimity. Consciously aware of this aesthetic construct,[49] she strives towards the union of the two:

> [The Marquis de St Claire's] chateau was situated in one of those delightful vallies [*sic*] of the Swiss cantons, in which the beautiful and the sublime are so happily united; where the magnificent features of the scenery are contrasted, and their effect heightened by the blooming luxuriance of woods and pasturage, by the gentle winding of the stream, and the peaceful aspect of the cottage. (*Udolpho*, 143–4)

Part of Ann Radcliffe's aesthetic plan of campaign was to contrast 'the Sublime' with 'the Ridiculous'. She employed humour and self-satire far more than did her rivals. She may have been familiar with James Beattie's 'Essay on Laughter and Ludicrous Composition', which was written in the year of her birth; her relative Dr Samuel Hallifax was among the subscribers to the 1776 *Essays* which contain this work, and as previously noted, her uncle Bentley was acquainted with Beattie's patron Mrs Montagu. Ann Radcliffe's lower-class characters systematically follow Beattie's rules for humorous writing: (1) juxtaposition of opposites; (2) incongruity of cause and effect; (3) false comparison founded on similitude; and (4) union of meanness with dignity.[50] This fourth principle, which Beattie illustrates with the example of Don Quixote and Sancho Panza, is the one exploited most fully by Ann Radcliffe (notably in the characterization of Vivaldi and Paulo in *The Italian*), especially in the use of mean language applied to important ideas, mock-heroic burlesque and provincial barbarisms. She herself admits that the loquaciousness of her comic characters is tedious, but felt it was *her duty as an artist* to create comic hyperbole as the humorous analogue to the sublime. Ann Radcliffe's (attempt at) humour has not attracted much critical attention, but the systematic way it is constructed should alert us to the possibility that her sublimity also has rational sources and does not rise unmediated from the depths of her unconscious.

Ann Radcliffe regularly cited Beattie's *The Minstrel; or, The Progress of Genius* (1771, 1774) in her epigraphs, notably in *The Mysteries of Udolpho* –

And oft the craggy cliff he loved to climb,
When all in mist the world below was lost.
What dreadful pleasure! there to stand sublime,
Like shipwreck'd mariner on desert coast.[51]

– and she seems to have read his *Dissertations Moral and Critical* (1783), in which the importance of association in creating images of the sublime is emphasized. Darkness, the howling wind and the creaking of rusty hinges bring to mind childhood stories about ghosts and goblins, superstitious credulity and 'the dreams of a distempered fancy'.[52] Emily in *Udolpho* is possessed by Fancy, the demonic muse, and thus her 'dream of a distempered imagination' resembles 'one of those frightful fictions, in which the wild genius of the poets sometimes delighted' (296). William Duff in *An Essay on Original Genius* (1767) speaks of

the word ENTHUSIASM, which is almost universally taken in a bad sense; and, being conceived to proceed from an overheated and distempered imagination, is supposed to imply weakness, superstition, and madness. ENTHUSIASM, in this modern sense, is in no respect a qualification of a Poet; in the ancient sense, which implied a kind of divine INSPIRATION, or an ardor of Fancy wrought up to Transport, we not only admit, but deem it an essential one. . . . A glowing ardor of Imagination is indeed . . . the very soul of Poetry. It is the principal source of INSPIRATION; and the Poet who is possessed of it, like the *Delphian* Priestess, is animated with a kind of DIVINE FURY.[53]

Similar phrasings concerning the relationship of sublime enthusiasm to 'the illusions of a distempered imagination' (*Udolpho*, 95)[54] recur throughout Ann Radcliffe's novels – and also in works by contemporary novelists and critics, as it was central to aesthetic discourse from about 1760 to 1820. Within the romantic constructs of the novel it is necessary to show that Emily's 'momentary madness' (102) is in the same category as 'that high enthusiasm, which wakes the poet's dream'. Eighteenth-century physicians classified mental illness into two broad types of madness: Raving and Melancholy (that is manic and depressive). Ann Radcliffe skilfully exploits this clinical conception in *The Mysteries of Udolpho*: in the context of the novel's celebration of the 'romantic imagination' (342), she takes great care to distinguish between Emily's poetic visionary madness and the manic-depressive personality attributed to Sister Agnes, who 'had for some months shewn symptoms of a dejected mind, nay, of a disturbed imagination. Her mood was very unequal; sometimes she was sunk in calm melancholy, and, at others, as I have been told, she betrayed all the symptoms of frantic madness' (290). Agnes is a perfect example of the eighteenth-century medical model of psychological disorder: 'she was frantic and melancholy by quick alternatives; then, she sunk into a deep and settled melancholy, which still, however, has, at times, been interrupted by fits of wildness' (577). All of the genuine horrors of mental alienation are adroitly projected from Emily onto Sister Agnes, who functions as an aesthetic scapegoat whereby Emily is purged of madness ('the horrors', 643) and permitted to celebrate the delightful terrors ('the wild genius', 296) of the Gothic–Romantic imagination.

Portrait of the Artist

———— • ————

Only five days after William Radcliffe's appointment as editor of the *Gazetteer* in January 1791, he had arranged for his wife's poem 'Song of a Spirit' to be published anonymously in its pages, even though the paper was not known for publishing poetry:

> The following Poem does not stand in need of any prefatory recommendation. As it is, however, meant to be re-published in a work, now preparing by the Authoress, we are bound to acknowledge that we have only the loan of it for a day.[1]

The poem was signed 'Adeline' and reappeared towards the end of that year in *The Romance of the Forest*, as a composition by the heroine Adeline. The novel was published anonymously, but Ann Radcliffe's name appeared on the title page of the second edition, which came out around April 1792, at which time she also gracefully acknowledged the previous publication of the poem:

ADVERTISEMENT

> It is proper to mention that some of the little Poems inserted in the following Pages have appeared, by permission of the Author, in the GAZETTEER.

Only this one poem by Ann Radcliffe has been traced in the pages of the *Gazetteer*, but there may well have been others among the issues of the paper that have not survived. William was increasing his paper's coverage of the French Revolution and its support for Fox: 'The rise in stocks . . . is occasioned by the confidence of the country not in Ministry, but in the wisdom and strength of Opposition.'[2] The paper acknowledged that in the public mind it was seen as a supporter of the Whig cause.[3]

The Romance of the Forest received widespread critical acclaim. The *Critical Review* recognized the manner of *The Old English Baron* and the model of *The Castle of Otranto*, but felt that 'all the horrid train of images' were managed with skill and consistency. 'One great mark of the author's talents is, that the events are concealed with the utmost art.' The mysterious author was described only as 'the Authoress of "A Sicilian Romance"' on the title page of the first edition; in a footnote added at the last minute to the review, the critic notes that the second edition has just come out, in which 'she styles herself Ann Ratcliffe, and we have no authority for prefixing Miss or Mrs'. He apologized for praising the book so highly, and ended on a prophetic note: 'The lady is wholly unknown to us, and probably will ever continue so.'[4]

Ann Radcliffe gives her novel a specious historical framework on the opening page: 'Whoever has read Guyot de Pitaval, the most faithful of those writers who record the proceedings in the Parliamentary Courts of Paris, during the seventeenth century, must surely remember the striking story of Pierre de la Motte, and the Marquis Phillipe de Montalt'.[5] The allusion is not directly to François Gayot de Pitaval's *Causes célèbres et intéressants* (1734), but to the English translation of this work by Charlotte Smith, entitled *The Romance of Real Life* (1787) – Smith similarly misspells de Pitaval's name as 'Guyot'. But this is merely an example of Ann Radcliffe's technique of cultural colouring: in fact de Pitaval's work contains neither 'the striking story' of de la Motte and de Montalt, nor any other tale that remotely resembles the story of *The Romance of the Forest*. Pierre de la Motte was notorious for the 'queen's necklace' trial in the 1780s involving the Comtesse de la Motte – a suit far more recent than de Pitaval.[6] No 'Marquis di Montalt' has been traced.

Ann Radcliffe's immediate predecessors were more influential. For example, a trapdoor leads to a long-sealed room in which a large chest is discovered to contain a skeleton, just as in Clara Reeve's *The Old English Baron*. La Motte resembles Father Anthony in Sophia Lee's *The Recess*, and the apartment which Adeline discovers connected to her room via a trapdoor is obviously Lee's 'Recess': 'she was convinced by its structure that it was part of the ancient foundation. A shattered casement, placed high from the floor, seemed to be the only opening to admit light' (114–15).

It has been suggested that an important source for the novel was the original French edition of François-Guillaume Ducray-Duminil's *Alexis, ou la maisonnette dans les bois* (1789), a *roman noir* with numerous parallels such as a subterranean vault in a forest, dark passageways, flickering lights, a black chamber and a voice from the tomb.[7] However, Duminil's novel was first translated into English when it was serialized in the *Lady's Magazine* between March 1791 and July 1793, and *The Romance of the Forest* was not published until late 1791 (I cannot determine the exact date). In June 1791 appeared the chapter in which Alexis is 'tormented by ominous dreams. I saw my father pierced with stabs, stretching out his hand to me';[8] followed in November by 'The Subterraneous Temple', which centred on the cavern in the forest: 'The floor and columns were of black marble, and on the ceiling hung a lamp which cast a deadly gleam. In the centre of the temple several steps led to a magnificent tomb; above it he saw a picture, representing a woman with a child in her lap.'[9] Thus parts of the English translation could have been the direct source, and if Mrs Radcliffe were impatient with the slow appearance of the serialization, she could have asked her husband, who was fluent in French, to translate interesting passages for her from the original. Adeline's sequence of bloody dreams has been given a psychosexual interpretation,[10] but since the source may be Ducray-Duminil's *Alexis*, it is difficult to establish how a psychoanalytical approach can be relevant specifically to Ann Radcliffe rather than to Ducray-Duminil. What is notable is that the dreams are the means by which Adeline becomes an agent of retribution, the avenger of her real father's murder (346–7). Eventually she discovers at the heart of the abbey an ancient suite of apartments terminating in a chamber 'exactly like that where her dream had represented the dying person' (115), where she discovers the manuscript that relates the melancholy story of the dead man of her dream, who turns out to be her real father, murdered by Montalt. Despite the universal consensus that Ann Radcliffe invented, and is the prime exemplar of, 'the explained supernatural', these dreams are clear instances of the *unexplained* supernatural.

A long digression on the family of La Luc in their idyllic retreat illustrating 'the philosophy of nature, directed by common sense' (245) has prompted many critics to read *The Romance of the Forest* as a Rousseauesque *Bildungsroman*. Chloe Chard proves beyond doubt that Ann Radcliffe was familiar with Rousseau's *Julie; ou, la Nouvelle Héloïse* and *Émile* – or more precisely William Kenrick's translations *Eloisa* (1761) and *Emilius and Sophia* (1762) (there is no evidence that she read the French originals). The allusions to (Kenrick's translations of) Rousseau lay thick on the ground. The philanthropy that flows from the château to the village of Leloncourt 'united the inhabitants in the sweet and firm bonds of social compact' (277), that is the social contract where wisdom and happiness dwell together. Like her uncle Bentley, Ann Radcliffe agreed intellectually with much of Rousseau's philosophy, though it was not always congruent with her romantic inclinations. La Luc's niece Clara quickly passes from nature to culture: 'From being delighted with the observance of nature, she grew pleased with seeing her finely imitated, and soon displayed a taste for poetry and painting. When she was about sixteen she often selected from her father's library those of the Italian poets most celebrated for picturesque beauty' (249). It was of course her uncle's library, rather than her father's, which would hold such books. Her love of music causes her to ignore her philanthropic duties to the poor; she tries to control her inclinations but soon succumbs to temptation: 'The beauty of the hour awakened all her genius; she never played with such expression before . . . "No! nothing was ever so delightful as to play on the lute beneath her acacias, on the margin of the lake, by moon-light!"' (252). This conflict, never resolved, might seem to illustrate a moral conflict between duty and pleasure, or indulgence and restraint. But it is really an aesthetic conflict, a conflict between the obligations of the artistic person to one's family and friends and the expression of one's genius.

Ann Radcliffe's novels are really *Künstlerroman*, whose central importance lay in the fact that their heroines are themselves literary creators, not passive women whose sole function is to be either educated or abused by men, or whose sole duty is to society. Even more than its predecessors, *The Romance of the Forest* is replete with the vocabulary of aesthetic discourse and innumerable references to 'the sublime', 'obscurity', 'gloomy grandeur' and 'striking contrast'. The earliest extended critique of Ann Radcliffe's work noted that 'in the most distressing circumstances her heroines find time to compose sonnets'.[11] The Radcliffean heroine is a poet, and all experience is grist to her mill. *The Romance of the Forest* is a portrait of the artist as a Gothic heroine. Adeline's maturation is an advancement from one library to another, from one poetic inspiration to another, from receptivity to creativity. Adeline quickly takes the place of – and outstrips – Clara in La Luc's educational programme. Whereas in Clara we find 'the bloom of beauty, with the most perfect simplicity of heart', in Adeline we encounter 'a genius deserving of the highest culture' (277). Adeline's mind is 'eager for knowledge, and susceptible of all the energies of genius' (260). Adeline is a self-portrait of Ann Radcliffe as a woman of courage, wit, presence of mind and command of countenance – a sensible and practical girl. But also, and more importantly, she is a self-portrait of Ann Radcliffe the self-confident author, who sets out an unabashed and feminist claim to genius as well as mere beauty and virtue: 'The observations and general behaviour of Adeline already bespoke a good understanding and an amiable heart, but she had yet more – she had genius' (28).

For Ann Radcliffe, 'genius' means the genius of the inspired poet in possession of a high degree of creative – original or originating rather than imitative – imagination. Jacqueline Howard focuses upon the contemporary discourse about 'genius' in relation to *The Mysteries of Udolpho* and Emily's construction of herself as a sublime poet, and the same discourse can be seen at work in *Romance of the Forest*. Howard quotes from William Duff's *An Essay on Original Genius* (1767) many passages which adumbrate Ann Radcliffe's use of the concept:

Duff at this time, moreover, sanctioned 'the invention of supernatural characters ... and the exhibition of them, with their proper attitudes and offices' as 'the highest efforts and the most pregnant proofs of truly ORIGINAL GENIUS'. . . . 'True Genius', according to this theorist, 'is removed from the din and tumult of business and care'; it blossoms best 'in the peaceful vale of rural tranquility'. . . . Finally, for Duff, Genius is indicated by such 'properties' as 'vivid and picturesque description', 'sublimity', 'irregular greatness', 'wildness of Imagination', and 'Enthusiasm' – all of which . . . [are] deemed by her late eighteenth-century critics to be prominent features of Radcliffe's romances.[12]

By the end of the novel, Adeline has become in effect a professional poet. Almost every morning she goes down to the seashore where she climbs the bank and composes a poem (eleven altogether), the subject of which is usually the nature of 'fancy'. Adeline very frequently 'muses' or sits 'musing' – that is makes herself receptive to the Muse. Like any professional poet, she uses her predecessors' works as a stimulus by taking 'a volume of Shakespear or Milton' from La Luc's library on her rambles. With book in hand, she climbs to the top of a 'wild eminence', a rocky cliff above a lake, listens to the murmurs of the pines 'and conspired with the visions of the poet to lull her to forgetfulness of grief' (261). But that is not all: her proactive engagement with the Muse leads directly to her composing poetry. She conscientiously studies the models in her chosen profession, such as 'that rich effusion of Shakespeare's genius, "A Midsummer Night's Dream"', before proceeding to write her own poem 'Titania to Her Love' (284–5). The final crown in her *oeuvre* is an ode 'To the Nightingale' (298–9), a choice of subject designed to leave no doubt as to her literary credentials.

Adeline, the artist, is constantly 'imagining' what will happen to her or, especially, to Theodore: 'the image of Theodore, dying by the hands of the Marquis, now rose to her imagination' (196); 'She pictured to herself the dark damp dungeon where he lay, loaded with chains, and pale with sickness and grief' (217); 'The idea of Theodore suffering – Theodore dying – was for ever present to her imagination' (228). Theodore is simply the poet's muse, an object upon which Adeline can focus her (faintly sadomasochistic) 'melancholy imagination' (336). Like many a male poet's mistress, he is not a lover or even a person, but an image, an icon, which serves as the visible proof of the poet's creativity.

The most important resolutions in the novel are neither moral nor psychological, but aesthetic. The 'spot formed for solitary delight' mentioned earlier had been 'a green summit, which appeared, among the savage rocks that environed it, like the blossom on the thorn' (273) – prefiguring the image of 'beauty sleeping in the lap of horror'. The marriage of Adeline and Theodore – the blossom and the thorn – leads to their marital villa, symbolizing the union of the aesthetic opposites of nature and art, the wild and the cultured, the individual and the social, the sublime and the beautiful:

> The chateau was characterized by an air of simplicity and taste, rather than of magnificence, which however was the chief trait in the surrounding scene. The chateau was almost encircled with woods, which forming a grand amphitheatre swept down to the water's edge, and abounded with wild and romantic walks. Here nature was suffered to sport in all her beautiful luxuriance, except where here, and there, the hand of art formed the foliage to admit a view of the blue waters of the lake, with the white sail that glided by, or of the distant mountains. In front of the chateau the woods opened to a lawn, and the eye was suffered to wander over the lake, whose bosom presented an ever moving picture, while its varied margin sprinkled with villas, woods, and towns, and crowned beyond with the snowy and sublime alps rising point behind point in awful confusion, exhibited a scenery of almost unequalled magnificence. (362)

Adeline is the Poet/Genius, closely modelled upon Edwin, the hero of James Beattie's *The Minstrel; or, The Progress of Genius* (1779) (quoted five times in *The Romance of the Forest*, and seven times in *The Mysteries of Udolpho*), who loves to wander in lonely vales, dreaming of graves and corpses and ghosts, letting his Fancy roam till sleep brings entrancing visions. The heroine, however complacent and proper to outward appearances, has come to embrace the powers of superstition that were perceived as fearful in the previous novel:

> Queen of the solemn thought – mysterious Night!
>   Whose step is darkness, and whose voice is fear!
> Thy shades I welcome with severe delight,
>   And hail thy hollow gales, that sigh so dear!
> (*Romance of the Forest*, 83)

A major characteristic of the Gothic poet's creativity is the cultivation of a susceptibility to the irrational: 'While she sat musing, her fancy, which now wandered in the regions of terror, gradually subdued reason. . . . Her imagination refused any longer the controul of reason, and, turning her eyes, a figure, whose exact form she could not distinguish, appeared to pass along an obscure part of the chamber' (134). For the Gothic novelist, as for Collins (in his 'Ode to Fear' quoted in the epigraph to the eleventh chapter of the novel), 'fancy lifts the veil' between the known world and the world of shadows (152).

Ann Radcliffe explores one of the basic images of female creativity: the forest recess. James Beattie had noted that the great poets found inspiration in the archetypal forest: 'No parts of Tasso are read with greater relish, than where he describes the darkness, silence, and other horrors, of the enchanted forest' (book 13 of *Jerusalem Delivered*); Milton in *Comus* was similarly enamoured of 'forests and enchantments drear', and asserts that 'forests in every age must have had attractive horrors'.[13] For Ann Radcliffe the forest symbolizes the 'wild illusions of creative mind' which break down and then reshape the structures of society and civilization. The journey into its dark interior parallels the artist's discovery of her own creative powers. For La Motte the forest is merely a refuge from his creditors, but for Adeline it nourishes her creative energies. For La Motte the forest is a perplexing 'labyrinth' (21), while for Adeline it is the sacred grove. As they enter more deeply into the forest, La Motte steadily succumbs and tries to extricate himself, while Adeline's spirits gradually rise. The male contracts while the female expands. La Motte wishes to press on, but the forest takes an active role in shattering the fabric of society: 'the hind wheel rising upon the stump of an old tree, which the darkness had prevented Peter from observing, the carriage was in an instant overturned' (17). Unable to proceed further, they are forced to spend the night in the ruined Abbey of Saint Clair. As they explore the sublime pile, 'Adeline, who had hitherto remained in silence, now uttered an exclamation of mingled admiration and fear. A kind of pleasing dread thrilled her bosom, and filled all her soul' (18).

When Adeline rises next morning and looks out of her window upon the forest and sees the 'inconceivable splendour' of the rising sun and the awakening of nature she involuntarily utters a prayer to the benevolent Father of all. Her unconscious powers of creativity are given birth. This sequestered spot is of course the rediscovered garden of Eden, an allegory supported by a Shakespearean quotation: 'Are not these woods/More free from peril than the envious court?/Here feel we but the penalty of Adam' (33, quoting *As You Like It*, II. i. 3–5).

The Romance of the Forest was in its third edition by November 1792, which testifies to its popularity. Not one critic would argue with the opinion of the *English Review* that this romance 'must certainly be allowed to rank among the first class'.[14] Sir Walter Scott affirmed that the public was fascinated by Ann Radcliffe's ability to awaken the sense of mystery and suspense: 'every reader felt the force, from the sage in his study, to the group which assembled round the evening taper, to seek a solace from the toils of ordinary life by an excursion into the regions of imagination'.[15] Within a very short period there were 'few readers of novels who have not been delighted with her *Romance of the Forest*'.[16] Mrs Radcliffe's novel became the vogue with its middle-class readership. Maria Edgeworth wrote to her cousin Sophy Ruxton from Clifton near Bristol on 14 August 1792, asking if her aunt, Mrs Ruxton, had seen it yet:

> It has been the fashionable novel here, everybody read and talked of it; we were much interested in some parts of it. It is something in the style of the *Castle of Otranto*, and the horrible parts are we thought well worked up, but it is very difficult to keep Horror breathless with his mouth wide open through three volumes.[17]

The Romance of the Forest played a significant role in spreading the popularity of the very genre of 'romance'. It quickly established itself as a classic of modern romantic novel writing, and was plundered by imitators. A reviewer in 1794 noted that the 'strange farrago' of *The Romance of the Cavern; or, the History of Fitz-Henry and James* (by George Walker, 1792) was 'copied from various popular novels. The Romance of the Forest gave it the name; the Recess its heroes; and Ferdinand Count Fathom has supplied some of its most interesting events.'[18] The *Critical Review*, which for years had published a Monthly Catalogue of 'Novels', for the first time in March 1794 expanded the heading to 'Novels and Romances'.[19] Further editions appeared in 1794, 1795, 1796 and later.[20] Familiarity with the novel was also spread through excerpts, beginning with the journal *Monthly Extracts*, in which Chapters 1 and 2 appeared as 'Character of Pierre de La Motte', and Chapter 15 as 'Memoirs of the Family of La Luc' (3, August 1792).

Even after the unparalleled success of *The Mysteries of Udolpho*, many readers remembered with fondness the poetic beauty of *The Romance of the Forest* and maintained that it was Ann Radcliffe's best novel. Modern critics would not disagree with the view expressed by Dunlop in 1814 that 'the apparently supernatural circumstances are accounted for at the end of the romance in such a manner as scarcely to disappoint the reader, or to appear inadequate to the emotions of surprise and terror, which had been raised in the course of the work'.[21] Mrs Barbauld in 1810 compared the scene in which the Marquis Montalt reveals to La Motte that he plans to kill Adeline to the scene in which King John requests Hubert to murder Arthur (*King John*, III. iii) – and judged that Mrs Radcliffe was more skilful and more realistic than Shakespeare.[22]

The novel was dramatized by James Boaden as *Fontainville Forest*, and produced at Covent Garden on 25 March 1794, designed specifically to compete with a production of Handel's Oratorios with which Kemble was opening his New Drury Lane Theatre that season. The *pièce de résistance* of Boaden's medieval set was the appearance of a spectre inspired by Fuseli's painting of Hamlet in the Shakespeare Gallery.[23] Not to be outdone, New

Drury Lane followed with *Macbeth* on 21 April that year, with John Philip Kemble and Mrs Siddons in the title roles. But Covent Garden drew the crowds back with Henry Siddon's dramatization of *A Sicilian Romance; or, The Apparition of the Cliffs, an Opera* – based upon Mrs Radcliffe's previous novel – which was acted by Middleton for his benefit several times between March and May.[24] Thus Ann Radcliffe competed with Shakespeare for the favour of the public.

One last, and bizarre, response to *The Romance of the Forest* remains to be considered: the belief that it was a divine prophecy. Many people had been thrown into a mental turmoil by the events of the French Revolution, particularly during the Terror of 1794, when *The Mysteries of Udolpho* was published. Mrs Piozzi noted that at the time her circle were reading the novel:

> the people are gaping for Wonders of every kind, and expect Marvels in the Natural World to keep Pace with the strange Events observed in the *Civil & Political* World. *Some odd* Things will I trust casually be talked of here & there for a long time, as *Signs & Wonders* are to most people the sure & only Tests of approaching End.[25]

One of the manifestations of this millennialism was the belief that ancient prophecies were being fulfilled. Even Mrs Piozzi, an educated middle-class woman, began a serious study of the prophecies in Revelations and Isaiah.[26] Prophetic publications became so numerous that the *Monthly Review* had to introduce the separate heading of 'Modern Prophecies' under which to review them.[27] One such pamphlet was the *Testimony of the Authenticity of the Prophecies of Richard Brothers*, the follower of Joanna Southcott. For people like these, Mrs Radcliffe was more than just an exemplar of the spirit of the times: she was herself a prophetess. The most extraordinary reading of *The Romance of the Forest* was the critical commentary allegedly authored by none other than God Himself.

Joanna Southcott, the great Sibyl in this age of revolution, was herself partly responsible for popularizing the word 'mysteries', of which her prophecies were the elucidations. She was the Lamb's Wife, the Woman clothed with the Sun, who claimed to be appointed the mother of the true Messiah.[28] In 1803, some six years after she first began receiving communications from the 'Small Still Voice' of God, one of her followers, the Revd T. P. Foley, brought Mrs Radcliffe's novel to her attention, in the belief that God had directed him to this novel as part of a divine plan. He was probably struck by Adeline's prophetic dreams and her express wish that she were a prophet: 'O! could I dive into futurity and behold the events which await me!' (100–1). For Southcott's 100,000 followers, even Gothic novels were instructive 'histories', one way by which God communicated to man. William Blake offered similar allegorical/prophetic interpretations of literary works, and his friend the engraver William Sharp was one of Southcott's followers. The Spirit told Joanna that 'I caused that history to be in his [Foley's] hand/As I knew that Such Dangers would be in your Land.' The result was a divine analysis dated 13 August 1803, consisting of twenty-eight lines of prose and 208 lines of rimed couplets, *dictated by the Spirit of God*, in an unpublished manuscript now in the Miriam Lutcher Stark Library at the University of Texas in Austin.[29]

According to the Spirit, Ann Radcliffe's romance was 'wisely Imagined and wisely Printed'; its purpose was 'to show Vice in its true colours, and how long it hath power to go on without Discovery, before their Crimes are fully ripe and how Judgments overtake them in the end'. The story is a 'History', that is an allegory, of the tribulations of Southcott's followers and a prophecy of God's divine plan. Phillipe de Montalt is the 'type' or 'Likeness' of Satan, and Adeline represents Joanna. The criminals hired by Montalt are the henchmen of Satan, those guilty of satirical and slanderous attacks upon Joanna's claim to be visited by the Holy Spirit. The mystery over the identity of Adeline's father, according to the Spirit, parallels Joanna's choice between acknowledging conventional society as her parent or the 'Voice' of her true Father. Just as Montalt is brought to trial for murdering Adeline's father and trying to murder her, so the time is coming when Satan will be tried for murdering Christ, when Southcott and her followers will triumph:

I say like the Novel the End will be here
And all Such triumph of Joy they will turn
Look back on the Days they in Silence did mourn
Fearing their Foe Should them Wholly Destroy
And 'tis in these Dangers that I shall enjoy
My *Friends* to *Deliver* My *Foes* for to *fall*.

On the broader historical level, Montalt is an allegory of corrupt France (and the French people who had murdered their king and replaced him with Napoleon) attempting to destroy Adeline who represents England. The novel is thus a political prophecy that although England will suffer at the hands of the French, like Adeline it will never be defeated. The inference is that Ann Radcliffe was divinely inspired to write the novel to reveal God's plan to deliver England in general, and Southcott's virtuous brotherhood in particular. Thus, ironically, she was seen to carry on the tradition of her uncle Jebb's 'prophesying protestantism'.

Unrivalled Genius

———— • ————

William Radcliffe's career with the *Gazetteer* was short-lived. In January 1792 his salary as editor was increased to £4 4s (that is 4 guineas) per week, and in October to 5 guineas per week.[1] In February William proposed that a shop be engaged for the distribution of the newspaper in Bath – an idea perhaps suggested by his father-in-law William Ward – and premises were procured by March.[2] Over the next year about seven hundred copies were dispatched to Bath each month, for a sale of only two dozen copies a day (sales in London were 1,500–1,900 a month). This was not profitable in itself, but they persevered with the Bath circulation in order to attract London advertisers. The need for revenue was pressing; William and his colleague Mr Beauchamp were instructed by the management committee 'at all times to exclude such matter as may not appear to Mr Radcliffe and himself either immediately interesting or Pressing in favour of Advertisements'.[3] An increasing emphasis upon cultural affairs, poems, anecdotes and readers' correspondence signalled an effort to attract advertisers; the front page was dominated by advertisements for the theatres and opera houses. William Radcliffe probably wrote the bulk of the copy, to judge by the relatively large expenditure of £1 6s every few months for 'Pens for Mr Radcliffe'.[4]

Although William's salary had been raised to 5 guineas a week in October, on 31 December 1792 John Egerton informed the management committee that 'Mr Radcliffe had acquainted him, that he had entered into a connection with another Paper, which would occasion him to relinquish his engagement with the Gazetteer, as soon as possible'. Perhaps William objected to the proprietors' decision to decrease the size of the theatre advertisements, to virtually eliminate the appended theatre reviews, and even to combine two theatres into a single advertisement in order to save the duty on them.[5] Whatever the case, the parting was not amicable: on 2 January 1793 it was 'Resolved that Mr Beauchamp be directed, to pay Mr Radcliffe up to

Saturday Jan. 12ᵗʰ and to acquaint him; that his *late professions* towards the Gazetteer, compared with his *present conduct*; render the Proprietors extremely desirous, of putting an End, to any further connection with him.'[6]

The first thing they did was to engage a Mr Wiley to translate the French papers, which shows precisely which part of William's job was deemed most essential.[7] Journals competed to meet the public appetite for news about the French Revolution, and William Radcliffe's experience – editor-in-chief of a somewhat radical paper, parliamentary reporter, French translator – would have been valued by others. We do not know what paper he established a connection with, if any. I believe that he did not obtain the employment which he had hoped for, that his announcement had been premature and that he was supported by his wife's earnings for the next year and a half. The fact that he travelled with her for several months, through Holland and Germany and then the Lake District, in the summer and autumn of 1794, suggests that he was unemployed until well after the publication of his wife's greatest novel.

We can safely say that *The Mysteries of Udolpho* was officially published on Thursday 8 May 1794. The earliest advertisement for the novel appeared in the *London Chronicle* for 22–24 April 1794 (the paper was published three times a week): '*In a few Days will be published*, In Four very large Volumes Twelves, THE MYSTERIES OF UDOLPHO. A Romance; interspersed with some Pieces of Poetry, &c. By Ann Radcliffe, Author of the Romance of the Forest, &c. Printed for G. G. and J. Robinson, Paternoster-row.' The same advertisement was repeated in the issue for 26–29 April. Advance advertisements also appeared in *The Times* for 2 and 8 May. The actual date of publication has been confused by the appearance of advertisements announcing 'This day is published' in the *Star* on 9 May, in the *Courier, and Evening Gazette* on 10 May and in *The Times* on 21 May and again on 23 May. The advertisements in the *London Chronicle* are the most precise: in the issue for 1–3 May it was advertised as being published 'On Thursday next'; this was repeated in the issue for 3–6 May; in the issue for Thursday 8 May to Saturday 10 May the advertisement was appropriately changed to 'This Day was published . . . Price One Pound in boards . . .'. (The *London Chronicle* rather blotted its record for accuracy by repeating the same advertisement in the issue for 19–21 June, but it was common practice to rerun such advertisements for up to two or even three months after publication.) Similarly the first advertisement in the *St James's Chronicle* stated 'This Day was published' in the issue for 8–10 May. No novel would have been officially published on a Saturday (i.e. 10 May), and in the 1790s as well as in the 1970s, Thursday is the standard day for publishing magazines and books. Matthew Gregory Lewis was able to obtain a copy before crossing the Channel and to have finished reading it by 18 May, three days after arriving at the Hague.[8]

The Mysteries of Udolpho was more frequently advertised than any other novel in the *London Chronicle* during 1794, demonstrating that the Robinsons were intent on recouping their investment. Payments from Messrs Robinson for advertising the book were recorded in the ledger of the *Gazetteer* for 24 and 26 April, 3, 6 and 9 May, and 10, 17, 24 and 31 October – which strongly suggests a second printing in October.[9]

On 9 May 1794 Hookham and Carpenter simultaneously published the fourth edition of *The Romance of the Forest* – which contained Ann Radcliffe's dedication to the Duchess of Leeds – together with James Boaden's *Fontainville Forest* (the dramatic adaptation of *The Romance of the Forest*) and the second editions of both *A Sicilian Romance* and *The Castles of Athlin and Dunbayne*. Hookham and Carpenter took out advertisements for their four books in the *St James's Chronicle*, beginning in the issue for 8–10 April, and a long advertisement (complete with two quotations from *Macbeth*) in the *Courier, and Evening Gazette* for Saturday 10 May 1794. The near-simultaneous publication of *The Mysteries of Udolpho*, *Fontainville Forest* and the three reissued novels was linked so as to elevate a hot property to celebrity status and to have the greatest possible impact upon the public.

For the copyright to this novel Ann Radcliffe was paid the then considerable sum of £500. The contract for the publishing rights has mysteriously survived and is now in the Sadleir–Black Collection in the University of Virginia Library. It was one of the last additions made by Robert K. Black to his Gothic collection, purchased apparently from a basement bookshop in Newark, New Jersey, in the mid-1940s.[10] The contract was dated 11 March 1794, and gave the Radcliffes' address as 'Brownlow Street Holborn'. Apparently they were living in rented accommodation, for they are not listed in the poor rates books for Brownlow Street, Parish of St Andrew. Possibly they stayed with the Brownlow Street ratepayer named George Burton, who may have been related to Robert Hallifax's brother-in-law Edmund Burton, and to David Longman Burton whom the Radcliffes visited in Lincolnshire later that year.[11]

William and Ann both had to sign the contract, because married women had no legal status for agreements regarding property, intellectual or otherwise:

> William Radcliffe and Ann his wife agree to sell and deliver unto the said George Robinson for himself and Company a certain Manuscript Romance, written by the said Anne [*sic*] Radcliffe, entitled 'the Mysteries of Udolpho' and the whole benefit therefrom and interest therein for which said Manuscript the said George Robinson for himself and Company agrees to pay unto the said William and Ann Radcliffe on their order the sum of five hundred pounds . . .

One hundred pounds would be paid within three months or upon publication if earlier, followed by four further payments of £100 at two-month intervals. William and Ann signed a receipt on 10 May 1794, acknowledging receipt of £100 and the four notes payable at two, four, six and eight months for £100 each, 'in full for the Copy Right of the Mysteries of Udolpho'.[12]

The obituary which appeared in the *New Monthly Magazine* was mistaken in asserting that the Robinsons gave her £1,000 for it, and that Cadell and Davies gave her £1,500 for *The Italian*, but correctly pointed out that 'they were well repaid for their speculation, the work being universally sought for, and many large editions rapidly sold'.[13] For a Gothic novel, the sum of £500 was unbelievably high: the authors of the three-volume Minerva novels usually received only £10 to £20.[14] It is well known that Jane Austen received only £10 for her parody of Ann Radcliffe's Gothic fiction, *Northanger Abbey*. Shelley expected to get £60 for his three-volume Gothic romance *St Irvyne*, but it had to be published at his own expense in 1811.[15] George Robinson paid Mrs Inchbald £200 in 1790 for her novel *A Simple Story*, and in 1796 he bought her novel *Nature and Art* for only £150. Robinson argued that 'Two volumes in twelves, that, at trade price, could not yield the publisher four shillings per copy, required more than one impression to bring him any profit upon the outlay.' From this copyright fee the actress invested £88 15s, which gave her £5 per annum.[16] Charles Maturin did manage to obtain £500 for *Melmoth the Wanderer* – but that was published a full generation after *Udolpho*.[17]

Mrs Radcliffe's royalty caught the public imagination, and even twenty years later, a contributor to the *Gentleman's Magazine* was moved to remark upon the '£1,000' paid to her for *Udolpho*.[18] The French biographical works also cited these figures, thus enhancing her reputation across the Channel.[19] Such an amount was 'at that time so unusually large a sum for a work of imagination, that old Mr Cadell, than whom no man was more experienced in such matters, when he was told that 500*l.* had been given, offered a wager of 10*l.* that it was not the fact'.[20] No doubt Robinson confirmed the sum to Cadell and also the fact that it was well spent, for Cadell's firm subsequently outbid competitors and paid Mrs Radcliffe £800 so that they could publish *The Italian* (though it was widely believed they paid £1,500 for it).

During the late 1790s and early 1800s, a single person could live quietly in the country on £200 per annum, and a young couple with two servants could manage fairly well on £500. In 1788 Eleanor Butler and Sarah Ponsonby, the Ladies of Llangollen, supported themselves and four servants, in Welsh retirement, for an expenditure of £444 13s 2d.[21] Around 1791 Anna Seward was supporting a fair-sized household on a 'moderate' yearly income of £400, though in 1794 her urban friend Harriet Bowdler considered that amount to be 'comparative poverty'.[22] By the end of 1792 William Radcliffe had been earning 5 guineas per week, or £274 per year; if he was employed at all in 1794 his annual income still would have been much lower than the amount his wife earned from her novel. At the very least, the royalty for *The Mysteries of Udolpho* enabled the Radcliffes to take a trip abroad, and to buy a house on their return home.

A more important consequence of the large royalty was its cultural impact: serious money dignified what might otherwise have been dismissed as yet another silly novel. Literature, the patrimony of men, already under threat by working women novelists such as Charlotte Smith, was struck another humiliating blow: never before had such an amount been paid to a woman, and the male literary establishment was astonished. The antiquarian Joseph Ritson knew the sum was £500 as early as 8 March 1794 – three days before Mrs Radcliffe signed the contract – when he wrote to a friend, with a degree of envy:

> novel-writing is certainly in high estimation. Mrs Radcliffe, Author of 'The Romance of the Forest', has one at present in the hands of Robinsons for which she asks five hundred pounds, though it is but to consist of four volumes. Godwin also, and I believe, Holcroft, have each one in the press. In short, one would suppose all the world to be novel readers, though, for my part, I must with shame confess I never look into one.[23]

Ritson's friend William Godwin may have been the source for this information, or even Robinson himself.[24] Dr Charles Burney, who was also acquainted with the major publishers, similarly knew of this extraordinary royalty before the book was published, and reported it to his daughter Fanny, who was pleased for her literary colleague, but envious: 'I am very glad for Mrs Radcliffe & her £500 & I *act* "think of That, Master Brooke!" if *so*.'[25] The allusion is to Shakespeare's *Merry Wives of Windsor* (III. v. 108), when Falstaff expresses his indignation to Ford, disguised as Master Brook, at being dumped into the Thames with the dirty clothes – i.e. Fanny Burney is indignant about being paid so little in comparison. It was shortly after this that she began her own semi-Gothic 'Grand Work' *Camilla*, though it remained untitled for a year: 'I like well the idea of giving *no name at all*, – Why should not I have my mystery, as well as Udolpho?'[26] The royalty paid to Mrs Radcliffe for a work of four volumes totalling 1,797 pages and 292,000 words[27] was weighed as Fanny Burney planned how to market *Camilla* most lucratively:

> I wish to know whether, if I part with the Copy right, it would not be rather an *advantage* to the Publisher to have *5* volumes instead of *4*, or else *4* large as Udolpho, as *he* may then raise to non-subscribers. . . . If we print ultimately for ourselves, according to our original plan, we always meant to make 4 *Udolphoish*

volumes, & reprint the Edition that succeeds the subscription in *6* volumes duod[mo] common, for a raised price.'[28]

Mrs Radcliffe's novel thus played a pivotal role in the professional marketing of fiction by women.

The Mysteries of Udolpho is one of the great works of European literature; it has prompted a rich range of modern criticism, and is capable of sustaining analysis and appreciation on many different levels, from the most traditional historical contextualization to the most advanced semiotics and neo-Freudian interpretations. My own reading of the sexual anxieties of the novel will be reserved for Chapter 11. For the moment, I wish to concentrate here on the historical context of the novel, particularly on the influence of contemporary aesthetic theory and the romance tradition.

The Mysteries of Udolpho is, above all, a cultural artefact. The landscapes that made this novel so famous are really strings of iconic mood-words and aesthetic terms rather than genuine descriptions of scenery: 'solitary silence . . . tremendous precipices . . . gloomy grandeur . . . dreadful sublimity'.[29] Radcliffe's major characteristic is an epic chiaroscuro, as in her breath-taking set-pieces of Alpine scenery, which have never been surpassed:

> From Beaujeu the road had constantly ascended, conducting the travellers into the higher regions of the air, where immense glaciers exhibited their frozen horrors, and eternal snow whitened the summits of the mountains. . . . Over these crags rose others of stupendous height, and fantastic shape; some shooting into cones; others impending far over their base, in huge masses of granite, along whose broken ridges was often lodged a weight of snow, that, trembling even to the vibration of a sound, threatened to bear destruction in its course to the vale. Around, on every side, far as the eye could penetrate, were seen only forms of grandeur – the long perspective of mountain-tops, tinged with ethereal blue, or white with snow; vallies [*sic*] of ice, and forests of gloomy fir. (42–3)

The landscape becomes an *objet d'art*, given a cultural dimension by allusions to artists such as Salvator Rosa (30) and Domenichino (377), and by Emily's own practice of drawing miniature landscapes. Ann Radcliffe's landscapes follow strict rules of classification: the room in the west turret of Château-le-Blanc has three windows which 'presented each a separate and beautiful prospect', and we understand immediately that Languedoc to the north illustrates the Beautiful, the Pyrenees to the west exemplify the Sublime and Roussillon to the south represents the Picturesque (479). In the grounds of the château an octagonal pleasure pavilion serves as a camera obscura: one window opens upon 'a romantic glade' and 'woody recesses', one discloses 'the distant summits of the Pyrenées'; a third fronts the grey towers of the château 'and a picturesque part of its ruin'; a fourth affords 'a glimpse of the green pastures and villages' of the Aude; 'the grand objects of a fifth window' show 'the bold cliffs' over the shore; and the sixth reveals 'the wild scenery of the woods'. These six windows illustrate respectively Forest Scenery, the Sublime, the Picturesque, the Beautiful (Poussin), the Grand (Claude) and the Horrid. The remaining two windows are wisely not referred to – according to contemporary classifications they would have to illustrate the Grotesque and the Ludicrous.

The novel is replete with cultural images, wholly unlike any other novel until the cultivation of recherché allusions in the Decadent novel a century later. Ample exhibition of Mrs Radcliffe's reading of the English classics is provided by the epigraphs and quotations from Thomson's *Castle of Indolence*, Shakespeare's *Hamlet*, *Julius Caesar*, *Macbeth* and *A Midsummer Night's Dream*, Beattie's *The Minstrel*, Collins's *Ode to Fear*, Goldsmith's *The Traveller*, Gray's *The Bard*, Mason's *Caractacus*, Milton's *Comus*, *Il Penseroso* and *Lycidas*, Ossian, Pope's translation of Homer, Rogers's *Pleasures of Memory*, Frank Sayers's *Moina* (a 'Dramatic Sketch of Northern Mythology' influenced by Ossian and Mason) and others – some seventy-five quotations plus eighteen complete poems composed by the characters themselves. In few other literary works has literature itself been the pre-eminent subject. For all its horrors, the novel is an extraordinary affirmation of faith in civilization and the liberal arts.

Monsieur St Aubert's library is 'enriched by a collection of the best books in the ancient and modern languages' (3); he taught his daughter 'Latin and English, chiefly that she might understand the sublimity of their best poets' (6) – who presumably include the poets reviewed by Thomas Warton in his *History of English Poetry* (1774–81): Gower, Chaucer, Spenser, Sackville's *Gorboduc* and various romances, such as *Guy of Warwick*, *Sir Bevis* and *Richard Coeur de Lion*. Emily has a room of her own, 'which contained her books, her drawings, her musical instruments', where she 'exercised herself in elegant arts' (3). In Valancourt's simple room we discover 'volumes of Homer, Horace, and Petrarch' (35).

In Venice, Emily hears the gondoliers and minstrels singing 'the verses of Ariosto. They sung of the wars of the Moors against Charlemagne, and then of the woes of Orlando: afterwards the measure changed, and the melancholy sweetness of Petrarch succeeded' (177). At the castello di Udolpho, culture is inverted: Ludovico, lover of the servant Annette, is a satirical portrait of Ariosto – the Divine Ludovico. It was he who in Venice sang the verses of Ariosto overheard by Emily; now in Udolpho, Annette explains that he 'used to sing such sweet verses about Orlandos and about

the Black-a-moors, too; and Charly – Charly – magne, yes, that was the name'
(247). In Udolpho Emily can no longer overcome anxiety through culture:
she 'took down from her little library a volume of her favourite Ariosto; but
his wild imagery and rich invention could not long enchant her attention;
his spells did not reach her heart, and over her sleeping fancy they played,
without awakening it' (284).

Creativity blossoms again at Château-le-Blanc. As Blanche draws near to
the château she dreams of tales of chivalry, 'legends, to which she had once
or twice obtained access in the library of her convent, that, like many others,
belonging to the monks, was stored with these reliques of romantic fiction'
(468). We catch the allusion to Bishop Percy's *Reliques of Ancient English Poetry*
(1765). Château-le-Blanc is appropriately hung with tapestries which
'depictured scenes from some of the antient Provençal romances' (469, 532)
and 'scenes from the wars of Troy' (474), while its ancient wing contains a
suite of apartments of faded magnificence, with Venetian pier glasses and
'grand furniture . . . made after the fashion of some in the Louvre' (532).
Ann Radcliffe may be remembering the impressions of her uncle Bentley,
who visited Paris in 1776 and reported that 'The famous Louvre is an
incomprehensible jumble of magnificence and meaness [*sic*] – of grandeur
and bad taste – and ruins.'[30]

In the château's haunted chamber, Ludovico passes the time while
waiting for the ghost to appear by reading 'a volume of old Provençal tales'
(549), lent to him by Dorothée, who had retrieved it from 'an obscure corner'
of the Marquis de Villeroi's library (a possible allusion to Bentley's library).
This gives Ann Radcliffe the opportunity to defend 'that love, so natural to
the human mind, of whatever is able to distend its faculties with wonder and
astonishment' (549), and she uses her undisguised authorial voice to celebrate
tales of mystery and imagination:

> The fictions of the Provençal writers, whether drawn from the Arabian legends,
> brought by the Saracens into Spain, or recounting the chivalric exploits
> performed by the crusaders, whom the Troubadors accompanied to the east,
> were generally splendid and always marvellous, both in scenery and incident;
> and it is not wonderful, that Dorothée and Ludovico should be fascinated by
> inventions, which had captivated the careless imagination in every rank of
> society, in a former age. (551–2)

'The Provençal Tale' turns out to be a rendition of the story of Sir Bevys of
Lancaster as contained in Warton's *History of English Poetry*. Ann Radcliffe's
knowledge of the Provençal troubadours comes from Warton's lengthy study
of how they 'followed their barons in prodigious multitudes to the conquest
of Jerusalem', and helped create the origins of romance:

Undoubtedly the Provencial bards contributed much to the progress of Italian literature. . . . They introduced a love of reading, and diffused a general and popular taste for poetry, by writing in a language intelligible to the ladies and the people. Their verses being conveyed in a familiar tongue, became the chief amusement of princes and feudal lords, whose courts had now begun to assume an air of greater brilliancy: a circumstance which necessarily gave great encouragement to their profession, and by rendering these arts of ingenious entertainment universally fashionable, imperceptibly laid the foundation of polite literature.[31]

Clara Reeve picked up this justification for her own history, *The Progress of Romance* (1785), a work which Mrs Radcliffe also almost certainly read: 'Romance may not improperly be called the polite literature of early ages, and they have been the favourite amusements of later times.'[32]

In the final pages of the novel, Annette, whom I see as a comic metonym for Ann Radcliffe, looks down from the corridor into the gaily decorated hall, and 'almost fancied herself in an enchanted palace, and declared, that she had not met with any place, which charmed her so much, since she read the fairy tales; nay, that the fairies themselves, at their nightly revels in this old hall, could display nothing finer' (671). When all the mysteries have been elucidated, the great hall of Château-le-Blanc 'was hung with superb new tapestry, representing the exploits of Charlemagne and his twelve peers; here, were seen the Saracens, with their horrible visors, advancing to battle; and there, were displayed the wild solemnities of incantation, and the necromantic feats, exhibited by the magician *Jarl* before the Emperor' (670–1). Oddly enough, no one has recognized that the source of this allusion is Warton's *History of English Poetry*: the romances of Charlemagne and Arthur have been decorated by the Scandinavian skalds, and in one unidentified saga 'Jarl, a magician of Saxland, exhibits his feats of necromancy before Charlemagne.'[33] Ann Radcliffe lifted this sentence almost verbatim and applied it in her typically ingenious, cleverly teasing, manner.

As we read these final pages it suddenly becomes clear that the novel has been an allegorical fantasia upon the romances excerpted in Warton's *History*, and the magical tableaux in Handel's *Rinaldo*, Tasso's *Jerusalem Delivered* and John Hoole's translation of Ariosto's *Orlando Furioso*.[34] The castle of Udolpho is the enchanted castle of the necromancer Atalantes:

From steep to steep, from wood to wood they pass'd,
Till fam'd Pyrene's hills they reach'd at last.
. . .
Thence from the summit shew'd a rough descent,
That winding to the lower valley went,

Where, in the midst, a rocky mountain stood
On which aloft the fort of steel they view'd,
That rear'd to heaven, with such stupendous height,
Made all beneath seem little in its flight.
Behold th'enchanter's tower (Brunello said)
In which the knights and dames are prisoners made.

(vol. 4, 74–5, 78–86)

The Paladin Astolpho and Duke Rodolpho have left their trace in the name
of the castle (though 'the wealthy Adolpho' in a romantic story in the *Lady's
Magazine* in 1792 may also be a source[35]). Emily combines both Angelica and
the virgin Bradamante, whose lover Rogero is seduced by the enchantress
Alcina. The story of Ariodante (via Handel's opera as well as Ariosto) makes
its contribution to the story, after some gender transpositions: Valancourt is
the pathetic maiden Genevra, seemingly seduced by the guileful Duke
Polinisso (Montoni), to the great distress of her lover Ariodante (Emily).
These tableaux are overlaid with scenes from Tasso's *Rinaldo* (especially as
dramatized by Handel) and *Jerusalem Delivered* (also translated by John
Hoole): Lady Laurentini is the sorceress Armida, who lives in her magic
castle on the summit of the mountain guarded by monsters. This beautiful
witch, like Lady Laurentini, is the pivot upon which all the action turns;
Armida invokes the Furies just as does Lady Laurentini in her incarnation
as mad Sister Agnes, who it transpires is the source of the mysterious music.
Rinaldo is the figure behind Count Morano, Tancredi has gone into the
making of the Count de Villefort and Almirena is mirrored in the Marchioness
de Villeroi.

In contrast to all this romance is a solid strain of realism. Jacqueline Howard
argues that the sublime poems that Emily writes are the medium through
which her romantic sensibility is linked 'to freedom, assertiveness, and
transgression of propriety'.[36] Economic concerns are not so 'paramount' in
Radcliffe's work as some modern critics like to suggest, but the importance
of carefully tending one's inheritance is a significant theme. Emily is
mortified to learn that the property which she inherits from her father is to
be controlled by her capricious uncle and aunt, and that she 'was to be
considered as a dependent, not only by her aunt, but by her aunt's servants'
(121) – a feeling perhaps experienced by Nancy Ward upon first entering
the residence of her uncle Bentley. Women are the real sources of power and
wealth in the novel. Lady Laurentini is the rightful owner of Udolpho;
Montoni has dubiously usurped and squandered her wealth and property.
But Emily's aunt had cleverly contrived to have most of her possessions

privately reserved for herself in the marriage settlement rather than her husband, and refuses to sign over her estates to him. She takes steps to ensure that Emily will inherit her property, and Emily tries to keep this inheritance inviolable. Emily sensibly advises Mme Montoni that 'so long as you keep this, you may look forward to it as a resource, at least, that will afford you a competence, should the Signor's future conduct compel you to sue for separation' (283) – a rather practical consideration of the possibility of divorce in a novel of such high romance. For all her fearfulness, Emily is as tough and pragmatic as they come. Property looms larger than love in *The Mysteries of Udolpho*, and the last half of the novel is mainly concerned with her consolidation of her property rights.[37]

The terrifying economic consequences of Madame Montoni's marriage are a more pressing concern to Emily. Madame Montoni, for her refusal to transfer her property to her husband, is cruelly imprisoned and eventually starved to death. Like Madame Montoni, Emily steadfastly keeps for herself that which is hers. She similarly asserts the female's right to own – and enjoy the use of – property: 'The law, in the present instance, gives me the estates in question, and my own hand shall never betray my right' (381). The knowledge that she has become a woman of property is what enables Emily to experience her own power over Montoni. Threatened by the importunities of Signor Verezzi, she eventually signs her estates away, but when she recovers safety, the first thing she does is solicit the help of Count De Villefort to successfully recover them. 'Propriety' originally described the moral sensibility attainable specifically by the property-owning classes.

By the end of the novel, Emily 'found herself mistress of a large fortune' (619), which she uses to relieve the wants of her former and current tenants. She recovers her aunt Montoni's estates, and regains La Vallée and her father's *maternal* estate; she sells her estate at Toulouse in order to regain from M. Quesnel her father's paternal domain, in which she installs Annette as housekeeper and Ludovico as steward (637); as the niece of the Marchioness de Villeroi she inherits one-third of the property of Signora Laurentini/Sister Agnes (655), though she passes it on to M. Bonnac, whose wife is descended from the family of Udolpho; Valancourt's brother gives Emily and Valancourt part of his rich domain, all of which will eventually descend to Valancourt. Thus everyone regains their birthright, their property.

The general public was fascinated by the very title of *The Mysteries of Udolpho*, and rushed upon it with an eager curiosity. 'When a family was numerous, the volumes flew, and were sometimes torn, from hand to hand, and the complaints of those whose studies were thus interrupted, were a general tribute to the genius of the author.'[38] Mrs Radcliffe's novels, and this one in particular, came to symbolize remembered youth. They epitomized the early innocence of romanticism, and were remembered as a prelapsarian world of lost happiness. There is something deeply nostalgic about their evocation of a romantic past. Hazlitt, in his 1819 lectures at the Surrey Institution, concluded that 'her great power lies in describing the indefinable, and embodying a phantom. She makes her readers twice children.'[39] Thomas Moore, in a similarly nostalgic manner, singled out the summer vacation of 1794 before he entered Trinity College, Dublin, as 'the part of my life the most happy and the most *poetical* (for all was yet in fancy and in promise with me)'. During this vacation he visited with his friend Beresford Burston, jun. at the latter's father's country seat, 'and there, in reading Mrs Radcliffe's romances, and listening, while I read, to Haydn's music, – for my friend's sisters played tolerably on the harpsichord, – dreamt away my time in that sort of vague happiness which a young mind conjures up for itself so easily'.[40]

At the opposite end of the scale, Dr Joseph Warton, Headmaster of Winchester College, who was seventy-two years old when the novel appeared, told his friend George Robinson, the publisher, that he was so fascinated 'he could not go to bed till he had finished it, and that he actually sat up the greater part of the night for that purpose'.[41] In France, a similar story was told about Napoleon's General Maximilien Foy.[42] We can also be fairly certain that Horace Walpole, now seventy-seven years old, read *The Mysteries of Udolpho* shortly after its publication. On 4 September 1794 he replied to a letter from the Countess of Upper Ossory praising Gothic romances. This date, together with a reference to the explained supernatural for which Mrs Radcliffe was noted, would suggest that *Udolpho* was high on the Countess's list, and on Walpole's: 'I have read some of the descriptive verbose tales, of which your Ladyship says I was the patriarch by several mothers. All I can say for myself is that I do not think my concubines have produced issue more natural for excluding the aid of anything marvellous.'[43]

Hester Lynch (Thrale) Piozzi and her family and friends read *The Mysteries of Udolpho* during August (possibly late July) 1794, and when she went on holiday to Denbigh, North Wales, Mrs Piozzi regretted not having brought a copy with her to amuse what little literary acquaintance she could find there. 'I reproach myself daily that I forgot to bring them down The Mysteries of Udolpho: it would have such an effect read by owl-light among the old arcades of our ruined Castle here.'[44] (Later she also owned a copy of *The Italian*.[45]) During that summer the Reign of Terror was at its height in France, and Mrs Piozzi and her correspondent recognized a revolution in reading as well as in the political world:

> as you say, love seems banished from the novels, where *terror* (as in the Convention,) becomes the *order of the day*. Miss Radcliffe however plays that game best which all are striving to play well. . . . Her tricks used to fright Mrs

Siddons and me very much; but when somebody said her book was like Macbeth, 'Ay,' replied H.L.P., 'about as like Peppermint Water is to good French Brandy.'[46]

The first obituaries of Mrs Radcliffe recognized that *The Mysteries of Udolpho* was 'one of the most extraordinary compositions in the circle of literature'.[47] In its various editions, from the inexpensive British Novelists' edition by Mrs Barbauld to Limbard's more expensive illustrated version and then Ballantyne's edition, the novel could be found in virtually every private library. Everyone who was *serieux* about literature knew something about *The Mysteries of Udolpho*, if only through its appearance in the literary journals, where reviews sometimes were a mere pretext for lengthy extracts (for example, a 6,000-word excerpt appeared in the June 1794 edition of the *European Magazine* and was then reprinted in the July and August issues of the *Hibernian*). Clara Reeve had complained about such 'pilfering practices' many years earlier.[48]

The lead review in the *Critical Review* opened with a quotation from Gray's *Progress of Poesy* (vol. 3, 9–12) in order to rank Ann Radcliffe with William Shakespeare, than which no higher praise was possible:

> Thine too these golden keys, immortal boy!
> This can unlock the gate of joy,
> Of horror, that and thrilling fears,
> Or ope the sacred source of sympathetic tears.

> Such were the presents of the Muse to the infant Shakspeare, and though perhaps to no other mortal has she been so lavish of her gifts, the keys referring to the third line Mrs Radcliffe must be allowed to be completely in possession of.[49]

Her power of keeping the reader at a high pitch of interest was praised, but the reviewer nevertheless complained that the nature descriptions and poetry, however good individually, pall through over-abundance, that the manners are anachronistic for the chosen period, that the talkative maid is an overworked character type and that 'the adventures do not sufficiently point to one centre'. These counterbalancing criticisms offended one reader, from whom the periodical 'received a remonstrance' in October or November.[50] This gave the reviewer the opportunity to set the record straight:

> It never could be our intention to depreciate the genius of Mrs Radcliffe; for if our Correspondent will re-examine the introductory sentences of the Review

in question, he will find such a compliment paid to the powers of her imagination as we seldom condescend to pay to any writer whatever.

It could not be our intention to speak slightingly of a work which all must admire, and which we have no hesitation in pronouncing 'The most interesting novel in the English language.'

. . . But, . . . we must be allowed to point out whatever appears faulty in the most unexceptionable productions; . . . It does not at all destroy the merit of Udolpho to say that it is not perfect.

Only two lines from the 'remonstrance' are quoted, but it is interesting that they show how the reader attempted to establish the novelist's literary respectability by comparing her to Virgil and her work to Edward Gibbon's *Decline and Fall of the Roman Empire*:

The circumstance to which we objected in the Mysteries of Udolpho, was an exuberance of description. We agree, 'that not many of our readers would consider this as a fault;' on the contrary, we allow that many of the best writers of antiquity, and Virgil himself, the most correct of them all, have fallen into a similar error. – Our Correspondent, however, must consider that we were criticising for the world in general; and though it is true, that 'Mr Gibbon's history is liable to the same objection,' and though it does not derogate, on the whole, from the charms of that elegant work, yet it is an error in composition, against which writers in general ought to be on their guard, and young writers in particular, who, without the same powers as Mr Gibbon or Mrs Radcliffe, may chuse to imitate them even in their defects. . . . Far be from us the base and malignant gratification of giving pain to any writer whatever! and least of all to one, in whom (if we are rightly informed) the highest endowments of the imagination are enriched by the more substantial excellence of amiable manners, and genius is accompanied by its best ornament, modesty.

This reader, whose remonstrance was considered to be serious enough to require a public reply – and an apology – was surely William Radcliffe. Who else could testify that the 'amiable' and 'modest' author was 'pained' by the criticisms? The reader exhibits William Radcliffe's characteristic touchiness regarding questions as to his wife's propriety. And as a newspaper editor, he knew how to issue a veiled threat for libel.

The idea that Coleridge wrote this review has proven irresistible to many modern critics, and is still currently held by most, although it was convincingly disproved in 1951, and again in 1972, and ought to be laid to rest. Coleridge in late 1796 had been busy drafting reviews of Gothic novels for the *Critical Review*:

indeed I am almost weary of the Terrible, having been an hireling in the Critical Review for these last six or eight months – I have been lately reviewing the Monk, the Italian, Hubert de Sevrac [by Mary Robinson] &c. &c. & &c. – in all of which dungeons, and old castles, & solitary Houses by the Sea Side, & Caverns, & Woods, & extraordinary characters, & all the tribe of Horror & Mystery, have crowded on me – even to surfeiting.[51]

Unfortunately only his review of Lewis's *The Monk* was published; and the others were destroyed, as Coleridge himself states. As he explained later, he had written half a dozen reviews which he thought devilishly clever and severe, 'but a Remark made by Miss Wordsworth[,] to whom I had in full expectation of gaining a laugh of applause read one of my Judgments[,] occasioned my committing the whole Batch to the Fire'.[52] In other words, Dorothy Wordsworth was so offended by Coleridge's (possibly sexist) ridicule that he desisted.[53] Coleridge was still at Cambridge and had not even begun any review work when the criticism of *The Mysteries of Udolpho* was published. In contrast to that reviewer's praise, we know that for Coleridge Ann Radcliffe's style was a touchstone of bad taste. For example, he felt that 'the death of Mignon and the incidents in the castle [in *Wilhelm Meister*] are sort of Radcliffe scenes unworthy of the exquisite earlier parts'.[54] Part of the reason why Coleridge disliked Scott's *Lady of the Lake* was because it reminded him of the artificial conventions used by Mrs Radcliffe:

> I amused myself a day or two ago on reading a Romance in Mrs Radcliff's [*sic*] style with making out a scheme, which was to serve for all romances a priori – only varying the proportions – A Baron or Baroness ignorant of their Birth, and in some dependent situation – Castle – on a Rock – a Sepulchre – at some distance from the Rock – Deserted Rooms – Underground Passages – Pictures – a ghost, so believed – or – a written record – blood on it! – A wonderful Cut throat – &c. &c. &c.[55]

William Enfield, the last tutor at Warrington Academy before it was dissolved in 1783, and latterly the Unitarian minister of the Octagon Dissenting Congregation in Norwich,[56] is believed to be the author of the review in the *Monthly Review*, in which he did not hesitate to declare the novel to be

> distinguished by a rich vein of invention, which supplies an endless variety of incidents to fill the imagination of the reader. . . . [She] has contrived to produce as powerful an effect as if the invisible world had been obedient to her magic spell, and the reader experiences in perfection the strange luxury of artificial terror. . . . A story so well contrived to hold curiosity in pleasing suspence, and

at the same time to agitate the soul with strong emotions of sympathetic terror, has seldom been produced.[57]

As mentioned earlier, the Rational Dissenting view did not exclude an appreciation for terrible magic.

The pleasure which the reviewer for the *Analytical Review* had already anticipated, from having read her previous novel, was 'far surpassed': 'the whole work is calculated to give the author a distinguished place among fine writers'.[58] The general consensus was that Ann Radcliffe's style surpassed all of her contemporaries in its fertility of invention, power of suggestion and descriptive brilliance. One early reviewer thought it difficult to do justice to 'the precision and singular beauty of her style:

> We think her Mysteries of Udolpho a model of pure English, animated by the finest inspirations of the muse of romance. Her landscapes are, indeed, sometimes gorgeous, and hazy, but we would refer to her Venetian scenes for some of the most finished pictures that are to be found in any language.

She was a mistress of enchantment, calling up romantic feelings 'with the power of a magician'.[59]

Sir Walter Scott felt that a second reading of a Radcliffe novel was no longer possible once one had been 'admitted behind the scenes at the conclusion of the first'.[60] This betrays Scott's historicist prejudice, and is not borne out by experience or the testimony of readers. Henry Crabb Robinson read *The Mysteries of Udolpho* soon after it was published; he re-perused it 'with Delight' in 1798; and reread it a third time with pleasure more than thirty years later, in 1829:

> though not so strongly as in youth, this romance even now is capable of diverting my attention from objects that would seem to be irresistible in their demands. . . . Finished *Udolpho*, which I ought not to have begun. Yet towards the end it indisposed me to any other occupation.[61]

Hazlitt testified that his impressions of the full moon or the sighing of the autumn wind were 'owing to a repeated perusal of the Romance of the Forest and the Mysteries of Udolpho'.[62] Charles Bucke, one of Mrs Radcliffe's most fervent admirers, read it through nine times and was still charmed whenever he thought of it.[63]

𝔓icturesque 𝔗ours

———— • ————

The royalties for *The Mysteries of Udolpho* enabled Mrs Radcliffe to explore that scenery which she had heretofore only imagined. The result would be *A Journey Made in the Summer of 1794, through Holland and the Western Frontier of Germany, with a Return Down the Rhine: To Which Are Added Observations during a Tour to the Lakes of Lancashire, Westmoreland, and Cumberland* (published by Robinson in June 1795, and later that year in Dublin and in a French translation). Extracts were published in the *Lady's Magazine* and the *Scots Magazine*.[1]

In the preface to *A Journey*, dated 20 May 1795, Mrs Radcliffe explained that she would use the pronoun 'we' because her trip was made 'in the company of her nearest relative and friend'. She wanted her husband's name to appear as joint author, but he felt that the appearance of his name on the title page 'would have implied a greater share in the work than he was entitled to, and would have been too much of a novelty'.[2] One reviewer sarcastically observed that Mrs Radcliffe 'is a great deal more complaisant and gallant than another female traveller, Mrs Piozzi, who takes no notice of her husband, although poor Piozzi, no doubt, joined in the emotions of his travelling governess, as well as Mr Radcliffe'.[3]

Mrs Radcliffe explained that her husband was primarily responsible for the political and economic remarks, though she does not otherwise distance herself from them: if she did not share her husband's democratic sentiments, she would not have published them under her name. These sentiments are notably republican. For example, they observe that many of the inhabitants of Frankfurt 'declared to us, that they had a substantial, practical freedom; and we thought a testimony to their actual enjoyments more valuable than any formal acknowledgments of their rights' (228). Thriving merchants in Rotterdam remind the authors that commerce 'is the permanent defender of freedom and knowledge against military glory and politics' (12). Their arrival in Manchester provokes William to condemn 'the dreadful guilt of the Slave Trade' (377). On the last leg of the trip the Radcliffes made a pilgrimage to the top of the ancient mount facing the castle in Kendal, on which stands the obelisk erected in 1788 to commemorate the centenary of the Revolution of 1688, and launched into a praise of Liberty of which Joseph Priestley – and even Tom Paine – would have approved:

> At a time, when the memory of that revolution is reviled, and the praises of liberty itself endeavoured to be suppressed by the artifice of imputing to it the crimes of anarchy, it was impossible to omit any act of veneration to the blessings of this event. Being thus led to ascend the hill, we had a view of the country, over which it presides; a scene simple, great and free as the spirit revered amidst it. (389)[4]

In 1793 Charlotte Smith had ironically observed that a living writer who quoted lines from Thomson on liberty would be accused of expressing 'sentiments of dangerous tendency'.[5] In 1795 it required a brave spirit indeed to celebrate publicly any sort of revolution.

This defence of liberty may be linked to Radcliffe's Unitarian background. Webb observes that 'In the dark days of the war [with France] and for long thereafter, the Unitarians seemed almost the sole open defenders of the legacy from Rational Dissent.'[6] Bogue and Bennett in 1812 noted that the Birmingham riots inspired widespread fear among the Dissenters, who were attacked by both clergy and government:

> In almost all the speeches, papers, pamphlets, and volumes of the ministerial party, in which liberty was not kept entirely out of view, it was spoken of in a way which would lead people to imagine that they must beware of it as a dangerous inmate. The mad deeds of the French were exposed in colours sufficiently glaring, but instead of considering these as a gross abuse of liberty, they were employed as weapons to destroy it, and an attack was by these means made against liberty itself.[7]

As Miles notes, the *Journey* 'provides the most emphatic evidence of Radcliffe's own political opinions at a juncture when the public mood had shifted sharply against the optimism of 1791 and 1792. . . . Radcliffe's cool reaffirmation of Price's dissenting principles in 1795 may be taken as an index of deep political belief.'[8]

Hardly a year before Mrs Radcliffe made her remarks on liberty, Priestley had been driven from Britain as a political/religious refugee. The Radcliffes visited relatives in Nottingham in autumn 1794 (as discussed below) and would have known that in June of that year that city's 'Unitarian cotton manufacturer Robert Dennison, had the workshops attached to his mill set on fire' because he was a signatory to the anti-war petition.[9] The previous two years marked the peak of anti-Unitarian violence. In April 1792 mobs attacked the homes and mills of Unitarians in Nottingham; in June the doors of Unitarian meeting-houses in Manchester were battered down; in November the mills of the Unitarian cotton manufacture in Belper belonging to William Strutt were flooded, and his books were burned, because he had tried to distribute copies of Paine's *Rights of Man* to his workers.[10] Watts notes the famous trials of the period:

> Unitarians who criticized Church or State were particularly exposed to charges of seditious libel. Thomas Fyshe Palmer, minister to a Unitarian meeting in Dundee, was sentenced in 1793 to seven years' transportation to Botany Bay for his part in publishing a pamphlet in favour of parliamentary reform. . . . James Belcher, a Unitarian bookseller in Birmingham, was also imprisoned in 1793 for selling the works of Thomas Paine. Jeremiah Joyce, tutor to the sons of the Earl of Stanhope and future secretary of the Unitarian Society, was arrested in 1794 and held for twenty-three weeks on suspicion of treason.[11]

Seen in their contemporary context, Ann Radcliffe's views on the issue of liberty are more defiant than apologetic. Her public assertion that the English disgust with the Terror in France should be kept in perspective could not have been made without an awareness that many of her contemporaries would revile her for her position; she is taking a stand that places her in the Wollstonecraft school.

Holland was of interest to Mrs Radcliffe because of her Dutch ancestors, though there was little alternative, as Britain was now actively pursuing the war with France. France had already invaded Holland, and for Mrs Radcliffe to travel in Germany and Holland during such turbulent times demonstrates that her 'retiring disposition was not due to timidity'.[12] She and her husband embarked at Harwich, and sailed to Helvoetsluys. They reached The Hague just as the garlands used to ornament the palace in May were being taken down (36); and they went to an evening service at a Dutch church in Harlem 'on the 4th of June' (55) – a Wednesday in 1794. The previous Sunday (1 June) they attended a service at an English Protestant chapel in The Hague; their arrival in Holland had been three days earlier, which would have been 29 May. They had therefore left England about a fortnight after signing the receipt for the first instalment of royalties for *The Mysteries of Udolpho* on 10 May.

Details of the journey seem to have been arranged through some of Mrs Radcliffe's eminent relations. The frequency with which the Radcliffes attend church services and make a point of speaking to the incumbents suggests that they had letters of introduction from Dr Samuel Hallifax, Bishop of St Asaph. On their first night in Helvoetsluys they stayed at an inn kept by English people, and slept (separately) in two crib-like beds let into the wainscot. One of the two English churches in Rotterdam was under the jurisdiction of the Bishop of London (11); they moved within the English community as much as possible, and kept in touch with a network of bankers to meet their expenses. When they dined at Messrs Bethman, the chief bankers of Frankfurt, the presence of nine or ten English people made it unnecessary to speak French, a fact which Mrs Radcliffe especially notes, presumably relieved at not having to struggle with a tongue in which she was not fluent.

The journey was the fulfilment of a dream nurtured by creating the French, Swiss and Italian scenery in *The Mysteries of Udolpho*. However, Ann Radcliffe's very *British* Gothic sensibility – illustrated by her usual range of references to Collins's *Ode to Evening* (88–9), Johnson's preface to Shakespeare (135), Milton's Eden (263) and *Comus* (452), Pope's *Eloisa to Abelard* ('Black Melancholy . . . breathes a browner horror') (309), Mrs Barbauld's 'The Invitation: To Miss B*****' (*Poems*, 1773) (383), Ossian's 'song of spirits' (393, 422) and Mason's *Caractacus* (447) – was not much gratified on the Continent. The tomb of William of Orange in the Nieuwe Kerk at Delft prompted her to reflect upon 'the transientness of human worth and happiness' (23), but the stately classical church had 'nothing of the "dim religious light," that sooths [*sic*] the mind in Gothic structure' (25; the phrase is Milton's: *Il Penseroso*, l. 152). Dutch Renaissance had little appeal: the Stadthouse of Rotterdam despite its fantastic ornament, 'has been built too early to have the advantages of modern elegance, and too late for the sanction of ancient dignity' (12). She was, however, impressed by the majestic plainness of Cologne Cathedral, 'free from the incongruous ornaments usual in Romish churches' (111); there she caught sight of a mysterious woman covered in loose black drapery, 'rendered more interesting by her situation beneath the broken arches and shattered fret-work of a painted window, through which the rays of the sun scarcely penetrated to break the shade she had chosen' (112). This visit inspired the opening scene of *The Italian*, in which a mysterious assassin is glimpsed pacing in the shadows of the portico of the church of Santa Maria del Pianto, the interior of which is obviously more characteristic of Cologne than any church in Naples, having 'nothing of the shewy ornament and general splendor, which distinguish the churches of Italy . . . but it exhibited a simplicity and grandeur of design' (*The Italian*, 2).

On Trinity Sunday they visited a convent of the order of Clarisse in Cologne, whose members take a vow, not only to renounce the world, but their dearest friends . . . lest some lingering remains of filial affection should tempt an unhappy nun to lift the veil of separation between herself and her mother, she is not allowed to speak even with her, but in the presence of the abbess. Accounts of such horrible perversions of human reason make the blood thrill and the teeth chatter. (109)

Some of the anti-Catholic impressions formed on this visit would find their way into *The Italian*.

Although the sublimity of Switzerland was the goal of the journey, it began appropriately with the Picturesque and the Beautiful. At Goodesberg they ascended the mountain in the evening, to its ancient ruined citadel, to watch the sunset and indulge in cultural reverie:

> It was a still and beautiful evening, in which no shade remained of the thunder clouds, that passed in the day. To the west, under the glow of the sun-set, the landscape melted into the horizon in tints so soft, so clear, so delicately roseate as Claude only could have painted. Viewed, as we then saw it, beyond a deep and dark arch of the ruin, its effect was enchanting; it was to the eye, what the finest strains of Paisiello are to the heart, or the poetry of Collins is to the fancy – all tender, sweet, elegant and glowing. (138–9)

Near Goodesberg are the Seven Mountains, on three of which (Drakenfels, Wolkenbourg and Lowenbourg) were the castles (two still visible as ruins) that provided a story of great interest to Mrs Radcliffe. Three brothers have a sister named Adelaide who falls in love with the knight Roland; they pretend Roland has been killed in the war of Palestine, and Adelaide goes into a convent. Roland returns, too late, and builds his castle overlooking the island where Adelaide's monastery is situated. Mrs Radcliffe may well have made a special pilgrimage to this site, for, as she triumphantly explains, 'This is the story, on which the wild and vivid imagination of Ariosto is said to have founded his Orlando' (145).

The Valley of Andernach is characterized by 'grandeur, beauty and barren sublimity, united in a singular manner' (154); luxuriant woods and cheerful villages 'mingl[ed] in striking contrast . . . with the horrors of untamed nature' (155). At Friburg, on the border with Switzerland, Mrs Radcliffe caught her first glimpse of the immensity and sublimity 'of a country of all others in Europe the most astonishing and grand', which Rousseau had popularized in his *Confessions* and which she had so beautifully imagined in her novels. But through it all runs her characteristic strain of melancholy: 'Yet while we yield to the awful pleasure which this eternal vastness inspires, we feel the insignificance of our temporary nature, and, seeming more than ever conscious by what a slender system our existence is upheld, somewhat of dejection and anxiety mingle with our admiration' (273).

Unfortunately the Sublime collapsed into the Ridiculous. At the gate of Friburg, a frontier post with an Austrian garrison, they handed in their German passport, which had been provided by M. de Schwartzkoff, the Hanoverian minister at Frankfurt. The functionary to whom they gave this returned to their inn without it, and it transpired that what he had passed on to the authorities to be examined was their *voiturier*, a travel pass that had been prepared at Mentz. Though this pass was for Basel in Switzerland, it was incorrectly marked 'returning to England' because it had been prepared at the same time as that of 'two English artists, then on their return from Rome' (276) whom they had met in Frankfurt, and who were indeed on their return journey to England. The Radcliffes tried to explain the error to the Lieutenant de Place, 'an illiterate Piedmontese in the Austrian service' (275), but he affected to believe that their name was not Radcliffe, but a German name resembling it:

> Neither my Lord Grenville's [original passport, written in French], or M. de Schwartzkoff's passports, our letters from London to families in Switzerland, nor one of credit from the Messrs Hopes of Amsterdam to the Banking-house of Porta at Lausanne, all of which he pretended to examine, could remove this discerning suspicion as to our country. (275)

Mrs Radcliffe was terrified at the thought of being in the power of this petty military official, whose actions seemed to her to be malicious as well as obstinate. She could not bear the idea of staying at an inn while he pretended to investigate their claim by contacting authorities elsewhere. She panicked. Rather than risk further injustice, they resolved to return immediately to Mentz, where the Prussian authorities sent off an official complaint to the Austrian authorities at Friburg, but this was the end of the adventure. Thus a journey of 600 miles ended in bathos.

It was, however, a lucky escape, for had they gone on to Switzerland their eventual return would have been endangered by the French invasion. Mrs Radcliffe records that all the towns of the Palatine were filling up with refugees and hospital wagons bearing the wounded and dying. Many towns were still half-ruined from the war of the preceding two years and the French invasion that was even now taking place. Mentz was now a depot for the Prussian army on the Rhine, the half-ruined towers of its churches, bombed during the siege of 1792–3, still standing but blackened by flames. Oppenheim, which they passed through in July 1794, fell to the French in October. Worms, similarly wretched with its burned palace and church, was a camp full of troops because the frontier posts were a very short distance away; here they saw the wounded Prince of Anhalt Plessis arrive in a wagon. Franckenthal was plundered by the French only a few weeks before the Radcliffes passed through. The Elector's palace in Mannheim was a desolate suite of apartments, 'like the skeleton of grandeur', because the furniture and paintings had been removed and packed away in anticipation of an approaching bombardment (250–1). Cologne was in a state of crisis and military confusion, for the French had entered Brussels and were advancing upon Liege and Maastricht. As the Radcliffes sailed past Dusseldorf their boatman sensibly refused to stop despite being threatened with gunfire.

They were relieved to get back to 'the neatness, the civility, the comforts, quietness, and even the good humour and intelligence to be easily found in Holland' (345), but Nimeguen was thronged with fugitives from Flanders, and Mrs Radcliffe was grieved to see the nuns forced to live in boats moored to the banks of the river. After a fortnight spent in Helvoetsluys waiting for a convenient passage – the English transports were full of wounded soldiers and there was a threat from French frigates and privateers – they managed to get safe passage to Deal on board an American ship. The following year, when people were reading the *Journey*, France invaded Holland and occupied Amsterdam, and annexed Belgium, and the upheavals in France lead to the abolition of the Revolutionary Tribunal and the constitution of the Directory.

Home at last, the Radcliffes were 'struck by the superior appearance and manners of the people to those of the countries we had been lately accustomed to' (370). Mrs Radcliffe frankly did not like Abroad. The German scenery was magnificent, but she felt that the cities were wretched and the people dreadful. The best lodgings in the Valley of Andernach were felt to be not up to the clean standards of any common English half-way house between London and Canterbury (159). They were cheated by coach drivers and required to pay unnecessary tolls. For all her professed admiration for gloomy grandeur, Mrs Radcliffe loathed 'the squalidness and decay, that characterise German towns' (171). Limbourg, like many towns, was 'another collection of houses, like tombs, or forsaken hospitals' (172); at their inn they were appalled by 'the sullenness and then the ferocious malignity of a German landlord and his wife' (172). William Radcliffe observed that 'There is little individual prosperity in Germany, little diffusion of intelligence, manners, or even of the means for comfort' (342). The peasantry was debased, and there were few wealthy individuals or patrons whose income was not wholly absorbed by political and military expenses, 'and though, in an advanced state of society, or in opulent nations, what is called patronage is seldom necessary, and must, perhaps, be as injurious to the happiness as it is to the dignity of those who receive it', nevertheless the lack of such liberality discouraged advances in the arts, intellect and science (344).

One reviewer of the *Journey* noted the 'illiberality' of Mrs Radcliffe's sentiment that Englishmen ought to avoid friendships with the natives. She betrayed the xenophobia typical of the English person abroad: 'This fair writer appears to have travelled under the strong impression of attachment to her native country.'[13] The *Journey* makes it clear that Mrs Radcliffe was almost virulently anti-Roman Catholic, despite her Gothic aesthetics, as when she ridicules the relics in the Capuchin monastery church of Bonn. The *Journey* was singled out for praise in the *British Critic*,[14] but their critic underlined the real flaw of the work: 'We are surprised that Mrs R. did not glean more anecdotes in her way, having passed through places which had recently been the theatres of such extraordinary events.'[15] The *Analytical Review* likewise wished that she had 'more frequently sought occasions of describing living manners'.[16] The *English Review* justly observed that she possessed 'great candour, as well as sensibility and humanity of disposition', but lamented the 'tedious descriptions of the setting and rising sun, moon light, grey obscurities, breathless air, tall sails, &c. &c'.[17] But the gathering of aesthetic sensations was the overriding motive for all of Ann Radcliffe's endeavours.

The Radcliffes were back in London during late August or early September 1794, and during a brief respite before going on to the Lake District Mrs Radcliffe allowed herself to be lionized for the first – and last – time. During her travels abroad, *The Mysteries of Udolpho* achieved an unprecedented popularity. Even the conservative *British Critic*, more used to reviewing philosophy and poetry and *belles-lettres* than popular novels, felt honoured to be able to review the work:

> Mrs Radcliffe had before obtained considerable reputation, from the cultivation of this branch of literature, and we are happy that it has fallen to our province to record one of the best and most interesting of her works. We wish to render all possible honour to her talents.[18]

To celebrate the novelist's triumphant return, the publisher George Robinson gave a literary dinner at his home to mark the success of *The Mysteries of Udolpho*. One of the guests invited to meet the great enchantress was Mrs Inchbald, the actress whose touching novel *A Simple Story* had been published by Robinson in 1790. During 1792 she had read *The Romance of the Forest*;[19] she greatly admired Mrs Radcliffe, and was in the process of writing her Rousseauesque novel *Nature and Romance* (published in 1796). There were two highlights in her life in 1794. One was her introduction, through Mrs Siddons, to Sir Thomas Lawrence, already acquiring fame as a painter of the fashionable, for whom she sat in July:

Nor second to this, in whatever way we look at it, was the invitation to Mr
Robinson's, which introduced her to the mighty magician of Udolpho, the very
accomplished Mrs Radcliffe; and, if *terror* be the grand source of the sublime,
the most *fertile* in its employment among the sons and daughters of fiction. She
sported in it as a congenial element; and, fearless herself, held every imagination,
aged or youthful, alike enthralled by her mysteries.[20]

Mrs Inchbald's biographer James Boaden goes on to testify that Mrs Radcliffe
was one of the 'valuable additions to her personal friends' this year. However,
there is no further evidence that the friendship developed, nor any indication
that the two women ever met again. Mrs Inchbald was a Unitarian (until the
very end of her life), and a close friend of William Godwin (there was jealousy
between her and Mary Wollstonecraft, and she bitterly broke off the
friendship when Godwin married Wollstonecraft). They may have had much
in common intellectually, but it is not likely that the novelist would have
cultivated the friendship of someone so daring and free as the actress. Mrs
Inchbald was probably Robinson's mistress, and as she is the only guest
noted, it may in fact have been a quite private dinner rather than a public
occasion. Beyond this, Mrs Radcliffe was fundamentally unsociable, perhaps
through false gentility as well as shyness, and she shrank back from such an
adventure.

Ann Radcliffe could not endure the personal contact attendant upon
celebrity, so she drew the veil and vanished from sight. Talfourd explained
that

> a scrupulous self-respect . . . induced her sedulously to avoid the appearance
> of reception, on account of her literary fame. The very thought of appearing
> in person as the author of her romances shocked the delicacy of her mind. To
> the publication of her works she was constrained by the force of her own genius;
> but nothing could tempt her to publish *herself*; or to sink for a moment, the
> gentlewoman in the novelist.[21]

Talfourd's rationalization does not altogether account for her sequestration:
had Ann Radcliffe allowed herself to be lionized, within a very short time she,
like Mrs Inchbald, would have moved in the decidedly *gentle* circle which
included Mrs Siddons and the Kembles, Lord and Lady Mount-Edgecombe,
Mrs Barbauld, Mrs Opie, the Sheridans, Sir Francis Burdett, Lady Mount-
Cashel, Horne Tooke, the Abercorns, the Castlereaghs and her (less gentle)
fellow Gothicists Holcroft, Lewis and Godwin.[22]

Soon after this event Mrs Radcliffe relinquished society, and set off in
pursuit of the delights of nature. All of the pictorial skill that she had been
saving up for Switzerland now had to be unleashed on the lesser beauties of

the Lake District. She and her husband probably began this northern tour in late September, and they may well have accompanied her parents William and Ann Ward on a trip to Nottingham to stay with some of her relatives.

William Radcliffe was not replaced by any strong leader in the editorial department of the *Gazetteer*, and his departure marked the beginning of the newspaper's decline. In April 1794 the proprietors had had to increase the price of the paper by a halfpenny, which further damaged sales. On 25 September the management committee, in a desperate move to improve the situation, 'Resolved (Nem. Con.) to apply to Mr Radcliffe; to know of him, whether he can again undertake the Office of being Editor to the Paper.'[23] This overture does not seem to have reached William Radcliffe, and another meeting of the committee on 5 November 'Resolved that Mr Beauchamp be desired to write a letter to Mr Radcliffe to know if it would be agreeable to him to undertake the Editorship of the Gazetteer, provided there should be a Vacancy. Mssrs. Robinson will probably be able to convey a letter to Mr Radcliffe.'[24] The Treasurer of the committee, John Watkins, in mid-November, wrote a letter which was sent (perhaps by Robinson) to William Ward, and received Ward's reply from Chesterfield dated 18 November:

> Sir,
>
> *I last night Rec*[d] *your Letter directed to me at Nottingham, w*[th] *place I have Left near a month, & come to spend some time at Chesterfield.*
>
> *I believe my Son & Daughter are in Lancashire, but the Last Letter I Rec*[d] *from them, my Daughter say'd they was going very soon into Yorkshire, to visit some Relations they have their.*
>
> *I shall write to my Daughter by this days post & acquaint them with the Contents of your Letter & dare say you will hear from M*[r] *Radcliffe very soon.*
>
> > *from Sir,*
> > *Your Most Humb*[le] *Ser*[vt].
> > *W*[m] *Ward*[25]

But the committee of the *Gazetteer*, having heard nothing from William Radcliffe, on 19 November appointed Mr Gordon as editor-in-chief. It was not until December that William was to reply to Mr Watkins:

> Broughton Dec[r] 1st
> 1794
>
> Sir,
>
> *We have received a letter from Mrs Ward, which mentions an application from you to know my address, and that Mr Ward has replied you would probably soon hear from myself.*

I, therefore, shall wait here till Saturday next, for the purpose of receiving any communication, which you may choose to make, with more certainty than if it was addressed to me, during an excursion, which we are about to take into Yorkshire; and I add my present address –

    at the Rev[d] David Longman Burton's,
        Broughton, near Brigg,
        Lincolnshire.

The post, which arrives here, on Saturday, leaves London, on Thursday. I am, Sir,

    Your obedient humble Serv[t]
    W. Radcliffe.[26]

The Radcliffes' northern tour must have lasted for at least three months. Mrs Radcliffe's parents had given up the Wedgwood showrooms in Bath at the beginning of 1793 and had retired to Chesterfield.[27] Before they found a place to settle, they may have been 'shared out' among relatives in Nottingham. Samuel and John Jebb had come from Mansfield, Nottinghamshire, and some of Mrs Radcliffe's Jebb relations probably resided in Nottingham. The goal in Yorkshire may have been Sheffield, the area to which the Oates family traced their roots prior to their connection with the Jebb family. Mrs Radcliffe also had Yorkshire relations through her great-grandmother Elizabeth Gilliver. In Lincolnshire Revd David Longman Burton may have been related to Edmund Burton, friend of Mrs Radcliffe's relation Robert Hallifax. But they are not likely to have resided for long with someone who was not a closer relation. Revd Burton may well have been a relation of William Radcliffe, for his mother Deborah Radcliffe was to die at Burton's vicarage in Broughton in 1809, which suggests that he may have been her brother, with whom she stayed after the death of her husband.

People, manners and anecdotes are almost wholly absent from Ann Radcliffe's account of her northern tour, which was a field-study trip devoted almost obsessively to an analysis of the Sublime. Her summing up of the 'characters of the three great lakes' becomes a *reductio ad absurdum* in Gilpin's mechanistic manner:

> Windermere: Diffusiveness, stately beauty, and, at the upper end, magnificence.
> Ullswater: Severe grandeur and sublimity; . . .
> Derwentwater: Fantastic wildness and romantic beauty . . . (477)

Although Mrs Radcliffe refers to the official theorists such as Sir Joshua Reynolds and Edmund Burke (420–1), she travels like the Ossianic heroine of her novels, searching for the Sublime and even the Demonic, as if growing into her public persona as the great enchantress. A figure glimpsed through the smoke issuing from a lime kiln in Middleton Dale 'looks like the Witch of the Dale, on an edge of her cauldron, watching the works of incantation' (376), an allusion to the Witch of Wokey-Hole which Percy's *Reliques* associated with 'the Sybils Cave in Italy'.[28] The vale of Ullswater 'is the very abode for Milton's Comus, "deep skilled in all his mother's witcheries"' (456). The vast moorlands near Keswick are 'the very region, which the wild fancy of a poet, like Shakespeare, would people with witches, and shew them at their incantations, calling spirits from the clouds and spectres from the earth' (440). She visited the prehistoric stone circle at Castlerigg:

> well suited to the deep and wild mysteries of the Druids. Here, at moon-light, every Druid, summoned by that terrible horn, never awakened but upon high occasions, and descending from his mountain, or secret cave, might assemble without intrusion from one sacrilegious footstep, and celebrate a midnight festival by a savage sacrifice. (446)

This is deliciously strong stuff, derived from the Celtic mythology in Frank Sayers's *Poems*, published in 1789 and 1792, and fully annotated by the author with references to the Druids' human sacrifices, Hela the goddess of death, the Prophetess in her cave, the three Fatal Sisters and their web of Fate, Glasor's golden bough and the Twilight of the Gods. Mrs Radcliffe was also heavily influenced by William Mason's Druidic drama *Caractacus* (1759), which she quotes six times in her novels. Mason's poem, notable for including female Druids, was a stirring defence of the native rights of the free-born Briton, the kind of poetry which Bentley liked, and she probably first read it while staying with her uncle.

The antiquarian impulse that would eventually overwhelm Ann Radcliffe's imagination begins to emerge on this trip. She took with her a copy of Thomas Gray's *Journal* (1775), which recorded his own trip to the Lake District and Yorkshire in 1769; she examines the vale of the Lune from precisely the same viewpoint as that noticed by Gray (381), and mentions that Gray had remarked on the tombs in the church in Kendal when she views the chapel of the Stricklands (387). She stayed at Old Buchanan's Inn in Penrith, because it had been recommended by Gray (433) – a quarter of a century earlier! She also took with her, or acquired on the journey, a copy of Thomas West's *Antiquities of Furness* (1774), which she acknowledged as her source for some of the historical details about Furness Abbey near Lancaster, an archetype of romantic beauty that was the goal of many picturesque travellers, and whose ivy-clad walls graced a piece in Wedgwood & Bentley's Imperial Russian dinner service.[29]

The very first place Mrs Radcliffe visited was Hardwick Hall in her native Derbyshire, seat of the Duke of Devonshire. The 'lofty grandeur' of its great rooms recalls the spacious abandoned apartments of her novels, with 'tall windows, which half subdue the light they admit' (372). The legend of Mary's imprisonment was rehearsed, and her tapestry work was praised; 'the furniture is known by other proofs, than its appearance, to remain as she left it' (373). (Hardwick Hall was not built until after Mary's death, but the legend of her imprisonment there persists to this day.)

Various castles were visited on this trip, including Lancaster Castle with its new Gothic additions, Lyulph's Tower, the Duke of Norfolk's new Gothic mansion, and Brougham Castle in the Vale of Eden, said to be where Sir Philip Sidney wrote *Arcadia*, whose dungeons especially inspired her:

> Dungeons, secret passages and heavy iron rings remain to hint of unhappy wretches, who were, perhaps, rescued only by death from these horrible engines of a tyrant's will. The bones probably of such victims are laid beneath the damp earth of these vaults. (427)

Much of her next novel, *The Italian*, would take place in such a dungeon.

There were many admirers of the *Journey*, including the famous Ladies of Llangollen. The poet Anna Seward wrote to Lady Eleanor Butler on 4 February 1796:

> It gratifies me, that your Ladyship's and Miss Ponsonby's ideas are similar to mine on Mrs Radcliffe's Tour. I was assured you would be peculiarly impressed by the description of Hardwicke, of the Lakes, and by the sombre picture of the solitary tide-man, passing his cheerless life on the edge of lonely seas. Nor less striking the descriptions of the waste desolation this ruinous war has produced in Germany. The political observations are not many, but they are just and pointed.[30]

She went on to suggest, mistakenly, that the furniture and objects in the little confessional supposedly occupied by Mary Stewart at Hardwick inspired the idea behind the Marchioness's apartment in *The Mysteries of Udolpho* – it would be truer to say that the novel influenced Mrs Radcliffe's depiction of Hardwick. Thomas Green, who had made his own picturesque tours, and who had studied Burke on the Sublime and Uvedale Price and Gilpin on the Picturesque, read the *Journey* in 1800 and was much gratified to find his expectations amply fulfilled: 'Her pictures, though somewhat overwrought and heavy compared with the expressive etchings of Gray, exhibit as clear distinct and forcible images to the mind's eye, as it is well possible for words to convey.'[31] Excerpts from her *Journey* were reprinted not only in the reviews but also in the Addenda to the posthumous edition of Thomas West's *Guide to the Lakes in Cumberland, Westmorland, and Lancashire* (1802).[32] This was only fitting, for Mrs Radcliffe probably employed the first edition of West's guide (1788), with its directions to 'stations' from which picturesque prospects were guaranteed.

It was specifically a reading of Ann Radcliffe's description of Furness and its abbey which led De Quincey to call her 'the great enchantress', and the *Journey* inspired him to abscond from Manchester to the Lakes.[33] The *Journey* influenced picturesque travellers and topographical writers as much as her novels influenced creative writers. Joseph Farington's massive project *Britannia Depicta* contains paraphrases and direct quotations from Mrs Radcliffe's tour. In the volume on Cumberland (1816) the engraving of Derwentwater from Brough Top is accompanied by a lengthy quotation from Radcliffe's description of the scene, and Farington's drawing is clearly based upon her description of the view 'expanding within an amphitheatre of mountains'. The description accompanying an engraving of Castle Crag and Bowder-Stone is also a paraphrase of Mrs Radcliffe's own description: 'The solemn stillness that reigns around, is only broken by the remote sounds of unseen cataracts, dashing from precipice to precipice, and sometimes by the voices of mountaineer children, shouting a far off, and pleasing themselves with rousing the echoes of the rocks.'[34]

Ebenezer Rhodes in his *Peak Scenery* (1819) cited Mrs Radcliffe's 'Northern Tour' in support of the view that the furniture in the apartments of Hardwick Hall remained exactly as Mary Queen of Scots had left it.[35] Rhodes's description of his first sight of Haddon Hall, near Bakewell in Derbyshire, matched by a plate engraved by John Greig, is modelled upon Emily's first vision of Udolpho:

> The day was gloomy, and the sombre effect of the sky, together with the dark unvaried tone that prevailed, increased the solemnity of the scene. A transient ray of sunny light moved gently over Haddon as we beheld it, and gradually unfolded its architectural detail: it was a momentary gleam, at whose bright touch the landscape glowed with beauty; too soon it passed away! a thicker gloom succeeded, and again involved the whole in shadow.[36]

Most of Mrs Radcliffe's contemporaries, including Rhodes, believed that the castle of Udolpho was based upon Haddon Hall, a rumour whose origin and influence will be traced in Chapter 15.

Ann Radcliffe's scenery entered the collective mind as much as her haunted castles. The traveller William Maton in an unpublished travel journal noted that a visit in 1799 to Lyulph's Tower on the banks of Ullswater 'reminded us, in every particular, of the airy castles described in romances', such as those 'from the pen of a Radcliffe'.[37] Henry Matthews made the following comment in his diary for 21 May 1818: 'Wild Romantic road over the Apennines; – which reminded me of Mrs Radcliffe's descriptions in her Romance of Udolpho.'[38] Louis Simond in his *Voyage en Italie* (1827) also saw scenes which reminded him of Mrs Radcliffe.[39] The popular journalist and traveller Richard Ford in his *Gatherings from Spain* (1846) complained that there was as much 'bandittiphobia' in travel writing 'as in one of Mrs Ratcliffe's [*sic*] romances' (Chapter 16). Sydney Owenson's (Lady Morgan's) description of 'the horrible grandeurs of the Alps' seems to be partly derived from *Udolpho*.[40] It would be some years before the classic picturesque travellers such as Mrs Radcliffe would be superseded by Murray's handbooks.

John Sheppard, while visiting Venice in 1816, remarked that 'its name alone is fraught with an indefineable charm, were it only for the associations linked with it by our Shakespeare, and by the "mighty magician of Udolpho."'[41] Another visitor to Venice in 1816 or 1817 stood on the bridge of the Rialto and thought, quite naturally, of *The Merchant of Venice* – and *The Mysteries of Udolpho*:

> This is not the only spot at Venice which recalls fiction, poetry, and romance, to the mind. Shakespeare, Otway, and – in spite of many inaccuracies – Mrs Radcliffe, rise up every where in the shape of their heroes and heroines. The very situation of the city – the very names of the surrounding objects, constantly recall them.[42]

The most famous recollection of Mrs Radcliffe's description of Venice occurs in Byron's *Childe Harold*:

> I loved her from my boyhood; she to me
> Was as a fairy city of the heart,
> Rising like water-columns from the sea,
> Of joy the sojourn, and of wealth the mart;
> And Otway, Radcliffe, Schiller, Shakespeare's art,
> Had stamp'd her image in me . . .
>
> (Canto IV (1818), stanza xviii)

John Keats probably read Radcliffe's *Journey* in March 1818, as he sat indoors in Teignmouth during the long rainy spell at the beginning of his tour of Devonshire. He told a friend what to expect from his letters: 'I am going among Scenery whence I intend to tip you the Damosel Radcliffe – I'll cavern you, and grotto you, and waterfall you, and wood you, and water you, and immense-rock you, and tremendous sound you, and solitude you.'[43]

Talfourd insists that Mrs Radcliffe's journey through Holland and Germany in the summer of 1794 'was the first and only occasion, on which she quitted England'.[44] Her novels are so un-English and exotic that no one could believe that she had not travelled in France and particularly Italy, and there been inspired by images for *The Mysteries of Udolpho*. The author of the first full obituary wrongly asserted that the *Journey* contained the narrative of her travels in France and Italy as well as Germany.[45] Most of the early critics believed that Mrs Radcliffe had made her journey in 1793 and had published it in 1794.[46] Sir Walter Scott knew that the *Journey* was published after *Udolpho*, but supposed that *Udolpho* was 'at least corrected' as it was going through the press in order to incorporate some of the impressions she had gained from her travels.[47] An article on the periodical press in the *Edinburgh Review* for May 1823 revealed that

> The Editor of the Englishman for many years was a Mr Radcliffe. He had been formerly attached to some of our embassies into Italy, where his lady accompanied him; and here she imbibed that taste for picturesque scenery, and the obscure and wild superstitions of mouldering castles, of which she has made so beautiful a use in her Romances.[48]

The author of the obituary in the *Annual Biography* denied the claim:

> The unrivalled force and richness with which Mrs Radcliffe depicted the countries, – Italy, Switzerland, and the South of France, – in which the scene of her principal romances is laid, naturally induced a general belief that she had visited them. A recent traveller in those countries, of some celebrity, was so impressed with this idea, that he frequently refers to Mrs Radcliffe's descriptions, as evidently derived from personal observation. . . . The fact, however, is, that neither Mr nor Mrs Radcliffe was ever in Italy at all; nor on the Continent until the year 1794.[49]

All these views are not merely interesting errors, but evidence of how powers of description can be more convincing than powers of observation.

T·E·N

The Mighty Magician

———— • ————

The year 1795 opened with a New Year's Day performance at Covent Garden of Miles Peter Andrews's *The Mysteries of the Castle*, a dramatization based upon *A Sicilian Romance* which also included characters drawn from *The Mysteries of Udolpho*. Mrs Radcliffe's fame increased steadily, while her husband's career advanced by fits and starts. Protracted negotiations between William Radcliffe and the *Gazetteer* included the opportunity for William to acquire the newspaper. On 11 February 1795 the committee 'requested that Mssrs. Payne & Sheperson should wait on Mr Radcliffe & settle with him the Terms of his commencing Editor & Proprietor'.[1] He was appointed editor on 1 March, although he did not become one of the proprietors. On 18 March the committee encouraged him to endeavour to increase business with the principal advertisers.[2] The sales of the newspaper were now only half what they had been at the time of his departure, and despite his return they continued to decline. William fell ill due to overwork and stress, and on 22 August, fewer than six months after his reappointment, he offered his resignation:

> Sir,
>
> *Having been advised, that the late hours, which are necessarily kept by the Editor of a Morning Paper, have been injurious to my health and are likely to be so, I am to intreat you to present my respects to the Proprietors of the Gazetteer and my thanks for their favours and civilities towards me, together with my resignation of my situation, which I make with the reluctance, due to their handsome conduct in my behalf and especially to their indulgence, during my illness.*[3]

The company's last payment to William Radcliffe was made on 7 September 1795. (The *Gazetteer* continued to suffer a loss. In 1796 the paper was reformed under new partners. After complicated negotiations and setbacks,

Mary Vint became sole proprietor from April 1797 to 20 September 1797, when the copyright was bought up by the *Morning Post*, and the *Gazetteer* ceased to exist as a separate entity.[4])

Soon William Radcliffe was negotiating for the purchase of the *English Chronicle or Universal Evening Post*, a paper that was published every Tuesday, Thursday and Saturday,[5] sometimes called 'the Englishman'.[6] The colophon for the issue published on 22 March 1796 makes the new ownership clear: 'London: Printed by J. Norris for W. Radcliffe, Blake Court, Catharine-Street, where literary communications & Advertisements are received.' Just as his wife's £500 royalties from *The Mysteries of Udolpho* helped him through the troubled months of 1794–5, so perhaps an advance on her £800 royalties for *The Italian* (published towards the end of 1796) may have assisted him in acquiring the *English Chronicle*. The offices were situated at 3 Catherine Street, the Strand, and contained two presses, according to Radcliffe's declaration in August 1799 complying with requirements of the Seditious Societies Act.[7]

After the Radcliffes returned from their trip to the Lake District – or at least before their account of this trip was published – they bought their own house in London, at No. 5, Melina Place, near St George's Fields in Southwark.[8] The short terrace of fifteen houses had large front gardens, and was virtually a rural residence at the time, when the area had many open fields and market gardens, with street names such as Nursery Row, Prospect Place and Pleasant Retreat.[9] Nevertheless it was only about one and one-quarter miles from the newspaper office across the Thames, a not unreasonable walking distance.

It was while residing here that Ann Radcliffe wrote *The Italian*, which was published towards the end of 1796, by the firm of Cadell and Davies. Their books were noted for being finely produced and bound, and their market was the middle and upper classes.[10] They published many of Gilpin's picturesque travels, and noted editions of Ariosto, Metastasio and Tasso. After the unexampled praise of *The Mysteries of Udolpho*, Ann Radcliffe perhaps felt it was time to seek a 'high-class' publisher. They paid her the extraordinarily large royalty of £800 (exaggerated to £1,500 in some public accounts).[11]

The search for sources for *The Italian* has been no more productive than for any other of Ann Radcliffe's novels. Among the books given to Ellena by Olivia in the novel are 'a volume or two of Guicciardini's history' (94), that is Francesco Guicciardini's *L'historia d'Italia* (1561), a sober multi-volume political history in which neither Ellena nor Ann Radcliffe are likely to have had much interest, chosen merely as a period detail. Vivaldi's mini-history of the savage delights of Emperor Claudius, who built an aqueduct and lake for the sake of a naval battle, in which hundreds of slaves perished for his amusement (160), is certainly inspired by Dryden's *Alexander's Feast*. It has been argued that the novel draws upon a translation of Philippus van Limborch's *The History of the Inquisition*,[12] mainly because Limborch's description of the executioner ('His Head and Face are all hid with a long black Cowl, only two little Holes being left in it for him to see thro'. . . . looks like the very Devil' (vol. 2, 217–18)) resembles Ann Radcliffe's description of the assistants of the Inquisition ('Their faces were entirely concealed beneath a very peculiar kind of cowl, which descended from the head to the feet; and their eyes only were visible through small openings contrived for the sight. . . . their appearance was worthy of demons (310)). Limborch's *History*, a large-format scholarly work, was published in 1731 (and abridged in 1734), and by 1797 would be found only in the collection of an antiquarian. I doubt that Ann Radcliffe ever read it, otherwise she would have exploited its dramatic details to a much greater extent.[13]

There are only faint traces of Pierre Jean Grosley's *New Observations on Italy and Its Inhabitants* (a work which definitely influenced *The Mysteries of Udolpho*), as in Vivaldi's first sight of Rome, and the pilgrims in the woods of Rugieri. But as noted by Tompkins, Ann Radcliffe has curiously dated the novel to 1758: precisely the year that Grosley was in Rome when he observed that the Inquisition had passed no capital sentence for a hundred years; she has therefore perversely chosen a date when the scenes she described could *not* have occurred. Her attitude to history was cavalier.

The suggestion that *The Italian* is inspired by Monvel's play *Les Victimes cloitrées*, perhaps via Matthew Gregory Lewis's use of that play in *The Monk* (1796), also remains unproven.[14] On the other hand, there is no doubt that *The Mysteries of Udolpho* was an inspiration of prime importance for the young author. Lewis had been struggling for some time with his novel, rewriting it and nearly abandoning it in despair, when fate in the form of Ann Radcliffe came to the rescue. He wrote to his mother on 18 May 1794:

> I have again taken up my Romance, and perhaps by this time Ten years I may make shift to finish it fit for throwing into the fire. I was induced to go on with it by reading 'the Mysteries of Udolpho', which is in my opinion one of the most interesting Books that ever have been published.[15]

Lewis perceived a strong resemblance between himself and Montoni.

The Italian is often claimed to be a 'response' to *The Monk*, but direct borrowings are negligible.[16] The real forebear for Schedoni was Ann Radcliffe's own Montoni, and the wicked Marchesa di Vivaldi is an amplification of the Marchioness in *A Sicilian Romance*; Schedoni's near murder of Ellena is modelled not upon Ambrosio's near rape of Antonia, but upon the murder of Duncan in Shakespeare's *Macbeth*. There are far more differences between *The Monk* and *The Italian* than similarities.[17] Mrs Radcliffe, unlike Lewis, shows that guilt and depravity can be constructed upon the desire for absolute power rather than mere sexuality, and their source is ultimately human rather than demonic. Disturbing and pervasive references to torture, 'half-stifled groans, as of a person in agony' (197), 'sickening anguish' (127) and 'horrible perversions' (198) point up how far Ann Radcliffe has moved from the *frisson* of terror to the agony of horror, but in my view this can be attributed to the suffering she witnessed in the Palatinate in 1794. The sordidness of the village where Ellena and Schedoni subsequently stop on their continuing journey back to Naples is probably inspired by some of the derelict villages Mrs Radcliffe passed through in the Palatinate, just as the decayed fortresses upon lofty acclivities seen upon the approach to Spalatro's house may have been inspired by her Rhine journey.

Charles Bucke, who met Mrs Radcliffe during the last years of her life, testified that 'She was a great admirer of Schiller's Robbers.'[18] The fiendish imagery of *The Robbers* (English translation 1792)[19] may account for the Lewisian flavour of *The Italian* (its influence upon Lewis is well documented). McIntyre suggests that Schiller's *Der Geisterseher* was a possible source for the trip on the Brenta described in *The Mysteries of Udolpho*; this would mean that Mrs Radcliffe knew the original German, which is very doubtful.[20] The first half of *Der Geisterseher* was translated by D. Boileau in 1795 as *The Ghost-Seer, or Apparitionist*, and it is easier to establish that the translator was influenced by Ann Radcliffe's description! Several references from this translation in turn found their way into *The Italian*, such as the resemblance of the peculiar physiognomy of the Armenian ('each passion seemed, by turns, to have exercised its ravages on it, and to have left it successively. Nothing remained but the calm piercing look of a person deeply skilled in the science of man; but it was such a look as abashed everyone on whom it was directed'[21]) to that of Schedoni ('It bore the traces of many passions, which seemed to have fixed the features they no longer animated. . . . his eyes were so piercing that they seemed to penetrate, at a single glance, into the hearts of men, and to read their most secret thoughts; few persons could support their scrutiny, or even endure to meet them twice' (35)). A similar description occurs in two 1796 translations of Karl Grosse's *Der Genius*, Joseph Trapp's *The Genius* and Peter Will's *Horrid Mysteries*.[22]

Ann Radcliffe's artistic development is more strongly marked than that of many writers. Each successive novel is palpably more skilfully constructed than its predecessor. Sarah Josepha Hale put the case most elegantly: 'we are struck with the evident progress of her mind, and the gradual mastery her will obtained over the resources of her imagination'.[23] *The Italian* is the work of a master craftsman; we sense the joy of professional authorship which guides each stroke of the pen. The narrative is structured with consummate ease, and clues planted with dexterity stimulate the intellectual pleasure of the detective novel, of which it is the prototype.[24] The author has become an expert novelist, never at a loss as to what comes next; one horror follows another in a clear and consistent manner, and a series of professionally calibrated *coups de théâtre* build up to a powerful climax. The introductory chapter describing the mysterious figure on the portico of the church is a *tour de force* whose 'half intimations of veiled and secret horrors' are justly singled out for praise by Scott, among many others subsequently.[25] In these few pages the framework of the whole novel – the confessional – is established with such dazzling technical proficiency that we are more than a little amused by the author's playful assertion that the narrative which follows 'was written by a student of Padua': 'You will perceive from the work, that this student was very young, as to the arts of composition' (4). Such a passage is a perfect example of 'the ingenious Mrs Radcliffe' and the teasing games she plays with her readers.

It was this novel in particular which prompted Nathan Drake to proclaim Mrs Radcliffe 'the Shakespeare of Romance Writers':

> every nerve vibrates with pity and terror . . . : every word, every action of the shocked and self-accusing Confessor, whose character is marked with traits almost super-human, appal yet delight the reader, and it is difficult to ascertain whether ardent curiosity, intense commiseration, or apprehension that suspends almost the faculty of breathing, be, in the progress of this well-written story, most powerfully excited.[26]

The poetic fertility of *The Mysteries of Udolpho* has been superseded by narrative virtuosity in *The Italian*; the hitherto nearly uncontrolled wellsprings of the imagination are now directed into the most fruitful channels. Lyrical descriptions of the landscape are distributed with judicious economy rather than luxurious profusion, though with a few strokes of her brush Ann Radcliffe can still paint a symphony in sepia and silver. The novel has many magic scenes of beauty – and, like *The Mysteries of Udolpho*, numerous references to magic, magical spells and the charm of magic. But poetic reverie has been replaced by dramatic action, and one feels that she has put aside Thomson, Beattie and Mason in favour of the Elizabethan and Jacobean dramatists (though direct sources are difficult to identify). The first biographer of Monk Lewis felt that Ann Radcliffe's characters were 'so vividly delineated, that she well deserves the epithet . . . of a "Sculptor Novelist"'.[27] We do not share that view today, but the stock figures of the earlier novels have certainly given way in *The Italian* to characters of greater depth and variety. Schedoni is psychologically the most complex, and the most fully human character in Ann Radcliffe's novels. In his portrayal she exhibits a deeper understanding of that amalgam of anger, hypocrisy and guilt – in a word, perversion – that governs his actions as well as those of the Marchesa, Spalatro and the torturers of the Inquisition.

It cannot be established exactly how Ann Radcliffe's contemporaries read any political message in the novel. She explicitly compares the prisons of the Inquisition to those of the Bastille, but this can be interpreted either 'as die-hard radicalism' of radical Dissenters or 'as a patriotic assault on Catholicism' of conservative Protestants.[28] Most readers, now as then, appreciate primarily the psychology of the novel. *The Italian* is a complex study of despair, or 'unavailing pity' (128). The portal of the Inquisition is opened by 'Grim-visaged comfortless Despair' (196), an outright personification from Gray's *Ode on a Distant Prospect of Eton College*. Despair lay at the heart of the novel: over the inner apartment of the Inquisition is 'an inscription in Hebrew characters, traced in blood-colour. Dante's inscription on the entrance of the infernal regions, would have been suitable to a place, where every circumstance and feature seemed to say, *"Hope, that comes to all, comes not here!"'* (200). More than a hundred occurrences of the words 'remorse', 'guilt' and 'despair' could be cited. 'The Confessional of the Black Penitents' is a richly evocative subtitle, and visual and symbolic images of the confessional appear throughout the book. In the powerful scene in which the Marchesa finally screws up her courage to make explicit her request that Schedoni assassinate Ellena, she notices the awful inscription above the confessional – *'God hears thee!'* – and is interrupted by the requiem for the dead, which strikes despair into her heart (176–8). But any suggestion that confession leads to forgiveness of sins is not seriously put forward or examined. Like Milton's Satan, Schedoni is a fallen angel, a crippled devil – an icon of the demonic sublime.

As in all of Ann Radcliffe's works, the psychological and moral themes are communicated through cultural images. Aesthetic artifice is everywhere in evidence, and employed with self-conscious calculation. In a typical set-piece, the *'coup-d'oeil* was striking and grand': fifty nuns in delicate veils are 'contrasted by the severe majesty of the lady Abbess'; visitors in their gaily coloured Neapolitan habit 'opposed well with the dark drapery of the ecclesiastics' outside the grate, whose countenances are 'arranged' into a palette of aesthetic categories – 'the grave, the austere, the solemn, and the gloomy, intermingling with the light, the blooming, and the debonaire' (130). Later, Ellena, Vivaldi, a venerable priest and a harsh-visaged ruffian 'formed altogether a group worthy of the pencil' (185). The artistic landscape is observed with scientific aids: one scene is described 'as through a telescope reversed' (63), and the ships gliding across the Bay of Naples are perceived 'as in a camera obscura' (292).

Whereas *The Mysteries of Udolpho* was dominated by landscape painting and poetry, *The Italian* is filled with music and sound, to an astonishing degree. Visual images of the *memento mori* in the former novel are replaced here by aural images of the requiem for the dead. In no contemporary novel, English or foreign, do music and sound play such important and prominent roles. The 'sweetness and fine expression' (5) of Ellena di Rosalba's singing first attracts the attention of Vicentio di Vivaldi, who is himself 'a fine tenor' and is 'passionately fond of music' (17). It was probably such singing in church which first brought Ann Ward to the attention of William Radcliffe. Music is also celebrated for its appeal to the irrational, the buried self, for Ann Radcliffe was among those who, during the latter part of the eighteenth century, turned away from the Augustan view of music as either a mere decoration or a licentious temptation. Vivaldi follows Ellena to her villa, where 'the hollow murmurs' and 'the groans' of Vesuvius rumble in the background (10–11), where he hears the deep chanting of a requiem for the dying, and then hears Ellena herself 'performing the midnight hymn to the Virgin' (11). Ellena is abducted and carried off to a monastery, where she is deeply impressed by the vesper service of the monks:

> it was a music which might be said to win on silence, and was in perfect unison with her feelings; solemn, deep, and full, it swelled in holy peels, and rolled away in murmurs, which attention pursued to the last faint note that melted into air. Ellena's heart owned the power of this high minstrelsy . . . (65)

In the cave containing the shrine of Our Lady of Mount Carmel, the central Delphic emblem of the novel, Vivaldi hears the solemn harmony of mass being celebrated in the connecting convent: 'It was such full and entrancing music as frequently swells in the high festivals of the Sicilian church, and is adapted to inspire that sublime enthusiasm, which sometimes elevates its disciples' (117). The peal of the organ suddenly ceases, and is replaced by the solemn tolling of a bell, 'the knell of death', which accompanies a stately march of nuns 'moving in time to the slow minstrelsy'. Mrs Radcliffe's travels in the Palatinate contributed to a more realistic picture of Roman Catholicism than in her preceding novels, and may have suggested this haunting music. Montague Summers does, however, point out some incongruities: the vesper bell ought not to ring for evening mass, a Carmelite nun ought not to be clad in white drapery and an abbess ought not to wear a mitre on her head![29] The Daughters of Pity, with whom Ellena is finally safely lodged, 'particularly excelled in music' of an exquisite simplicity (300), in marked contrast to the assemblies with the gay and frivolous strains of the Marchesa's favourite composer, who unfortunately is not identified (165).

The second chapter of the second volume, with an epigraph citing the singing of Milton's 'unletter'd Swain', is dominated by the rustic sound world of the shepherd's horn, the hautboy and pastoral drum (149), and the melancholy song of fishermen near the shore. This chapter is in effect a musical interlude, dominated by 'merry sounds' (163) symbolizing Ellena's newfound freedom after escaping from the convent. Ellena's dark journey from the desolate house by the seashore to the ruined palace of the Baróne di Cambrusca and then to a village where the carnival is being celebrated is 'like coming out of purgatory into paradise' (173), and is constructed as a series of sharply contrasted sounds: from Spalatro's house where 'no sounds were heard, except such as seemed to characterize solitude, and impress it's awful power more deeply on the heart' (255) – the *inferno*; through the faint cries and feeble groans and distant gunshots among the ruins – the *purgatorio*; to the strains of revelry, tambourines and flutes of the carnival – the *paradiso*. When Vivaldi is imprisoned and questioned by the Inquisition, a black mantle is thrown over his head, which cuts off his sight and restricts the subsequent inquisition entirely to *aural* imagery – a brilliant experimental *tour de force* which concentrates the mind exclusively upon sounds.

Numerous examples could be cited of 'the music of spirits' and 'celestial airs' (144) which guard the heroine in her tribulations. Music obviously affords keen pleasure to the author, who we know enjoyed organ music and singing, especially Handel. Mrs Radcliffe was herself as hypersensitive to the mysterious music of mortality as any of her heroines, as in her experience on returning from an excursion near Mannheim in 1794:

> at the close of evening, the soldiers at the gates are frequently heard chanting martial songs in parts and chorus; a sonorous music in severe unison with the solemnity of the hour and the imperfect forms, that meet the eye, of sentinels keeping watch beneath the dusky gateways, while their brethern, reposing on the benches without, mingle their voices in the deep chorus. Rude and simple as are these strains, they are often singularly impressive, and touch the imagination with something approaching to horror, when the circumstances of the place are remembered, and it is considered how soon these men, sent to inflict death on others, may themselves be thrown into the unnumbered heap of the military slain. (*A Journey Made in 1794*, 257)

The general consensus among reviewers was that *The Italian* demonstrated Ann Radcliffe's great improvement in skill, if not in genius.[30] The first obituarist noted that 'though generally read, [it] did not increase her reputation'.[31] A perceptive critic recognized that *The Italian* was both less diffuse and more reflective than her previous works, but nevertheless concluded that the most notable feature of the novel was the Radcliffean hallmark of mysterious terror: 'We are made to wonder, only to wonder; but the spell, by which we are led, again and again, round the same magic circle, is the spell of genius.'[32] The 'specimens', quoted almost entire by the reviewers, included the scene in which the Marchesa hires Schedoni to assassinate Ellena; descriptions of Schedoni; the story of Marco Torma as relayed to Schedoni; Spalatro's lonely house by the shore of the Adriatic; and the scene when Schedoni nearly stabs Ellena. The major scenes thus achieved widespread dissemination even among those who never read the novel itself.

The greatest impetus to Ann Radcliffe's fame was its recognition by the distinguished scholar Thomas James Mathias, highly respected editor of Gray and Librarian to the monarch at Buckingham Palace. In his satire *The Pursuits of Literature, or What You Will*, the first part of which appeared in 1794, one section attacks popular literature such as Charlotte Smith's *Celestina*:

> Is it for me to creep, or soar, or doze,
> In Modish song, or fashionable prose:
> To pen with garreteers obscure and shabby
> Inscriptive nonsense in a fancied *Abbey*.

In the second edition (1796) the reference to *Celestina* is given an appropriate annotation (the extensive footnotes were the real occasion of the satire's popularity):

> Put for almost any modern novel. Mrs Charlotte Smith, Mrs Inchbald, Mrs Mary Robinson, Mrs &c. &c. though all of them are ingenious ladies, yet they are too frequently *whining* or *frisking* in novels, till our girls' heads turn wild with impossible adventures, and now and then are tainted with democracy.

There is no reference to Mrs Radcliffe until the third edition of Part 1, which was published shortly after August 1797, when the note goes on to cite 'Mrs Anne [*sic*] Radcliffe' as an honourable exception to those 'unsexed female writers' (alluding to Lady Macbeth's invocation 'unsex me here') who 'instruct, or confuse, us and themselves, in the labyrinth of politics, or turn us wild with Gallic frenzy'. This date would suggest that the publicity surrounding the publication of *The Italian* (though that novel is not mentioned) prompted Mathias to read *The Mysteries of Udolpho* and to qualify his satire on ingenious lady novelists:

– Not so the mighty magician of *The Mysteries of Udolpho*, bred and nourished by the Florentine Muses in their sacred solitary caverns, amid the paler shrines of Gothic superstition and in all the dreariness of inchantment: a poetess whom Ariosto would with rapture have acknowledged, as the

> La nudrita
> Damigella Trivulzia AL SACRO SPECO. O.F. c. 46.[33]

John Hoole in his translation of *Orlando Furioso* had annotated this quotation thus:

> Trivulzia, a virgin of Milan, who at fourteen years of age gave surprising marks of genius; she was learned in the Latin and Greek languages, and from her excellence in poetry is said by the poet to have been bred in the cave of Apollo, where the Sybils delivered their oracles in verse.[34]

This clinched the status of Ann Radcliffe as poetess and prophetess.

Mathias's quotation highlights the fact that Ariosto and Radcliffe could be spoken of in the same breath. Modern readers make a mistake in always comparing Radcliffe to other novelists; it is more illuminating to compare her – as did her contemporaries – to the dramatic and epic poets Ariosto, Shakespeare and Milton. The 'poetic' rather than 'novelistic' features of her *oeuvre* deserve far greater attention than they are given in modern Radcliffe criticism. Radcliffe drew upon theoretical writings by Warton, Reeve and Barbauld to place her works within the tradition of ancient romance and to implicitly defend them from the charges of vulgarity and sensationalism associated with 'modern novels'. Her work was really beyond political analysis. Even Mary Hays recognized three kinds of novels: novels of sensibility and virtue like *Clarissa*, which claim to be realistic but are really prescriptive; novels like *Caleb Williams*, which naturalistically portray life as it really exists; and romance, whose value 'consists principally in the display of a picturesque fancy, and the creative powers of a fertile and inventive genius'.[35] As I attempted to show in an earlier chapter, *The Mysteries of Udolpho*, perhaps the most poetic novel in the English language, is consciously structured in the manner of an epic poem, specifically Ariosto's *Orlando Furioso* and Tasso's *Jerusalem Delivered*. The great French novelist Stendhal in a letter to his sister Pauline in 1804 ranked Mrs Radcliffe in the same class as Homer, Tasso and Ariosto: 'Fais tout au monde pour faire lire au Gaëtan *Roland le Furieux*, l'*Iliade*, les *Mystères d'Udolphe*, *Cleveland*, la *Pharsale* de Lucain . . . Mais surtout l'*Iliade*, la *Jérusalem*, *Roland* et le *Confessionnal des Pénitents noirs [The Italian]*.'[36] Ann Radcliffe's references to Ariosto established a literary convention; in Mary Robinson's *Hubert de Sevrac* (1796) the abandoned château Montnoir has a wonderful Gothic library on whose shelves is a volume of Ariosto which serves as the spring which opens a secret panel, and thus becomes literally the key to the world of romance.[37]

Mathias's encomium was highly gratifying to Mrs Radcliffe, though she is said not to have been aware of it until more than twelve months after its publication, and then only because she met with it by accident.[38] (In fact it is possible that she was aware of his comments as soon as they were made, and that 'twelve months after' simply indicates that the obituarist did not realize that the praise did not occur until the third edition.) The littérateur Nathan Drake, who praised Mrs Radcliffe for her contribution to Gothic mythology and a taste for the terrible, and who defended her from the charge of encouraging dangerous incredulity, in 1798 cited in full the passage from the seventh edition of *The Pursuits of Literature* in support of his own commendation, though he was unaware of its author.[39] Mathias's authorship of the satire was revealed at the beginning of 1798, with the publication of *The Sphinx's Head Broken: or, a Poetical Epistle, with Notes, to Thomas James M*th**s, Cl*rk to the Q***n's Tr**s*r*r: Proving Him to be the Author of the Pursuits of Literature*, and confirmed shortly afterwards in *Literary Memoirs of Living Authors of Great Britain*,[40] so it should have been widely known towards the end of that year, when it was possibly brought to Mrs Radcliffe's attention.

As Sir Walter Scott pointed out, the value of Mathias's tribute was enhanced by the knowledge that he was perfectly acquainted with the manners and language of Italy (his own Italian poetry was highly regarded), and by inference judged Mrs Radcliffe's use of the Italian scene to be correct.[41] His canonizing praise of the 'mighty magician' of Udolpho was of incalculable importance: henceforth it was quoted in full (often via Scott's quotation) in virtually every extended comment upon Mrs Radcliffe, not only during her lifetime, but throughout the nineteenth century and most of the twentieth.[42] It was the imprimatur which ensured her literary immortality. It has also had the less fortunate effect of characterizing her as a reactionary exception to her more radical sisters. Only the critic of the *Monthly Mirror* paused to notice that the skill with which she drew her characters in this novel may have been influenced by the recent 'philosophical romances' – the radical political novels – of Godwin, Holcroft and Bage.[43]

Ann Radcliffe's reputation was such that she was read as avidly by learned gentlemen as by young men and women. Mathias reflected a taste current among men more often associated with High Culture than for delving into Gothic romance. The scholar Henry Francis Cary, who read voluminously in the classics and in scholarly works in French, Italian, Latin and Greek, and who would become the Assistant Librarian at the British Museum in

1826, read *The Italian* shortly after it came out, during his twenty-fifth year, to satisfy his curiosity as to what all the fuss was about. He was quite struck by the 'unmixed sensation of horror' in *The Italian*, but had to give the palm to the more correct taste of Mackenzie's *Julia de Roubigné*.[44] The littérateur Thomas Green was also more at home devouring the classics and the modern masters, but throughout 1797, in his twenty-eighth year, he enlivened his studies by adopting a Gothic programme of reading. This included Walpole's *Castle of Otranto* and *The Mysterious Mother*, Burke's *On the Sublime and Beautiful* and Ann Radcliffe's *The Italian*. He was familiar with her previous work, and felt that this new novel 'will maintain, but not extend' her reputation. For her vivid descriptions of nature, delineation of strong dark characters and the excitation of horror, 'I know not that Mrs R. has any equal: but she languishes in spinning the thread of the narrative on which these excellencies are strung'. He recognized that Godwin was guilty of plagiarism in his novel *St Leon*: 'the account of the interrogatories at the Inquisition, with the decoy employed there, are directly and impudently stolen from Mrs Radcliffe'.[45]

The Italian greatly appealed to upward-reaching middle-class women such as Mrs Hartley, unmarried daughter of Dr David Hartley, philosopher and physician, friend of Joseph Priestley and Dr Jebb, who settled in Bath. Her brother, with whom she lived at Belvedere, Bath, was a good friend of Benjamin Franklin, and a Liberal, and she was acquainted with Fanny Burney, Mrs Ord and other Bluestockings, and the Bowdlers. She 'converse[d] very much with books', which she borrowed from a library as she could not afford to buy them. She wrote to Sir William Weller Pepys on 4 November 1797:

> I have since read a lighter work; but of beautiful imagination, interesting scenes, and true genius, 'The Italian', or the Confessional of the black Penitents. I hope you like it and that you read it with as much eagerness as I do; Mrs Radcliffe's works, seem to me more like Epic poems, than ordinary romances. She equals any author that I ever read, in fertility of imagination, intricacy of plot, and consistency of character.[46]

Mrs Hartley's reference to epic poems suggests that she had Mathias's recent praise in mind.

Radcliffean romance was decidedly in vogue: *The Italian* was so popular that for a time 'cloaks, slouched hats, and black whiskers [became] fashionable amongst young gentlemen'.[47] Boaden's dramatization of Mrs Radcliffe's latest novel, as *The Italian Monk*, opened at the Haymarket on 15 August 1797 and was performed twelve times during the season.[48] Boaden absurdly reclaimed Schedoni and restored him to domestic happiness, and the piece was diversified with music and songs by Colman. The actor Mr

Palmer, when he took leave of the acting profession a year or two later, took Boaden aside and said that 'he could not quit London without in a particular manner thanking me for the part of Schedoni'.[49]

It was probably the public fame of *The Italian* that led the artist Giuseppi Marchi to seek out and visit Mrs Radcliffe, resulting in an all-too-rare insight into her life at the time. Marchi had been Sir Joshua Reynolds's assistant since the age of fifteen, and had followed his coffin just behind the chief mourner at his funeral in 1792. He had become a scholar and sculptor in his own right, and had saved enough money to live decently upon his retirement.[50] Marchi's friend the engraver Joseph Farington noted the occasion in his diary for 28 August 1797:

> Marchi called – He dined yesterday with Mr & Mrs Radcliffe the Authoress – She is daughter to Mr Ward who was a Bookseller at Bath. Mrs Radcliffe is 27 or 8 years old, a pretty face. Marchi told her of Johnson & Goldsmith coming to see Sir Joshua Reynolds, she said, those were fine times. Mr Radcliffe was educated at Oxford – He is now Editor of an Evening paper, for which He paid £1000 – He is abt. 30 years old and democratically inclined. They reside at No. 7 Melina Place – St Georges fields.[51]

(The correct address was No. 5.[52]) Marchi portrays the couple some five years younger than they really were. Mrs Radcliffe's one recorded remark is characteristic of her respect for the olden days: 'those were fine times'. Marchi's information that Mr Ward was a bookseller is not the kind of error one makes apropos of nothing: Mrs Radcliffe has given her father a more literary character and has suppressed the fact that he was a ceramic merchant. Moderate respectability has given way to pretensions to culture, or at least to a more romantic construct of her persona. It is especially worth noting that William Radcliffe's democratic views were conspicuous enough to be remarked upon after a single dinner with him.

By 1798 the critical consensus was that Ann Radcliffe was entitled 'to rank among the first novel-writers of her age'.[53] And yet *The Italian* was to be the last work published during her lifetime. There is no sign at all that she was 'written out'; on the contrary, melodrama had given way to dramatic assurance, and her characterization was deepening. Mrs Barbauld observed: 'if she wishes to rise in the horrors of her next, she must place her scene in the infernal regions'.[54] It therefore comes as a shock to see her jettison the full-bodied dark romanticism she had attained in favour of the archaeologizing of her last novel *Gaston de Blondeville*, published post-humously. The great mystery in Ann Radcliffe's life is the question: what – or who – compelled her to abandon her muse?

Behind the Veil

———— • ————

William Hazlitt remarked that 'Mrs Radcliffe's heroes and lovers are perfect in their kind; nobody can find any fault with them, for nobody knows anything about them'.[1] The same can be said of her villains, who are stock characters from melodrama. But despite literary conventions, family relationships are more complex in Ann Radcliffe's novels than in the works of many of her contemporaries, and several of her character types have recognizably 'realistic' features that go beyond the rhetoric of Gothic fiction and literary tradition. Every novel has two parallel family households and two geographical settings – surely a result of living in two distinct households at a critical point in her childhood. The substitute parents of the orphaned/ abducted heroine (or hero in the case of the first novel) existed in reality, in the person of Thomas Bentley and his household. Discussions about the relationship of the life to the work too easily spin on the circle of using the life to illustrate the novels to illustrate the life. But if the known facts of the life can be shown to have parallels in the novels, then it is reasonable to assume that often-repeated features of the novels may illuminate the author's otherwise unknown inner life. However, it must be acknowledged that the lines of analysis followed in this chapter are frankly speculative.

Ann Radcliffe seems to have cleverly planted clues about her own life in her fiction, as in her very specific references to dates and ages. In *The Romance of the Forest* Adeline first meets her suitor Louis La Motte when he 'was now in his twenty-third year' (68); it may be more than just a coincidence that William Radcliffe was twenty-three years old when he married Ann Ward, and the description of Louis La Motte – an imperfect figure rather than an idealized hero – may be a portrait of William: 'his person was manly and his air military; his manners were unaffected and graceful, rather than dignified; and though his features were irregular, they composed a countenance, which, having seen it once, you would seek again' (68). *The Italian* opens in the year

1764 – the year of Ann Radcliffe's birth. *The Mysteries of Udolpho* may contain an extravagant autobiographical allegory: Emily was born in 1564 (if she is the daughter of the Marchioness, as many clues intend us to conclude[2]) and met Valancourt in 1584 when she was twenty, while Ann Ward was born in 1764 and met William Radcliffe in 1784 when she was also twenty. Emily meets him on a walking holiday, a favourite pastime of William and Ann Radcliffe. Because of his humble income, Emily resolves to support him with her own inheritance, just as Mrs Radcliffe seems to have supported her husband during the early years of their marriage. He is familiar with the classical rather than the romantic poets, and 'read aloud works of genius and taste' to her (140), just as William read classical passages aloud to his wife, and perhaps similarly condescended to improve her knowledge and correct her taste (585). But he lacks imagination (just as Vivaldi in *The Italian* is gently satirized for lacking both humour and imagination). Eugenia DeLamotte points out that all the preparations for Emily's marriage to Valancourt are suddenly transformed into preparations for the marriage of her aunt to Montoni, and Valancourt mysteriously disappears: the subsequent nightmare view of the marriage of Montoni and Emily's aunt may dramatize Emily's anxieties about marrying Valancourt[3] – and Ann Radcliffe's anxieties about marrying William Radcliffe. Like her, Emily sings simple and lively airs (51), is impressed by organ music, composes poetry and loves the work of Ariosto, indulges in pensive melancholy and travels in search of sublime landscapes: surely this most realistic and fully rounded character in Ann Radcliffe's fiction can be identified with her author.

The young novelist, having little social experience and no circulation in the drawing rooms of the fashionable, exploited her family for her characters, sometimes by splitting them into pairs of opposites, sometimes just by utilizing the duplications of her two-household childhood. In *A Sicilian Romance*, the Marquis of Mazzini's first wife Louisa Bernini, second daughter of Count Della Salario, is said to have died young – as did Hannah Oates, second daughter of James Oates, who died less than two years after marrying Bentley. The lady to whom the Marquis committed the education of his daughters, Mme de Menon, 'who was distantly related to the late marchioness',[4] takes her place in Mazzini's household, just as Elizabeth Oates took over the role of housekeeper after the death of her sister Hannah. Mazzini's two daughters Emilia and Julia may derive their names from Rousseau's *Émile* and *Julie ou La Nouvelle Heloise*, but Emilia (and Emily in *Udolpho*) may have been chosen to link with Ann Radcliffe's grandmother Amelia Oates and her ancestor Amelia De Witt. The two girls have to give up their lovely apartments to the new wife and Mme de Menon is forced to leave, just as Bentley's new wife Mary Stamford displaced Elizabeth Oates, and in effect sent her packing, back to Chesterfield. (The cardboard figures of Ferdinand, Marquis of Mazzini, his second wife Maria de Vellorno and Hippolitus are too shallowly characterized to be said to really 'represent' Thomas Bentley, Mary Stamford and William Radcliffe.)

Eighteen-year-old Julia, like all Ann Radcliffe's heroines, thought of herself as possessing 'symptoms of genius', and she 'discovered an early taste for books' (vol. 1, 10). She felt 'excluded' from the busy scenes of life (vol. 1, 14), and her melancholy seems to derive from a childhood disillusionment:

> The weakness of humanity is never willingly perceived by young minds. It is painful to know, that we are operated upon by objects whose impressions are variable as they are indefinable . . . When at length this unwelcome truth is received into the mind, we at first reject, with disgust, every appearance of good, we disdain to partake of a happiness which we cannot always command, and we not unfrequently sink into a temporary despair. (vol. 1, 44–5)

An authorial aside in *The Castles of Athlin and Dunbayne* reveals a similar pessimism about childhood illusions:

> When first we enter on the theatre of the world, and begin to notice the objects that surround us, young imagination heightens every scene, and the warm heart expands to all around it. The happy benevolence of our feelings prompts us to believe that every body is good, and excites our wonder why every body is not happy. . . . As we advance in life, . . . we are led reluctantly to truth through the paths of experience; and the objects of our fond attention are viewed with a severer eye. Here an altered scene appears; – frowns where late were smiles; deep shades where late was sunshine; mean passions, or disgusting apathy stain the features of the principal figures.[5]

The story itself makes no attempt to develop the idea that perceptions are deepened by experience; the theme of the novel is simply that virtue triumphs over vice. This gratuitous passage seems to contain purely auto-biographical reflections upon the author's childhood. Although the terrors of each novel are experienced within the second family into which the heroine is abducted, her basic unhappiness had already been prompted by her involvement with her first family. Adeline's personal experience of human nature is largely negative: 'during my whole life I have never known a friend' (*The Romance of the Forest*, 242). Her own parents – possibly like Nancy Ward's – never reach out to support her; on the contrary, they abandon her to her misery. Although books supply an enthusiastic joy for these heroines, they also serve as tools for suppressing their emotions. Adeline 'sought a refuge from her own reflections in the more pleasing ones to be derived from books' (96); 'When her mind was discomposed by the behaviour of Madame La Motte, or by a retrospection of her early misfortunes, a book was the opiate that lulled it to repose' (82). Self-repression is characteristic of Ann Radcliffe's heroines. The feelings they want most to repress seem to be connected to a discovery of the meanness of their parents and a sense of having been abandoned (and remaining unloved) by them.

These 'early misfortunes' predate the heroine's relationship with the wicked villain, which is usually the object of critical attention; I suggest that Ann Radcliffe's relationship with her mother is the central issue of the 'family drama' in her novels. In *The Castles of Athlin and Dunbayne* the Countess Matilda is a characteristic Radcliffean mother figure: weak, ineffectual and manic-depressive, full of a grief which lapses into mental disorder requiring the attention of a physician. Similarly in *The Romance of the Forest*, Madame La Motte is brooding and ill-humoured for no apparent reason, which suggests that this trait was observed all too frequently by the novelist. The uneasy relations between the La Mottes are not happy. Madame La Motte persecutes her impatient husband with conjectures and suspicions; she is 'harrassed with anxiety' (92), but is also a petty tyrant herself (79). The betrayal of trust within the family induces the heroine's pessimism: 'To a generous mind few circumstances are more afflicting than a discovery of perfidy in those whom we have trusted', observes the author, and Adeline pathetically exclaims, 'Am I doomed to find every body deceitful?' (118). Ann Radcliffe seems not to have established any bonds of friendship throughout her life, perhaps concluding, like Adeline, that 'no person is to be trusted' (118).

It seems not unreasonable to look to the author for the roots of her heroines' disquiet. Talfourd believed that 'the passions, the affections, the hopes of her characters are essentially her's; born of her own heart; figured from the tracings of her own brain'.[6] Ann Radcliffe's novels betray pessimism, repression and a sense of frustration and confinement. A melancholy beyond the requirements of fashion – never successfully matched by her imitators – is everywhere in evidence. A peculiar characteristic of her novels is that the protagonist is on the verge of madness. Even in the first novel, *The Castles of Athlin and Dunbayne*, Osbert's indignation and pity over the murder of his father 'exasperated his brain almost to madness' (39). Almost identically, in *A Sicilian Romance* the Marchioness Mazzini is so jealous over Hippolitus's love for Julia that 'her brain was at length exasperated almost to madness' (vol. 1, 100). It has been said that 'it would take considerable blindness to avoid noticing the diagnoses of insanity which are offered on every page' of *The Mysteries of Udolpho*.[7] Ann Radcliffe's close psychological scrutiny of Emily's highly strung sensibility and 'distempered imagination' (95)[8] – in a word, incipient mental disorder –is one of the novel's claims to realism rather than romance. Emily exhibits symptoms of temporary insanity throughout the novel, apparently caused by her strenuous effort to suppress strong feelings and maintain a dignified self-control. 'Emily wished to trip along the turf, so green and bright with dew, and to taste the full delight of that liberty, which the izard [the Pyrenean antelope] seemed to enjoy as he bounded along the brow of the cliffs' (36), but the free spirit is hedged round with apprehension, anxiety and restraint. Constant tension and repression force her 'to try whether exercise and the open air would not relieve the intense pain that bound her temples' (151). Oppressed by anxiety, she often 'breathed with difficulty' (329, 360, 406, 432, 521). But contrary to the stereotypical perception of Gothic heroines, Emily rarely faints; just as her aunt Montoni goes into epileptic fits rather than swooning, Emily falls into autistic trances, as when she tries to suppress her desire for Montoni's death: 'A damp chillness came over her; her sight became confused; she knew not what had passed, or where she was' (318). After seeing a corpse which she believes to be that of her dead aunt, she 'often fixed a wild and vacant look on Annette, and, when she spoke, either did not hear her, or answered from the purpose. Long fits of abstraction succeeded', followed by temporary amnesia (350). When Valancourt offers to elope with her, the conflict between desire and propriety transports her into a cataleptic state and 'her reason had suffered a transient suspension' (155). (Similarly, Julia in *A Sicilian Romance* is subjected to such a degree of harassment that she experiences 'a temporary suspension of reason' (vol. 1, 142).) Even after her escape from Udolpho, Emily goes into profound reveries unlinked to specific causes, and remains 'unconscious of all around her' (416) or sinks into 'a kind of musing stillness' (453). This paralysis of acute anxiety is quite specific to Ann Radcliffe's novels and cannot be dismissed as a mere Gothic 'convention'.

Because Gothic novels confront issues of horror and sexual violence, it is common to interpret them using the tools of Freudian (and more recently Lacanian) psychoanalysis, treating literary style as a matrix of strategies for dealing with taboo material (such as repetition, compulsion, splitting, projection, sublimation and so on). Daniel Cottom suggests that Ann Radcliffe's idealization of a neurasthenic sensibility is itself evidence of a severe internal conflict, and David Punter suggests that *The Italian* 'fits in' with Melanie Klein's analysis of narcissism and the child's fantasies about the father inside the mother.[9] Gothic novels of course are not simply case studies of internalized hysteria and paranoia, but interpretations based upon psychoanalytical (rather than sociological or aesthetic) theories do have a compelling attraction.

The characteristic duplications of settings and parental characters (split into good/evil pairs) in Ann Radcliffe's novels might suggest the use of projection to cope with a problem of childhood abuse. Nevertheless, too much Radcliffe criticism has concerned itself with a supposed incest theme in her novels. Montoni in *The Mysteries of Udolpho* is little more than the archetypal wicked stepfather of nursery tales. There is no evidence to support the reading that Emily loves Montoni on a subconscious level, even though their debate over power, control and possession in a sense takes the form of a sexual contest.[10] Kenneth Graham's view that Montoni is Emily's 'Demon-Lover', an erotic fantasy, is a rather male chauvinist interpretation.[11] The text does not suggest that Montoni and Emily have any physical desire for one another. Emily's initial attraction to Montoni is simply a marker of her aesthetic judgement, paralleling the late eighteenth-century response to Milton's Satan, as explained in Beattie's *Dissertations Moral and Critical* (1783): 'the test of sublimity is not moral approbation but that pleasurable astonishment wherewith certain things strike the beholder' – Emily grants sublimity its due, even in an immoral vessel. The threat of the Radcliffean villain is primarily physical, economic and social, and the female fear of violation or rape merely 'lends power and vocabulary to their menace, especially for the fearful reader'.[12]

The central relationship in *The Mysteries of Udolpho* does not concern father and daughter, but mother and daughter: Emily tears aside the mysterious black veil and penetrates the recess of the mother figure, who is simultaneously the Shadow, the Other. Emily is male-willed, fascinated by powerful and passionate women such as Lady Laurentini/Sister Agnes and the Marchioness de Villeroi, and courted by young women such as the peasant girl Maddelina, 'whose gentle countenance and manners soothed her more than any circumstance she had known for many months' (418), and eighteen-year-old Lady Blanche, who 'became impatient for her new friend' when Emily spends some time in the convent: 'She had now no person, to whom she could express her admiration and communicate her pleasures, no eye, that sparkled to her smile, or countenance, that reflected her happiness' (495). Similarly, in a fleeting early episode in the novel, Emily is attracted to a Venetian girl, Signora Herminia, who sings and plays on her lute, 'with her veil half thrown back', whose picture Emily draws and gives to her 'as a pledge of her friendship' (188). Emily is similarly attracted to the Lady Abbess, whose veil is 'thrown half back' (484), suggesting some half-hidden mystery.

As the rays of the moon gleam upon Emily's face, partly shaded by a thin black veil, we see that she has 'the contour of a Madonna, with the sensibility of a Magdalen' (184): she is purity and passion united, and it is difficult to believe that Ann Radcliffe did not fully comprehend that she was characterizing her heroine as both virgin and whore. She would have been aware from reading Brydone that 'the blessed Virgin . . . has long been constituted universal legatee, and executrix to all the antient goddesses . . . and what was Venus or Proserpine, is now Mary Magdalene, or the Virgin'.[13] In the haunted apartment at Château-le-Blanc, in the death chamber itself, is the Marchioness de Villeroi's 'long black veil, which, as Emily took it up to examine, she perceived was dropping to pieces with age' (533). Dorothée, in an impulsive gesture to test the effect of the striking resemblance between the Marchioness and Emily, casts the veil upon her: 'Dorothée wept again, and then, taking up the veil, threw it suddenly over Emily, who shuddered to find it wrapped round her, descending even to her feet' (534). Emily frantically endeavours 'to throw off' the veil, in a desperate attempt to deny the mother/daughter union. The scene is immediately followed by a grotesque parody of childbirth as she gazes upon the black counterpane covering the Marchioness's deathbed:

> The edge of the white pillow only appeared above the blackness of the pall, but, as her eyes wandered over the pall itself, she fancied she saw it move. Without speaking, she caught Dorothée's arm, who, surprised by the action, and by the look of terror that accompanied it, turned her eyes from Emily to the bed, where, in the next moment she, too, saw the pall slowly lifted, and fall again. . . . the pall was more violently agitated than before; but Emily, somewhat ashamed of her terrors, stepped back to the bed, willing to be convinced that the wind only had occasioned her alarm; when, as she gazed within the curtains, the pall moved again, and, in the next moment, the apparition of a human countenance rose above it. (535–6)

It transpires that this is merely a smuggler who is deliberately frightening away the intruders so his smuggling activities will remain undiscovered, but the symbolism is more difficult to explain away. We can well imagine that one of the first things to be impressed upon Nancy Ward when she went to stay with her uncle Bentley was that her aunt Hannah had died in childbirth; her parents would have discussed this family tragedy before her departure, and there would have been painful reminders of the event or a retelling of the story once she arrived in Chelsea. In one sense she felt herself to be the orphan of this aunt, but her own childlessness may reflect a fear of death in childbirth. Emily's room in Udolpho is called a 'double chamber' (234) because passages are hollowed out of the thick walls surrounding it. Thus suspended within an outer shell, it is a womb, and Emily is the infant. The unlockable staircase door inspires not so much the fear of rape, as the fear of being torn from the womb; abduction is a metaphor for birth rather than sexual assault. The castle of Udolpho itself is not so much an image of 'patriarchal' tyranny as an emblem of the female allegories of Fate, Solitude, Silence, Secrecy. Its gateway is described in terms of the breasts, belly and hips of the mother:[14]

> The gateway before her, leading into the courts, was of gigantic size, and was defended by two round towers, crowned by overhanging turrets. . . . The towers

were united by a curtain, pierced and embattled also, below which appeared
the pointed arch of an huge portcullis, surmounting the gates . . . an ancient
servant of the castle appeared, forcing back the huge folds of the portal, to
admit his lord. (227)

At the forbidden centre of this novel – as well as Ann Radcliffe's other
novels – is 'the spectral presence of a dead-undead mother, archaic and all-
encompassing, a ghost signifying the problematics of female identity which
the heroine must confront'.[15] The female's attitude to the maternal body is
ambivalent, because it is the source of her power even as it threatens to
engulf her. Although the Gothic heroine seems to be trapped in the
castle/abbey, within this maternal body she also can explore her own body
and develop her own identity. Ann Radcliffe's heroines are particularly
noteworthy for the obsessive curiosity that compels them to search out every
nook and cranny of this 'pre-Oedipal' labyrinth, with an apparent determination to encounter its imaginary horrors. They realize, subliminally, that
the mother at the centre of the labyrinth is the ultimate source of their
horrors. But, instead of slaying this minotaur and growing up, they identify
with it; they voluntarily regress to the source of their magical power.

Terry Castle argues that from the eighteenth century onwards there has
been a significant link between phantasms and lesbian desire in the literature
of women: 'the metaphor has functioned as the necessary psychological and
rhetorical means for objectifying – and ultimately embracing – that which
otherwise could not be acknowledged'. Specifically, lesbian desire is the
'repressed idea' expressed objectively as the image of the dead/undead
mother; the Freudian 'act of negation' transforms the desire into a spectre
or apparitional figure, thereby denying the carnal aspects of lesbian love,
while at the same time revering the desire itself as a haunting reverie.[16] In
an intriguing essay Castle demonstrates 'the supernaturalization of everyday
life' in the *The Mysteries of Udolpho*, in which 'the lover is always a *revenant*'.[17]
The characters are haunted by spectral images of the beloved: St Aubert
feels the 'presence' of his dead wife; La Voisin can 'sometimes almost fancy'
he sees his dead wife; Emily is 'haunted' by her father's living image in the
landscape; and variations of the word 'haunted' are frequently applied to her
lovers Valancourt and Du Pont. Emily's hallucinatory self-absorption
transforms all other characters into phantoms of an internalized image.
Through nostalgia, elegy and reverie she transmutes death into reunion
rather than separation, and at the end of the novel she returns to a world
where the dead continue to live in memory. Grief confers immortality, as
the visionary dead become perfect comforters. Ultimately objects and icons
become more important than real people, and the pleasure of grief produces
an indifference to real life outside oneself. Castle is partly following Freud's

suggestion that there is an intimate relationship between chronic grief or melancholy, self-love and erotic ambivalence (his essay 'Mourning and melancholia', 1917). Claire Kahane, also following Freud, suggests that in Gothic novels by women the lesbian/erotic bond between mother and daughter is displaced by searching secret rooms, and that grotesque, distorted body images indicate a sense of being somehow freakish or unnatural: this is what obscurity is designed to obscure.[18] The paradigm for this interpretation is the androgynous wax figure (believed to be a woman, discovered to be a man) behind the black veil.

The woman behind the veil is the mother, with whom Emily is sexually fascinated. Emily's chaste dignity mirrors her sexually self-sufficient narcissism: she gazes into the pool and sees herself-as-mother and herself-as-daughter. The demon lover of *The Mysteries of Udolpho* is the Romantic imagination: if Emily invites rape, it is not by Montoni, but by the goddess Fancy. The repeated doublings in the novel produce an allegorical repletion, what Camille Paglia would call 'a redundant proliferation of homologous identities in a matrix of sexual ambiguity'.[19] More specifically this is the matrix of narcissism, and more specifically still, the matrix of female narcissism, in which triplings rather than doublings proliferate: *Diva triformis*; mother, self, daughter; Hecate, Artemis, Diana; the Sublime, the Picturesque, the Beautiful. Many of the women in the novel are projections of Emily as virginal mother goddess, especially the three sets of triplicates: Emily as a young girl, Maddelina and Lady Blanche; Emily as a young woman, the Marchioness de Villeroi and Lady Laurentini; Emily as a Madonna, the Abbess and Sister Agnes. The novel is dominated by three trios of older woman, female servant and younger girl. The compulsive search through secret rooms is an erotic pursuit; in the context of the novel it connotes lesbian incest between daughter and mother: mother as tormentor (Udolpho), mother as protector (Château-le-Blanc), mother as self (La Valée).

The true mysteries of Udolpho are suppressed rather than explained. Of course the 'nameless deed' hinted at in the epigraph to the novel is explained away in the concluding pages, for propriety clouds the revelations of the author's imagination. Ann Radcliffe opens the window on the forbidden, but half closes it again to make her novel acceptable to respectable readers. She concludes with the comforting moral that innocence will finally triumph over misfortune, which is patently untrue with regard to the Marchioness and Mme Montoni, both innocent yet both cruelly murdered.[20] Coral Ann Howells finds a feminist pleasure in such 'Radcliffean duplicity', which clearly discloses that the hero does *not* succeed in rescuing the heroine, that women are sexual, that women are silenced by brute force as much as by decorum: 'It is a case of writing in and then masking divergent views (while leaving both in the text!).'[21]

How does *The Italian* betray Ann Radcliffe's personal psychodrama? The central erotic moment comes when Schedoni is about to plunge the dagger into the sleeping Ellena: 'Her dress perplexed him; it would interrupt the blow, and he stooped to examine whether he could turn her robe aside, without waking her. . . . vengeance nerved his arm, and drawing aside the lawn from her bosom, he once more raised it to strike' – only to be frozen in terror when he sees a miniature of himself hanging at her neck, and believes her to be his own daughter (234). The thin gauze patently would not impede the dullest dagger – the imagery is frankly prurient, just as when Hippolitus comes upon the unconscious Julia in *A Sicilian Romance*: 'Her face was concealed in her robe; and the long auburn tresses which fell in beautiful luxuriance over her bosom, served to veil a part of the glowing beauty which the disorder of her dress would have revealed' (vol. 2, 132). Similarly, in *The Romance of the Forest*: 'The negligence of [Adeline's] dress, loosened for the purpose of freer respiration, discovered those glowing charms, which her auburn tresses, that fell in profusion over her bosom, shaded, but could not conceal' (87). These are characteristic instances of what feminists today call 'the male gaze' – though here they are created by a female author for the interest of what she must have known was a predominantly female readership. Contemporaries indeed noted that 'Her genius was of the sterling kind, and partook much of the masculine character'.[22]

Modern readers, over-receptive to 'incest themes', detect in this last scene (and a later scene when Schedoni subsequently sits with Ellena and tries to make amends by expressing a paternal solicitude towards her, which she mistakes for the advances of a seducer) a father/uncle about to murder/rape his daughter/niece. But contemporary readers would have recognized that the scene signified the guilt of familial murder. Ann Radcliffe's Shakespearean source should be obvious despite the gender transpositions: to use the title of a painting exhibited at the Royal Academy in 1790, *Lady Macbeth Prevented from Stabbing the King by His Resemblance to Her Father As He Sleeps*.[23] *Macbeth*, Shakespeare's study of guilt and remorse, lends important scenes to *The Italian*. When Schedoni is within a few paces of Ellena's sleeping form, she 'raised herself, and he started back as if a sudden spectre had crossed him' (218). His henchman Spalatro, as when Macbeth sees the bloody 'dagger of the mind', has a supernatural vision (never explained away) of a blood-stained finger beckoning him to an act he fears to perform (231–2). In the context of these Shakespearian allusions, Schedoni plays the role of *Lady* Macbeth, urging her husband on, then finishing off the deed: 'Give me the dagger, then,' cries the Confessor (231). Schedoni is to Ellena what Lady Macbeth is to Duncan. In formal literary terms this Father plays the role of Shakespeare's 'unsex'd female', and we should also bear in mind that he is acting as the agent of the Marchesa. In a sense he can be seen as the heroine's 'wicked mother' as well as 'wicked uncle'. This central passage concerns the nature of identity and illustrates the complex relationship between self and other. Schedoni's suspended murder of Ellena does not suggest heterosexual incest pure and simple. The traditional view that the uncle is a 'displacement' for the father in the 'trauma of incest' seems inadequate even for the earlier novels; here it is possible that the uncle is a displacement of the unacceptable face of the mother that the heroine (or novelist) wishes to suppress.

The relationship between Ellena and Sister Olivia adumbrates the problematical relationship between Ann Radcliffe and her own mother. Her ambivalent attitude is illustrated by the projection of the wicked mother archetype upon the mother of Vivaldi, the Marchesa, a proud woman 'of violent passions, haughty, vindictive, yet crafty and deceitful' (7) – a figure whom we have seen in the previous novels. This projection enables Ann Radcliffe to portray Signora Bianchi, the aunt, as the good mother, but even that attempt at resolving the problem does not fully satisfy her, and she disposes of Bianchi quickly, thus making Ellena an 'orphan' twice over. The Countess di Bruno, alias Sister Olivia, whom Ellena in due course discovers to be her real mother, is an idealized mother, goodness personified. But the reason for ambivalence towards her is not hard to find: the Countess, by allowing herself to be supposed dead in order not to bring ignominy upon her house by revealing that her brother-in-law had murdered her husband, had in effect *abandoned* her daughter, albeit into the care of her sister Bianchi, just as Ann Oates Ward abandoned her daughter to the care of her sister Elizabeth Oates. 'Of this event, or of her mother, Ellena had no remembrance; for the kindness of Bianchi had obliterated from her mind the loss and the griefs of her early infancy' (241) (just as Adeline tried to suppress remembrance of her 'early misfortunes' in *The Romance of the Forest*). This fictional projection may be Ann Radcliffe's attempt to resolve a love/hate relationship with her own mother.

An epigraph from Shakespeare's *Twelfth Night* establishes the provenance of Olivia's name – and something of the homosexual ambience of the novel (Olivia falls in love with Viola disguised as a boy). Ellena 'no longer returned her caresses' (378) when she is surprised to learn that Olivia is her mother, and the nature of her love is transformed into filial love. But this does not mask the fact that the real love interest in *The Italian* is the relationship between Ellena and Olivia, nor does the conventionally familial nature of that relationship discount its lesbian undertones. This is the final development of the lesbian theme that first appeared in *The Romance of the Forest*, when Adeline wakes from a fever to discover her protector Clara La Luc: 'the bed curtain on one side was gently undrawn by a beautiful girl. . . . Adeline gazed in silent admiration upon the most interesting female countenance she had ever seen' (243). The first meeting between Ellena and Olivia is an even more highly charged depiction of erotic love at first sight:

> the nun passed close by Ellena, who threw back her veil, and fixed upon her a look so supplicating and expressive, that the nun paused, and in her turn regarded the novice, not with surprize only, but with a mixture of curiosity and compassion. A faint blush crossed her cheek, her spirits seemed to faulter, and she was unwilling to withdraw her eyes from Ellena . . . .
> 'She is very handsome,' said Ellena. (87)

Their relationship develops quickly. Olivia gives Ellena an unambiguous love-token: 'a knot of fragrant flowers' (94) and a volume of Tasso. When Ellena finally escapes the convent, by disguising herself in Olivia's veil, their separation is the parting of lovers, explicitly recognized as such by Vivaldi:

> 'Farewel, dear Ellena!' said Olivia, 'may the protection of heaven never leave you!'
> The fears of Ellena now gave way to affectionate sorrow, as, weeping on the bosom of the nun, she said 'farewel! O farewel, my dear, my tender friend! I must never, never see you more, but I shall always love you; and you have promised, that I shall hear from you; remember the convent della Pieta!'
> 'You should have settled this matter within,' said Jeronimo, 'we have been here these two hours already.'
> 'Ah Ellena!' said Vivaldi, as he gently disengaged her from the nun, 'do I then hold only the second place in your heart?' . . .
> 'I envy your friend those tears,' said he, 'and feel jealous of the tenderness that excites them. Weep no more, my Ellena.' (135–6)

The argument that it is anachronistic to read modern same-sex desire into the so-called early modern 'friendship tradition' cannot be sustained; contemporary feelings about romantic friendships did not judge them to be merely conventional.[24] Vivaldi's clearly articulated jealousy undermines any 'purely literary' interpretation we may wish to place upon such sentiments. It is a mistake to dismiss the reality behind such feelings simply on the basis that they form part of the sentimental friendship literature of the late eighteenth and early nineteenth centuries. As Emma Donoghue observes, 'Elizabeth Mavor resurrected the phrase "romantic friendship" in 1971 specifically to shield the Ladies of Llangollen from being called lesbians. It has become a popular term among historians, often invoked to neutralise and de-sexualise textual evidence.'[25] It is not true that all of the contemporaries of the Ladies of Llangollen believed that they were just romantic friends: in 1992 Liz Stanley 'unearthed an unpublished diary in which Hester

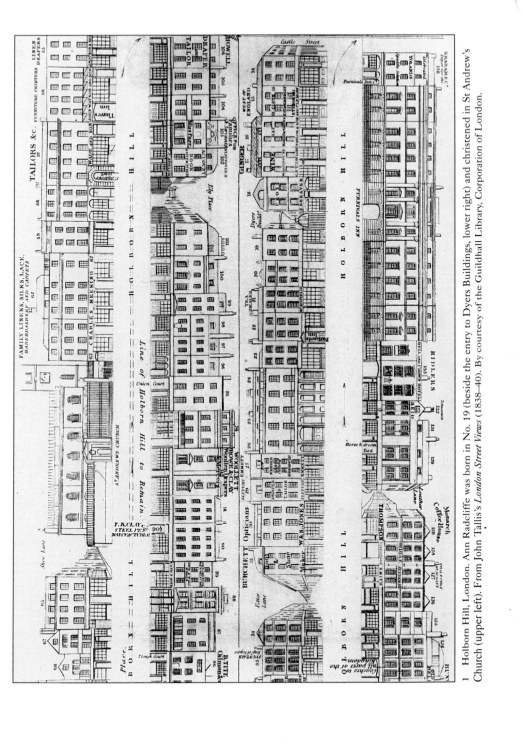

1 Holborn Hill, London. Ann Radcliffe was born in No. 19 (beside the entry to Dyers Buildings, lower right) and christened in St Andrew's Church (upper left). From John Tallis's *London Street Views* (1838–40). By courtesy of the Guildhall Library, Corporation of London.

2 Monument to Thomas Bentley in St Nicholas Church, Chiswick, designed by James Stuart and sculpted by Thomas Scheemakers, 1780. Watercolour sketch by T. Trotter, 1796. Courtesy London Borough of Hounslow Leisure Services Department: Heritage and Tourism: Chiswick Library.

3   Carisbrooke Castle, Isle of Wight, a possible model for the Castle of Udolpho. Engraving in Brayley and Woolnoth's *The Ancient Castles of England and Wales* (1825). By courtesy of the Guildhall Library, Corporation of London.

4   Haddon Hall, Derbyshire, the legendary inspiration for Château-le-Blanc in *The Mysteries of Udolpho*. From Ebenezer Rhodes's *Peak Scenery* (1819). By courtesy of the Guildhall Library, Corporation of London.

5　Adeline flees from a mysterious figure in the ruined cloister. Woodcut from Radcliffe's *The Romance of the Forest* (Limbird's 1832 edition). By permission of the British Library 1560/1178(1).

6　Sister Olivia is recognized by the old servant Beatrice and reveals herself as Ellena's mother. Woodcut from Radcliffe's *The Italian* (Limbird's 1832 edition). By permission of the British Library 1560/1178(2).

7 Contract for *The Mysteries of Udolpho*, dated 11 March 1794, and the Receipt. By courtesy of The Sadleir-Black Gothic Novel Collection, Special Collections Department, University of Virginia Library.

Frontispiece

vide Vol 2 Chap 23.

8   Frontispiece to Anne Ker's _Adeline St Julian; or, The Midnight Hour_ (1800), an example of 'the Radcliffe school'. By permission of the British Library 12614.aa.11.

9   Netley Abbey, Hampshire. Sepia illustration in John Hassell's *Tour of the Isle of Wight* (1790). By courtesy of the Guildhall Library, Corporation of London.

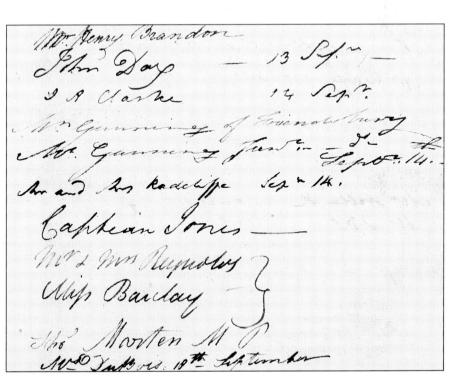

10   Mr and Mrs Radcliffe enter their names in the Knole Visitors' Book, 14 September 1807, for the pleasure of the Duke of Dorset. By permission of Robert Sackville West and The Trustees of Knole Estates.

11 Ann Radcliffe's last entries in her Commonplace Book, 12 November 1822, twelve weeks before her death. By courtesy of the Trustees of the Boston Public Library.

Thrale [whose daughter once visited the ladies] describes the Ladies of Llangollen as "damned Sapphists" and claims that women were reluctant to stay the night with the Ladies unless accompanied by men'.[26] Even more to the point, Anne Lister, herself a lesbian, visited the famous Ladies in 1822 and recorded in her diary: 'I cannot help thinking that surely it was not Platonic. Heaven forgive me, but I look within myself & doubt.'[27] This kind of evidence suggests the necessity of re-evaluating the so-called literary conventions of female friendship documented by Lillian Faderman in *Surpassing the Love of Men* (1981).[28] Although Faderman must have been aware of Lister's remark, she ignored it when compiling her anthology of lesbian literature *Chloe plus Olivia* (1994), wherein she continues to base her non-sexual interpretation of romantic friendship specifically upon the error that Hester Thrale considered the Ladies to be *only* 'fair and noble recluses' and 'charming cottagers' rather than sapphists.[29]

Ellena and Vivaldi have no contact with one another for more than two hundred pages; their reunion is abrupt and conventional, recounted in two brief paragraphs (408). In contrast, two full pages are required to report the reunion, after a much shorter separation, of Ellena and Olivia. This is the reunion of lovers:

> [Ellena] perceived several persons advancing in the shady distance. Among the voices, as they drew nearer, she distinguished one whose interesting tone engaged all her attention, and began also to awaken memory. She listened, wondered, doubted, hoped, and feared! . . . Ellena thought she could not be deceived in those tender accents, so full of intelligence, so expressive of sensibility and refinement. She proceeded with quicker steps, yet faltered as she drew near the group . . .
>
> The voice spoke again; it pronounced her name; pronounced it with the tremblings of tenderness and impatience, and Ellena scarcely dared to trust her senses, when she beheld Olivia, the nun of San Stefano, in the cloisters of the Della Pieta!
>
> Ellena could find no words to express her joy and surprise on beholding her preserver in safety, and in these quiet groves; but Olivia repaid all the affectionate caresses of her young friend . . . (369–70).

The potent symbol of the veil is even more pervasive in *The Italian* than in *The Mysteries of Udolpho*. Like the grated partition which separates the confessor and the penitent in the confessional, it reveals the buried self.[30] An epigraph sums up its erotic allure:

> That lawn conceals her beauty
> As the thin cloud, just silver'd by the rays,

The trembling moon: think ye 'tis shrouded from
The curious eye? (129)

The veil with its 'artful folds' (118) enhances rather than conceals female
sexual attractiveness; it is frequently wafted aside by a breeze or 'thrown
half back' – an unmistakably erotic gesture, used also in *The Mysteries of
Udolpho*. Vivaldi is variously 'fascinated', 'excited', 'rapt' and 'embarrassed'
by Ellena's veil. But the transposed gender relationship between Schedoni-
as-Lady-Macbeth and Ellena-as-Duncan should alert us to the possibility
that the sexuality with which the veil is suffused is not heterosexuality
narrowly defined, but rather a narcissistic and quasi-lesbian sexuality.[31] Ellena
is attracted to the veiled Olivia in exactly the same way as Vivaldi is attracted
to the veiled Ellena: 'Her face was concealed by a black veil, whose
transparency, however, permitted the fairness of her complexion to
appear. . . . When the hymn had ceased, she . . . throw[s] back her veil',
discovering herself to Ellena, then drops it again to indicate the impropriety
of any expression of affection in public (86–8). Eventually Olivia's veil will
be preserved by Ellena 'as a sacred relique' (257) – a virtual fetish. The
conventional heterosexual marriage of Ellena and Vivaldi (which,
incidentally, is complemented by the same-sex crypto-marriage of Vivaldi
and Paulo[32]) does not negate a lesbian subtext to Ann Radcliffe's novels, for
as Jane Spencer points out, *The Romance of the Forest*, *The Mysteries of Udolpho*
and *The Italian* all 'end with defeat for the authoritarian male and the
heroine's marriage to a feminized hero'.[33] George Haggerty also points out
that 'Theodore plays on Adeline's emotions precisely to the degree that he
is restrained, controlled, victimized and emasculated. To the degree, that is,
that Theodore becomes *like a woman*, he is attractive to the heroine of *The
Romance of the Forest*.'[34] Valancourt in *The Mysteries of Udolpho* is so sensitive
that he has been called one of Ann Radcliffe's finest *heroines*; Emily's
gardener shoots him, and he reappears with his arm in a sling, having atoned
for his apparent infidelity by being symbolically castrated. In *The Italian*,
Vivaldi passes much of his time blinded by a hood – a classic symbol of
castration.

Exactly what relationship all this bears to Ann Radcliffe's personal life
can never satisfactorily be answered in view of the paucity of available
information about her. While I would not baldly claim that 'Ann Radcliffe
was a lesbian', the possibility that some degree of lesbian desire (unacted
upon) was part of her character seems to me to cast at least a little light upon
the mysteries of her life and work. The evidence is entirely circumstantial,
but is worth summarizing. The countervailing heterosexual evidence is
largely absent: she bore her husband no children, and expresses no interest
in children in her writing; marriage as such is not a subject of her novels (as

it is, for example, in novels by her imitator Regina Maria Roche, and many other contemporary novels, Gothic as well as sentimental and realistic), and many of them illustrate bad or disastrous marriages. The (heterosexual) love interest in the novels is conspicuously guarded by an exaggerated sense of propriety and self-control suggesting sexual coldness, and her heroes are effeminized before being accepted as suitors. On the other hand, her heroines express keen interest in women, and develop romantic female friendships containing features that go beyond the traditional treatment of such relationships in the genre (such as the hero's explicit jealousy of such relationships). The primary interest in the novels – the heroine's search for the mother – can be interpreted in an erotic sense using traditional psychoanalytical tools, and a link between homosexuality and melancholia is a standard psychoanalytical premise. Last, Ann Radcliffe's contemporaries remarked upon the 'masculine' features of her art, and it is clear from her novels, her journals and her poetry that she identified with the masculine creative power of Shakespeare and Prospero the magician.

T·W·E·L·V·E

Horrid Mysteries

———— • ————

Because William Radcliffe in his contribution to the 1824 obituary of his wife says that her aunt 'was accomplished "according to the moderation," – may I say, the *wise* moderation? – of that day',[1] we may be tempted to judge him as a reactionary. Many people adopt increasingly conservative political opinions as they grow older, and like Wordsworth he might conceivably have shifted from revolutionary to reactionary views in response to the excesses of the French Revolution. But it is often the case that men are simultaneously egalitarian and antifeminist. Thomas Paine's *Rights of Man* were just that, which is why Mary Wollstonecraft redressed the balance by proposing the *Rights of Woman*. In any case we must remember that William Radcliffe was radical enough to be called 'democratically inclined' by Marchi, who visited the Radcliffes in August 1797; his republican feelings must have been pronounced for them to have been thought worthy of remark after the course of a single evening meal. If he had not succumbed to the onslaught against radicalism by 1797, his views are hardly likely to have been reversed during the course of the next few years, which is when Ann Radcliffe must have taken the decision to cease writing for publication.

Whatever his motivation may have been, there is evidence that William Radcliffe had a direct hand in forcing his wife to abandon the excesses of Gothic fiction. This accusation is made against him by Charlotte Smith in a letter written sometime in 1802, when she was bemoaning the 'woeful times for Authors!': 'Mrs Ratcliffe [*sic*] is restrained by the authority of her husband from calling any more "spirits from the vasty deep" of her imagination'.[2] Charlotte Smith, who had good reason to dislike husbands, may be retailing a rumour that was conveyed to her through her publishers Cadell and Davies, with whom she corresponded regularly, the same firm who had paid her rival £800 for *The Italian* and who presumably kept requesting a sequel but were rebuffed. Nevertheless, everything we know about William Radcliffe suggests that it would be unfair to blame him solely for his wife's silence. He was her staunchest supporter and encourager. His statement that she was 'hurt' by the criticism of Scott and others rings true, and we can be certain that she was as 'tremblingly alive' to criticism as any of her heroines. One can easily believe that, like Emily, she must have possessed 'a mind, that fears to trust its own powers; which, possessing a nice judgment, and inclining to believe, that every other person perceives still more critically, fears to commit itself to censure, and seeks shelter in the obscurity of silence' (*Udolpho*, 118). My view is that William wished to shield her from abusive attacks by reactionary critics. We must take Mrs Radcliffe's hypersensitivity into account when noting criticism of her work: if her husband ever did suggest that she retire from the field, surely it was advice given for her own peace of mind.

The earliest obituary summed up the majority view regarding the celebrated novelist's sequestration:

> The anonymous criticisms which appeared upon [her] work, the imitations of her style and manner by various literary adventurers, the publication of some other novels under a name slightly varied for the purpose of imposing on the public, and the flippant use of the term 'Radcliffe school', by scribblers of all classes, tended altogether to disgust her with the world, and create a depression of spirits, which led her for many years, in a considerable degree, to seclude herself from society. It is understood that she had written other works, which, on these accounts, she witheld [*sic*] from publication, in spite of the solicitude of her friends, and of tempting offers made her by various publishers.[3]

William Radcliffe noted how gratified his wife had been to receive the unsolicited praise of professional critics, the greatest scholars of the age and even statesmen; he felt that the censure upon her work came

> chiefly from the writers of other novels or romances, whose candour upon the subject may be suspected; . . . [but she observed] that those who betrayed a wish to expel her violently from the field of literature, or at least to close it roughly against her as she retired, seldom failed to imitate her in one part of their works, after having endeavoured to proscribe her by another.[4]

The feeblest of these attackers/imitators passed unnoticed, 'but there were others', her husband hints darkly, writers of repute whose meanness of heart matched the greatness of their talents.

Sir Walter Scott similarly declared that the criticism of her was inflicted, 'in more than one case, by persons of genius, who followed the same pursuit with herself'.[5] This observation is rather disingenuous, because among those writers of genius who inflicted such hurt upon Mrs Radcliffe was Scott himself. He attacked what he called the 'Radcliffe school' in 1810, in an anonymous criticism of Maturin's *The Fatal Revenge*. He said Maturin employed 'all the usual accoutrements from the property-room of Mrs Radcliffe', but what was worse, like her and her imitators, Maturin resolved his story by giving simple natural causes to all of the apparently mystic and marvellous incidents: 'we fling back upon the Radcliffe school their flat and ridiculous explanations, and plainly tell them that they must either confine themselves to ordinary and natural events, or find adequate causes for those horrors and mysteries in which they love to involve us'.[6] Mrs Radcliffe, an enthusiastic reader of all of the Waverley novels as they appeared, was very hurt by Scott's 'slighting' of her in the preface to *Waverley* (1814), according to her husband.[7] The subtitle of this archetypal antiquarian novel, *'Tis Sixty Years Since*, was chosen very carefully so as to emphasize that it was neither a romance of chivalry nor a tale of modern manners. Scott explained in his preface that if he had called it *A Tale of Other Days* he feared that his readers would have anticipated

> a castle scarce less than that of Udolpho, of which the eastern wing had been long uninhabited, and the keys either lost or consigned to the care of some aged butler or housekeeper, whose trembling steps, about the middle of the second volume, were doomed to guide the hero, or heroine, to the ruinous precincts. Would not the owl have shrieked and the cricket cried in my very title-page? and could it have been possible for me, with a moderate attention to decorum, to introduce any scene more lively than might be produced by the jocularity of a clownish but faithful valet, or the garrulous narrative of the heroine's fille-de-chambre, when rehearsing the stories of blood and horror which she had heard in the servants' hall?[8]

These are cheap jibes at the lower-class characters who were the mainstay of regional fiction for which Scott himself was to become so famous. Ironically, Scott was later accused by Wordsworth of the 'want of taste which is universal among modern novels of the Radcliffe school'.[9] This phrase was first used in a review of Joseph Fox's *Santa-Maria; or, The Mysterious Pregnancy* (1797): prompted by Fox's praise of Mrs Radcliffe in his own Prefatory Epistle to his novel, the anonymous reviewer described Fox as a 'pupil of the Radcliffe school' who exhibited all of her defects and none of her beauties.[10]

Northanger Abbey, Jane Austen's satire upon Gothic novels, to which *The Mysteries of Udolpho* serves all too often as a mere footnote, is sometimes credited with killing off the Gothic tradition. Austen began her novel in 1798, but by the time it was published, posthumously, in 1818 the tradition was already in terminal decline,[11] and Mrs Radcliffe had ceased writing long before that date.

Charlotte Smith almost certainly perceived a rival in the person of Ann Radcliffe, and attacked her subtly. Mrs Smith's *The Banished Man* appeared in 1794 with an 'Avis au Lecteur' oddly printed at the beginning of its second volume, presumably because it was written slightly later than the preface to the first volume, which had already been typeset: dated 30 July 1794, it seems to have been prompted by an awareness of the popularity of *The Mysteries of Udolpho*. In this 'advice' Mrs Smith claims that the Gothic architecture strewn across the modern novel has all been stolen from her:

> For my own part, who can now no longer build chateaux even en [*sic*] Espagne, I find that Mowbray Castle, Grasmere Abbey, the castle of Rock-March, the castle of Hauteville, and Rayland Hall, have taken so many of my materials to construct, that I hardly have a watch tower, a Gothic arch, a cedar parlour, or a long gallery, an illuminated window, or a ruined chapel, left to help myself. . . . But my ingenious contemporaries have fully possessed themselves of every bastion and buttress – of every tower and turret – of every gallery and gateway, together with all their furniture and ivy mantles, and mossy battlements; tapestry, and old pictures; owls, bats, and ravens . . .[12]

She wryly goes on to profess that she is not interested in satisfying 'the idlest readers of a circulating library' with fables 'that only a distempered imagination can produce', nor does she wish to write about apparitions or haunted houses, as do her 'ingenious contemporaries', for 'I have no talents that way'. Terms such as 'distempered imagination' and 'ingenious' seem to be pointedly aimed at Mrs Radcliffe (though she does not mention her by name), and to suggest both madness and plagiarism.

A prime candidate for being one of those writers who had cynically attempted to push Ann Radcliffe from the field of literature while at the same time imitating her works is Anna Maria Mackenzie. Her Radcliffean novel *Mysteries Elucidated* (1795) (published by the Minerva Press, which catered for an audience thirsty for Delicious Shudders) has a remarkable prefatory address 'To the Readers of Modern Romance'. Here Mackenzie unmistakably refers to Mrs Radcliffe, the 'modern genius' who 'has lately outsoared' Frances Burney, Clara Reeve, *et al.*, and who has

> contrived to give her story the highest colouring of unfettered invention, by a choice of fictious [*sic*] subjects, which naturally affords a greater latitude to the excentricities of a brilliant imagination, spurning the trammels of sober reason, and forcing, as it were, the willing slave of terror, to adopt the enthusiasm of ideas, which, like the description they are cloath'd in, are all wild, vast, and terrific.

But Miss Mackenzie has a serious reservation, a reservation which all of the more prudent and less romantic readers of Mrs Radcliffe felt: that the excitement can be maintained only by a succession of increasingly horrible images, so 'there is some reason to fear unhappy effects on the young and ductile mind. Indeed, were I possessed of powers equal to that truly ingenious author, I should be cautious of giving them that unbounded licence'.[13] One critic felt it necessary to defend Mrs Radcliffe, and observed that Mackenzie's censure was 'trite' and 'futile': 'our present youth are not likely to be injured by supernatural terrors . . . the powers displayed in the works alluded to, have raised the writer above invidious or petty attacks'.[14]

Another writer of talent who attacked Ann Radcliffe was Mary Wollstonecraft, a novelist herself as well as a propagandist for women's rights. An important passage in her novel *The Wrongs of Woman, or Maria* (1798) is clearly an attack upon Radcliffe even though she is not mentioned by name:

> Abodes of horror have frequently been described, and castles, filled with spectres and chimeras, conjured up by the magic spell of genius to harrow the soul, and absorb the wondering mind. But, formed of such stuff as dreams are made of, what were they to the mansion of despair, in one corner of which Maria sat, endeavouring to recall her scattered thoughts! . . . the terrific inhabitants [of the madhouse where she has been imprisoned], whose groans and shrieks were no unsubstantial sounds of whistling winds, or startled birds, modulated by a romantic fancy, which amuse while they affright; but such tones of misery as carry a dreadful certainty directly to the heart.[15]

For Ann Radcliffe to have been attacked from within her own Dissenting culture was particularly ironic.

Clara McIntyre in 1920 expressed the view – repeated in nearly all modern Radcliffe criticism[16] – that the censure of her novels, including *The Italian*, was never sufficiently scathing to have shocked her into silence. She was never subjected, for example, to attacks similar to those unleashed upon Mrs Barbauld's political poem on freedom, *Eighteen Hundred and Eleven* (1812), which were so severe and distressing that Barbauld ceased writing and even abandoned preparations for the publication of her collected works. But the supposed absence of harsh criticism of Ann Radcliffe is true only with regard to the reviews dealing specifically with her actual novels. McIntyre does not sufficiently take into account the deluge of commentaries which attacked Mrs Radcliffe by implication – clearly alluding to her without mentioning her name – and the glancing blows that rained upon her in condemnation of her imitators' works.

The critical assault upon Ann Radcliffe began properly in August 1797 when a critic calling himself 'a Jacobin Novelist, Greenwich' wrote a letter to the editor of the *Monthly Magazine* satirizing 'The Terrorist System of Novel Writing'.[17] He denounced 'the wonderful revolution' that had transformed the writing of novels, whose writers had adopted Robespierre's 'SYSTEM OF TERROR' and thereby maintained tyrannic sway over young readers in circulating libraries, boarding schools and watering places, their aim being 'to frighten and instruct'. The main thrust of his argument was that it required no skill at all to cater for the modern taste for terror. Any lady's maid could conduct her reader in a cold sweat through four volumes by following a few simple rules, consisting mainly of the heroine's curious investigation of decayed apartments hung with old tapestries, or flights along subterranean passages. When the heroine lifts the veil she discovers not a waxwork figure but 'the tremendous solution of all her difficulties, the awful word HONORIFICABILITATUDINIBUSQUE!!!' In other words, fame and celebrity are exposed as the secret aim of the novelist, and Mrs Radcliffe in particular.

In a follow-up to this article, a contributor signing himself 'E' admitted that Mrs Radcliffe was one of those 'writers of genius, who have succeeded in the terrible', but that parts of her work are 'fair game for ridicule', and her innumerable imitators were responsible for that new species of novel 'the hobgoblin-romance'. He hoped that writers of superior talents would tackle a higher style of composition. Although he acknowledged it was unfair for women to be more dependent than men upon the opinions of others, he nevertheless concluded that 'a woman who has sense enough to make a fair estimate of her own interests and happiness, will be prudently inclined to sacrifice the hope of fame, to avoid the possibility of odium'.[18] The advice seems aimed at Mrs Radcliffe, and she took it.

We may find these satires rather laughable today, but they were regarded as serious challenges to Mrs Radcliffe's morals and her art. Her avid admirer Thomas Green, though amused by the original article, felt compelled to agree with the serious point behind the ridicule. 'It seems hard, but it is true, that original excellence in any department of writing, by provoking scurvy imitation, has a natural tendency to bring disgrace upon itself.'[19] Though this judgement was not published until 1810, and Mrs Radcliffe may never have seen it, it does reflect the ungenerous majority view. A reviewer in 1834 succinctly summarized the case: 'Mrs Radcliffe has shared the fate of many an inventor. She has been made answerable for the sins of her imitators.'[20]

In particular, she was tarred with the same brush applied to her most sinful imitator Matthew Gregory Lewis. Although *The Italian* was widely praised, from 1797 to 1800 the critical reviewers endeavoured to protect the public from the immoral bias of Gothic romance, prompted largely by the reaction against the impiety and obscenity of Lewis's *The Monk*. The *Monthly Magazine* in August 1797 praised the 'rich treat' of Radcliffe's 'highly-wrought romance', but then went on immediately to note the indecorum of the 'voluptuous revelry' in Lewis's 'terrific and luxurious tale'.[21] Everyone recognized the inescapable link between the two novelists; it became common to speak of them in the very same breath, and the moment Lewisian impropriety became attached to Radcliffe's name, the battle to preserve her decorum was doomed.

An early reviewer of *The Monk* felt that 'the convent prison resembles the inflictions of Mrs Radcliffe'; he praised what he recognized as Lewis's plagiarisms from *The Romance of the Forest*, but nevertheless concluded that *The Monk* was 'totally unfit for general circulation.'[22] Another critic noted that in Lewis's drama *The Castle Spectre* 'Mr L.'s obligations, indeed, to Mrs Radcliffe are every where so apparent in the work under our review, that we may reasonably question, whether his castle would have been raised, if her romantic edifices had not previously been constructed.'[23] Mathias's attack upon Lewis in *The Pursuits of Literature* was virulent, but representative (and, it must be said, accurate): lewdness was matched with blasphemy when in the novel Ambrosio remarks that 'the annals of a brothel would scarcely furnish a greater choice of indecent expressions' than the Bible; Mathias felt that this was '*actionable at Common Law*', pointing out that as an elected Member of Parliament Lewis was supposed to defend the religion of the state. Lewis expurgated future editions of his novel.[24] The fact that this edition of *The Pursuits of Literature* also contained the unqualified praise of Mrs Radcliffe hardly helped to reassure orthodox commentators that her works comprised an altogether different class of Gothic romance.

Reviewers attacking other writers' novels very frequently shot an arrow across Mrs Radcliffe's bow. It was said of Stephen Cullen's *The Castle of Inchvally*: 'The success of several deservedly popular novels and romances has occasioned the reading public to be pestered with innumerable tales of distressed lovers, enchanted castles, &c. &c.'[25] Of *Austenburn Castle*: 'Since Mrs Radcliffe's justly admired and successful romances, the press has teemed with stories of haunted castles and visionary terrors.'[26] Charlotte Smith's *Montalbert* was part of 'the inundation of romantic horrors with which the press has lately groaned'.[27] Novels of common life and common sense were increasingly praised as alternatives: Mrs Parsons's *Women as They Are* 'may be safely recommended to those young persons whose taste has not been vitiated by an absurd attachment to what is unnatural or mysterious'.[28] Similarly the stories in Charlotte Smith's *The Young Philosopher* 'do not agitate like the mysterious horrors of Mrs Radcliffe', but are true to nature and delightful.[29]

The anonymous seventeen-year-old author of *Eloise de Montblanc* (1796) sought to fend off criticism in her preface: 'And when too she recollects the perfect Pen of a Burney, a Radcliffe, a Bennet[t], or a Smith, she shrinks at meeting the scrutinizing Eye of Criticism.'[30] Sarah Lansdale Tenterden likewise attempted to disarm criticism with a modest admission of inexperience in her introduction to *Manfredi, Baron of St Osmund* (1796): 'It may be considered as presumption in a young authoress to venture her little productions abroad in the world, when there are so many works extant of Radcliffe's, Smith's, Bennett's and Burney's, who so greatly excel in this species of composition' (vol. I, p. vi). But the reviewer dismissed her work nonetheless: 'The lady seems to be a disciple of Mrs Radcliffe, and to describe horrors and spectres, in a style which approaches already to the height of the terrific. Nevertheless, it is possible that better occupations might be found, than that of describing such scenes.'[31]

By 1800, when the new reactionary periodical the *Anti-Jacobin Review and Magazine* condescended to 'honour' *The Italian* with a review, the novel was found to be 'rather German than English', and the reviewer expressed 'many weighty objections' to the work. So by the turn of the century the reputation of *The Mysteries of Udolpho* was losing its magic, and the great enchantress no longer overawed self-righteous critics who acknowledged that their sole purpose was now to point out the 'moral tendency' of novels.[32]

Adaptations of Gothic novels for the stage contributed to the backlash against the insidious effects of the terror novel. Mrs Radcliffe and 'Monk' Lewis were frequently pillaged for the terrors of the theatre, and the age of high Gothic melodrama was just gathering pace: in 1808 Ferdinand Fullerton Weston's opera *Castle of Udolpho* was founded upon a selection of crimes from *The Mysteries of Udolpho*. Lewis's play *The Castle Spectre* was enormously popular: 'we cannot but regard the success of this piece, and of others of a similar class, as truly humiliating to the pride of our national taste'.[33] One 'Academicus' waxed indignant that such melodramas were being foisted upon 'the good sense of a British audience'; he tried to convince his readers that the Cock Lane Ghost, *Aladdin and His Wonderful Lamp* and *The Castle Spectre*, however suitable for children in the nursery, 'are not to be endured by men of sense and judgment'; he hoped specifically to 'dissolve the spell ... [of] even the mighty magician of *Udolpho*'.[34]

It would take a long time to dislodge the view that the novels of 'the ingenious and amiable Mrs Anne Radcliffe' were moral and especially 'commendable and thank-worthy'.[35] But the 'anti-novelists' steadily gained the day. In the pages of the annual *Flowers of Literature*, which began publication in the first decade of the new century, we find a recurring indecision as to whether or not Ann Radcliffe should be held responsible for goblin-mongering. The authors, Revd F. Prevost and F. Blagdon, reprint a passage from the respectable Dr Barrow's *Essay on Education*, noting that there are exceptions to the usual run of trashy novels:

> The novels of Fielding, of Richardson, and of Radcliffe no man of taste will peruse without pleasure, and no man of reflection without improvement. But

far different from these are the volumes that usually crowd the shelves of a
circulating library, or are seen tumbling on the sofas of a fashionable drawing-
room. It is not the occasional perusal of the best, but the habitual reading of
the worst, which it is the wish of every wise and good man to censure and
restrain.[36]

But Dr Barrow's opinion was that of a slightly earlier generation. Prevost
and Blagdon recognized that *The Romance of the Forest* was 'a creation of
genius', but they nevertheless 'would wish to see banished from our
literature those *hobgobliana*, which the German school first suggested, and
which Mrs Ratcliffe [*sic*], by her superior talents, rendered popular'.[37] In
1803 they launched their attack upon terror novels with an 'Invective against
Novelist Goblin-Mongers': 'O ye goblin-mongers! ye wholesale dealers in
the frightful! is it not cruel to present to the imagination of a lovely female
such horrid images, as skulls with the worms crawling in and out of their
eyeless sockets?'[38] This of course pointedly refers to the waxwork figure
behind the black veil in *The Mysteries of Udolpho*, and is thus a direct attack
upon Ann Radcliffe. 'It is the continual influx of those wretched novel-
writings, and the rare appearance of the good, that has brought this branch
of literature into such merited disrepute. The generality of people hold
them, with reason, in great contempt.' We know that Ann Radcliffe had not
altogether ceased writing, though she had turned her pen to a less terrifying
romance, and was on the point of publishing *Gaston de Blondeville* in 1803,
and that the manuscript had even been given to the publishers but had
suddenly been withdrawn (to be discussed in Chapter 14). It may have been
her reading of this attack on goblin-mongers that finally tipped the balance
in favour of withdrawal and absolute silence. Succeeding issues of *Flowers
of Literature* attacked and ridiculed the Gothic novel, and culminated in
1807 with an attack upon Charlotte Dacre's *Zofloya; or, The Moor* (1806):
'Abounding with caverns, groans, shrieks, murders, hobgoblins, and all the
wretched mummery of the Radcliffean school'.[39] The reference to Mrs
Radcliffe was immediately preceded by the observation that, with the
exception of M. G. Lewis, 'the *grossest* and *most immoral* novelists of the
present day, are *women*!'

   This is not the place to document in detail Ann Radcliffe's influence upon
two or three dozen novelists who have been largely forgotten today,[40] but it
is important to demonstrate that her name was inextricably linked to the
Terrorist School by her contemporaries. All of her trademarks and set-pieces
quickly found their way into a host of novels pandering to popular taste.
Within months of *Udolpho*'s publication, Eliza Parsons turned out *Lucy*, a
shamelessly plagiarized hotchpotch of Radcliffean details.[41] (Jane Austen
would later enjoy satirizing Mrs Parsons's two novels, *Castle of Wolfenbach*

and *The Mysterious Warning.*) In Anne Ker's *The Heiress di Montalde; or, The Castle of Bezanto* (1799) Palmira's loquacious servant Lisette is modelled upon Ann Radcliffe's Annette, and their interactions plagiarize scenes from her novel. It has a nice literary joke: a portrait depicts the original owner of the castle, Signora Emilia di Udino – surely this is Emily of Udolpho! Mrs Ker's next romance *Adeline St Julian; or, The Midnight Hour* (1800) borrows the name of the heroine and the forest scenes from *The Romance of the Forest*, a description of Languedoc with its forest haunted by a mysterious lady singer from *The Mysteries of Udolpho* and the Inquisition and torture scenes from *The Italian*. What is particularly interesting about *Adeline St Julian* is its prefatory dedication to Lady Jerningham (who once insisted that she saw 'a woman in white' in one of Horace Walpole's trees;[42] Edward Jerningham was a correspondent of Anna Seward and Hester Lynch Piozzi). The dedication demonstrates how important a model was Ann Radcliffe even though she is not mentioned by name. Mrs Ker defends the production of romances, because in earlier epochs

> the trials of the human heart may be more strongly depicted, and the sympathy of the reader excited in the same degree, towards afflicted virtue and persecuted merit. . . . In those times the vicious had much more frequent opportunities of pouring affliction on the good. There is, therefore, a greater variety of events to be selected for the purpose of exemplifying this great moral – 'That the power of the wicked is transient, and their punishment certain; and that innocence, though oppressed by injustice, if supported by patience, shall finally triumph over misfortune.'[43]

This passage is a quotation of the penultimate paragraph of *The Mysteries of Udolpho*:

> O! useful may it be to have shewn, that, though the vicious can sometimes pour affliction upon the good, their power is transient and their punishment certain; and that innocence, though oppressed by injustice, shall, supported by patience, finally triumph over misfortune!

Though the quotation is not identified, neither is it disguised: Lady Jerningham was expected to appreciate the reference, and encouraged to accord some Radcliffean approbation to her follower. Mrs Ker patently exploits not only the popularity of the Gothic novel but also the high moral ground on which Mrs Radcliffe was perceived to stand. Lady Jerningham's daughter Charlotte, Lady Bedingfeld, was the intimate friend of Matilda Betham, author of 'Lines to Mrs Radcliffe, on first reading The Mysteries of Udolpho', published in *The Athenaeum* in 1807:

ENCHANTRESS! whose transcendant powers,
With ease, the massy fabric raise –
. . .

Accept the tribute of a heart,
Which thou hast often made to glow
With transport, oft with terror start,
Or sink at strains of solemn woe![44]

Matilda Betham also corresponded with Coleridge, Lamb, Southey and the
Ladies of Llangollen. Britain's 'Lesbian poetess' (Coleridge's praise[45]) in
her collected *Poems* (1808) also addressed verses to Miss Ponsonby, whom
she knew. It seems odd to publicly address a poem to Mrs Radcliffe if she
had not personally known her, but there is no documented connection[46]
(other contributors to *The Athenaeum* addressed poems to Charlotte Smith
seemingly without the benefit of her personal acquaintance).

Ann Radcliffe was the 'great exemplar' of terror, and the critics recognized
immediately that *The Mysteries of Udolpho* had 'given birth to several humble
imitations', by men as well as women, such as John Bird's *The Castle of
Hardayne*,[47] John Palmer, jun.'s *The Haunted Cavern; a Caledonian Tale* (1795)[48]
and Miles Peter Andrews's *The Mysteries of the Castle* (1795), though, as one
reviewer remarked, 'we fear that lady will not feel herself flattered by the
relationship'.[49] Many of Mrs Isabella Kelly's novels, as a reviewer noted of
The Abbey of St Asaph, were 'In humble imitation of the well-known novels
of Mrs Radcliffe',[50] and few imitators were felt to be up to the mark. In the
incidents of Anna Maria Mackenzie's *Dusseldorf; or, The Fratricide*, 'the writer
imitates those of Mrs Radcliffe; but she is far from being equal to that lady
in this branch of composition'.[51] The tale of Regina Maria Roche's *Clermont*
'reminds us, without any great pleasure, of Mrs Radcliffe's romances'.[52] Mrs
Robinson's *Hubert de Sevrac* was recognized as 'an imitation of Mrs Radcliffe's
romances, but without any resemblance that may not be attained by a
common pen. . . . But it may be necessary to apprise novel-writers, in general,
that this taste is declining, and that real life and manners will soon assert
their charms.'[53]

It has been said that 'the history of popular fiction throughout the 1790s,
is largely a chronicle of novelists striving to shape their romances in Mrs
Radcliffe's successful mold'.[54] Jane Austen's aunt Cassandra Cooke, in the
preface to her *Battleridge* (1799) (By a Lady of Quality), makes the point:
'She is the Queen of the *tremenduous* [*sic*]; and alas! is most copiously, most
inadequately imitated by almost every writer since her *Romance of the Forest*
appeared.'[55] About a third of all the novels published between 1796 and 1806,
and many serials in ladies' magazines, had scenes inspired by *A Sicilian
Romance* and *The Romance of the Forest*.[56] Thinly disguised redactions of her

books were serialized as shilling shockers, with everything stripped away except the sensational, which thereby appeared even more gross in the absence of Ann Radcliffe's restraining sentiment.[57] In Isaac Crookenden's chapbook *The Vindictive Monk; or The Fatal Ring* (1802) Sceloni is obviously modelled upon Schedoni.[58] The plot abbreviates that of *The Italian*, except that Sceloni now works for a lascivious nobleman rather than a wicked Marchesa, and the scene in which Sceloni is about to plunge a dagger into the sleeping hero is plagiarized from Schedoni's forestalled murder of Ellena. Ann Radcliffe's more interesting and more imaginative plot is thus conventionalized and refocused for the adolescent boy. More reputable writers brazenly declared their sources even in their titles: Ann Ker's *Adeline St Julian* (1799), Mary Houghton's *The Mysteries of the Forest* (1810), Catherine Ward's *The Mysteries of St Clair* (1824), T. J. Horsley Curties's *The Monk of Udolpho* (1807), Catherine Harwood's *The Castle of Vivaldi; or, The Mysterious Injunction* (1810) – the list of derivative adaptations and anonymous plagiarisms could be continued indefinitely: Ann Radcliffe's hideous progeny is enormous. As Clara McIntyre observes, 'a lady of any literary conscience might well have a sense of guilt at being responsible for such a following'.[59]

Sentimental and Gothic novels, which seemed to celebrate the breakdown of authority and to savour of Dissenting enthusiasm, fell into marked disfavour and loss of prestige among the Established classes around the turn of the century. Those whose position in the rising middle classes was not quite secure reinforced their status by opting for the mainstream literature of social manners and rejecting the sorts of books they had grown up on, a taste for which they now ascribed to the lower classes. Class consciousness informed many literary judgements. The review of *Ranspach, or Mysteries of a Castle* is typical: 'The class of readers among whom this book will circulate, will probably not object to confusion of costume, inaccuracy of diction, or incoherence of narrative.'[60] Even in the supposedly classless society of America, Gothic fiction was relegated to the lower orders, as in Royall Tyler's *The Algerine Captive* (1797):

> Dolly, the dairy maid, and Jonathan, the hired man, threw aside the ballad of the cruel stepmother, over which they had often wept in concert, and now amused themselves into so agreeable a terrour, with the haunted houses and hobgoblins of Mrs Ratcliffe [*sic*], that they were both afraid to sleep alone.[61]

Presumably Tyler was familiar with the attack on 'the hobgoblin-romance' in contemporary British periodicals.

Hugh Murray (whose pedestrian judgements reflect the commonly accepted opinions of several generations of literary critics) praised Mrs

Radcliffe as 'one of the most original and powerful writers of the present age', and recognized 'the superiority of her genius', but nevertheless confessed embarrassment at being so affected:

> The pleasure, indeed, which this affords, though natural, is not of a very high order; and, till her time, was confined chiefly to the nursery. Nor is it of a very improving nature, but, on the contrary, tends rather to weaken the mind, and make it liable to superstitious apprehensions.[62]

Another commentator on taste, while acknowledging that 'the ingenuity of Mrs Radcliffe cannot be too much admired', went on to express virulently sexist views about the general run of novels: 'they are the wretched productions of brain-sick females just escaped from boarding schools, or of miserable garretteers, who want genius and learning to gain a livelihood in any other department of literature'.[63] The imputation of vulgarity may have been the most wounding arrow obliquely striking at Mrs Radcliffe. Coleridge's pompous review of *The Monk* cast aspersions upon the entire Gothic genre:

> We trust . . . that satiety will banish what good sense should have prevented; and that . . . the public will learn, by the multitude of the manufacturers, with how little expense of thought or imagination this species of composition is manufactured. . . . Figures that shock the imagination, and narratives that mangle the feeling, rarely discover *genius*, and always betray a low and vulgar *taste.*[64]

Criticism of the vulgar classes is also a major feature of the many burlesques of Ann Radcliffe's works, whose highly mannered style was instantly recognizable and therefore easily parodied. The most horrifying incidents in *The Mysteries of Udolpho* were turned on their heads and lampooned in anti-Gothic novels such as Mrs F. C. Patrick's *More Ghosts!* (1798), as in this allusion to the black coverlet in the death chamber of Château-le-Blanc:

> 'Yes, Sir,' said the housekeeper, who had read the Castle of Adolphus, 'and I said that smugglers, for aught we know, might have come thro' a hole in your Honour's bed, and so have carried you off, and forced your Honour to turn smuggler in your old age, as such things have been.'[65]

William Beckford's burlesque novel *Azemia* (1797) – which he published under the pseudonym Miss Jacquetta Agneta Mariana Jenks, of Bellegrove Priory, Wales[66] – contains several unmistakable allusions to the romances of

Mrs Radcliffe, his 'justly-celebrated prototype'.[67] But Beckford acknowledges that the creator of the genre is herself beyond satire, and he pays a remarkable tribute to her genius:

> With less diffidence, though still with greater humility, I have ventured with shuddering feet into the World of Spirits, in modest emulation of the soul-petrifying Ratcliffe [sic] – but, alas!
>
> 'Within that circle none dare walk but she.'
>
> Even if I *had* ever had the fortune to see a *real natural ghost*, I could never describe it with half the terrific apparatus that fair Magician can conjure up in some dozen or two of pages, interspersed with convents, arches, pillars, cypresses, and banditti-bearing cliffs, beetling over yawning and sepulchral caverns. Her pictures,
>
> 'Dark as Poussin, and as Salvator wild,'
>
> can only be faintly copied; – to rival them is impossible.[68]

The *Monthly Mirror* considered *Azemia* to be 'the hasty production of a person of talent' and attributed it to Robert Merry (better known as 'Della Crusca').[69] The reviewer quoted from the 'burlesque imitation of a celebrated romance writer's descriptive passages', alluding of course to Ann Radcliffe. In 1804 Mrs Piozzi belatedly came across the *Monthly Mirror*'s 1797 review of the novel, herself believed the author to be Robert Merry, and noted that she was an object of his ridicule: 'His principal 'Spite was against Mrs Radcliffe as it appears – but he lash'd Cumberland & me en passant.'[70] If William Radcliffe similarly believed *Azemia* to be by Robert Merry, then Merry may be one of those writers of reputation whom he felt had inflicted injury upon his wife.

Full-scale burlesques based upon Radcliffe's works include *Rosella, or Modern Occurrences* by Mary Charlton (1799), *Romance Readers and Romance Writers* by Sarah Green (1810) and *The Heroine, or Adventures of Cherubina* by Eaton Stannard Barrett (1813) – which 'very much amused' Jane Austen: 'It is a delightful burlesque, particularly on the Radcliffe style'.[71] Barrett parodies and explicitly refers to *A Sicilian Romance*, *The Romance of the Forest*, *The Italian* and especially the set-pieces of *The Mysteries of Udolpho*. Parody becomes outright plagiarism as Barrett describes Lady Sympathina – 'Her face has the contour of a Madona [sic], and the sensibility of a Magdalen'[72] – and the tapestry in a Gothic apartment: 'worked in colourless and rotten worsted and depicting scenes from the Provençal Romances; – the deeds of Charlemagne and his twelve peers; the Crusaders, Troubadours, and Saracens; and the Necromantic feats of the Magician Jurl [sic]'.[73] Barrett's parody provides ample testimony to the abiding popularity of Ann Radcliffe's novels. His allusion to 'an amorous Verezzi, an insinuating Cavigni, an abandoned Orsino' (vol. 3, 178) takes it for granted that *Udolpho* is as fresh in the reader's mind as the day it was first published nearly twenty years earlier. The real damage was caused by the ease with which Radcliffean Gothic was transposed into lower-class vulgarity. For one who genuinely valued culture and the imagination as highly as did Mrs Radcliffe, the exposure of her genteel pretensions may have been more intolerable than any exposure of her stylistic weaknesses. What Ann Radcliffe conceived as epic romances became diminished as sentimental, sensational, vulgar – and Jacobin – novels.

Many connections were made between 'the Radcliffe school' and 'the Wollstonecraft school', linked via 'the Terrorist school'. Part of the attack against Ann Radcliffe was that her works fostered republican sympathies, a not wholly unfair view. The egalitarian individualism of her Dissenting background and her husband's politics can be detected in many of her characters. Vivaldi stands up to his father: 'there are some few instances in which it is virtuous to disobey' (*Italian*, 30). Ellena and Vivaldi celebrate their marriage by throwing open their estate to persons of all ranks: 'this entertainment was not given to persons of distinction only, for both Vivaldi and Ellena had wished that all the tenants of the domain should partake of it, and share the abundant happiness which themselves possessed' (413). Even the sublime mountain scenery of Ann Radcliffe's landscapes, her hallmark, was suspect. The Goddess of Liberty was 'the mountain Goddess' for Anna Laetitia Barbauld, who in her poem 'Corsica' (1773) portrayed gallant little Corsica valiantly striving against the French in order to achieve its freedom.

The notorious Marquis de Sade declared in 1800 that Ann Radcliffe's novels carried the torch of liberty, and that Gothic novels were 'the inevitable fruit of the revolutionary shocks felt by the whole of Europe'.[74] William Hazlitt explicitly associated Mrs Radcliffe with the disorder of the Revolution: her mouldering castles 'derived part of their interest, no doubt, from the supposed tottering state of all old structures at the time'.[75] As a woman with a Unitarian cultural background, her moral values were bourgeois, while her aesthetic–emotional values were on the side of revolution.[76]

For ten years from about 1792 'a very marked political reaction towards a conscious conservatism' increased in England.[77] Reformist movements virtually ground to a halt. Unitarians in particular were classed as Radical Dissenters, sympathetic to the principles of the French Revolution. Anything innovative or progressive was evidence of democratic tendencies. Other women besides Mrs Radcliffe were persuaded to stop writing. Mrs Barbauld's otherwise liberal brother Dr Aikin argued in *Letters for Literary Ladies* (1795) that women *dare not* sacrifice reputation to fame. The subjective individualism of the Gothic novel, and Ann Radcliffe's subversive novels in particular, became highly suspect to a society reacting against the excesses of freedom and desperately trying to re-establish the security of universal principles of behaviour.

Many modern critics share Marilyn Butler's view that Mrs Radcliffe was a revolutionary despite herself: 'While not supporting nor presumably consciously sharing the feminist ideological position, Ann Radcliffe pushes further than anyone yet the novel's technique for seeing the world through explicitly female eyes.'[78] However, Butler's assumption that she could not have been 'consciously' feminist is quite mistaken, as she does not take into account Ann Radcliffe's Dissenting background and her husband's acknowledged republican sympathies. As Janet Todd has pointed out, Mary Wollstonecraft, Mary Hays, Helen Maria Williams, Anna Laetitia Barbauld, Elizabeth Inchbald and Charlotte Smith 'were all nurtured in Dissenting circles'.[79] Moreover, most of these women came from specifically Unitarian circles: 'Priestley and Price and the Aikins, though they took care to act as if they spoke for Dissent in general, in fact spoke only for that small but influential minority which characteristically pretended to be Presbyterian while being in fact Arian and Unitarian.'[80] Mrs Barbauld, like other Unitarians with pro-French, pro-American and anti-slavery sympathies, positively rejoiced in the label 'Democrat' – and to this list we must add Ann Radcliffe, nurtured by her Unitarian uncles Thomas Bentley and Dr Jebb and their circles.[81]

As Janet Todd notes, the Dissenters' struggle for full political rights in the late eighteenth century, their stress upon the vernacular over the privileged discourse of Latin, their emphasis upon self-expression and the educational institutions they had to found because they were excluded by the two universities – all these emphases 'would help develop female political consciousness'. Excluded from many civil rights, it is not surprising that the Dissenters were especially attracted to the French Revolution.[82] If the facts of Ann Radcliffe's life had been better known to her contemporaries, a firm link between her and Mary Wollstonecraft would have been discovered in the person of Joseph Priestley, whom Hazlitt later dubbed 'the Voltaire of Unitarianism', a man notorious for his radical political and religious views, and a good friend of her uncle Bentley. The Birmingham riots that began on 14 July 1791 were provoked by the holding of a dinner to celebrate the second anniversary of the storming of the Bastille; Priestley's Old Meeting-House was the first meeting-house burned down by rioteers cheering for 'Church and

King'; this was then followed by the New Meeting-House, and the sacking of his house and the destruction of his books and scientific apparatus.[83] Priestley escaped death by hiding at his son-in-law's home, and then fled to London. During three days of riots some hundred Dissenters' homes were burned down. King George III, though he lamented the riots, was said to have been 'pleased that Priestley is the sufferer for the doctrines he and his party has instilled'.[84] Mrs Barbauld wrote to Dr Priestley on 29 December 1792: 'Burns not thy cheek indignant, when thy name,/On which delighted science lov'd to dwell,/Becomes the bandied theme of hooting crowds?'[85]

In the 1760s Priestley was one of the best friends of Ann Radcliffe's uncle Thomas Bentley, and also a friend of her uncle John Jebb. Jebb and Priestley were both attacked as avaricious hypocrites in the satire *Orpheus, Priest of Nature, and Prophet of Infidelity* (1781).[86] In the late 1780s, though now based in Philadelphia, Priestley was a prominent member of the circle of radical intellectuals and supporters of the American Revolution which included Thomas Paine, William Godwin and Mary Wollstonecraft. In the 22–24 April 1794 issue of the *London Chronicle*, which carries the earliest advertisement for *The Mysteries of Udolpho*, there is also an advertisement for Priestley's sermon 'The Use of Christianity, Especially in Difficult Times', which was the farewell discourse he preached at Hackney on 20 March 1792. He had tried to re-establish himself in London, but received little support. His wife had been distressed that feeling was running so high against them: 'so violent is the spirit of party, that it is hardly possible to get a servant, and those we have are exposed to so much abuse from the neighbours of the lowest class, that it is as much as they can bear'.[87] His sons emigrated to America in June 1793 and he followed in June 1794, a political/religious refugee. Priestley's *An History of Early Opinions Concerning Jesus Christ . . . Proving that the Christian Church was at First Unitarian* – a historical study of Scripture designed to prove that Christ was not divine and that atonement had no value – provoked outcry from pulpit and press when it was published in 1786 and was still generating controversy shortly before Ann Radcliffe's death.[88] Unitarianism and Rational Dissent were eclipsed by the rise of Evangelicalism and anti-French reaction. No successors replaced Price and Priestley, and most of the Unitarian academies had closed by 1800 through lack of students and financial problems. Many Unitarians themselves followed the inevitable trend of their beliefs: Arthur Aikin, after three generations of Unitarian ministers, in 1795 renounced Christianity and became a Deist, devoting himself to literature and science, and many chapels metamorphosed from Unitarianism to humanism.[89]

The Italian may not occupy the same shelf as *A Vindication of the Rights of Woman* (1792), but Ann Radcliffe is no more willing to accept the notion of female inferiority than Mary Wollstonecraft. In fact Ellena's defiance of the

Abbess is very nearly republican, articulated with as much resolution as Wollstonecraft could require (and expressed in terms no more stilted than those in Wollstonecraft's own novels):

> Fear, shame, and indignation, alternately assailed her; and the sting of offended honour, on being suspected, and thus accused of having voluntarily disturbed the tranquillity, and sought the alliance of any family, and especially of one who disdained her, struck forcibly to her heart, till the pride of conscious worth revived her courage and fortified her patience, and she demanded by whose will she had been torn from her home, and by whose authority she was now detained, as it appeared, a prisoner.
>
> The Abbess, unaccustomed to have her power opposed, or her words questioned, was for a moment too indignant to reply; and Ellena observed, but no longer with dismay, the brooding tempest ready to burst over her head. . . . (67–8)
>
> Her judgment approved of the frankness, with which she had asserted her rights, and of the firmness, with which she had reproved a woman, who had dared to demand respect from the very victim of her cruelty and oppression. (85)

A prominent member of the Wollstonecraft school did in fact suggest that Ann Radcliffe shared the ideology of women's rights. Mary Hays, whose first publication in 1792 defended the Dissenters' right to public worship, who knew Joseph Priestley and was a good friend of Godwin and a promoter of works by Godwin and Wollstonecraft, in the preface to her feminist novel *Memoirs of Emma Courtney* (1796) holds up Ann Radcliffe as one who celebrates rather than condemns passion, and accords her an important place among the developers of psychological analysis:

> The most interesting, and the most useful, fictions, are perhaps, such, as delineating the progress, and tracing the consequences, of one strong, indulged, passion, or prejudice, afford materials, by which the philosopher may calculate the powers of the human mind, and learn the springs which set it in motion – 'Understanding, and talents,' says Helvetius, 'being nothing more, in men, than the produce of their desires, and particular situations.' Of the passion of terror Mrs Radcliffe has made admirable use in her ingenious romances. – In the novel of Caleb Williams, curiosity in the hero, and the love of reputation in the soul-moving character of Falkland, fostered into ruling passions, are drawn with a masterly hand.[90]

I do not know if Mary Hays, through her friendship with Priestley, knew that Ann Radcliffe was herself part of the Unitarian Dissenting culture that was being characterized as republican and Jacobin, though fortunately the Establishment, and the mob, had little inkling of it. *Caleb Williams* was published a few weeks after *The Mysteries of Udolpho*,[91] so there was no direct influence between them, but many people perceived that they came from the same cauldron of revolutionary ideas. Allan Cunningham remarked that 'William Godwin is the Anne Radcliffe of moral order and social law'.[92] Godwin in his novel took the deterministic aspect of Hartley's theory of association to its logical conclusion, and he and many Unitarians were branded as 'necessitarians' (that is 'determinists', who believed that a necessary chain of events and circumstances dictated one's life and character). Miles suggests that 'As necessitarians were perceived as atheistical Jacobins intent on destroying Christian and "family" values, they tended to bring associationism into disrepute',[93] a suspicion probably increased when Hartley himself defended the French Revolution in 1794 in *Argument on the French Revolution and the Means of Peace*. Thus, 'Whereas "sensibility" was a universal language of aesthetic response in the pre-Romantic period, by 1800 it was being systematically reviled.'[94]

With plenty of quotations from Godwin, Wollstonecraft, Rousseau, Matthew Gregory Lewis and Thomas Holcroft, Mary Hays defends free thinking, free speaking and the right to celebrate a character who loves virtue while being enslaved by passion – in other words she has written a 'Jacobin' novel combining sexual freedom and radical politics. Mary Hays and Mary Wollstonecraft – and Ann Radcliffe – recognized in the ideology of sensibility a source of feminine power that justified its dangers, a kind of freedom within imprisonment.[95] Wollstonecraft has exactly the same ambiguous valuation of the 'distempered imagination' as Ann Radcliffe; while apparently condemning 'wild emotions', Wollstonecraft nevertheless excuses 'the romantic passion, which is the concomitant of genius', noting that the works of Shakespeare and Milton 'were not the ravings of imbecility, the sickly effusions of distempered brains; but the exuberance of fancy, that "in a fine phrenzy" wandering, was not continually reminded of its material shackles'.[96] By the end of the century the cult of sensibility was associated with Jacobinism and attacked by reactionary journals such as the *Anti-Jacobin Review*. In its issue of 9 July 1798 George Canning lambasts sensibility as the child of a sickly fancy, effeminacy, Frenchness, Rousseau, dramatic and un-English nature description and autobiographical self-obsession – *all of which* could apply to the trio of Mary Wollstonecraft, Mary Hays and Ann Radcliffe.[97]

References to Ann Radcliffe in the prefaces of novels by women, as in Hays's *Emma Courtney* and other examples noted above, have not been accorded sufficient notice by modern feminist critics. The key position occupied by Burney in inspiring the ambition of women writers in the 1780s was taken by Ann Radcliffe in the 1790s. She was a pivotal figure in the developing battle between men and women for recognition as novelists, and the very name of Ann Radcliffe in the hands of women writers became a metonym for the equal genius, if not superiority, of female novelists. For literary men to belittle the efforts of literary women – as they did increasingly from the late 1790s – it would become necessary to denounce specifically the work of Ann Radcliffe. Women writers could not be pigeonholed once again within the limits of the pathetic rather than the sublime without dealing with the Radcliffe anomaly. Mrs Radcliffe's name was repeatedly linked with the Amazons of the age, even when she was mentioned, by her admirers and apologists, as an exception to the rule. Mathias, who had been unstinting in his praise of her in *The Pursuits of Literature*, was stung into reactionary caution by Godwin's revelation of Wollstonecraft's seemingly licentious private life in the *Memoirs of the Author of a Vindication of the Rights of Women* (November 1798), which Mathias called 'a manual of speculative debauchery'. Like most men, Mathias hated the modern Minervas and Bellonas of French revolutionary thought:

> the poetry of Mrs Charlotte Smith, and the sombrous fancy and high-wrought imagery of Mrs Radcliffe, cannot be mentioned without admiration. But when female writers *forget the character* and delicacy of their sex; when they take the trumpet of democracy, and let loose the spirit of gross licentiousness, moral and political, in contempt of those laws, which are their best shield, and of that religion, which has invariably befriended and protected them; the duty which is owing to the defence of our country, and of all female virtue, comfort, and happiness, calls for strong animadversion.[98]

The Revd Richard Polwhele, in direct response to the Wollstonecraft *Memoirs* and in support of Mathias, published his virulently antifeminist poem 'The Unsex'd Females' (1798), attacking Wollstonecraft, 'whom no decorum checks', Mary Hays, Mrs Barbauld, Mary Robinson, Charlotte Smith, Ann Yearsley, Helen Maria Williams, Angelica Kaufman, Emma Crew – and Ann Radcliffe's spirited aunt Ann Jebb. (Incidentally, Wollstonecraft and Mrs Jebb share company among the subscribers to Ann Batten Cristall's *Poetical Sketches*, 1795.) Like Mathias, Polwhele specifically excluded Mrs Radcliffe from this Freedom-fired band, and included her instead among the praiseworthy women inspired by a particularly *female* genius, along with Montague, Carter, Chapone, Seward, Piozzi, Beauclerk, Burney and Hannah More.[99] Polwhele was a friend of Anna Seward and called her attention to the poem, a commendatory passage from which was quoted in a short biography of Seward in 1804, as evidence of Seward's virtue.[100] In marked contrast, no reference to Polwhele's poem would be made in Ann

Radcliffe's biography. Mrs Radcliffe cannot have relished her name being drawn into the debate at all, certainly not to be held up as an opponent of female freedom – an adversary to her own aunt.

Polwhele sent the poem to his friend John Whitaker who dutifully prepared a review for the *Anti-Jacobin*, which concluded with a rousing appeal to nationalism: 'we are happy to see one of the first poets of the day . . . employing his poetical talents at this awful crisis of Church and State, in vindication of all that is dear to us as Britons and as Christians'.[101] Lengthy excerpts from his poem were reprinted in New York in 1800, with a preface upon 'impious Amazons'.[102] Polwhele's correspondence with his cronies in the literary and Anglican establishment provides ample evidence of the conspiracy to suppress the radicalism (and 'Methodist' individualism) of the 1790s, and to put women writers in their proper place.

The new conservatism reinforced the view that in a woman, superiority of talent evidenced imprudence of conduct. Most of the women who wrote during the Romantic age were revolutionary only in the single respect of insisting upon equality between men and women.[103] Any woman who devoted herself more to writing than to marriage and children was dubbed a virago. Most of the attacks upon the Terrorist School were blatantly sexist attacks upon women, who were viewed as interlopers on a male playing-field:

Ye female scribes! who write without a blot,
'Mysterious Warnings' of – the Lord knows what;
O quit this trade, exert your proper skill,
Resume the needle, and lay down the quill.[104]

The Revd Caleb Colton recognized that *The Mysteries of Udolpho* and *The Romance of the Forest* were 'the two mightiest efforts of a female pen', in effect describing Ann Radcliffe as a virago; he would not grant such masculine goals to Hannah Cowley, whose poetry he praised specifically because it was feminine poetry, and whom he advised not to attempt anything epic:

Such mighty deeds transcend a woman's pen,
The rage of combat is a theme for men;
As soon her hand might rule the scythed Car,
As *justly* paint th'infuriate scenes of War.
In the light sock with sportive ease she treads,
Or graceful follows where fair Burney leads;
Or, with the Enchantress from the Tuscan cave,
Whence wizard Bards oft charm'd their Arno's wave,
Seeks, with the hurried step and gaze of fear,

Udolpho's turrets, and the forest drear;
But let her not attempt Ulysses' bow,
Nor rashly strive Achilles' lance to throw.[105]

This remarkable downgrading of the female writer is nowhere better seen than the shift from William Duff's 1767 *An Essay on Original Genius* to the same author's 1807 *Letters on the Intellectual and Moral Character of Women*, the latter work being a reactionary attack on Wollstonecraft's 'contumacious spirit of a combatant'. Jacqueline Howard sums up the transition:

> In an emphatic delimiting of his earlier democratic study of original genius, he downgraded the quality of imagination in women to being 'more gay and sprightly than in men', but 'less vigorous and extensive'. Moreover, he was now careful to tell women that they had no prior claim to that 'power of deep musing thought, and that sublime melancholy which is the inseparable concomitant of genius'. With such firm position of the capacities of 'female genius', it is no accident that by 1818, the year of publication of Mary Shelley's *Frankenstein*, genius had come to be closely associated with the male Romantic poet, who took upon himself a God-like role – as 'legislator' for mankind.[106]

The two adjectives most frequently applied to Ann Radcliffe were 'genius' and 'ingenious', both masculine terms. She herself had applied the term 'genius' to her heroines, and her most admiring critics called her a 'genius'. Those critics who did not quite like to admit her equality with men called her 'ingenious', and by her death the term 'genius' had been reclaimed to apply mainly to men. Like many of the viragos, she invaded the masculine preserve by staking out her claim to an unfettered imagination. In the first collected edition of her novels after her death, she is cited as having struck a blow for freedom and feminism:

> In nothing, perhaps, is the contrast between the present and preceding ages more striking, than in the character of British females, who, in our times, have burst those boundaries which the 'lords of the creation' had fixed, and boldly contested with them in the fields of Literature. . . . It has, however, been reserved to the present age for woman to maintain her just rank in the creation; to exchange the distaff for the pen; and to wield the latter with as much force, and as much elegance, as had ever been done by the other sex.[107]

Mrs Radcliffe was one of the women responsible for this sea change in the rights of literary women. She excelled 'in wielding the magic wand, and creating regions of her own, where she might rove "a chartered libertine"'.[108]

One last candidate for those novelists who attempted to push Ann Radcliffe from the field is T. J. Horsley Curties, who readily acknowledged his indebtedness to her in the preface to *Ancient Records, or, The Abbey of Saint Oswythe*, published by William Lane's Minerva Press in 1801. He even bragged that both this novel and its predecessor *Ethelwina, or The House of Fitz-Auburne* (1799)

> owe all their story to the imagery of, perhaps, a too heated imagination. Its mysteries – its terrific illusions – its very errors must be attributed to a love of Romance, caught from an enthusiastic admiration of *Udolpho*'s unrivalled Foundress. – He follows her through all the venerable gloom of horrors, not as a kindred spirit, but contented, as a shadow, in attending her footsteps.[109]

Curties observed that this species of romance had been 'feebly attacked' of late, and he protested that novelists should be allowed to mine their subterranean caverns unmolested. He then shamefully stabs his mentor in the back, by asserting that female novelists ought to behave like proper ladies and cease writing Gothic fiction altogether, leaving the field open to him and other male writers:

> Ought the female Novelist, in order to display a *complete* knowledge of human nature, to degrade that delicate timidity, that shrinking innocence which is the loveliest boast of womanhood in drawing characters which would ruin her reputation to be acquainted with? – Ought she to describe scenes which bashful modesty would blush to conceive an idea, much less avow a knowledge of? – Oh no! let the chaste pen of female delicacy disdain such unworthy subjects; – leave to the other sex a description of grovelling incidents, debased characters, and low pursuits: – there is still a range wide and vast enough for fanciful imagination; but when female invention will employ itself in images of the grosser sort, it is a fatal prediction of relaxed morals, and a species of – at least – LITERARY PROSTITUTION.[110]

So there we have it: Mrs Radcliffe as a whore – the basic insult by which men regained the throne of the novel in the nineteenth century.

T·H·I·R·T·E·E·N

The Gothic Tourist

——— • ———

In February 1802 William Radcliffe's newspaper the *English Chronicle (or, Universal Evening Post)* merged with another respected paper and was renamed the *English Chronicle and Whitehall Evening Post*,[1] under which name it continued until 1843.[2] With a reputation for good news-gathering, through a large network of correspondents, the paper achieved a substantial circulation at home and was distributed on the Continent.[3] William Radcliffe was proud to be associated with the newspaper, which accordingly was allowed some prominence in Talfourd's memoir. There is no evidence to confirm a report that at a later date Radcliffe also became part proprietor and editor of the *Morning Herald* – a claim contained in a farrago of nonsense including the statements that he 'renounced his employment in our embassy in Italy' in order to enter journalism, that he began editing in 1762 (two years before his birth!) and that he employed Edmund Burke on his staff.[4]

In their leisure time Mr and Mrs Radcliffe took up with enthusiasm the middle-class fashion for excursions to coastal resorts that began during the closing decade of the eighteenth century.[5] For the middling classes the Gothic Tour of Southern England substituted for the Grand Tour of the Continent. Mrs Radcliffe's pleasure in simply going for a ride is documented by the only extant letter from her:

My Dear Miss Williamson,

The carriage is at door, and I have only time to say, that the books are arrived, and that we shall have great pleasure in seeing you on Wednesday. Pray come early, that we may have a ride.

Sincerely Yours,
A. Radcliffe[6]

The letter is undated, and could have been written any time after her marriage. I do not know who Miss Williamson is, and it is impossible to speculate on the circumstances of the letter. All we can extract from it is evidence of good spirits and a pleasure in books and travelling.

Talfourd explains that Mrs Radcliffe particularly enjoyed 'unbroken leisure and frequent travelling; and, as her income was increased by the death of relatives, she retained the same plan of living, only extending its scale of innocent luxury'.[7] This suggests that she was a frequent traveller *before 1797*, when she first inherited money, from her aunt Elizabeth. Mrs Radcliffe did not record her travels before 1794, so we do not know what sights visited earlier might have had an influence upon *The Mysteries of Udolpho*. But from various asides in the *Journey* we can deduce that prior to 1794 she visited Oxford (53), Nottingham (84) and Canterbury (159). In her journal describing a holiday in 1800 the ruined towers of Pevensey Castle remind her of Newark Castle, for which no visit is recorded.[8] Newark Castle, on the banks of the Trent in Nottinghamshire, is noted for its towered gatehouse, and is one of the castles possibly seen prior to the creation of Udolpho.

Mrs Radcliffe was a keen enthusiast for seaside holidays, almost certainly long before her enjoyable trip to the seaside village of Schevening near The Hague (*Journey*, 46–7). The first trips recorded in her journals published by Talfourd, which date from 1797, are to the Kent coast. She notes that Sandgate Castle is 'built low like Sandwich castle': presumably therefore she had previously visited the east coast of Kent – Deal, Sandwich, Ramsgate, Margate. Talfourd says that 'she was extremely partial' to Dover on the south coast; although only two visits to Dover are recorded, Talfourd's testimony, and undated posthumous poems which feature Dover and Shakespeare's Cliff, indicate that she visited it frequently from an early date. I would suggest that Dover Castle may have provided the inspiration for massive castles on the sea in her earliest novels. During the period 1770–90 Dover Castle was not yet encroached upon by houses creeping up the hill; as illustrated in *Buck's Antiquities* it is an exceedingly romantic castle with a large gateway on the top of a hill at the edge of the sea, which could well have been the model for the castle of Athlin on its Scottish loch, or the castle in *A Sicilian Romance* with its terrace overlooking the straits of Messina.

Mrs Radcliffe's trips concentrated on the broad valley of the Medway, popularized by Samuel Ireland's *Picturesque Views on the River Medway* and *Picturesque Views on the River Thames*. She and her husband made two holidays each year, lasting ten to fourteen days, usually to the seaside, and she kept a travel journal for each of these, which she read for the amusement of her husband. She always took numerous books with her on these trips, probably collections of English poetry and the latest memoirs, and guidebooks such as Hassell's *Picturesque Rides and Walks, with Excursions by Water, Thirty Miles Round the British Metropolis* (1817). When Talfourd began editing her posthumous works, he was impressed more by these journals than by the unpublished poetry or fiction, according to his friend Mary Russell Mitford: 'Mr Talfourd says that by far the finest things he has seen of hers are her manuscript notes on different journeys in England – simple, graphical, without a single word to spare – and with a Cobbett-like power of putting a scene before your eyes. Some few of these will be incorporated in the Memoirs, but not nearly all.'[9]

The £50 left to Ann Radcliffe by her aunt Elizabeth Oates, who died in the summer of 1797, was hardly enough to have 'freed' her, though she may have used the bequest to finance a trip to the seaside that year. The first journal from which Talfourd took excerpts recorded details of a trip to Dover in September 1797.[10] This first trip may serve as a paradigm of all of her trips, and I shall not record the details of all of them. The Radcliffes began their tour on 1 September – just a few days after their dinner for Giuseppe Marchi. As they descended towards Rochester she was struck by the 'solemn appearance of the castle, with its square ghastly walls and their hollow eyes, rising over a bank of the Medway, grey and massive and floorless; nothing remaining but the shell'. She usually describes castles more enthusiastically than cathedrals or churches. The couple made their way in the gig through the long narrow streets of Rochester, then climbed the steep hill that gives magnificent views over Chatham and its busy docks. She recognized one of the sloops as one they had seen sailing on the Thames by Greenhithe – Mrs Radcliffe was something of a ship-spotter.

They stayed overnight in Sittingbourne, and on the following day set out for Canterbury, whose cathedral 'looked very tall and solemn, like a spectre of ancient times, and seemed to hint of what it had witnessed'. There is no mention specifically of visiting the cathedral, but on a trip to Winchester Cathedral in 1798 she refers to the impression of the immense length of Canterbury Cathedral that one gains especially from inside. After dinner they proceeded to Dover over Barham Downs, noting the 'rich little valleys' and the 'noble mansions and parks' on the rising grounds. The next day they climbed to a fortified point below Dover Castle:

> The most grand and striking circumstances, as we stood on the point, were –
> the vast sea-view – the long shades on its surface of soft green, deepening
> exquisitely into purple; but, above all, that downy tint of light blue, that
> sometimes prevailed over the whole scene, and even faintly tinged the French
> coast, at a distance. Sometimes, too, a white sail passed in a distant gloom,
> while all between was softly shadowed; . . . the solemn sound of the tide,
> breaking immediately below, and answered, as it were, at measured intervals,
> along the whole coast; this circumstance inexpressibly grand; the sound more
> solemn and hollow than when heard on the beach below.

Such descriptions of distant sound and fine gradations of light occupy much space in all of her travel journals, and are mirrored in her imaginative writing. Mrs Radcliffe's travel journals rather resemble exercise books. She carefully records everything a responsible tourist ought to record, according due emphasis to details to be remembered afterwards, especially the most 'striking circumstances' and 'picturesque objects'. Hardly any human figures move against the scenic background. She seems especially to enjoy things seen and heard *at a distance*.

On 4 September they climbed Shakespeare's Cliff, and leaned over the railing to look down upon the precipice and the sea far below. At the very top the railing gave way and 'bushes of hawthorn, massed with yellow, alone fence the precipice. Putting our hands on the ground, we peeped over, ledge below ledge, abrupt down.' It is characteristic of Mrs Radcliffe that she always climbed to the very top of a precipice or turret in order to gain the sublimest view possible; like her heroines, if there was anything more to see, she was game to see it. The Radcliffes were energetic travellers. Late that afternoon they set off for Hythe, ten miles distant, along the high sea-cliffs, which they eventually reached in the deepening dusk, after passing through the narrow streets of Folkestone, noting en route the ancient round towers of Sandgate Castle and the grey towers and Gothic windows of Hythe's ancient church.

Ann Radcliffe's parents visited her in the summer of 1798, during a particularly hot, dry June, and William Ward died at Melina Place on 24 July. After making the arrangements, Ann accompanied her mother to Chesterfield to settle her with relations. Under her father's will, Edward Cheselden of Somerby, Leicester (whom William Radcliffe speculated was a nephew of the celebrated surgeon), and Revd William Brown of Burrough (son of his mother's sister Deborah) were appointed to hold his land and real estate at Houghton on the Hill, near Leicester, in trust 'to the use of my Daughter the wife of William Radcliffe Gentleman' for the term of her life. Subsequently, this would pass to William Radcliffe for the term of his life, and then to their children (this last provision was included as a standard clause by the solicitor, though perhaps William Ward had some faint hope that his daughter would have issue – she was still younger than his wife had been when their daughter was born), and then to Ann the wife of Edward Wilmot of Lansdown Court in Bath if she survived his daughter and son-in-law. His land and real estate in Bruntingthorpe alias Westrotes-war, ten miles directly south of Leicester, were left to his wife for her life, and to his daughter and son-in-law if they survived her. Ann Ward also received all his goods and chattels (including the house in Bath), and was made his sole executrix.[11] He was buried in the churchyard in Gray's Inn Lane, St Andrew's Parish, London.

In 1798 the Radcliffes made an excursion to Portsmouth and the Isle of Wight. The tour began on 20 September, two months after the death of her father, to which she does not refer. Deborah Rogers suggests that this trip was made 'Perhaps as a diversion from the grief caused by her father's death', and that the trip to the southern coast in 1800 was 'Perhaps again to escape feelings of grief' at her mother's death.[12] But the simple fact is that Mrs Radcliffe took her regular annual vacations as usual, and no specific motivation can be attributed to any particular holiday. We might expect sadness after such recent bereavement, but on the contrary her journal reveals a sense of freedom and exhilaration. Talfourd felt that 'she seems to have particularly enjoyed' this tour[13] – a tour in which Mrs Radcliffe appears to be quite 'normal', wholly without the Gothic trappings of her persona. From Portsmouth they sailed to the Isle of Wight, where they spent a day rambling. They planned to stay in Ryde, but the accommodation at the neat inn was so inadequate they decided to return in an open boat to Portsmouth. 'After taking a hasty dish of very good tea, went down a rough causeway, where many people were hurrying to the same boat, and such a crowd collected as alarmed me.' How ironic that a woman who could re-create the terrors of the Inquisition should recoil at the horrors of an overcrowded boat. 'A small party was, however, soon made up for a second boat; when, with little sails and two oars, we launched among the peaceful waters.' Distant lights on the ships appeared like glow-worms through the deepening evening, and they heard the 'faint and melancholy sweetness' of French horns coming from Monckton Fort. After landing, they went for a moonlight walk along the rampart, then supped and slept at the Fountain, 'after a day the most delightful of the whole tour'.

They returned to London via Winchester, where they visited the venerable cathedral. What especially caught Mrs Radcliffe's imagination was the altarpiece by Benjamin West, of *Lazarus Rising from the Dead*, and her description suggests a piety not found in the novels:

The face well expresses the wanness and sharpness of death; but it might have been much more descriptive of reviving life, beginning to steal upon the languor of death; and of surprize and joyful hope, on beholding our SAVIOUR. The attitude of Lazarus is indeed such, that he might be taken for a person dying rather than one returning to life. The countenance of our SAVIOUR is full of placid benevolence; but the action should have been more expressive of command – of command, without effort. The principal female figure, who supports Lazarus, is clear, beautiful and natural; she looks up to our SAVIOUR, with tears of awe and gratitude; but the grief and anxiety she has suffered are not yet entirely chased from her countenance by joy and thankfulness; their impression was too deep to be suddenly effaced, though the cause of them is removed. The faces of the spectators do not sufficiently speak astonishment, awe and adoration, except that of one, seen remotely and obscurely, as if pressing forward more fully to ascertain the fact.

Mrs Radcliffe's detailed strictures suggest that she shared William Gilpin's rather poor opinion of the painting, though she does not refer to his criticism in *Observations on the Western Parts of England* which appeared in the spring of 1798, and which she perhaps had not yet read. Gilpin disliked the composition, the colouring and the lack of varied expressions, and felt that the figure at the foot of Lazarus resembled nothing so much as *une femme accouchée*.[14] Mrs Radcliffe's critical judgement and vocabulary when dealing with paintings are limited to an evaluation of realism and the representation of emotions in portraits; comments on aesthetic structure and contrast are reserved for the natural landscape. It may strike us as odd that this painting does not prompt a reflection upon her father's death, as though that recent event was of little importance to her.

I believe that she must have visited the Isle of Wight well before this first recorded trip in 1798, possibly as early as 1790, when she may also have visited Netley Abbey near Southampton. One of the major, unmissable, sights on the island is Carisbrooke Castle, dating from the twelfth century. It is near Newport at the centre of the island, and we know that she travelled along the Newport road during a subsequent visit; indeed it was impossible not to do so. From the fact that Mrs Radcliffe does *not* describe this castle in any of her published journals, I infer that she had visited it on a previous occasion, and did not revisit it on her later trips. It is hardly credible that she would have gone to the Isle of Wight without visiting Carisbrooke Castle. The grated window high in the wall of the room in which Charles I was imprisoned would have been pointed out to tourists.[15] Mrs Radcliffe would have appreciated the story that among the small collection of books which consoled the King during his imprisonment were Tasso's *Jerusalem Delivered* and Spenser's *Faerie Queene*.[16]

The interior of the castle does not resemble that of Udolpho – indeed no castle or country house in England has the marble pillars and staircase or larchwood panelling that firmly tie Udolpho to the Apennines. But the exterior has a number of features that we might associate with the castle of Udolpho: a keep approached by a flight of seventy-one steps, with a decayed staircase leading to its summit, and, most notably, a pair of circular walls forming a double chamber at its centre – Emily's room in Udolpho is called a 'double chamber' (234), because passages are hollowed out of the thick walls surrounding it. The ruins of a guardhouse stand below, as well as the chapel of St Nicholas, which was erected in 1738 on the ruins of an ancient chapel, and extensive twelfth-century decayed ramparts. From 1790 to 1798 numerous paintings of the castle and its gateway were exhibited at the Royal Academy. Illustrations of the castle in the picturesque literature of the day are very impressive, and I believe that the great gateway almost certainly inspired the awesome portal of the castle of Udolpho – if only by way of prints in the shops.[17] The massive vaulted gateway, a little thirteenth/ fourteenth-century castle in itself, matches nearly exactly the entrance to Udolpho: a large (if not 'gigantic') gate flanked by two drum towers, embattled, 'united by a curtain, pierced and embattled also, below which appeared the pointed arch of an huge portcullis', with huge folding wooden doors. (The circular towers today lack overhanging turrets, but prints reconstructing the ancient form of the castle may have illustrated them.)

One feature of the castle that would have appealed to Mrs Radcliffe was the fact that for thirty years in the mid-thirteenth century it was ruled by a woman, the widowed Countess Isabella, and visitors today still climb the steps to the window seat she had built for herself in the wall of her private chamber, from which she surveyed the valley below, just as did Emily from her chamber in Udolpho.

No excursions are recorded for 1799, but in April Mrs Radcliffe went into the country for a prolonged period, due to the ill health apparently of her husband, of an unspecified nature. One of the lost opportunities for literary intercourse was her apparent decision – pleading her husband's ill health as an excuse – to spurn the advances of Mrs Carter in 1799.

Elizabeth Carter, friend of Dr Johnson, Hannah More, Elizabeth Montagu and many notables in the literary and intellectual world, was the archetypal *bas bleu*. Her brilliant translation of Epictetus remained unsurpassed for many years, but she was also good-natured and sensible. Like many of the late Augustans, she was sensitive to the appeal of romantic melancholy and sublime scenery, and she visited the gloomy ruins of Fountains Abbey and the solemn shades of Rippon Minster in 1781, when Ann Radcliffe was but a girl.[18] She had homes in South Lodge, Bath, and in Deal. She became an avid reader of novels in the 1790s, preferring romance to realism, though the work had to be moral. Her nephew and first biographer noted that 'Mrs Carter highly approved of many that have since been written by authors of considerable genius, as well as of strict morals, such as Mrs West and Mrs Radcliffe, and others who might be named; and she found the reading of such works a very pleasing relaxation from her severer studies.'[19] She wrote to Mrs Montagu in 1790: 'I have been reading with much pleasure the "Sicilian Romance". The language is elegant, the scenery exquisitely painted, and moral good, and the conduct and conclusion of the fable, I think, original. Have you read it? And do you know the name of the authoress? I do not.'[20] She correctly surmised that the author was a woman, and devoured Ann Radcliffe's other novels as they were published. Joseph Farington noted in his diary on 15 September 1794 that 'Lady B[eaumont] recd. a letter to-day from Mrs Carter, who expresses herself in a very strong manner in favour of the "*Mysteries of Udolpho*" and of the talents of Mrs Radcliffe, the author.'[21]

According to the testimony of her nephew, Mrs Carter disapproved of the novels of Charlotte Smith, and was partial to the novels of Mrs D'Arblay and Mrs West:

> But of all authors of this class, Mrs Carter thought most highly of Mrs Radcliffe, and was most delighted with the perusal of her Romances. The good tendency of all her works, the virtues of her principal characters, supported on the solid foundation of religion, the elegance of her style, and her accurate, as well as vivid, delineations of the beauties of nature, appeared to her such as to raise Mrs Radcliffe to a degree of eminence far superior to any writer of romance of the present day.[22]

Although Mrs Carter cultivated refined, knowledgeable, virtuous people rather than literary folk, she nevertheless made a special effort to become acquainted with Mrs Radcliffe. This would have been a great mark of distinction for the novelist, and ample testimony of her respectability, despite having been drawn into the widening whirlpool of the German school of horror. In April 1799 Mrs Carter wrote to Ann Radcliffe: 'If Mrs Radcliffe is not engaged, Mrs Carter will have the pleasure of calling upon her about twelve o'clock tomorrow morning.' This was sent with a covering letter from Henrietta Maria Bowdler from Bath, dated 18 April 1799:

> *Dear Madam,*
>
> *I venture to give you this trouble, at the request of Mrs Carter, whose admirable talents, and far more admirable virtues, are too well known to need any introduction from me. She very much wishes to have the pleasure of knowing you; and will deliver this letter, if she has the good fortune of finding you at home. As I am persuaded the acquaintance must afford mutual satisfaction, I could not refuse the request with which Mrs Carter honoured me; though it is made on the supposition of my having some degree of interest with you, to which I have no claim, except from the very sincere admiration I have ever felt for your talents, and the regard and esteem with which I am, dear Madam,*
>
> > *Your obliged and affectionate humble servant,*
>
> > *H. M. Bowdler*
>
> *P.S. If Mrs Carter does not deliver this letter herself, she will, I believe, take an early opportunity of waiting on you, with a very amiable friend of mine, Miss Shipley, who has promised to carry her in her carriage.[23]*

Henrietta Maria (Harriet) Bowdler (1754–1830) was the sister of the man who 'bowdlerized' Shakespeare's plays to make them less dangerous for young readers. Less of a prude than her brother, she was nevertheless an advocate of good works, and contributed to the education of the young with books such as *The Proper Employment of Time Talents and Fortune*. She was a very good friend of Anna Seward, and of Sarah Ponsonby and Eleanor Butler. She frequently wrote to the Ladies of Llangollen with Bath gossip, and in a letter written around 1809 she revealed that *The Mysteries of Udolpho* was one of her favourite, albeit less demanding, novels.[24]

Although the letter of introduction from Harriet Bowdler to Mrs Radcliffe makes no claim to intimate friendship between the two women, it nevertheless holds out the probability of some slight acquaintance. There are no other grounds for writing such a letter – an introduction from a total stranger would hardly be proper. Perhaps the two women met briefly when Mrs Radcliffe returned to Bath to help her mother arrange her affairs after the death of her husband. Miss Bowdler, like Mrs Radcliffe, led a sequestered life, being 'afflicted with a disorder which rendered her incapable of enjoying society'.[25] Mrs Carter's letter received a rather curt reply from the novelist:

Mrs Radcliffe is extremely sorry that an engagement to go into the country to-morrow, for some time, on account of Mr R's state of health, which is very critical, will deprive her of the honour intended her by Mrs Carter; for which she requests Mrs C. to believe that she has a full and proper respect.[26]

William Radcliffe had previously been unwell due to overwork, and this may refer to a recurrence of some frailty in his constitution. On the other hand, it may be a complete fabrication. I am not sure why Mrs Radcliffe may have wished to conceal the fact, but I suspect that the real reason why the Radcliffes left town was the critically declining state of health of her mother. Ann Oates Ward was so ill as to draft her final will on 4 April 1799, in Bath, and she would die on 14 March 1800, in Chesterfield. Mrs Radcliffe probably travelled to Bath on the day after writing her letter to Mrs Carter, and then brought her mother back to Chesterfield, which explains why a meeting between the two celebrated authors was impossible at the time. The stiff formality of her response is remarkable, nor did Mrs Radcliffe follow it up after her return to London.

Mrs Carter, not surprisingly, never renewed the request for an acquaintance, though she lived until 1806. Pennington in his 1807 memoir of Mrs Carter inadvertently implied that it was Mrs Carter who did not wish to know Mrs Radcliffe; immediately after praising the novelist, he went on to say that 'Of her, however, she had no personal knowledge, any more than of Mrs Smith; but she was well acquainted with Mrs D'Arblay, whose worthy and respectable father, Dr Burney, she had long known, and slightly with Mrs West, of whose character she thought as highly as she did of her works.'[27]

This implies that Mrs Carter did not think Mrs Radcliffe worthy of her acquaintance, and seems to rank her with the less reputable Charlotte Smith as opposed to the virtuous Mrs D'Arblay and Mrs West. The possible rebuff was exacerbated when Pennington went on to say that 'at no period of her life was Mrs Carter particularly anxious to be known to literary persons', that she herself did not enjoy being sought out on account of her literary reputation, and that she spurned to read works by writers whose characters betrayed 'the least tendency towards levelling and democratic principles'. Mrs Radcliffe, not unreasonably, found these remarks less than satisfying when she read them in 1807. She feared that they would be misconstrued by others as well, and it gave her some 'uneasiness' according to her husband. He was quite right to point out that 'the remark may be misunderstood to imply that Mrs Carter had rejected, or avoided, or would have rejected, or avoided, that acquaintance',[28] and he quite properly demonstrated that the case was just the opposite.

All of this was to create a mountain out of a molehill, but the incident nevertheless indicates the singular apprehensiveness of the novelist's sensibilities. It was an uneasiness which William Radcliffe remembered when he wrote his wife's obituary many years later, when he took the opportunity to publish the correspondence in order to set the record straight. After reading this correspondence in the 1824 obituary, Dr Pennington sent William Radcliffe 'a most handsome letter', presumably to reassure him that no such interpretation had been intended by his slightly careless remark.[29] We do not know if Pennington in turn objected to the impression created by William Radcliffe that his wife had rejected the acquaintance with Mrs Carter.

While Mrs Radcliffe was caring for her husband in the country, and possibly also her mother, society was busy speculating about whether she was the author of the latest sensational production, *The Plays on the Passions* (1798), published anonymously, and not discovered to be by Joanna Baillie until 1800. Baillie's series of sensational melodramas focused upon 'one strong, indulged, passion' as advocated by Mary Hays in the preface to *Emma Courtney* (in which she discussed Radcliffe and Godwin). *De Monfort*, the first in the series, representing the passion of hatred, owed many debts to Shakespeare, although Elizabeth Inchbald recognized that it was written to be read by someone who had studied dramas in books rather than in the theatre.[30] De Monfort, like many of Ann Radcliffe's villains, is a maniac distracted by a secret grief. The play is really a revenge tragedy, and its monks, nuns, Gothic chapels, heavy groans and especially the sensationalistic disclosure of the bloody corpse in the final scene remind one more of Lewis than Ann Radcliffe. But when Anna Seward first read *De Monfort* in June 1799 she thought instantly of Mrs Radcliffe, as she told her friend Revd Whalley:

The situations in the close are of soul-harrowing strength and horror. It appears indubitable that the sublime, though exceptional novel, Caleb Williams, was the origin of Mrs Radcliffe's design of writing plays illustrative of the passions, and the mischiefs that result from the absorbing dominion of any one of them . . . but it is most true what Mrs Jackson observes, that, in all Mrs Radcliffe's writings, attentive only to terrific effects, she bestows no care upon their causes, and rashly cuts the knot of probability which she seems to want patience to untie. One has heard of a labouring mountain bringing forth a mouse: In Mrs R.'s writings mice bring forth mountains.[31]

Seward also wrote to Miss Ponsonby, one of the Ladies of Llangollen:

My literary friend and correspondent, Mrs Jackson, whose taste is highly just and discriminating, also speaks of them [the *Plays on the Passions*] in a style which creates considerable predilection. . . . she says: 'Before their author was known, I observed so much of the power and defects of Mrs Radcliffe's compositions in these dramas, as to believe them hers; and I hear she owns them.'[32]

However, by October Seward was acknowledging to Revd Whalley that 'My literary friends now assert that they are not Mrs Radcliffe's; and, indeed, though the defects and merits of the plans and characters are each of her complexion, yet I always thought the masterly nature of several of the single speeches above her powers, as comparing them with her novels.'[33] And to another literary friend she wrote: 'The literary world now asserts that the Plays on the Passions are not Mrs Radcliffe's.'[34] It is not known if the Ladies of Llangollen eventually discovered the real author of *De Monfort* when Joanna Baillie made herself known later in 1800, or through an acknowledgement of mistaken identity from Miss Seward.

The rumour about Ann Radcliffe's authorship of these plays had been circulating very widely. During the first week of March 1799 Mrs Hester Lynch Piozzi, taking the waters in Bath, passed much time in a 'brilliant Constellation of agreable Companions' consisting of the Miss Mores, the Miss Lees, Mrs Jackson, Mrs Pennington, Miles Peter Andrews, Mrs Siddons and Mrs Whalley.[35] She remembered meeting with these literary friends at the Miss Lees's house in Bath, where they tried to decide if *De Monfort* was written by a man or a woman.[36] Mrs Piozzi maintained the minority view that the author was a woman. On 5 April she wrote to tell Penelope Pennington that Mrs Jackson's 'conjectures about the Play were right after all. Mrs Radcliffe owns herself Author, as Susan Thrale writes me word, and Jane de Montfort will come out immediately.'[37] Mrs Piozzi was not corresponding with Anna Seward at this date (though she did so later). On this occasion the news came direct from her daughter Susan, who was residing in London. But Susan had visited the Ladies of Llangollen, who perhaps had relayed to her the rumour communicated to them by Anna Seward, acting as intermediary for Mrs Jackson. Thus the rumour that began with Mrs Jackson was 'confirmed' by Mrs Jackson through an intermediary – the usual way that rumours are confirmed. The Ladies of Llangollen were probably also the source for the correction of the rumour, as Hester Lynch Piozzi wrote to Penelope Pennington on 29 May 1799: 'The intelligence concerning Mrs Radcliffe's having written that play on hatred seems to have been premature.'[38] It is likely that Mrs Piozzi would have conveyed this confirmatory intelligence to the Lees and their Bath circle as soon as she heard it. The fact that neither Mrs Piozzi nor the Miss Lees seem to have made any connection between Ann Ward and Mrs Ann Radcliffe during the circulation of this rumour incidentally confirms that they had never met her.

The elusive Eliza E. Jackson, the instigator of the rumour, was a friend of Seward's friend Revd T. S. Whalley. She lived in Bath from 1789 to 1791, and moved to London in 1792, but returned frequently to stay in Bath; Seward stayed with her in Bath in August 1791.[39] Mrs Piozzi revealed that she came from Jamaica (presumably the English plantation colony there), and that her husband had lost his life while saving his wife and children from a fire aboard a ship.[40] She was very plain, very sensible and extremely intelligent, 'greatly beloved & respected in many a Coterie of London & Bath'.[41] She had a heart attack ('the Palsy') in December 1791.[42] Anna Seward noted that early in life her hand was hopelessly injured in a mysterious accident. Her children included Henry, Thomas, another son and a daughter. At a slightly later date she resided in Weymouth and in Turville Court, Oxfordshire. She was living in Edinburgh when Seward last wrote to her in June 1806, and Walter Scott was to have visited her in 1807. She was the author of a comedy, and of *Dialogues on the Doctrine and Duties of Christianity, for the Instruction of the Young*, printed in Edinburgh in 1806. In the dedication and preface she signs herself 'E. E. Jackson'. The work owes a great deal to Hannah More's *Strictures on the Modern System of Female Education*, and an abundance of scriptural studies and sermons. The most interesting aspect of the book from our point of view is its list of subscribers. Among the lesser nobility we also find the names of the Lee sisters, Hannah More, Mrs Piozzi, Mrs Siddons, Miss Seward and 'Miss Oates, Lancaster' – one of Mrs Radcliffe's cousins. Ann Radcliffe may have been distressed by the intimation of a sort of family betrayal if Mrs Jackson's knowledge of her came through her relation. (She seems to have died around 1829 or 1830.)

It is probable that Mrs Jackson was acquainted with Henrietta Bowdler, who had tried unsuccessfully to introduce Mrs Carter to Mrs Radcliffe. The list of subscribers to the *Poems* (1799) of the Bath resident Mary Alcock included Thomas Bowdler, Miss Bowdler, Mrs H. Bowdler (three copies), Francis Jackson, Mrs Jackson and Miss Jackson (that is Mrs Jackson and her two children). In a prose-piece called 'The Scribbler' Mrs Alcock castigates the blasphemy and obscenity of *The Monk*, and the 'inundation of hobgoblin nonsense, of haunted castles, mysterious caverns, yawning graves, bleeding ghosts, &c.' and the dangerous tendency of such works upon young ladies who frequent the circulating libraries.[43] So this little coterie of literary ladies comprised a kind of conspiracy of ill will towards Mrs Radcliffe.

Mrs Radcliffe's mother Ann Oates Ward had prepared her will in Bath on 4 April 1799, though she was back in Chesterfield by the time of her death on 14 March 1800. The Radcliffes had given up Melina Place when they went 'into the country' – the poor rate assessment for 5 July 1799 records that they were 'Gone'.[44] On their return, they bought a new house at China Terrace, Lambeth. The colophon of the *English Chronicle* for 30 December 1799 to 1 January 1800 noted that the newspaper was 'Printed and Published by and for W. Radcliffe, no. 3, Catharine Street, Strand (also of China Terrace, Lambeth).' 'Ratcliffe' first appears in the rate assessment for 28 February 1800; the property they occupied was listed as 'Empty' at the assessment for 11 December 1799, so presumably they moved in during late December.[45] Their new home, No. 2 China Terrace, was a short distance southwest of their old home, facing the same open field. A large common lawn fronted the terrace of ten substantial brick houses, each containing five 'cheerful Bed Rooms', three sitting rooms, good domestic offices and a garden.[46]

In her will Ann Oates Ward expressed the wish to be buried 'in a devout plain way' in Chesterfield Church next to her parents and her sisters (unless she should die in London, in which case she would consent to be buried near her husband in the burying ground in Gray's Inn Lane belonging to St Andrews, Holborn). William Radcliffe is curiously unsure about the exact date of Ann Radcliffe's second and last visit to Chesterfield, 'in the latter end of 1799, or the beginning of 1800, when she went to visit her mother, who was very ill, and who died shortly afterwards'.[47] Relations between him and his mother-in-law were probably cool. Ann Oates Ward left £50 to her good friend and live-in companion Mary Ling, together with 'one half of my wearing apparel of every sort', and her watch and the tortoiseshell case for it, if she should still be living with her at the time of her death; to 'my Good freinds Mr and Mrs Fletcher of the Circus Bath' she left 2 guineas apiece to buy something in remembrance of her; to Mr and Mrs Brown (presumably Revd William Brown of Burrough, trustee of her husband's estate) 'for all their care and attention' she left a ring bearing her crest; to her cousin Avery

Jebb and his wife Amelia she left the £50 inherited from her sister Hannah Oates, and her fifty shares in the canal (one of Bentley's projects) and all the interest due since 1778; and to her cousin Mrs Ann Jebb and her daughter, and her cousin Catherine Hallifax, each a ring.

Her trustees were her cousin Joshua Jebb and George Bossley of Chesterfield (probably a solicitor rather than a friend, as a blank space was left for his first name). They were entrusted with the task of administering the rents of the leasehold and dwelling house at No. 22, Milsom Street, Bath, and the £2,000 left to her by her husband plus his estate in Leicester, in trust for her daughter Ann Radcliffe wife of William Radcliffe, 'notwithstanding her roventure and as if she were solo and unmarried'. Such property was to be for Ann Radcliffe's 'sole and separate use and benefit exclusive of the said William Radcliffe her husband who is not to intermeddle therewith nor shall the same be subject to his Control Debts or Engagements'.[48] Clauses granting 'sole and separate' use were being inserted in many legal contracts around this time, in response to pressures for female property rights, but Ann Oates Ward's will exhibits unusual precautions against her property falling into the hands of her daughter's husband; 'intermeddle' is not a lawyer's term. The benefits of such property were to pass in due course to Ann Radcliffe's children should she have issue, failing which they would pass to *the trustees and their issue* – under no circumstances were they to pass to the benefit of William Radcliffe.

Ann Oates Ward's apparent belief that her daughter's husband would expropriate his wife's property for his own use may illustrate a personal enmity towards her son-in-law, or a general distrust based upon experience with her own husband, or both. Ann Radcliffe may have been aware of her mother's feelings on this subject for some time, for they closely match the sentiments of Mme Montoni on the issue of matrilinear inheritance in *The Mysteries of Udolpho*. What are the reasons for this extraordinary clause? Ann Radcliffe's parents would have known William as a young man who had experienced some difficulties at the *Gazetteer* and who had benefited from his wife's substantial royalties at a time when he may have been out of work. Perhaps his initial failure in getting on in the world, and his lack of gratitude at being helped by his wife, and perhaps even by his parents-in-law, explain why Ann's mother was so strict about her legacy being solely for the use of her daughter.

Ann Radcliffe also inherited all her mother's household furniture, books, silver plate and china, and all other goods and chattels.[49] This legacy, together with the property inherited from her father, left her agreeably affluent, but it is a mistake to suggest that Ann Radcliffe 'stopped writing for publication altogether when her mother's will made her financially comfortable'.[50] The main drawback to this motive is that it was never her purpose or need to write for money in the first place. Hers are not the kind of novels turned out on Charlotte Smith's production line. She wrote to express herself, or at least to amuse herself and her husband, and such motivation would persist despite her mother's will.

In July 1800 Mr and Mrs Radcliffe made another tour of the south coast, for a fortnight.[51] They visited Arundel Castle, whose lawns and woods exhibited 'grandeur, grace and beauty united'. At Worthing, she enjoyed watching the Brighton day-trippers: 'Dined at a pleasant hotel near the beach, with a grass-plot before it. Amused with numerous parties, who had come from Brighton in sociables, chariots and gigs, to dine, and who exhibited themselves on the grass-plot under our window.' Later, on a walk between Alfriston and Seaford on 19 July as the sun set, she reflected on the death of her parents:

> The silent course over this great scene awful – the departure melancholy. Oh God! thy great laws will one day be more fully known by thy creatures; we shall more fully understand Thee and ourselves. The GOD of order and of all this and of far greater grandeur, the Creator of that glorious sun, which never fails in its course, will not neglect us, His intelligent, though frail creatures, nor suffer us to perish, who have the consciousness of our mortal fate long before it arrives, and of HIM. He, who called us first from nothing, can again call us from death into life.
>
> In this month, on the 24th of July, my dear father died two years since: on the 14th of last March, my poor mother followed him: I am the last leaf on the tree! The melancholy greatness with which I was surrounded this evening, made me very sensible of this.

This strikes the most pious note of religious awe in Ann Radcliffe's writings, with an oddly despairing hope similar to that of Dr Johnson. Her sense of loss was perhaps triggered by the cumulative effect of losing both parents in a period of two years (and her aunt Elizabeth in 1797), coupled with her own childlessness, but the passage also illustrates a struggle to understand her own over-apprehensive temperament and morbid sensitivity.

The journey included Eastbourne, Beachy Head and Hastings, full of what Talfourd calls 'her little adventures', then a return along the coast to Dover, 'to which place she was extremely partial', and finally back to London.

In the autumn of 1800 Mrs Radcliffe spent a fortnight in Littlehampton, returning via Haslemere. Talfourd seems to imply that this trip was made without her husband; she probably made arrangements to stay in the Beach House where she had stayed with her husband the previous July. This seems to have been a sequestered reading holiday, perhaps prompted by a desire to follow in the footsteps of one of her favourite poets:

This is the country, from which Collins drew his first ideas, and fed his early taste for the wild and the grand.

> 'O! vales and wild-woods, would he say,
> In yonder grave your Druid lies.'   COLLINS

In the journal she also quotes from Goldsmith ('Where wilds immeasurably spread') and Shakespeare's *Cymbeline* ('Those high, wild hills and rough uneven roads'), which suggests that she had come well equipped with books to reinforce the sublime scenery.[52]

For three or four weeks from 27 September 1801 the Radcliffes made a tour of Southampton, Lyndhurst, Lymington and the Isle of Wight.[53] These travel notes are extensive and attractive, full of enthusiasm and energy. On the morning ride from Southampton to Lyndhurst she 'longed for the speed of a stag to bound along these lawns and endless forest glades'. They sailed in the packet to Yarmouth on the Isle of Wight and stayed in what is now the George Hotel, adjacent to Henry VIII's castle, on the site of King John's House, built as a residence by Admiral Holmes, who was appointed Governor of the island in 1688 following the Glorious Revolution.

On this holiday she was equipped with a telescope, which she used not only to search out the seabirds seated on their splintered summits and ledges, but to locate the cheerful white houses peeping out of the forest, the large white house of Mount Royal and Lyndhurst steeple. They made a sublime excursion to the Undercliffe and then walked the five miles to Steephill on 6 October: 'such a scene of ruin, as we never saw before. . . . a Druid scene of wildness and ruin'. The obligatory contrast of the Beautiful along the way was provided by 'the romantic and sweet village' of St Lawrence. At Steephill they stayed at the New Inn at the foot of St Boniface Downs. They would return to this site eleven years later. (The Bowdlers were holidaying on the Isle of Wight at the same time as the Radcliffes, but no meeting is recorded.[54])

It is clear that Ann Radcliffe had recently been reading some of the theoretical literature upon the Beautiful, the Picturesque and the Sublime, including specifically William Gilpin's *Observations on the Western Parts of England . . . to Which Are Added, a Few Remarks on the Picturesque Beauties of the Isle of Wight* (1798), and had been thinking about her own position in the aesthetic debate. She preferred the 'animated and beautiful scenery' of Ryde to the 'wild and romantic, rather than grand' scenery of the Undercliffe: 'Upon the whole, I prefer rich beauty [the Beautiful] to wild beauty [the Picturesque], unless accompanied by such shapes of grandeur as verge upon the sublime.' On the way to Lymington she had noted Gilpin's home near Boldre (where he was the vicar), and she was reminded again of the theorist of the Picturesque when she reached Salisbury and enjoyed a moonlight view of the 'sublime Cathedral, with its pointed roofs and its pinnacles and its noble spire. How could Mr Gilpin prefer a tower to it!'[55] She did nevertheless agree with Gilpin's description of the elegant Gothic clusters of the pillars, 'when Saxon heaviness first began to give way'.[56] Gilpin's *Observations* was obviously her vade-mecum on this trip. It would seem that she was preparing herself for a new novel.

F·O·U·R·T·E·E·N

Olden Times

Almost as if in deliberate reaction to her chauvinist critics, who felt that she had been led astray into German horrors and French Jacobinism, Ann Radcliffe's next novel was to be firmly rooted in English soil, its focus shifted from Catholic Italy to feudal England. Probably at the persuasion of her husband, who had written scholarly books, she turned away from the 'vasty deep' of the imagination towards the archaeology of historical fact.

The autumn tour of 1802 focused upon architectural antiquities, as though she were gathering the cultural details to match the scenic material gathered in the previous year. The couple visited Leicester and Warwick, and returned via Woodstock and Oxford, and Mrs Radcliffe's journals were filled with descriptions of 'great minuteness' regarding Kenilworth Castle, Warwick Castle and Blenheim Palace.[1] The painstakingly detailed notes demonstrate that guidebooks had been carefully consulted. Talfourd's short extracts show some typical Radcliffean concerns, such as the melancholy association between human mortality and the great and solemn ruin of Kenilworth, which

> spoke at once to the imagination, with the force and simplicity of truth, the nothingness and brevity of this life – 'generations have beheld us and passed away, as you now behold us, and shall pass away: they thought of the generations before them, as you now think of them, and as future ages shall think of you. We have witnessed this, yet we remain; the voices that revelled beneath us are heard no more, yet the winds of Heaven still sound in our ivy.'

Portions of this description, and of the succeeding description of Warwick Castle, were reproduced almost verbatim in the Introduction to *Gaston de Blondeville*. The possibility that she regularly drew upon her travel journals for her novels makes the absence of any earlier journals all the more frustrating. Warwick Castle was little more than a theatrical backdrop for literature – 'Before those great gates and underneath these towers, Shakespeare's ghost might have stalked; they are in the very character and spirit of such an apparition, grand and wild and strange.'[2] But the ruins of Kenilworth Castle particularly struck her imagination, and she studied its history soon after returning from her visit.

According to Talfourd she wrote *Gaston de Blondeville* in the winter of 1802/3. Talfourd, prompted by William Radcliffe, suggested that she wrote it merely to amuse herself and her husband, and then laid it aside, not intending it for the press, 'so disinclined had she become to publication'.[3] More correctly, as far as we can determine, the novel was not *withheld*, but *withdrawn* from publication. It was actually in the hands of a publisher and on the verge of being published, but was suddenly withdrawn (or possibly rejected) late in 1803. On 19 November 1803 the Philadelphia literary magazine the *Port Folio* published a report from one of its correspondents: 'It has been rumoured that Mrs Radcliffe has for some time been engaged in the composition of a Romance, of a very superior cast. We should be glad if any of our reading friends could ascertain the fact.'[4] Sir Walter Scott, referring to *St Alban's Abbey*, wrote in 1824 that 'we have some reason to believe, that arrangements were at one time almost concluded between Mrs Radcliffe and a highly respectable publishing-house, respecting a poetical romance, but were broken off in consequence of the author changing or delaying her intention of publication'.[5] In January 1826 the *Museum of Foreign Literature and Science* suggested, more or less, that the novel was withheld because Ann Radcliffe had had a nervous breakdown:

> Mr Colburn will shortly publish a Romance by Ann Radcliffe, author of 'The Mysteries of Udolpho' etc. This announcement will, no doubt excite the greatest interest among all classes of the 'reading public,' who will eagerly welcome a new and genuine work by the 'Great Enchantress,' whose pen has apparently been so long idle. The forthcoming Romance would have been published some years ago, had not the Author's nervous temperament, arising from the state of her health (which declined soon after the work in question was finished) made her hesitate to plunge again in the bustle of literary competition; and being in affluent circumstances, she could afford to indulge in the leisure and privacy she so much loved.[6]

It is hard to know if the *Museum* had access to private, accurate information; though published in Philadelphia and New York, it announced the forthcoming publication of her posthumous works even before they were publicized in England. The passage about her health was picked up for a review of *Gaston* in May 1826, but the English reviewer tellingly modified the reference to Mrs Radcliffe's 'nervous temperament' to 'delicate temperament'.[7] Talfourd's friend Mary Russell Mitford may have been the source of the information which was passed to Philadelphia in 1826; she had numerous American correspondents ever since the popular success of her book *Our Village* in America, and she was under less constraint to be tactful than Talfourd, the official biographer.

In his memoir Talfourd reports the very curious fact that several years after *Gaston* was written, Mrs Radcliffe,

> having forgotten many of the incidents, perused it with nearly the same interest as if it had been the production of a stranger. It was again laid aside; and in the latter part of life she repeated the experiment, but it did not absorb her attention as before, the former perusal having stamped the contents on her memory.[8]

The feeling that the novel was the work of a stranger might well be the result of experiencing a nervous breakdown immediately after writing it. Talfourd mentions no holiday tours during 1803 or 1804, an unusual gap in her journals which might be accounted for by illness (the other gap was 1799, when her mother and possibly her husband was ill). Some mental crisis may well have occurred at this time, not helped by the rumours of madness thrown out by writers in the preceding few years.

A weakening of Ann Radcliffe's imagination is certainly evident in her last novel. The narrative of *Gaston de Blondeville, or The Court of Henry III Keeping Festival in Ardenne* wholly lacks the energy and originality of her previous novels. It is little more than a costume romance, a historical pageant full of pseudo-medieval diction and archaeological tableaux. There are no surprises, no complications, no mystery, even though it contains genuinely supernatural events and the only real ghost in Radcliffe's work. Montague Summers rightly detects 'a certain languor in the narrative, as though it had been written with effort which had not quite succeeded'.[9] The attempt at authenticity is laboured: the author has read too much. Within the narrative itself there are references to the ballad of the Giant of Cornwall, the Chronicle of Charlemagne and re-creations of Provençal lays; tapestries depicting the stories of Troy, Priam, Queen Hecuba and Richard Coeur de Lion's deeds in Palestine; ancient authors such as the Venerable Bede and Marie de France; and even a direct quotation from Matthew of St Alban's description of the marriage of the Scottish King Alexander to King Henry's daughter. An analysis of the notes appended to the romance by William Radcliffe establishes the sources, often from volumes printed by the Society of Antiquaries.[10] Unfortunately Sir Walter Scott's *Kenilworth* was published five years before *Gaston de Blondeville*, and of course covered the identical subject; some reviewers found Ann Radcliffe's novel tiresome, because it was mistakenly considered to be a weak imitation of Scott's[11] – though its composition had *preceded* Scott by a dozen years.

To what extent was Ann Radcliffe 'the author' of *Gaston de Blondeville*? One of the first reviewers said he would not have believed she was the author had that fact not been authenticated by her husband.[12] Mrs Radcliffe herself was unable to recognize it as her own work when she read it at a later date. The tale of Gaston de Blondeville (considered separately from the Introduction, discussed below) possesses not a single hallmark of the author's hand. My own impression is that the narrative was a joint effort between husband and wife. William Radcliffe was obviously at his wife's elbow for every antiquarian paragraph of the novel.

Talfourd notes that Mrs Radcliffe never wholly abandoned the idea of publication, and occasionally reconsidered *Gaston*'s merits. The possibility that she may have revised it has not been raised by Radcliffe scholars. Parts of the Introduction – which *is* recognizably by Ann Radcliffe – were certainly written long *after* 1802/3, a fact not previously noticed. It contains a digression on the unique raised central hearth in the hall at Penshurst (44), which she did not visit until 1811, when she described it in her journals. Even more conclusive is the passage describing Windsor Castle Terrace, which is a reworking of the description written in her journal which Talfourd dates to sometime between 1812 and 1815, when she stayed in Windsor:

From the *Journal*:

We stood in the shade on the north terrace, where a platform projects over the precipice, and beheld a picture perfect in its kind. The massy tower at the end of the east terrace stood up high in shade; but immediately from behind it the moonlight spread, and showed the flat line of wall at the end of that terrace, with the figure of a sentinel moving against the light, as well as a profile of the dark precipice below. . . . No sound but the faint clinking of the soldier's accoutrements, as he paced on watch, and the remote voices of people turning the end of the east

From the Introduction to *Gaston*:

But, to return to Shakspeare, I have sometimes thought, as I walked in the deep shade of the North Terrace of Windsor Castle, when the moon shone on all beyond, that the scene must have been present in Shakespeare's mind, when he drew the night-scenes in Hamlet; . . . I have stood on the platform, which there projects over the precipice, and have heard only the measured step of a sentinel or the clink of his arms, and have seen his shadow passing by moonlight, at the foot of the high Eastern tower. . . . The very star – 'yon same star that's westward from terrace, appearing for a moment in the light there and vanishing. In a high window of the tower a light. Why is it so sublime to stand at the foot of a dark tower, and look up its height to the sky and the stars?

. . . Then the north terrace stretching and finally turning away from them towards the west, where high dark towers crown it. It was on this terrace, surely, that Shakespeare received the first hint of the time for the appearance of his ghost.[13]

the pole' – seemed to watch over the Western towers of the Terrace, whose high dark lines marked themselves upon the heavens. . . . Did you ever observe the fine effect of the Eastern tower when you stand near the Western end of the North terrace, and its tall profile rears itself upon the sky, from nearly the base to the battled top, the lowness of the parapet permitting this? It is most striking at night, when the stars appear, at different heights, upon its tall dark line, and when the sentinel on watch moves a shadowy figure at its foot.[14]

It seems clear that much of the Introduction was written *after* the novel and then tacked on to it. The style of the Introduction as a whole is markedly different from the style of the novel itself; there is clearly a disjunction between them, and the passages from the journals used in the novel are limited to its Introduction. I would date the bulk of the Introduction to sometime between 1811 and 1815 – 'the latter part of life' when Ann Radcliffe took up the manuscript of *Gaston de Blondeville* for the third time, after her return from Windsor, when she skilfully placed the story within a context that reasserted the 'spirits of the vasty deep' that she had forsworn in 1802–3.

The only interesting aspect about *Gaston de Blondeville* is this Introduction, which is far superior to the tale itself. Two English travellers, Willoughton the romantic enthusiast and Simpson the debunking philistine, stop to examine the ruins of Kenilworth on their way from Coventry to Warwick. The situation dramatizes an argument between Ann Radcliffe and her husband. Willoughton illustrates her whole approach to picturesque travel and her frank preference for the illusion over the reality:

'Alas!' said he, 'that enchanting vision is no more to be found, except in the very heart of a populous city and then neither by the glimmering of the dawn, nor by the glow of evening, but by the paltry light of stage-lamps. Yet there, surrounded by a noisy multitude, whose cat-calls often piped instead of the black-bird, I have found myself transported into the wildest region of poetry and solitude; while here, on the very spot which Shakspeare drew, I am suddenly let down from the full glow of my holiday-feelings into the plain reality of this work-a-day world.' (vol. 1, 5–6)

In his notes William Radcliffe observed that his wife similarly viewed the remains of Kenilworth 'with a mixture of admiration and disappointment' (vol. 3, 60). More to Willoughton's taste is the ruined banqueting hall. The melancholy of the scene speaks to him of 'the brevity and nothingness of this life' (vol. 1, 21), a passage picked up from her journal entry on Kenilworth. Willoughton's references point to the literary sources of Ann Radcliffe's (rather than her husband's) sense of the antique: Shakespeare, Milton, Gray, Beattie, Ovid and the romances of Charlemagne, Guy of Warwick, Amys and Amdion, Sir Tristram, Merlin's Prophecies, the Destruction of Troy and Richard Coeur de Lion excerpted in Warton's *History of English Poetry*.

The most important part of this Introduction is the 'grave dissertation on the illusions of the imagination' which represents Ann Radcliffe's critical summing up of her views on terror and the supernatural, a subject to which she had contributed so much. The self-contained essay was apparently lifted from the Introduction by Colburn, who published it separately in his *New Monthly Magazine*;[15] the position it should have occupied in the novel (vol. 1, p. 6) was slightly amended to account for its absence. Neither the essay nor the Introduction suffer any disjunction by this severance: it is even possible that Talfourd originally found the manuscript *already* in the form of a separate essay – prepared by Ann Radcliffe herself for later insertion into the Introduction rather than extracted from it.

Ann Radcliffe's critique systematically develops a theory of 'correspondent scenery' or 'accordant circumstances', illustrated with reference to Shakespeare. 'Accordant' is the mid-eighteenth-century critical term characterizing any type of writing which parallels a psychological mood without directly describing it: for example, Cawthorne in a poem quoted in *The Romance of the Forest* (245) speaks of the 'according music' with which Handel matches the emotions of his characters. Ann Radcliffe consciously adopted this technique in all of her novels, from the very first work *The Castles of Athlin and Dunbayne*, where Mary wanders through a wood 'whose awful glooms so well accorded with the pensive tone of her mind' (42), to *The Italian*, where music and sounds always 'characterize' – are in accord with – the mood of the characters. 'Local scenery', be it grand or gloomy, beautiful or sublime, is 'always in unison' with the characters, 'up-call[ing]' their 'corresponding feelings'. Correspondent Terror is illustrated by the storm that occurs as Cassius and the conspirators gather before the porch of Pompey's theatre in *Julius Caesar* (I. iii), 'when the sheeted dead were seen in the lightning to glide along the streets of Rome'. Correspondent Pity is illustrated in *Cymbeline* (IV. ii), when solemn music issues from the cave where Imogen reposes – 'All solemn things should answer solemn accidents'. Ann Radcliffe's exposition of Shakespeare's use of 'correspondent scenery', such as the desolate heath in *Macbeth*, is as skilfully sensitive as De Quincey's more famous essay 'On the knocking at the gate in Macbeth', and as poetic and imaginative as Wordsworth's 'correspondent breeze' (*Prelude*, Book First).

The critique stresses the importance of the creative evocation of the supernatural. Mrs Radcliffe condemns a theatrical production she had seen in which *Macbeth* was 'improved' by naturalism, by dressing the witches as 'downright Scotch-women', for she is more concerned with the higher poetic reality and is 'speaking of the only real witch – the witch of the poet; . . . The wild attire, the look *not of this earth*, are essential traits of supernatural agents, working evil in the darkness of mystery.' The other great instance of the sublime supernatural cited in this essay is of course the ghost scene in *Hamlet*, to which she gives a close critical analysis. Ann Radcliffe was no doubt familiar with Elizabeth Montagu's famous *Essay on the Writings and Genius of Shakespeare* (1778), which pointed out, for example, the 'correspondence' between the wandering star and the appearance of the ghost, and which firmly established the Romantic defence of the use of the supernatural by Tasso, Ariosto and Shakespeare: 'Ghosts, fairies, goblins, elves, were as propitious, were as assistant to Shakespeare, and gave as much of the sublime, and of the marvellous, to his fictions, as nymphs, satyrs, fawns, and even the triple Geryon, to the works of ancient bards.'[16]

Ann Radcliffe confidently declares that men like Dryden are deficient in the poetic sensibility because they are unresponsive to what she 'would call the picturesque in feeling': 'Such men may have high talents, wit, genius, judgment, but not the soul of poetry' as found in 'Shakspeare, Milton, Gray, Collins, Beattie, and a very few others, not excepting Thomson'. Curiously, Dryden is the *only* writer upon whom Ann Radcliffe ever passed a harsh judgement; probably she felt secure in this position because her uncle Bentley's friend Joseph Priestley was similarly severe: 'Instances of the most absurd rant, and such extravagance as is incompatible with every character, and with every passion, abound in Dryden's plays.'[17] It is manifest from this essay that she regarded herself as one of the 'great masters of imagination' along with Shakespeare and Milton.

Critics of the Gothic novel have given rather too much emphasis to Ann Radcliffe's famous distinction between horror and terror in this essay:

> Terror and horror are so far opposite, that the first expands the soul, and awakens the faculties to a high degree of life; the other contracts, freezes, and nearly annihilates them. I apprehend, that neither Shakspeare nor Milton by their fictions, nor Mr Burke by his reasoning, anywhere looked to positive horror as a source of the sublime, though they all agree that terror is a very high one; and where lies the great difference between horror and terror but in the uncertainty and obscurity, that accompany the first, respecting the dreaded evil?

In actual practice, she uses the words 'terror' and 'horror' interchangeably in her novels, and without distinction. But she has considered the subject in the light of the public reaction, and is attempting to defend her own novels by distinguishing sensibility and the 'terror' of the Radcliffe school from sensationalism and the 'horror' of the Lewis school. In her defence of Gilpin's principle that obscurity is necessary for the achievement of terror and the sublime, she does not mention Richard Payne Knight or Uvedale Price, but she does refer to 'the new school', so it is probable that she has kept up with contemporary aesthetic discussion of the picturesque.[18]

Mrs Radcliffe must have managed to reach Stonehenge in her later travels – which were predominantly antiquarian – for in the Introduction to *Gaston de Blondeville* Simpson protests at having been persuaded to accompany Willoughton on 'midnight rambles about Stonehenge' (vol. 1, 58). Talfourd cites extracts recording the Radcliffes' visits to Kent in June 1805 and, around 1806, Tewkesbury Abbey, where they were particularly keen to see the monument erected to the great Warwick in the choir.[19]

In autumn 1807 they visited the treasure house of Knole, in Sevenoaks, Kent, ancient seat of the Sackvilles and home to the Duchess Dowager of Dorset.[20] Talfourd says this was the second time they had visited Knole; the date of the first visit is not recorded, nor are there any journal notes for it other than the reference made during the visit to Blenheim in 1802. When they departed, they engaged in conversation with the old porter at the gate, who had lived in the area for fifty years: 'those were grand times; the late Dukes were very good, but things had got dearer then. When we were going, he desired Mr R. to write our names in the book, that my lord might have the *pleasure* of seeing who had been there.' In Victor Sage's view, 'For her, the paintings [at Knole] are, quite clearly, windows on to the Protestant succession, objective correlatives to her own imaginative piety.'[21] Sage's evidence is her description of one painting in particular:

> In a picture containing three portraits, that in the middle is of Luther. His bluff, blunt, strong habits of expression; his dauntless and persevering mind; his consciousness of the truth and importance of his cause, and his resolution to maintain it, are well expressed; strength and resolution in the chin. On his right is Melancthon, reasoning, acute, amiable. On his left, Pomeranius; a somewhat sly and monkish countenance.

The portrait of Erasmus is also described, with no apparent disapproval of the instigator of the Thirty-Nine Articles. However, we can be too selective in making any inferences. Her journal contains very detailed notes on about thirty-five portraits: of Giardini, Titian, Michelangelo, Queen Elizabeth,

Salisbury, Burleigh, Leicester, Lord Surrey, three Earls of Dorset, Pitt by Hoppner, Fletcher, Beaumont, Reynolds by himself, Dr Johnson, Goldsmith, Garrick, Swift, Pope, Otway, Dryden, Addison and others. (She parenthetically refers to a Rubens self-portrait seen 'at Buckingham House', so we know that she had visited the royal picture galleries at the Queen's House, which later became the core for Buckingham Palace.)

In his memoir Talfourd says that Mrs Radcliffe also went frequently to St Albans, 'the antiquities of which she explored with unwearied zeal'.[22] (Her uncle Bentley often stopped at St Albans on his journeys between London and Etruria.) In his notes to the posthumously published poetical romance *St Alban's Abbey*, which was the outcome of those visits, William Radcliffe relates an incident which establishes two specific visits to St Albans, in 1802 and 1808. During this last visit a helmet which had been 'dug up between the years 1802 and 1808' (which I take to mean after their first visit and shortly before their second trip) was shown to them, and the movement of the beaver was demonstrated by giving the helmet a few irreverent blows with the vestry poker.[23] This helmet, bearing traces of a damask pattern, is mentioned in the poem, so the composition of the poem can be dated to 1808–9. The poem runs to several hundred pages of turgid and morbid rhyming couplets. William Radcliffe's notes suggest that some twenty scholarly sources have been consulted, such as John Carter's *The Ancient Architecture of England* (1795),[24] Peter Newcome's *The History of the Ancient and Royal Foundation, Called the Abbey of St Alban* (1793–5), Richard Gough's *British Topography* (1780), and Browne Willis's *An History of the Mitred Parliamentary Abbies* (1718–19). The author's invocation to her newly adopted antiquarian muse, the 'Spirit of ancient days!', is tantamount to a confession of inadequacy:

> Teach me, in language simple and severe,
>
> . . .
>
> To paint th'awakening vision thou hast spread
> Before mine eyes – tale of the mighty dead!
>
> . . .
>
> Presumptuous wish! Ah! not to me are given
> Those antient keys, that ope the Poet's heaven,
> Golden and rustless! NOT TO ME ARE GIVEN! (vol. 3, 91–2)

In 1811 the Radcliffes visited Penshurst Place, west of Tunbridge Wells, and Mrs Radcliffe made extensive notes on the ancient seat of Sir Philip Sidney.[25] She was impressed by the 'grand, but gloomy' great hall with its blackened rafters, and the unique medieval survival of the centrally positioned fireplace roused her imagination with its precedents:

the bricks, raised half a foot, form a small octagon, on which, perhaps, Sir Philip Sydney and the knights his companions have often stood round the blazing fagots [sic], piled upon the same iron dogs, of enormous size, that still remain there. I think I see, in glimpses, the strong blaze of the wood flashing on their visages. The armour of Sir Philip himself, with helm (the vizor closed), stands at the back of an obscure gallery, and close beneath a high window, whose small frames admit a blunted, melancholy light. It stands like a spectre in arms, watching over the scene it once inhabited; and is admirably placed to touch the imagination, but not to gratify curiosity.[26]

This neatly sums up her own technique for tantalizing her readers.

The officious housekeeper gave them a tour of the apartments, and after seeing the nursery Mrs Radcliffe continued her pursuit of the sublime: '"Do the stairs near the nursery lead to the top of the turret?" – "I don't know, ma'am, but I'll see." I followed to the small platform, and looked over the battlements upon the wood and the valley. The view was pleasing, but not impressive, or extensive.' She may have been inspired to climb this turret by a reading of Charlotte Smith's 'Sonnet xlvi, Written at Penshurst, in Autumn 1788', beginning:

Ye Towers sublime, deserted now and drear,
Ye woods, deep sighing to the hollow blast,
The musing wanderer loves to linger near,
While History points to all your glories past.[27]

During this visit to Penshurst Mrs Radcliffe exhibits a somewhat condescending attitude towards the servant classes, reflected in her novels (for example, in *Gaston* some weak amusement is derived from the ignorance of the simple guide at Kenilworth, who talks about 'The Pleasant' when he means the *plaisance*, a banqueting-house). At Penshurst her mockery is specifically aimed at those who would pretend to a position higher than their rightful station. Two different concepts of the past collided in her husband's conversation with the housekeeper, and two different ways of regarding lineage:

Mrs Perry, the grandmother of the present Mr Sidney, who changed his name from Shelley, was a niece of Sydney, Earl of Leicester, and co-heiress with her sister, Lady Howard, of the Penshurst estates. The old housekeeper, who attended us, lamented much that Mr Sidney did not now live here, but hoped to see him return. She had been all her life on the spot, and told us what fine times she remembered when *Lady* Perry used to drive to the gate in a coach and six, and come down with such 'a sight of servants.' All the tenants used to come to meet her, and '*we girls*' (the speaker was a grandmother) used to stand all in a row to meet her. . . . 'Was she *Lady* Perry?' 'Yes, sir,' rather sharply, as if astonished that we could doubt it. 'Was she a *Lady* by birth?' 'Yes, sir,' more sharply, 'she *was* a Lady indeed.'[28]

Modern readers are perhaps not so sensitive to the housekeeper's impropriety in giving her mistress a rank to which she was not entitled by birth. Mrs Radcliffe is rather sarcastic as well as amused when the housekeeper points out the nursery, 'with a strong regret of *old times* – not those of Sir Philip Sydney, but of Lady Perry. . . . As I humoured her, she began, in the midst of her regrets, to apologize for her dress, and to lament that she had not had time to appear better.' The whole episode, which lacks the gloom and melancholy of most of her journals, is worked up into a humorous set-piece that could easily have formed part of a Waverley novel. Finally they pass back through the great hall to see the lofty kitchen:

> Here the good woman was at the climax of her regrets, and she shook her head and sighed often. 'It is a dismal place now, and what do I remember it in *Lady* Perry's time! I remember, when all them hooks,' pointing to rows of them that run, at a great height, over the wide and lofty chimney piece and round the roof, 'were hung with sides of bacon. And here was such a sight of servants running about, some one way, some another.' She then reverted to Lady P.'s coach and six, and the rejoicings that were to take place when she came down, and '*we girls* used to stand all in a row.' In short, one would have thought that nobody had ever lived in this mansion but Lady Perry. As to Sir Philip and the rest of the Sydneys, they were never thought of when she spoke of *old times* – a neglect which at first somewhat embarrassed me, who thought of them and old times as inseparable.

Construction of the Legend

———— • ————

Mrs Radcliffe did not die until 1823, in her fifty-ninth year, but virtually everyone believed she was dead long before that date. When she had not published another novel by 1800, her avid readers naturally believed that Fate rather than whim had removed her from public view. As each year passed, speculation increased as to the reasons for her inactivity. It was conjectured that her wild imagination had preyed upon itself, that her effort to create visions of horror had finally driven her into a lunatic asylum. Madness and death were the two great ideas that seized upon the public imagination.

It is rather an understatement to note that 'she who could allow herself to be proclaimed dead or insane and not remonstrate, was no ordinary woman'.[1] Ann Radcliffe did not simply remain aloof from fame and ambition: she disliked public notice to the point of eccentricity. Far from being indifferent to public opinion, on some occasions, according to her husband, she took strong measures to curtail the spread of her fame: 'It is within the knowledge of persons yet alive, that care was taken, and solicitations used, to prevent the issuing of any factitious commendation.'[2] Even on her occasional visits to the opera, she would sit in the pit, well wrapped up in warm clothing not simply for the sake of her health, but because she wished to be so muffled up as to escape observation.[3] As a literary editor noted in May 1823, unaware that Mrs Radcliffe had died only a few months earlier rather than a dozen years ago:

The fair authoress kept herself almost as much *incognito* as the Author of Waverley; nothing was known of her but her name in the title page. She never appeared in public, nor mingled in private society, but kept herself apart, like the sweet bird that sings its solitary notes, shrowded and unseen.[4]

It gradually dawns upon us that the mysterious legend of Ann Radcliffe was created not only by her admirers – and her detractors – but also by herself.

When Radcliffe's earlier novels began to be reissued – *Romance of the Forest* in Dublin in 1801 and in London in 1806, and *The Mysteries of Udolpho* in Dublin in 1800 and in London in 1803 and 1806 – it was obvious that no new novels would be forthcoming, and natural to conclude that their author was no longer among the living. As early as 1806 it was said in print that Mrs Radcliffe had died in 1800.[5] The rumours about her death really gathered pace after 1809, beginning innocently enough with the misunderstanding created by a brief obituary notice in the *Gentleman's Magazine* for 28 February 1809: 'At the rectory-house at Broughton, co. Lincoln, aged 71, Mrs Deborah Radcliffe, mother of the husband of the celebrated Authoress of several highly-esteemed Novels and other works.'[6] This obituary notice was wilfully misread, and in the retelling the novelist was substituted for her mother-in-law.

Virtually all of the early French biographical notices of Ann Radcliffe derive their mistaken notions about her death from this innocuous paragraph. Thus the first edition of the *Dictionnaire des Ouvrages Anonymes et Pseudonymes* blithely reported that she 'morte à Broughton près de Stemford, à l'âge de 71 ans au commencement de 1809'.[7] (As if to compound the mystery, the title page of this dictionary was mistakenly dated M.DCCC.VIII – one year *prior* to the reported death!) In a later edition she is said to have died 'à Linclico', a conflation of Lincolnshire, where her mother-in-law expired, and Pimlico, where the novelist in fact died.[8] Several French authorities were convinced that her last years were spent 'à Linclico, auprès Londres',[9] while others stated that she died 'à Brougton près Stampford' age seventy-one,[10] or 'à Brougthon près de Steinford' at the age of sixty-nine.[11] (The first English obituary said she died in her sixty-second year.[12]) The French took up the suggestion that her rivals, by the 'odieuse manoeuvre' of attributing disgusting works to her, forced her to renounce writing.[13]

One of the more humorous results of Ann Radcliffe's premature burial was the appearance of 'posthumous' works falsely attributed to her. French novelists in particular had no qualms about exploiting the cachet of their favourite authoress. *Le Tombeau* appeared in Paris in 1799, as an 'ouvrage posthume d'Anne Radcliffe', supposedly translated from English 'par H. Chaussier et Bizet', the real authors of the work.[14] Another, more interesting, work was *L'Hermite de la tombe mystérieuse, ou le fantôme du vieux château*, 'Anecdote, extraite des Anuales du treizième siècle, par Mme Anne Radcliffe, et trad. sur le manuscrit anglais, par le baron de L***', published in Paris in 1815 (and reprinted several times). Its author was the Baron de La Mothe-Langon, later La Mothe-Houdancourt; in his journal he noted that the first volume was finished on 3 August 1809,[15] so perhaps he was inspired by the rumours resulting from the announcement of the death of Mrs Radcliffe's mother-in-law earlier that year. Posing as the translator, he claimed that he had obtained the manuscript from a wounded Scottish soldier who was a relative of Mrs Radcliffe. La Mothe-Langon imitated Ann Radcliffe in many of his novels, and he placed the Gothic genre within its political revolutionary context in his preface to *Monastère des frères noirs* (1825):

> Des sensations fortes sont galeent nécessaires après les agitations politiques. . . .
> A la suite du règne exécrable de la Terreur, quand la France entière échappait
> à la hache du crime, les romans de Lewis, d'Anne Radcliffe, etc., furent
> recherchés avec avidité.[16]

Literally dozens of novels published in France, Germany and Holland claimed to be translations of manuscripts discovered among Mrs Radcliffe's posthumous papers (even before her actual death), such as *Comte le Vappa, ou le crime et le fatalisme* (1820), 'manuscrit trouvé dans le portefeuille d'Anne Radcliffe'.[17]

A particularly intriguing 'posthumous' work is a fugitive novel called *The Grave*. It is described in a humorous anecdote published in Boston in 1852, retailing events that were supposed to have occurred during 1809–11.[18] This anecdote, which evinces some knowledge about *Le Tombeau* ('The Grave') and the muddle over 'Linclico' in the French biographies, is a splendid example of the literary world's determination to create an imaginary life when denied access to the real facts. One day the journals are supposed to have announced the forthcoming publication of '*The Grave*, a posthumous work of Anne Radcliffe', but really by the young Robert Will, shrewdly conspiring with Mr Davies of Cadell and Davies. Unknown to them, Mrs Radcliffe was living a very retired life 'at Lincoln, a little village in the neighborhood of London', where she looked after her poultry yard and made the most delicious puddings, while her husband fished for trout in the nearby brooks. Contented housewife and patient angler, 'they both lived like retired grocers' – which is rather closer to the truth than the constructed mystery of Ann Radcliffe's life.

The reprints of *The Mysteries of Udolpho* and *A Sicilian Romance* by the firm of Longman in 1809,[19] following closely upon the heels of the misconstrued obituary notice, would have been interpreted as further proof of the novelist's demise, as well as stimulating further interest in her work. Late that year, probably in October, the Longman group published a travel book in which a reference to Mrs Radcliffe's insanity appeared in print for the first time: *Summer Excursions*, in the form of letters written by Elizabeth Isabella Spence, and addressed to the Dowager Countess of Winterton. In her travels through Derbyshire Miss Spence was much struck by 'an antique mansion seated on a bold eminence' surrounded by ruinous desolation, its 'high turrets [and] rude battlements, raised in gloomy pomp above the woods which half concealed it'. When she discovered this was Haddon Hall she made a point of visiting and describing it in detail, because the ancient mouldering edifice,

> exclusive of its being one of the finest specimens of antiquity this country produces, is the place Mrs Radcliffe has made the subject of her pen in describing the Castle of Udolpho. This circumstance alone would render it highly interesting to the admirers of her writings, and worthy of particular description.[20]

But it is her postscript to this letter which provides the juiciest gossip for the Dowager Countess of Winterton:

> To return to Mrs Radcliffe. The reader will, no doubt, regret with me that a lady whose original genius and wonderful imagination have insured her immortal fame, should have been obliged to retire into a remote part of Derbyshire under the most direful influence of deep-rooted and incurable melancholy. Her husband is a man of science and letters, I understand, concerned in some of the literary publications of the day.[21]

Elizabeth Spence's letter is dated 27 September from Chapel-en-le-Frith; her postscript is dated 30 September, from Stand-hall, which is where she was staying with her friends Mr J— and his sisters near Rochdale, Yorkshire.

It is clear that the castle of Udolpho was widely associated with Haddon Hall prior to Spence's visit, but the story about Mrs Radcliffe being incarcerated in a madhouse in Derbyshire seems to be of local origin. It is a curious coincidence, for Spence was not aware that Ann Radcliffe's family roots were in Derbyshire. Either the local hoteliers in Chapel-en-le-Frith promoted this story for the sake of increasing tourism (certainly they would have promoted the belief that Haddon Hall was the source for the castle of Udolpho), or Miss Spence's friends in Yorkshire told her of this story when she went to stay with them after leaving Derbyshire.

Elizabeth Isabella Spence, dubbed 'The Travelling Spinster' by the reviewers, made picturesque excursions to Malvern, the Wye Valley and the gloomy horrors of High Peak. An exasperated critic in *Blackwood's* suggested that 'Sir Richard Phillips, we believe, has been in the habit of sending off Miss Spence in Shandry-dans, and other vehicles, throughout the more picturesque regions of the island; and she, on her return, sells her literary bantlings to that generous and eccentric bibliopolist.' Richard Phillips published various books and periodicals, including the annual *Public Characters*, and together with the Unitarian John Aikin founded the *Monthly Magazine*[22] – a major outlet for Unitarian writers including Mary Hays, and a good source for Unitarian obituaries. Spence's descriptions were often inaccurate and even laughable.

Miss Spence's three-volume novel about fashionable life in Ilfracome, *A Traveller's Tale of the Last Century*, with its romantic scenery and descriptions of the 'broad turrets of a dilapidated Abbey, mingling amongst the dark sequestered woods', shows that she had read Ann Radcliffe's *A Sicilian Romance*.[23] The *Summer Excursions* was favourably reviewed in the *Gentleman's Magazine*, though the anecdote about Mrs Radcliffe is passed over in silence.[24] The book went through two editions in 1809, but no steps were taken to counter the gossip. The rumour spread by Elizabeth Spence was not publicly denied until after Mrs Radcliffe's death, by the editor of the *Annual Biography*, who says that the error about her visit to Italy while her husband was on an embassy there is trifling

> compared with one committed by the authoress of a book of travels through England; who, in noticing the Duke of Rutland's venerable and romantic seat in Derbyshire, called Haddon House, (on which Gilpin dwells with so much enthusiasm,) after saying that it was there that Mrs Radcliffe acquired her love of castles and ancient buildings, proceeds to observe, that that lady had for years fallen into a state of insanity, and was under confinement in Derbyshire! Mrs Radcliffe was in Derbyshire only on two occasions, and on both but for a few days; the one in 1798, when, after the death of her father, she accompanied her mother thither; the other in the latter end of 1799, or the beginning of 1800, when she went to visit her mother, who was very ill, and who died shortly afterwards. Haddon House she never saw; nor had she ever heard of it at the time of her earlier publications. With respect to the second part of the statement, it does really seem to be unpardonable, when we consider that the writer might have easily ascertained, had it been only by a reference to her publisher, that it was utterly destitute of truth, and that Mrs Radcliffe was frequently to be seen in the vicinity of the metropolis, in which she lived.[25]

Despite such pointers, Spence's work has not previously been identified as the source of this rumour.

Both of Mrs Radcliffe's parents had their roots in Derbyshire, and her relations the Jebbs dominated the life of Chesterfield. It is highly likely that some knowledge of places in Derbyshire would have influenced her books. Her visit to Hardwick Hall in 1794 clearly took place after the publication of *The Mysteries of Udolpho*, but the very fact that she went there so soon after publication suggests that she knew about it much earlier, and that it was a powerful attraction. She must also have known of the existence of Peverel's Castle of the Peak, on a steep and rocky eminence above the vast subterranean recess of the Peak Cavern, near Castleton. It was approached by a steep and nearly inaccessible zigzag path, and had a 50-foot keep containing the ruins of a narrow staircase winding to the roof. Evocative illustrations appeared in picturesque works, and most picturesque travellers were aware of the Wonders of the Peak.[26] Several scenes in Wedgwood & Bentley's Imperial Russian dinner service illustrate both the castle and the cavern. We do know that Mrs Radcliffe visited the great tourist attraction of Dovedale, for she wrote a poem 'To the River Dove' (published posthumously and therefore difficult to date).[27] In it she describes the gloomy cliffs and peaks and caverns which still make the two-mile stretch of Dovedale Gorge up the River Dove from Thorpe one of the most striking walks in the Peak National Park, though today the horde of ramblers would easily overcome any banditti who might issue from Reynard's Cave or the Dove Holes. The existence of Ann Radcliffe's poem must cast doubt upon William Radcliffe's testimony about his wife's short stays in Derbyshire. He claimed that she visited for only a few days, once in 1798 and again in early 1800. A trip to Dovedale from Chesterfield would have been a full day's outing, at a time when she was otherwise occupied by all the business entailed by the death of her father or the illness and death of her mother. The poem contains no hint of having been written at a time of grief.

Most scholars have rejected the rumour about Haddon Hall because of William Radcliffe's categorical disclaimer. But he is in fact mistaken: Ann Radcliffe *did* visit Derbyshire, well before she wrote her novels. In August 1776 she stayed with her uncle Bentley's wife's family in Derby, as revealed by her grandmother Amelia's letter to her dated 1 August 1776: 'To Miss Ward at Mr Stamfords in Derby', previously cited.[28] She was only in her thirteenth year at the time, but that is an ideal age at which to be charmed by the legend of the most romantic house in England. If she did not actually visit Haddon Hall, it is inconceivable that she could reside in nearby Derby without knowing of its existence. Haddon Hall was only a few miles further from Chesterfield than Hardwick, and one of the three great houses of the county (the third being Chatsworth).

Haddon Hall is picturesque rather than sublime, a manor house rather than a castle, and situated on a small limestone outcrop rather than atop an immense cliff. It is more welcoming than forbidding, and could never have been the model specifically for the castle of Udolpho. But in its years of desolate abandon, the medieval mansion could well have been the model for some of the gloomy interiors of the novel, especially the haunted apartment in Château-le-Blanc, which, like Haddon and unlike Udolpho, is embosomed in trees. Haddon Hall lay in a chrysalis of near ruin for two centuries, and was famous for its deserted apartments containing an antique state bed and decaying tapestries that were allowed to hang on the walls of the unoccupied house for two hundred years. Its equally famous elaborately panelled long gallery, with its grand door of ornate carvings leading to the ante-room of the orielled state bedchamber, might conceivably have suggested the long gallery in Château-le-Blanc, particularly the door off the great staircase leading into the ante-room of the saloon of the Marchioness, which is of such 'singular beauty' and 'delicate carvings' that the Count forbears to strike a blow against it (*Udolpho*, 560) – although the former is panelled with good English oak while the latter is panelled with larch, a surprisingly careful reference to its foreign site.

Haddon Hall was a stopping-point for all picturesque travellers in the Peak District. It presented a powerful image of domestic antiquity, and the notion that this venerable pile of embattled turrets should have inspired the most romantic castle in literature proved irresistible. Thus Ebenezer Rhodes, in his *Peak Scenery* (1819), noted that the Hall's 'massy walls and gloomy apartments, . . . its painted windows, admitting only a dubious light' serve as heady stimulants to the Gothic imagination, particularly that of its finest practitioner:

> Mrs Ann Radcliffe, who was a native of Derbyshire, often visited Haddon Hall, for the purpose of storing her imagination with those romantic ideas, and impressing upon it those sublime and awful pictures which she so much delighted to pourtray: some of the most gloomy scenery of her 'Mysteries of Udolpho' was studied within the walls of this ancient structure.[29]

Although *Peak Scenery* was published in 1819, Rhodes last visited Haddon Hall in 1816, and had been a frequent visitor up to that date; the association with Mrs Radcliffe was well in place by about 1812.

This volume of *Peak Scenery* was dedicated to the Duke of Rutland, the owner of Haddon Hall, whose family had abandoned their more ancient place of residence in favour of Belvoir Castle. If the Duke of Rutland had not already been encouraging the Radcliffe legend for some years past, he no doubt did so for the succeeding wave of tourists. When the lesbian diarist and adventuress Anne Lister stayed at the Duke's grand new inn, the Rutland Arms in Bakewell, in 1825, she found all four volumes of Rhodes's *Peak Scenery* placed conspicuously on the table, and noted in her diary that she 'Read there the account of Bakewell church, Haddon Hall, etc. Mrs Radcliffe (a native of Derbyshire) fond of the latter. Much there & there imagined much of the finest scenery of her "Mysteries of Udolpho".[30] We can deduce from another source that the housekeeper of Haddon Hall exploited this romantic association as she guided visitors around the hall. Elizabeth Selwyn, a keen picturesque traveller, visited Haddon Hall on 29 August 1820, and one can clearly sense the housekeeper/guide standing at her elbow reciting the most interesting statistics and anecdotes:

> There is a gallery 100 feet long, by 17; . . . There is not a vestige of furniture, but one state bed, and an old cradle, which belonged to the first Duke of Rutland. In one of the painted windows of the chapel the date is 1427. The principal apartments are hung with ancient arras, concealing the doors, which are of rudest workmanship. The gloomy apartments and general appearance of this antique edifice are said to have suggested to Mrs Radcliffe some of the traits she has introduced in her terrific descriptions of castles in 'Mysteries of Udolpho'.[31]

Nathaniel Carter, an American traveller who had little time for Gothic fiction, was presumably told of the connection during his visit to Haddon Hall in 1827:

> Although the day was remarkably bright, many of the passages and apartments wore the gloom of twilight. As Mrs Radcliffe is not a favourite in our country, it may be no recommendation of this interesting relic of other ages, to state that she borrowed from it much of her imagery in 'the Mysteries of Udolpho.'[32]

Peak Scenery's list of subscribers included King George III (who was in the throes of his own 'madness' at the time of its publication), the Dukes of Devonshire, Norfolk, Bedford and Marlborough, the Duchess of Dorset, Earls Fitzwilliam, Spencer and Grenville, the Earl of Elgin, Viscounts Milton and Kinnaird, the painter Sir Thomas Lawrence, the sculptor Francis Chantrey and his wife, the topographer John Britton, the literary critic Allan Cunningham, the industrialists Robert and Richard Arkwright, the architects Jeffrey Wyatt and Edward Blore and the directors of all the major publishing houses. Thus a wide selection of celebrities and important people in the literary, artistic and even political worlds was exposed to this anecdote about Ann Radcliffe. Some embellished the rumour. Sir Walter Scott heard that after Mrs Radcliffe visited Haddon Hall once, she insisted on returning so as to spend the night there, searching its hidden passages and deliberately cultivating the atmosphere for her mysterious Udolpho:

> although it was a place excellently worth her attention, and could hardly have been seen by her without suggesting some of those ideas in which her

imagination naturally revelled, yet we should suppose the mechanical aid to invention – the recipe for fine writing – the sleeping in a dismantled and unfurnished old house, was likely to be rewarded with nothing but a cold, and was an affectation of enthusiasm to which Mrs Radcliffe would have disdained to have recourse.[33]

A fellow Sheffield resident, Mary Sterndale, praised Rhodes's 'elegant work' in her own *Vignettes of Derbyshire* in 1824. Although she makes no reference to Mrs Radcliffe in her vignette of Haddon Hall, she does allude to the veiled picture in *The Mysteries of Udolpho* in her description of a visit to Tideswell Church, about six miles southwest of Chapel-en-le-Frith and about six miles northeast of Haddon Hall. In the south transept is

The vault of the Beeches, of Shaw, in Staffordshire, natives of Tideswell, the access to which is open. The coffin lid of the last who was there interred has a sliding board, beneath which, a plate of glass displays what would have appalled the stoutest heart in Udolpho, the countenance of the poor remains within.[34]

The allusion to *The Mysteries of Udolpho* may not be so far-fetched: Tideswell is a mile from Weston (modern spelling Wheston) – the place where Mrs Radcliffe's mother expressed a wish to be buried. There must be some family connection to the area, and we may wonder if Ann Radcliffe knew the church and its terrible vault.

In his memoir of 1826 Talfourd said that Mrs Radcliffe 'was amazed at an absurd report, that, haunted by the images of fear, with which she had thrilled her readers, she had sunk into a state of mental alienation'. The most galling rumour was that she had literally died insane: 'In an "Ode to Terror", with other effusions, published by a clergyman in 1810, Mrs Radcliffe is bemoaned, as having died in that species of mental derangement called "the horrors".'[35] This poem – not previously identified by Radcliffe scholars, despite Talfourd's pointers – was an 'Ode to Horror', which Revd Charles Apthorp Wheelwright, A.B. of Trinity College, Cambridge, included in his collection of *Poems* (1810). His almost malicious ode is a lugubrious survivor of Augustan allegory. Horror is personified as the goddess of insanity, pursuing her victims to the grave:

Nor to the restless child of pain
    Thy potent influence is confined,
Thy phantoms seize the ardent brain,
    And sweep the tract of mind.

As the pale spectres cross her way,
Lo! RADCLIFFE shudders with dismay,
And vainly struggling to be free,
Flies to the grasp of Death, from Madness and from thee.[36]

Wheelwright adds a footnote in case anyone believes he is being merely metaphorical:

Mrs Ann Radcliffe, the ingenious authoress of *the Italian, Mysteries of Udolpho*, &c. who had been *nursed by the Florentine Muses in all the gloom of Gothic superstition*, (Pursuits of Literature) is reported to have died under that species of mental derangement, known by the name of *the horrors*.[37]

The author had translated *Medea* and therefore felt qualified to speak about the nature of horror and obsession. He was also an Anglican clergyman, and believed that insanity caused by superstitious horror would be appropriately resolved in death, whereby the unfortunate victim would receive the grace of Heaven.

The Revd Wheelwright had been admitted as a pensioner at Trinity in 1804, and received his BA in 1809, so he was still a young man when he published his *Poems* and when he was ordained Deacon of London in September 1810. Mrs Radcliffe is the only contemporary writer to whom Wheelwright refers – the reference stands out in such extraordinary contrast amidst the translations of Seneca, Juvenal, Petrarch and Latin and Greek fragments, and paraphrases of the Scriptures, that he may have a specific, topical reason for it. Made Prebendary of Lincoln in 1811, he was also the Vicar of Castle Bytham and Rector of Little Bytham (1811–58) and Domestic Chaplain to the Dowager Lady Lilford.[38] Presumably Wheelwright already had some connection with Lincolnshire in 1810, for he dedicated his *Poems* to the Right Reverend George, Lord Bishop of Lincoln. Little Bytham is a few miles north of Stamford, where Mrs Radcliffe's mother-in-law died in 1809. Wheelwright thus may have gleaned the false report of the novelist's death from his future parishioners.

In a lengthy list of subscribers to Wheelwright's *Poems*, including dons, clergymen, bishops, earls, ladies and gentlemen, and fellows of Trinity Hall, Cambridge, we can note the names of Sir Richard Colt Hoare, Horace Mann of Trinity College, the Earl of Hardwick and John Nichols, editor of the *Gentleman's Magazine*. Wheelwright lived in Highbury, and a substantial number of the subscribers lived in Highbury and Islington (Nichols lived in nearby Canonbury); many residents of Bath and Bristol were also subscribers. The rumour about Mrs Radcliffe's madness therefore spread far and wide. A second edition was published in 1811, in two volumes, with no suppression of the 'Ode to Horror' or the footnote on her shocking expiry.

It is not surprising that Mrs Radcliffe should fall victim to the archetypal fantasy for which she herself was responsible in the creation of the mad Sister Agnes and the highly strung Emily of *Udolpho*. Even as late as 1824, according to Sir Walter Scott, some of her admirers

> are not yet undeceived, that, in consequence of brooding over the terrors which she depicted, her reason had at length been overturned, and that the Author of *The Mysteries of Udolpho* only existed as the melancholy inmate of a private mad-house. This report was so generally spread, and so confidently repeated in print, as well as in conversation, that the Editor [that is Scott himself] believed it for several years, until, greatly to his satisfaction, he learned from good authority that there neither was, nor ever had been, the most distant foundation for this unpleasing rumour.[39]

The French critics savoured her morbid sensibility, and were the first to position Ann Radcliffe on the dark side of Romanticism, likening her imaginative delirium to 'la Pythonisse sur le trépied sacré'.[40]

By 1811 the literary world believed Mrs Radcliffe to be either mad or dead, or both. Mary Russell Mitford was one of those in the younger generation of aspiring writers who firmly believed that she had died insane, until she eventually learned otherwise. One day Dr Mitford wrote to his daughter that he had seen Mrs Radcliffe being paid for some literary work. On 12 July 1811 Mary Russell Mitford wrote back to her father: '*The* Mrs Radcliffe has been dead some years. She died, poor woman, quite mad. It must have been another scribbler of that name, whom you saw receiving money. I wish to heaven anybody would give me some!'[41] Her phrase 'some years' may date the supposed death to 1809, perhaps arising from the notice of Mrs *Deborah* Radcliffe's death in that year. This case of mistaken identity is a puzzle. Dr Mitford's letter does not survive, but we can confidently say that the financial transaction which he witnessed took place in the offices of the printer-publisher John Valpy. Mitford was acting as his daughter's literary agent; in her letter to him dated 8 July she expresses dissatisfaction at the way Valpy has been advertising one of her books; in a postscript to her letter of 12 July she complains that 'John Valpy is quite entirely a fool! To think of offering us three copies of my book!' It is clear that Miss Mitford is resentful that Valpy has offered money to a certain Mrs Radcliffe but only author's complimentary copies to her. But why would John Valpy be giving some money to Mrs Radcliffe?

Valpy was the printer-publisher of many of the books issued by the 'Leviathan firm'[42] of Longman, Hurst, Rees, Orme and Brown. His offices were situated in Red Lion Passage.[43] Some of Mrs Radcliffe's novels were reprinted by Longman/Valpy, but she was not entitled to any royalties on these editions. Wheelwright's *Poems*, containing the infamous 'Ode to Horror', was reprinted in 1811 by John Valpy (Wheelwright occasionally contributed to Valpy's *Classical Journal*),[44] but it is hardly likely that Valpy offered Mrs Radcliffe financial compensation for the slander. The only reason why any payment should be made to *the* Mrs Radcliffe would be if she had written a book for him under another name, an intriguing prospect for which there is no evidence whatsoever.

It is more likely that Dr Mitford encountered the *other* Mrs Radcliffe, Mrs Mary Ann Radcliffe of the Wollstonecraft school. This lady's *Memoirs* were also published by Longman/Valpy in 1810 and reprinted in late 1811, when a critic was moved to comment upon the fact that some inferior writers were adopting names similar to those of their greater colleagues, and thereby imposing their own work upon the unsuspecting public; Mrs Radcliffe's name was one of those 'unwarrantably employed'.[45] The very name 'Mrs Radcliffe' was something to conjure by. Several novels bore on their title pages the name Mrs Radcliffe, or Radcliff, or Radcliffe, or Radclif, or Ratcliffe: for example, Mrs Elizabeth Ratcliffe's *The Mysterious Baron, or The Castle in the Forest, A Gothic Story* (1808) published by Newman at the Minerva Press. Mrs Mary Ann Radcliffe was genuinely entitled to style herself Mrs Radcliffe, and her publisher lost no opportunity to exploit the confusion with the greater novelist in promoting her work. Mary Ann Radcliffe's first novel *Radzivil* was published in 1790 by William Lane at the Minerva Press, as well as *The Fate of Velina de Guidova*, which is sometimes ascribed to her. These were both attributed to Ann Radcliffe in the Minerva Library Catalogues, exploiting the popularity of the younger novelist in the intervening years.[46] *Radclife's New Novelist's Pocket Magazine* appeared in 1802, a chapbook collection of tales compiled 'By Mrs Mary Anne Radclife, of Wimbledon in Surrey'. This was published in Edinburgh, and lasted for only two issues, so Mrs Radcliffe may never have heard of it.[47]

The very popular novel *Manfroné; or, The One-Handed Monk* (Longman, 1809) is attributed to Mary Anne Radcliffe, perhaps incorrectly, and was also attributed to Ann Radcliffe in most of its reprints.[48] The 1809 rumour of Mrs Radcliffe's death may have prompted Mary Ann Radcliffe to take up the mantle of the Great Enchantress. The second chapter of the novel opens with a direct imitation of the first view of the castle of Udolpho, Prince Manfroné (whose accent, like his severed hand, is dropped after the first chapter) resembles Schedoni with his brooding conscience, and Rosaline spends much of her time investigating deserted apartments with decayed bed hangings, her overwrought fancy inherited from Ann Radcliffe's Emily.

We do not know if Mrs Radcliffe was upset at being identified with the fierce republican sympathies expressed in Mary Ann Radcliffe's feminist tract *The Female Advocate; or, An Attempt to Recover the Rights of Women from Male*

Usurpation (written in 1792, but not published until 1799). It was specifically attributed to *the* Mrs Radcliffe in its French translation in 1799,[49] and presumably British readers made the same link. In her memoirs Mary Ann Radcliffe says she had intended to publish it anonymously, but her publisher 'strongly recommended giving my name to it. Whether, with a view to extend the sale, from the same name at that period standing high amongst the novel readers, – or from whatever other motive, is best known to himself.'[50] Obviously he wished to capitalize on the similarity of her name with that of the more famous Mrs Radcliffe. Valpy himself may have deliberately fostered this confusion on Dr Mitford.

The Memoirs of Mrs Mary Ann Radcliffe; in Familiar Letters to Her Female Friend (1810) inadvertently supported the rumours of Mrs Ann Radcliffe's death. This autobiography probably went into a second edition because it was thought to contain the memoirs of the mighty magician of Udolpho. The regret that Mrs Radcliffe's admirers must have experienced upon opening its pages is echoed by a reviewer of the work: 'We at first sight promised ourselves and our readers also, much satisfaction from presenting Memoirs of the very ingenious and much lamented Mrs Radcliffe, compiled by herself, but it seems that the lady here commemorated is, or rather was, a very different personage.'[51] Note nevertheless that the reviewer is certain of the death of the 'much lamented' Ann Radcliffe.

It is a curious coincidence that Mary Ann Radcliffe (whose husband was descended from James, Earl of Derwentwater) made a visit to the Duke of Rutland at Belvoir Castle, where she entered into (fruitless) negotiations with him concerning the exchange of land, upon which she hoped to build as a speculator in order to retrieve her financial situation.[52] If the Duke of Rutland was responsible for promoting the rumour about Mrs Radcliffe and his other property Haddon Hall, it is possible that he did not know that Ann Ward Radcliffe and Mary Ann Radcliffe were different women novelists, and that he assumed he knew *from personal acquaintance* that 'Mrs Radcliffe' *did* visit Haddon Hall, whether or not she was driven mad by its charms.

Incipient madness was part of the Radcliffe myth right from the beginning, even when Mathias compared her to the Sibyl of Apollo. Just as the Pythoness at Delphi induced her visions by inhaling narcotic vapours and devouring unsavoury leaves, so Mrs Radcliffe is supposed to have conjured up her nightmare terrors by eating raw vegetables before going to bed. Robert Macnish in *The Philosophy of Sleep* (1830) noted the influence of the stomach and liver upon one's dreams, and that indigestion was conducive to the most frightful visions:

> This fact was well known to the celebrated Mrs Radcliffe, who, for the purpose
> of filling her sleep with those phantoms of horror, which she has so forcibly

embodied in the 'Mysteries of Udolpho', and 'Romance of the Forest', is said to have supped upon the most indigestible substances; while Dryden and Fuseli, with the opposite view of obtaining splendid dreams, are reported to have eaten raw flesh.[53]

Raw meat and gin seem to have been the favoured forms of substance abuse, at least in the view of the American poet and traveller Bayard Taylor, who delivered a lecture on 'The Animal Man' in 1855: 'Byron, with all the shifting play of his wit, pathos, and passion, cannot wholly purify the pages of *Don Juan* from the smell of gin; and Mrs Radcliffe, in the nightmare horrors of her *Mysteries of Udolpho*, betrays the suppers of raw beef in which she indulged.'[54] Ann Radcliffe's eating habits have been embellished over the years, and by 1985 the offending fare had become 'undercooked pork chops'.[55]

While the rumours about confinement in Derbyshire were flying abroad, Talfourd claims that Mrs Radcliffe was in fact 'enjoying her wonted recreations and studies, with entire relish'.[56] As society speculated about her death and madness, she was studying the olden times at Penshurst, or having a pleasant seaside holiday in Portsmouth and the Isle of Wight. The only horror with which she had to cope was the bad service at the George Inn, Portsmouth, as noted in her travel journal around 10 October 1811:

> you could get nothing when you wanted it. We had fish brought without plates, and then plates without bread. All this owing to a vast throng of company, two hundred vessels or more being detained by winds, besides many ships of war. Nothing but ringing of bells and running about of waiters. If you ask a waiter a question, he begins a civil answer, but shuts the door before you have heard it all. It was very diverting to hear the different tones and measure of the ringings, particularly about supper time, and the next day about five, when every body happened to be dining at one and the same time, to hear them all ringing together, or in quick succession, in different keys and measure, according to the worn out, or better, patience of the ringer. These different keys enabled me to distinguish how often each bell was rung before it was answered; also the increasing impatience of the ringer, till, at the third, or fourth summons, the bell was in a downright passion. There was a mischievous amusement in this, after we had gone through the delay ourselves, and had gotten what we wanted.[57]

Many readers will wish that there were more of this delicate malice in Mrs Radcliffe's novels, and that their humour exhibited as sure a touch.

On 11 October they sailed on the packet for Ryde. Mrs Radcliffe took great interest in some of the crew and her fellow passengers, including two missionaries who would soon be going to Sierra Leone and Captain Reynolds,

> a plain, steady, grave seaman, of the old stamp; good sense, with a pious tender heart. Said he had carried, or that he was then about to carry, several hundred copies of the New Testament in the modern Greek, to be distributed under the direction of agents of the British and Foreign Bible Society.

She seems to have found such earnest piety gently amusing.[58]

This visit exhibits a powerful strain of melancholy as well as the sublime. At Portsmouth Mrs Radcliffe found the falling of the tide to be 'monotonous, not grand' as on previous visits. The dinner complications apparently aroused only a temporary liveliness in a wasteland of depression: 'Such life and bustle is inspiriting, for a little while.'[59] Later, settled at an inn on the Isle of Wight, the cadence of the sea reminded her of Shakespeare's *Tempest*:

> This resounding of the distant surge on a rocky shore might have given Shakspeare [*sic*] his idea when he makes Ferdinand, in the Tempest, hear, amidst the storm, bells ringing his father's dirge; a music which Ariel also commemorates, together with the sea-wave:–
>
> > 'Sea-nymphs hourly ring his knell,
> >   Ding, dong, bell!'[60]

During this autumn holiday they took several walks near Steephill and the Undercliffe, including the tiny church of St Lawrence. Behind this twelfth-century building, in 'a scene of extreme wildness, grandeur and solitude', Mrs Radcliffe took a childlike pleasure in hearing her voice echo beneath the cliffs. Echoes were an important element of Ossianic Romanticism; several chapters of Charles Bucke's *Philosophy of Nature* (1813) were devoted to echoes (Ossian was called 'the Son of the Rock'), and he mentions the Undercliffe in his chapter on the 'Character of Rocky Scenery'. The incident bears out her husband's testimony that she loved the sound of Greek, although she could not understand a word of it:

> Some of the shattered masses give most clear echoes: we stood before one, which repeated every syllable of several passages from the most sonorous languages, with an exactness of tone that was truly astonishing. It seemed as if a living spirit was in the rock, so near, so loud, and so exact! 'Speak to it, Horatio!' I could have listened to it for hours. How solemn is the voice of cliffs and seas! How great the style of Nature! how expressive! 'Speak to the rock!'

and again it gave every word, as if in sport or imitation, but with truth itself. How long had it slumbered in silence?[61]

The echo in the rock is being compared to the ghost of Hamlet's father. The previous Shakespearian reference was also to a dead father, as if Mrs Radcliffe especially cherished possible allusions to the death of her own father.

Although this last visit to her favourite holiday resort was an overall success, it was overshadowed by an unexplained sadness. Mrs Radcliffe's description of what was probably her last journey across the sea, back to Southampton from Cowes on 19 October, suggests that a wave of depression was rolling over her:

> How tranquil and grand the scene lay, beneath the gradually deepening shade! Still the dark shores and stately vessels kept their dignity upon the fading waters. How impressive the silence, and then how according the solemn strain, that died upon the waves from unseen and distant bugles, like a song of peace to the departing day! Another of those measured portions that make up our span of life, was gone; every one who gazed upon this scene, proud or humble, was a step nearer to the grave – yet none seemed conscious of it. The scene itself, great, benevolent, sublime – powerful, yet silent in its power – progressive and certain in its end, steadfast and full of a sublime repose: the scene itself spoke of its CREATOR.[62]

On this sober – and despairing – note the holiday ends. She would make one more trip the following year, but that would be her last long holiday, and shortly after her return she went into seclusion, not to a madhouse in Derbyshire, but to a cottage near Windsor Forest – where she remained sequestered for the next two-and-a-half years.

Sequestered at Windsor

Although Ann Radcliffe had been grossly libelled by Miss Spence and Revd Wheelwright, and their reports of her alleged madness were current among the very people whose respect she most valued, the rumours were not repudiated until well after her death. Talfourd says that 'Some of these rumours reached her; but she could not endure the thought of writing in the newspapers that she was not insane.'[1] No doubt such rumours were beneath her contempt. But it is curious that her 'scrupulous sense of propriety' would not at least permit her husband to take the necessary steps to defend her in print; he was, after all, a newspaper proprietor and ought to have known how to handle such matters with the necessary discretion. Rumours of a great deal less import were regularly refuted in the public journals: such refutations were in fact expressions of propriety. The original doubt remains unresolved: did Mrs Radcliffe remain silent on this matter because there was some element of truth in Elizabeth Spence's report that she suffered from 'deep-rooted and incurable melancholy'? 'Melancholy madness' is a condition we have come to associate with several of the writers and creative geniuses of the late eighteenth and early nineteenth centuries, including of course Charles Lamb, whose writings bear little trace of the paranoia evinced by the Gothic novelists. What contemporaries called the 'Blue Devils' was practically a fashionable literary disease.[2]

In St George's Fields, which faced the Radcliffe's home on China Terrace, the famous Dog and Duck tavern was demolished in 1811 to make way for the New Bethlehem Hospital. By 1815 London's premier lunatic asylum, with Colley Cibber's statues from the old hospital at Moorfields, representing Raving and Melancholy Madness, over its door, was situated across the road from Mrs Radcliffe's home – which perhaps is partly why she did not return to China Terrace in 1815 after her stay in Windsor, but moved to a new home in Pimlico. Most of the hospital's inmates were men, violent with Raving

Madness, paroxysms of frenzy and threatening behaviour, while the women were disordered by Melancholy Madness: despondency, dejection, depression and despair. Among both groups were many with imaginary fears of persecution. There were halfway houses at Hoxton and Bethnal Green, and forty licensed private asylums in London. In 1824 'insanity is so prevalent, . . . [that] all the private and public mad-houses are nearly filled with lunatics'.[3] The son of Bishop Hallifax, who figures in Mrs Radcliffe's prized lineage, was remembered by Sir Egerton Brydges as a tutor at King's and an eminent Greek student, 'who afterwards fell into the deplorable calamity of mental alienation'.[4] The consultant at Bethlehem Hospital noted 'the alarming increase of Insanity' from about 1790 to 1810, perhaps reflecting the turmoil in Europe.[5] Very few lunatics had haunted imaginations of the Gothic variety attributed to Mrs Radcliffe – which is really a literary construct – and there is no incontrovertible evidence that her Melancholia became severe enough to slip over into Mania, to use the only two divisions recognized by physicians at the time.

The *Annual Biography* obituary suggested that Ann Radcliffe's asthma during the last twelve years of her life 'occasioned a general loss of health, and consequent depression of spirits'.[6] But, as previously noted, the *New Monthly Magazine* obituary in May 1823 referred to her disgust with the world, 'a depression of spirits' for many years and seclusion from society 'followed by ill health'[7] – that is, suggesting that depression preceded rather than followed ill health. Talfourd when he wrote the memoir in 1826 omitted strong wording and phrases such as 'disgust with the world' and 'depression of spirits', and portrayed Ann Radcliffe's declining health in vague general terms. Presumably he was suppressing something.

The extraordinary degree to which Mrs Radcliffe had secluded herself from society was supplemented by the obsessively overprotective actions of her husband, and it can be difficult untangling the different motivations of man and wife. The affectionate husband has obviously concealed certain facts about his wife's condition. According to the *Annual Biography* obituary 'her only consolation was the unwearied attention of an affectionate husband, whose own intelligence enabled him to appreciate her worth'. This might suggest a serious state of long-term depression requiring assiduous care and encouragement by the only person who did not abandon hope for her recovery. Perhaps just as William Radcliffe tried to persuade his wife to stop imagining spirits of the vasty deep (during a minor nervous breakdown?) in 1802–3, so he now actively protected her reputation from an uncomprehending outside world as the nearly clinical depression evident in her journals in 1811 culminated in a major breakdown in the winter of 1812.

All of her heroines, like Julia in *A Sicilian Romance*, 'loved to indulge the melancholy of her heart in the solitude of the woods' (vol. 1, 96). We do not know enough about Ann Radcliffe's personal life to establish convincingly any 'causes' for her apparent melancholia. We cannot dismiss the possibility that it may simply be the result of an inborn temperament, as from an early age she seems to have been shy and withdrawn, becoming increasingly reclusive and hypersensitive to criticism in later life. If she suffered from an acute anxiety disorder that had a physiological cause such as some damage to the nervous system during childhood, the record certainly leaves no evidence of this (as it does, for example, for Sukey Wedgwood's physical symptoms of invalidism). Melancholic reverie pervades her novels to an uncommon degree, far beyond the requirements of literary convention. Robert Kiely feels that her works exhibit 'a sadness which is not merely fashionable. Especially after the death of her parents, her thoughts return again and again to death' and *intrude upon* rather than derive from her observations.[8] We should perhaps also hold out the possibility that she may have been affected by yet a third death in her family: Mrs John Jebb died on 20 January 1812 in her house in Half Moon Street, Piccadilly. She was interred in the Dissenter's burying ground in Bunhill Fields, immediately over the body of her husband (it is not known if Mrs Radcliffe attended her funeral).[9]

We can deduce that she began to be seriously unwell, from asthma if nothing else, from late 1810 or early 1811, just when the rumours of her madness and death were appearing in print. Possibly it was in search of some relief from the first asthma attacks that she visited the Isle of Wight in the autumn of 1811. Her visit to Malvern in October 1812 was unquestionably in search of healthy air, relaxation and exercise. Although she climbed the Malvern Hills with apparently no difficulty, this was the last time she was well enough to make an excursion of more than a single day's duration (until a fateful trip to Ramsgate ten years later, just prior to her death).

The Malvern excursion was to provide a source of anxiety in the shape of yet another false attribution. Mrs Radcliffe always took the latest literary productions with her when she travelled, to occupy her spare hours after walking and sightseeing. It was probably while she was in Malvern that she first dipped into the six volumes of the *Letters of Anna Seward: Written between the Years 1784 and 1807*, which had been published in Edinburgh in the previous year. Anna Seward was a poet of the old school; a line from her 'Monody on Major André' provides the epigraph of Chapter XX of Ann Radcliffe's *The Romance of the Forest*. The 'Swan of Lichfield', as Seward was dubbed, had been on friendly terms with Ann's Dissenting family. For example, she visited Joshua Jebb in Tapton in September 1796, when he was ninety-nine years old.[10] She was also acquainted with Dr John Jebb and his wife, whom she had met in Buxton in 1784, and was much distressed by news of Dr Jebb's death in 1786: 'Never were the graces of conciliation, resulting from warm and ingenuous benevolence, more engagingly blended with superior talents, and high-strung virtues, than in that extraordinary man.'[11] Her brother subscribed to Jebb's *Works* in 1787. Sadly, Seward's praise of Ann Radcliffe's novels was intermixed with stinging criticism of her lack of discrimination: in her view her talent had been devoted to purposes less moral than the great Richardson's; while 'her powers of scenic description are very considerable', she nevertheless lacks judgement and is unaware that the 'laboured exertion' of her powers leads to satiety. However, credit is given where credit is due: 'The object behind the mysterious veil, described at first only by saying what it is not, and the long deserted bed-chamber of the late Marchioness, form a very august exhibition of the terrible graces, who never frown with effect but when they are led by the hand of Genius.' Seward was less impressed with *The Italian*, feeling that the author's pen 'toils after the terrible'.[12]

The editor of the letters could not have realized that Ann Radcliffe was still alive in 1811, otherwise he would have suppressed the most hurtful passages. Mrs Radcliffe was highly distressed when she read Seward's letters to various friends expounding the view that not only was she the author of *Plays on the Passions*, but that she even claimed to be the author before the real author was discovered to be Joanna Baillie.[13] I have discussed the actual letters in their proper chronological place in Chapter 13, but we must now focus upon Mrs Radcliffe's response when she read them upon their publication. In no sense was the attribution in the letters of 1799 promulgated by their publication in 1811, because the letters that make it quite clear that Joanna Baillie was the real author are printed later in the same collection.[14] But William Radcliffe quite rightly pointed out that 'there was, however, no direct retraction of the alleged hearsay which Miss S. had thus chosen to leave upon record; and Mrs Radcliffe found little relief in the virtual refutation'.[15] In other words, the authorship was no longer at issue, but the allegation that Mrs Radcliffe had once claimed to be the author remained as a stain upon her character. Apparently indifferent to rumours of insanity and death, she was jealous of her reputation as an honourable author, and on at least this one occasion she actively took steps to rectify the rumour. According to her husband, she attempted to confront Mrs Jackson, who had originally relayed the claim to Miss Seward. From this edition of Seward's letters, Mrs Radcliffe knew that Mrs Jackson had written *Dialogues on the Doctrine and Duties of Christianity* and that she resided latterly in Edinburgh, but these facts nevertheless proved insufficient to trace her whereabouts in 1811:

She learned that Mrs Jackson, after having resided at Bath, had removed to Edinburgh. Mr Davies the bookseller, (of the eminent firm of Cadell and Davies,) who had opportunities of procuring information as to whatsoever was literary in Edinburgh, was requested to inquire whether Mrs Jackson was then in that city, in order that Mrs Radcliffe might ask from whom Mrs J. had heard the report. The answer to inquiries made at his request was, that the Mrs Jackson who appeared to be meant had left Edinburgh; that the place of her subsequent residence had not been learned; and that she was not even supposed to be living. Thus the subject was dropped; for to Miss Baillie herself Mrs Radcliffe could address nothing but protestations, which could not prove a negative, and which might be held intrusive; as there was no reason to suppose that that lady had ever credited the report. It was utterly untrue. The whole conduct of Mrs Radcliffe must have shown that she was incapable, not only of seeking, but of desiring any illegitimate fame, – of any indirect means of increasing the praise which she could not fail to know was given to her writings. . . . There was not the slightest pretence for the imputation. No person ever asked Mrs Radcliffe if she was the author of the Dramas; it was never hinted to her that they were conjectured to be hers; she never knew the report, except from Miss S.'s letters: she therefore could not give it even the indirect encouragement of designedly omitting to contradict it.[16]

Mrs Radcliffe had learned from Seward's letters that Mrs Jackson had befriended Sir Walter Scott while in Edinburgh, around 1807, and perhaps she feared that the great poet harboured suspicions about her integrity. She also would have known that Joanna Baillie became good friends with Mrs Carter, and she would have been distressed to think that this rumour must have circulated among the Bluestockings – as indeed it *had* circulated very widely, as previously shown.

William Radcliffe, every bit as scrupulous as his wife, wound himself into a convoluted knot trying to set the record straight. Robert Miles perceives an 'ideological character' in the Talfourd/Radcliffe memoir,[17] but the suppression of the radical Dissenting culture and the foregrounding of the genteel Anglican culture cannot be attributed solely to an inherent 'snobbishness' on the part of William Radcliffe, and irrespective of his estimation of the political sensibilities of his audience. Miles suggests that William's comments about his wife's pride in her 'superior' relatives and concern for propriety 'may simply reflect his snobbish values'[18] – but this ignores the outright evidence of the 'snobbish' values displayed by Ann Radcliffe in her journal entry describing the conversation with the vulgar housekeeper about 'Lady' Perry during the visit to Knole. Surely Miles is uncautious when he says that 'we have only his word for it that it was she, and not himself, who was most scandalised' by such blots upon her character as the rumour spread by Mrs Jackson. Her husband says that 'she had indeed often a very painful remembrance [of this circumstance], though her unwillingness to appear before the public in any sort of contention would not permit her to mention it otherwise than to a very few friends'.[19] Nevertheless Ann Radcliffe participated in efforts to remove this stain during her lifetime as much as did her husband after her death. William apologizes that he has 'been tedious upon this subject, but it was a great one with the deceased'[20] – which clearly indicates that it was she, more than he, who was scandalized. If we do not accept 'only William's word' for this, then we have to believe that he has lied and fabricated a whole series of specific details illustrating his wife's concern, which hardly seems likely. I see no reason to doubt, for example, William's statement that his wife was 'uneasy' about the reference to her in Pennington's biography of Mrs Carter. My view is that she did indeed react to Seward's charge with acute sensitivity, and that this is a measure of her ill health at the time. When Talfourd reported this incident in his 1826 memoir, he said that Mrs Radcliffe was 'tremblingly alive' to such rumours because of her seclusion from the world, and he referred to 'the singular apprehensiveness of her moral sense' as if to apologize for her overreaction.[21] Similarly, Sir Walter Scott reserved his astonishment for the inexplicably unchallenged reports of madness and death, and felt that such trifling rumours about authorship were fairly commonplace in comparison: 'the late Miss Seward would probably have suffered equally, had she been aware of the pain she inflicted by giving currency to a rumour so totally unfounded'.[22]

Everyone was too tactful to point out that Mrs Radcliffe was being paranoiac. For more than twelve years William Radcliffe remembered the reaction of his wife when she first read Seward's *Letters*, and he consulted the volumes again when writing the obituary, in order to quote the offending passages extensively and accurately. These letters must have preyed upon Mrs Radcliffe's mind constantly for the rest of her life, for the denial of this attribution forms the bulk of the obituary by her husband; indeed it seems to be the main reason for its composition. To clear her name was the last solemn testimony of his love for her: 'if it be possible that her spirit, now, as I humbly hope, beatified, can know what is passing here, may this asseveration of her innocence, solemnly made on her behalf, be one of its feeblest gratifications!'[23] The extended exposition of the incident bears witness to the fact that something crucial in the life of William and Ann Radcliffe is connected to her reading of Anna Seward's letters. I believe that it was her reading of these letters in late 1812, during a visit to Malvern, that triggered off a nervous breakdown. The obviously important position this incident occupies in the memory of her husband suggests to me that it was this that finally broke the highly-strung chords of her nervous temperament. Talfourd, as the official biographer, acknowledged that

> Mrs Radcliffe's greatest failing, if failing it can be termed, appears to have been the morbid delicacy of feeling which is acquired and nourished by living

in great retirement, and which generally induces individuals, particularly those of a nervous temperament, to attach an undue importance to trifles, for which, had they lived more in the world, they would not have cared.[24]

Talfourd thus skilfully conveys his own conclusion that Ann Radcliffe's behaviour at this time was neurotic. The conflict between propriety and imagination in her novels always occurs in the context of literary creativity, and this incident reveals how intimately her anxiety was connected to the problem of identifying herself as an author. The strangely intense language of William Radcliffe's 'asseveration of her innocence' suggests that he was defending another, unspoken, charge against his wife, namely that she had gone insane.

Immediately after returning from Malvern, Ann Radcliffe went into seclusion. According to Talfourd, 'From 1812 to 1815 inclusive, she passed much time at Windsor and its neighbourhood, and formed an intimate acquaintance with all the recesses of its forest.'[25] There she 'learned to smile' at those who consigned her to the madhouse or who charitably permitted her release in death from the terrors of her imagination. Talfourd passes over in silence the apparent fact that she retired to Windsor without the company of her husband. I suspect that Ann Radcliffe became the proverbial madwoman in the attic – that she was packed off to a quiet spot in Windsor to recover from a mental breakdown.

Despite the assertions in the obituaries regarding 'the unwearied attentions of an affectionate husband',[26] Mrs Radcliffe was probably attended in Windsor only by a servant, companion or nurse, while William continued to live in London. He carried on paying the rates on their home in China Terrace until the end of August 1815, when Mrs Radcliffe returned from Windsor and together they took a new home in Pimlico.[27] He would of course have visited her regularly, but the 23-mile journey could take four hours, so it was not practicable to commute. The Queen sometimes went to London in the morning and returned to Windsor around 8.30 p.m., but such day-trips were not frequent.

Mrs Radcliffe is said to have occupied 'a small cottage in the town'.[28] There is no reference to the Radcliffes in the poor rate ledgers. But for several years during her stay in Windsor, rates were paid by the households of Elizabeth Ward, Francis Ward and Thomas Ward/Ann Ward. Ann Ward lodged in a house at 10 Peascod Street, the main shopping street; she is obviously the widow or sister of Thomas Ward who paid the rates up to November 1811, and she remained the occupant at least until 1818. We might speculate that this Ann Ward was a relative of William Ward, either his sister or sister-in-law, and that Ann Ward Radcliffe resided with her after the death of Thomas Ward.[29]

While the world considered her fate as sealed, Mrs Radcliffe was exploring the forest of Windsor Great Park and strolling in the grounds of the castle. Windsor Terrace was a great promenade for the local inhabitants and visitors alike, and crowds gathered especially on Sunday evenings to observe the royal family going to the music room of the castle. The Long Walk was also popular for promenades, accompanied by military bands. Dr Burney in July 1799 described the Park as an Elysium for happy farmers, servants and tradespeople.[30]

During Mrs Radcliffe's retirement at Windsor, the castle was a *grand couvent* occupied by Princess Charlotte and her grandmother Augusta, the Princess Royal, and her maiden aunts, Princesses Elizabeth, Mary and Sophia. There was ample opportunity for riding and walking – indeed there was little else to do. Throughout 1813 the *Windsor and Eton Express* regularly reports the airings in the park taken by Princesses Elizabeth and Mary in the company of Lady Cranley, and Princess Charlotte in the company of Miss Knight, trips by the Queen and Princess Elizabeth to Frogmore, and rides in the Great Park by Princesses Charlotte, Augusta and Sophia.

Fanny, a mangy spaniel that Mrs Radcliffe had rescued in the streets of London, came as her companion to Windsor; she features in the anecdotes about dogs kept by noted personalities collected by John Thomas Smith, assistant to the sculptor Nollekens and eventually Keeper of the Prints and Drawings in the British Museum, in his rambling memoir *Nollekens and His Times* (1828) (Nollekens had died one month after Mrs Radcliffe):

> Mrs Radcliffe's attention was one day arrested by a boy who stood silently weeping under the gateway of the Little Stableyard, St James's; he held a cord, to the end of which a most miserable spectacle of a dog was tied, shivering between him and the wall. She requested to know the cause of his grief, and the poor little fellow, after sobbing for some time, with a modest reluctance stammered, 'my mo-mo-mo-mother insists upon my hanging Fan; she won't keep her because her skin is bare. Don't touch her, Ma'am, she has got the mange.' – 'Well, my little fellow, if you will walk back with me, I will not only give you half-a-crown, but will keep your dog, and you shall come and see it.'

Given proper care and attention, Fanny soon regained a fine coat, and was admired for her great beauty.[31]

The Princesses, who knew the fame of Mrs Radcliffe, recognized her in their walks at Windsor. The English fondness for dogs being what it is, Fanny in particular was 'often noticed by the late Queen and the Princesses, when walking with her mistress in Windsor Park, at the time Mrs Radcliffe had a small cottage in the town'. Smith relates the following incident as proof of Fanny's good breeding:

One of the Princesses' dogs, a spaniel exactly of Fanny's size, caught one end of a long bone, at the moment Fan had found it; who, instead of snarling as a dog generally does when an interloper attempts to carry off a prize, very good-temperedly complied with the playfulness of the Princess's dog by continuing to walk by her side, just like two horses in a curricle, each holding the extreme end of the bone, to the no small amusement of the royal equestrians, who frequently recognized and noticed Mrs Radcliffe as the Authoress and Fanny's mistress.[32]

While the Princesses were not engaged in their rides, they were occupied by (imagined) palace intrigue and reading. All of the Princesses, and the Queen, were of course eager to read *Camilla* by Fanny Burney, former Keeper of the Robes to the Queen; there were few impediments once the Bishop of Exeter sanctioned their reading of *Cecilia*, despite it being called a 'novel'.[33] Anne Ker's *The Heiress di Montalde* (1799) was dedicated with permission to Her Royal Highness The Princess Augusta Sophia, as was *Contrast* (1828) by Regina Maria Roche, author of a dozen Minerva Novels. The Princess of Wales's Lady-in-Waiting Lady Charlotte Bury was a good friend of Matthew Gregory Lewis, and an avid reader of *The Monk* and other tales of terror. The Princesses may have been introduced to Mrs Radcliffe by Princess Charlotte's governess the Duchess of Leeds. The Duchess of Leeds presumably read, or at least dipped into, *The Romance of the Forest* if not her other novels. The immense advance interest in *The Mysteries of Udolpho* had prompted Hookham and Carpenter to publish a fourth edition of *The Romance of the Forest* in early 1794, and Mrs Radcliffe had taken this opportunity to establish her *bona fides* as a proper lady by dedicating it to the Duchess of Leeds:[34]

> *Dedication*
> *To Her Grace*
> *The Duchess of Leeds.*
>
> *Madam,*
>
> *I am too grateful for the honour of being permitted to say that this work has Your GRACE's approbation, to misuse the opportunity now offered me of addressing you, by praise, which it would be presumption in me to offer, and which it is the privilege of Your GRACE's merits to disdain.*
>
> *Rather let me rejoice that the attention given in the following pages, to the cause of morality, has induced you to overlook the weakness of my endeavour to support it.*
>
> *I am*
>
> *Your GRACE's*
> *Obedient humble Servant,*
> *ANN RADCLIFFE*

The introduction between Ann Radcliffe and the Duchess of Leeds may have been effected by her publisher Hookham and Carpenter, for their entire booklist itself (with Radcliffe at its head) had been 'Dedicated (by Permission) to her GRACE the DUCHESS of LEEDS' in 1793.[35] The intimacy of the relationship between the Duchess and the novelist cannot be determined, but they may even have met at a performance of a Handel oratorio organized by the Duke of Leeds, for they had in common an intense enthusiasm for music. The Duchess, with her sisters, 'had been noticed for singing agreeably Handel's music'; an obituary of the Duke of Leeds (who died in 1799) noted that she 'chiefly attracted the attention of his grace by her peculiar taste and skill in music'.[36] Francis Godolphin (Osborne), the Duke of Leeds, was a member of Dr Charles Burney's club, and the Duchess was scheduled to sing at one of Dr Burney's parties, but did not follow it up because of her appointment as governess to the Princess of Wales, announced by *The Times* on 15 January 1813.[37]

Catherine Anguish, daughter of Thomas Anguish, one of the Masters in Chancery, became the Duke of Leeds's second wife in 1788.[38] She was born on 21 January 1764 and was thus within days of being Ann Radcliffe's exact contemporary. The Duke was Lord Lieutenant of the East Riding, Yorkshire, and Mrs Radcliffe and the Duchess may have had a mutual acquaintance in Yorkshire; perhaps it was when William and Ann visited relatives in Yorkshire in 1794 that the possibility of the dedication was proffered and accepted.

When Lady de Clifford resigned as governess to the seventeen-year-old Charlotte, Princess of Wales and heir to the throne, the Duchess of Leeds was appointed as her successor. Lady de Clifford left Windsor on Thursday 7 January 1813 and the Duchess of Leeds arrived on Friday to take up her two-year appointment.[39] She was appointed by the Prince Regent, in spite of the objections of Queen Caroline, through the recommendation of the Regent's friend Thomas, 2nd Earl of Chichester, whose wife was a daughter of the Duke of Leeds by his first wife.[40] She was upward striving and her false gentility somewhat matched that of Mrs Radcliffe. Because of her lowly birth – her father had been a Norfolk lawyer – she was regarded as an upstart. According to Lady Charlotte Bury, 'there were many epithets bestowed upon the Duchess of Leeds, such as "weak woman", and "a pinchbeck [i.e. counterfeit] duchess", &c., &c'.[41] Princess Charlotte despised her:

> The D of Leeds must [be] disagreable [*sic*] wherever she is, as she has no conversation, but stories of an hour's length; very *fidgety temper*, almost always ill, & keeping close to me whenever I am out in publick. . . . She is a *violent Tory. Her Part* at the Ball was quite *overacted*, for I have since heard she was *very grand* to several people. What can be expected of a *low woman* who has been *pushed up & never* found her *level?*[42]

The Princess's Lady Companion Cornelia Knight paints a rather more favourable picture of the Duchess, but the Duchess was a poor choice for controlling the rebellious Princess:

> the good Duchess of Leeds had no inclination to quarrel with anybody. Provided that she might ride two or three times a week at Hall's – a second-rate riding-school – on an old quiet horse for exercise, get into her shower-bath, and take calomel when she pleased, dine out, and go to all parties when invited, shake hands with everybody, and touch her salary, she cared for nothing more.[43]

Occasionally the Duchess organized children's balls at Windsor, and went to the summer fêtes given by Princess Elizabeth at her cottage, the Garden House, in Old Windsor. Princess Charlotte was herself intensely fond of music and novels, but in nearly all other respects her governess was her keeper rather than her companion. The Duchess followed close at her heels at all public engagements when at Warwick House in London, and accompanied her on most of her circumscribed rides and walks through Windsor Great Park and Forest.[44]

When the Regent and his agents failed to intimidate Princess Charlotte into marrying Prince William of Orange, the Duchess of Leeds and Miss Knight, and their servants, were ordered to resign, in July 1814. Lady Charlotte Bury's opinion is probably the most just: 'The Duchess of Leeds was an excellent quiet character, bent upon fulfilling her duty, but not suited to the stormy spirits with whom she had to deal.'[45] Her husband had died in 1799, age forty-eight, and she would die in 1837. Mrs Radcliffe and the Duchess arrived at Windsor at the same time, and departed within several months of one another, an intriguing coincidence.

Mrs Radcliffe may even have been an occasional visitor to the Castle or the Lower Lodge, or to Princess Elizabeth's romantic *cottage ornée* on the bank of the Thames at Old Windsor. References to Windsor in her posthumous works indicate that she had ready access to all parts of the royal estate at any time of the day or night, where she wandered freely by moonlight like the spectre in one of her novels.

Smith revealed that his informant for the anecdote about the Princess's dog was 'Miss Berry . . . who was greatly esteemed by Mrs Radcliffe'. Mary Berry was of course famous as Horace Walpole's literary executor: Mme de Stael declared her to be 'the cleverest woman in England'. 'It was said Miss Berry's parties were rather blue, and perhaps they were so'; she once stayed up all night on her return from a ball dressed in feathers and satin shoes, to read Joanna Baillie's *Plays on the Passions*.[46] She had a lesbian relationship with the sculptor Anne Seymour Damer, with whom she often travelled, and she performed in the amateur theatricals organized by Mrs Damer at

Strawberry Hill after Mrs Damer inherited Walpole's property.[47] Smith of course knew Miss Berry, because her companion Mrs Damer was a sculptor, just as was his master Nollekens. It is worth remarking that Giuseppe Marchi, who visited Mrs Radcliffe in 1797, was also a sculptor. Though Ann Radcliffe did not move in a 'literary circle', she may have moved on the periphery of an 'artistic circle'. Mary Berry sometimes visited Nollekens's studio, where she would have met Smith; for example, she went to his studio on 17 May 1811, while he was modelling a bust of her friend Lady Charlemont.[48] Mary Berry met the Princess of Wales in 1809, with whom she quickly became on intimate terms. The Princess of Wales visited her at Strawberry Hill in 1809, and from 1810 Mary Berry was a frequent dinner guest at Kensington Palace, where she became acquainted with the Duchess of Leeds. The Princess sat for Mrs Damer for her bust in January 1814, while Miss Berry was present.[49] She thus knew the Princess of Wales precisely during the period when Mrs Radcliffe resided at Windsor, so it seems likely that the anecdote about Fanny sharing a bone with the royal canine was relayed to Miss Berry directly by the Princess of Wales.

It does not seem likely that this fashionable socialite would have been a very close friend of Mrs Radcliffe – who we can be sure never went to a ball dressed in silver and white satin. But she and Miss Berry shared a common enthusiasm for art, and could have met, for example, at an exhibition of watercolours at the British Institution in Pall Mall. (Also, they both loved dogs.) They also shared a passion for 'Gothic Tours' to places such as Knole, Kenilworth and Warwick Castle, where Miss Berry and Mrs Damer spent five hours examining everything from the dungeon to the leads at the top of Caesar's Tower.[50] Mary Berry was a friend of George Robinson, Ann Radcliffe's publisher, and it is possible that an introduction had been made through him.

Whatever the case, it is extraordinary that this is the only testimony we have that Ann Radcliffe had a strong affection for anyone other than her husband or parents. Mary Berry is not mentioned in connection with the author by Radcliffe scholars, because the name of Smith's informant was suppressed in the second edition of his book the following year, and in all subsequent editions, a fact that has escaped notice in modern studies. It was probably Mary Berry who asked Smith or the publisher Henry Colburn to suppress the reference to herself, not because she did not wish to be linked with Mrs Radcliffe, nor because the anecdote was untrue (the anecdote remained unaltered), but because it would have been recognized that she had violated the confidence of the Princess of Wales. Or perhaps William Radcliffe, jealously watchful over his wife's reputation, asked Colburn, who had published his wife's posthumous works only two years earlier, to suppress the suggestion that his wife approved of the lesbian Twickenham set.

It is gratifying to discover that at the commencement of Mrs Radcliffe's residence in Windsor all the talk would have been about the ghost which had been sighted on the Terrace. In October 1812 a ghost appeared twice to the sentinel on duty. The sentinel made some passes at the spectre and demanded a response, to no avail. Breaking out into a cold sweat at having confronted the uncanny, the sentinel was almost literally scared to death. It took a while to calm him down, but he strenuously denied that it was his own reflection glimpsed in a window. The 'Terrace Ghost' occupied local discussion for quite some time, temporarily eclipsing the interest generated by the Berkshire county elections.[51] This may have inspired Ann Radcliffe's description of a moonlight walk along the Terrace of Windsor Castle with her husband (quoted in Chapter 14).

'At this time, she expressed her feelings in verse, rather than in prose', says Talfourd. Ann Radcliffe's genuinely *Posthumous Works*, edited by her husband and published together with *Gaston de Blondeville* in 1826, contain several poems which are clearly inspired by her stay in Windsor. 'Lines Written in a Bower at St Leonard's Hill' (vol. 4, 232–5), composed after reading a poem inscribed in the late Lady Elizabeth Lee's bower at St Leonard's Hill, the seat of her brother Earl Harcourt, are full of grief and fear of an early death. The poem is appropriately headed 'And I Too Was Once of Arcadia', from Poussin's famous painting in which the motto 'Et in Arcadia ego' is carved on a tomb prominently in the foreground. Lord Harcourt was the Warden of Windsor Forest, and the Dowager Lady Harcourt was a Lady-in-Waiting in late 1813; their home was frequently visited by the Princesses.

Ann Radcliffe's main occupation in Windsor was the composition of the long fairy epic *Edwy*,[52] in which the moon is frequently seen climbing above the towers on Windsor Terrace. William Radcliffe appended several footnotes to identify that some of the scenes took place near 'the Princess Elizabeth's late cottage at Old Windsor', the Maypole which 'formerly stood on the Green, before the gates of the Long Walk at Windsor' and 'the beautiful lodge at Sandpit Gate opening from the Western side of the Great Park'.[53] The central episode of the poem takes place on Midsummer's Eve along the enchantingly beautiful green alleys surrounding Virginia Water in Windsor Great Park. Her husband recalls that 'the Author was so frequently in the scenes alluded to, between the years 1810 and 1814, that the ideas, which this and the preceding and succeeding pieces show, may be safely dated from that period'.[54] William Radcliffe is less careful in his dating than Talfourd; they may have visited Windsor in 1810 and possibly even earlier, but the frequent moonlight scenes in the poem were probably written while Mrs Radcliffe was actually living in Windsor from 1812 to 1815 'inclusive' according to Talfourd. In *Edwy* Ann Radcliffe portrays herself as the Queen of the Night, voluntarily taking upon herself the enchantress persona ascribed to her by the critics:

> Where'er th'Enchantress points her wand,
>   Forth from the deep of darkness crowd
> Pale glimmering shapes, and silent stand
>   As waked from Death's unfolding shroud.

(Posthumous Works, iv, 268)

The first extended critique of Ann Radcliffe's work, in John Dunlop's *The History of Fiction* in 1814, is a summing up of the novelist in the sure knowledge that her *oeuvre* was complete. Dunlop consistently refers to her in the past tense: obviously her death is taken for granted by both writer and reader. It is worth noting that Ann Radcliffe's name does *not* appear in *A Biographical Dictionary of Living Authors*, published in 1816. If the publisher, Henry Colburn, had any reasons for believing that the great enchantress were still alive, she certainly would not have been omitted from this work.

The *coup de grâce* was the publication in 1815 of *The Poems of Mrs Ann Radcliffe*.[55] In the brief preface to this collection, the anonymous editor consistently refers to Mrs Radcliffe in the past tense: 'The genius of the author has been universally acknowledged. . . . That her genius was poetical, is proved by the beautiful and sublime descriptions of scenery with which her romances abound.'[56] This is clearly intended as a posthumous publication, and collects together all of the poems from *The Romance of the Forest* and *The Mysteries of Udolpho*.[57] The editor (whom I assume to be male, perhaps unjustly) took the occasion to append a selection of his own verse, an impertinence which would not have been taken had he believed Mrs Radcliffe to be still among the living. Insult was added to injury by his inclusion of his own poem titled 'Maniac's Song'. The collection was reissued in 1816 with the further addition of his 'Fragment' describing a nightmare vision full of clinically paranoic images:

> Methinks, at every step, the rolling viper,
> Bruised by my foot, will twist around my leg.
> The darkness seems condensing o'er my head,
> And somewhere near, I know, a dreadful chasm
> Yawns half across my path . . .[58]

Only two or three copies of the two editions of this very rare work are extant. It may have been suppressed or withdrawn very quickly, but it was never publicly challenged by William or Ann Radcliffe. There is no reference to the work in any of the obituaries, no disclaimer of authorship, no evidence that Ann Radcliffe was distressed at her work being pirated, no suggestion that she objected to being coupled with an inferior (and maniac) poet. If these poems were issued by an opportunist who was encouraged merely by rumours of her death, it seems unlikely that either William Radcliffe or Talfourd would not have identified the publication as being surreptitious. My inference is that the editor may have been a friend of the family, or even a relative, and that this publication may have been authorized by William Radcliffe and, as Michael Sadleir speculates,

> issued in anticipation of a death (or perhaps a permanent withdrawal from ordinary society) which unexpectedly did not take place. . . . Is it possible that Ann Radcliffe really *was* mentally afflicted; at one time seemed so ill that her death might momentarily be expected, or, at any rate, that no hope of recovery was entertained?[59]

The embarrassment which might have been caused upon a miraculous recovery – which would have occurred in the summer of 1815 when Mrs Radcliffe was found to be well enough to return to London from Windsor – would explain why the incident was passed over in silence by her husband and the official biographer. The final puzzle may be a mere coincidence: Michael Sadleir's copy of the 1816 edition of *The Poems*, in its original paper wrappers, bears on its title page the ownership signature 'J. Radcliffe 1828'.

The Final Years

———— • ————

William and Ann Radcliffe moved to No. 5 Stafford Row, Pimlico, in 1815. 'The situation in which they resided, during the last ten years, is one of the most cheerful round the metropolis.'[1] It was situated directly opposite Buckingham Palace: the rate books always listed the final occupant of Stafford Row as Her Majesty the Queen. William Radcliffe is first cited as residing there in the rate book compiled on 30 March 1816,[2] but the colophon of the *English Chronicle* for the issue for 13–15 July 1815 states that the newspaper was 'Printed & published for himself & Co. by W. Radcliffe, No. 3, Catharine-Street, Strand, (also of Stafford-Row, Pimlico).' That part of Stafford Row in which the Radcliffes' house was situated was demolished and is now occupied by the Buckingham Palace Hotel. However, plain but substantial three-storey brick houses contemporary with theirs survive further down the row, in what is now called Stafford Place.

Talfourd says that after Mrs Radcliffe returned from Windsor her curiosity was now satiated with her travels, and she became 'more attracted to the comforts of home'. One of these domestic comforts was canine. It was while residing at Stafford Row that she acquired one of her last dogs, a large spaniel whom she named 'Dash'. 'One day it happened, as Mr and Mrs Radcliffe were walking along the Strand, to visit the Exhibition of the Royal Academicians at Somerset-place, they saw a poor half-starved dog that had just been drawn upon the pavement, a coach-wheel having broken one of its legs.' Mrs Radcliffe, 'with her accustomed humanity', asked her husband to procure a coach, which took them and the dog 'to Stafford-row', where her careful attention restored the dog to perfect health.[3]

Obviously the stay in Windsor marked a threshold, after which Mrs Radcliffe – only fifty-one years old – was no longer fit to travel on long excursions, though she still relished the pleasures of touring in a more circumscribed manner.[4] She and William hired a carriage during the summer months, and made day-trips to beauty spots close to London, where they would dine and spend the day at a good inn, and then return home in the evening. Their favourite places of resort were Esher, Stanmore, Richmond, Southgate and especially Harrow, 'where they chose the room, not the largest, but which commands the richest prospect, and where Crawley Wood, near Ashridge, could be often distinctly seen'. These visits were pleasant but subdued, and it seems significant that Ann Radcliffe abandoned her habit of writing travel notes, something which would not have been impeded by merely asthmatic difficulties. I infer that after her apparent recuperation at Windsor, she was more or less sequestered by an ever-vigilant husband during this last decade of her life. Now would begin the process of beatification by her husband, who seems to have given up the *English Chronicle* during the latter part of his wife's illness.[5]

We have one first-hand report of Mrs Radcliffe's melancholy appearance during the last years of her life. This comes from the amiable and omnivorous littérateur Charles Bucke. He had acclaimed Mrs Radcliffe in *The Philosophy of Nature*, which he first published anonymously in 1813:

> For elegance of taste and sentiment, for the variety and strength, the beauty and amenity of her descriptions, Mrs Ratcliffe [*sic*] stands unrivalled, in her department of romance. It is impossible to read this enchanting writer without following her in all her magic windings, withersoever she is pleased to lead us.[6]

Bucke's study proved to be very popular, and Mrs Radcliffe probably read the expanded edition which appeared in 1821, retitled *On the Beauties, Harmonies, and Sublimities of Nature*, in which he first acknowledged himself as author. Here he praised the joys of rural retirement surrounded by a picturesque landscape which seemed to realize the beauties 'of Ariosto and Tasso, Spenser, and the "Genius of Udolpho"'. He added an even more gracious compliment by his assertion that she was 'bred in the schools of Dante and Ariosto, and whom the Muses recognize as the sister of Salvator Rosa'.[7] Mrs Radcliffe was so pleased by this that she wished to make the author's acquaintance. Bucke explained the event in a footnote to the third edition, published in 1837:

> For this criticism Mrs Ratcliffe [*sic*] was pleased to send me her thanks. Some time after, I was invited to supper. Her conversation was delightful! She sung *Adeste Fideles* with a voice mellow and melodious, but somewhat tremulous. Her countenance indicated melancholy. She had been, doubtless, in her youth, beautiful. She was a great admirer of Schiller's Robbers. Her favourite tragedy was Macbeth. Her favourite painters were, Salvator, Claude, and Gaspar Poussin: her favourite poets, after Shakespeare, Tasso, Spenser, and Milton. There was,

for many years, a report that this accomplished lady was afflicted with insanity. How the report came to be raised I know not; but, I believe, it never was the case. She had not only an elegant taste, but a comprehensive understanding.[8]

The parenthetical 'I believe' is a rather awkward way to dismiss a rumour, as if he is not altogether certain. Curiously enough, this edition was dedicated to the Duke of Rutland, whose seat at Haddon Hall was believed to be the model for the castle of Udolpho.

This supper must have taken place during Christmas 1821, to judge by Mrs Radcliffe's choice of song. She would certainly have enjoyed the adulation offered by her young admirer: 'I have read her *Romance of the Forest* four times; her *Italian* five times; her *Mysteries of Udolpho* nine times; and my imagination is, even now, always charmed whenever I think of either.' If she had read Bucke's *Amusements in Retirement* (1816), she would have been pleased by his relation of the story of her illustrious ancestors John and Cornelius De Witt.[9]

By a curious irony, after all the premature rumours of Mrs Radcliffe's death, less than a year before her actual demise she was rumoured to be planning a comeback, a report prompted by the ill-advised reappearance of old Madame Mara upon the stage. Madame Mara was celebrated for her singing of 'Mad Bess' from Purcell in Covent Garden, which she performed for many years even when her voice was no longer up to it.[10] She nevertheless reappeared in March 1822, when her declining powers were embarrassingly exposed to her expectant public. The contributor to *Blackwood's* claimed on this occasion to have

> heard a report, not in general circulation, that another old lady of equal fame in literature to that of Madame Mara in music, is about to resume her exertions, after a long interval, and to strive again at a species of composition which requires, above every thing, a fervid imagination, and a fresh and elastic fancy. I allude to Mrs Radcliff [*sic*], the author of Mysteries of Udolpho, who, it seems, is preparing a new romance. Whoever has tasted the melancholy sweetness and mystery of her writings, . . . will be uneasy at hearing she is about again to essay these things, and to vex the charm which has wrapped itself, I hope for ever, round her name.[11]

This rumour lends some support to my view that she revised *Gaston* for publication after returning from Windsor, specifically writing the Introduction which frames the romance.

According to the *Annual Biography*, 'During the last twelve years of her life, Mrs Radcliffe suffered greatly at intervals from a spasmodic asthma.'[12] This refers to the violent asthma attacks or spasms to which many asthma sufferers are subject. Mary Russell Mitford's mother suffered from the same illness less than a year after Ann Radcliffe's death, and Mitford's description of her mother's tribulations can help us to appreciate the author's own experience:

> My dear mother has had an attack of that terrible complaint, the spasmodic asthma, which continued for several months. The spasms came on every night at twelve or one o'clock, and continued for three or four hours with such violence that I have feared, night after night, that she would die in my arms. At last, the very great skill of a medical gentleman in this neighbourhood relieved her, though the remedies were so severe that for months she continued as weak as an infant, and the very first day that she thought herself well enough to venture to church she took cold, and the tremendous disorders reappeared, if possible with greater violence and greater obstinacy.[13]

The condition was not curable, and it is distressing to read a physician's list of putative remedies: 'Cathartics. – Emetics. – Diaphoretics. – Bleedings. – Diuretics. – Issues. – Anti-spasmodics. – Expectorants. – Blisters. – Inhaling of Vapors. – Oxygen. – Hydrogen. – Stomachics. – Absorbents. – Stimulants. – Bathing. – Tonics.'[14] None of these are very effective except for anti-spasmodics, such as vinegar, opium (which was highly recommended), ether and various tonics. The medicine Mrs Radcliffe took (discussed below) did include opium, but in quantities too small to account for any decay in her mental powers. A careful and weak diet was advised, and changes of air were often helpful: in fact 'there should be very particular enquiries made as to the nature of the situation in which the patient lives'.[15] Mrs Radcliffe's desire to live in 'open and airy situations' takes this advice to heart.

Like modern treatments for asthma, those of a century ago aimed to clear the air passages. A common antidote to violent asthma attacks was a herbal mixture called Stramonium. Other treatments for the distressing disorders of this illness, particularly the paroxysms during which the sufferer cannot breathe except by sitting bolt upright and exerting all his or her effort to do so, included mixtures of gum ammoniac and asafoetida, or Paregoric Elixir and Tincture asafoetida, or two drachms of gum ammoniacum dissolved in half a pint of Pennyroyal water and one ounce of oxymel of Squills.[16] Asafoetida is still used today as an anti-spasmodic, and gum ammoniac helps to clear catarrh. Inhalation of oxygen was a respite, but not a cure. The atmosphere was believed to be a compound of Oxygene air and Azotic air (the latter containing a high degree of mephitic fluid detrimental to health), and sometimes Carbonic acid air; the highest proportion of oxygenic air was to be found out of doors and not in confined hospital wards. Air as pure as possible was the most recommended treatment at the turn of the century, just as modern patients will benefit from breathing pure oxygen.[17]

There is no essential difference between 'humoural' asthma (brought on by colds) and 'spasmodic' asthma; the latter is simply more severe and constant, characterized by a stitch in the sides and a tightness across the breast even after the attack subsides. Dyspepsia, hypochondria, lowness of spirits and other nervous disorders were common symptoms.[18] Persons with melancholic temperaments were believed to be more susceptible to contracting the disease,[19] just as today the symptoms of asthma are often felt to be psychosomatic, in particular brought on by anxiety.

We do not need to speculate about Mrs Radcliffe's last illness, for there exists a remarkable document containing detailed descriptions of it: her own commonplace book, recording the progress of her health from May to October 1822. This is the only manuscript in Ann Radcliffe's own handwriting to have escaped oblivion. It was preserved through the diligent acquisition of two American collectors specializing in medical ephemera: Alexander Smets, who purchased it in 1842 from an unknown source, and James Orchard Halliwell-Phillipps, who bought it from Smets's estate, from whence it entered the Mellen Chamberlain collection, and now resides in the Boston Public Library.[20] It is an ordinary notebook, of blank pages bound in marbled boards, and the first half-a-dozen pages contain short passages copied from books which attracted her interest, such as Sir Walter Scott's *Life of Dryden*, Hughes's *Travels in Sicily, Greece and Albania* and Coxe's *Memoirs of the Duke of Marlborough*. It is especially interesting for containing her copy of a passage from Evelyn attacking the concept of the Established Church of England at the time of the 1688 Revolution – further evidence that Ann Radcliffe was a 'revolutionary' sympathizer even in the last year of her life:

> 'in all the declarations which have hitherto been published in pretended favour of the Church of England, there is not once the least mention of the Reformed, or Protestant Religion, that only of the *Church of England, as by Law established*, which Church the Papists tell us is the *Church of Rome* which is (say they) the Catholic Church of England, that only is established by law. The C. of England in the Reformed sense so established is but an usurped authority.' Evelyn's Letter to the Archbishop of Canterbury. Oct 7, 1688. (Folio 5)

Unfortunately what began as a commonplace book was quickly taken over to record the progress of the illness that would lead to her death. The first entry in this dismal record is her transcription of a prescription dated 17 May 1822 which a Mr Oliver (or Ollier) had given to her when she consulted him following a 'severe spasm'. Two more prescriptions from Oliver/Ollier follow, dated 18 and 23 May, then a prescription from a Dr Garthshore 'for keeping the stomach and bowels in good order', then a prescription from a Dr Berkeley given to a Mrs Morris – a friend or acquaintance with whom Mrs Radcliffe had shared her distress – 'for a cough with hard breathing. I found considerable relief from this. Two table spoonfuls three times a day. It caused perspiration and eased the breathing.' But the spasms continued, and from 28 May onward there follows a sequence of nine prescriptions from Dr Scudamore. Dr Charles Scudamore was a society physician; for example, in 1825 Anne Lister was treated for her venereal infection (acquired through lesbian sexual intercourse) by Dr Scudamore, who was in Buxton attending to various people including her aunt who had come to take the waters.[21] His actual prescriptions are pasted into the book, opposite Mrs Radcliffe's own expanded transcription of them,[22] together with her occasional comments on their effectiveness. For example, concerning a prescription dated 1 June: 'I took this medicine once during a spasm, 3 spoonfuls only, and after some time became gradually relieved, and breakfasted. I have generally *always* found *some* relief from warm tea, especially if I could eat a little.' Deborah Rogers emphasizes that several prescriptions testify to intestinal problems such as constipation: for example, the medications included Epsom salts and Liqu. Calcis used for dyspepsia and diarrhoea, but 'It is, of course, entirely possible that Radcliffe's various medications themselves contributed to intestinal difficulties.'[23]

Most of the prescriptions involved a purgative, and included both a draught (that is a cough mixture) and pills. For example, on 17 May the doctor prescribed pills made from a mercury salt and antimony powder in a rose base (*sub. hydrargyri, pulv. antimonialis, compact rosae galliae*). This is a diaphoretic to encourage perspiration, an expectorant and an emetic, a diuretic and purgative. Mercury is recommended for 'bilious' symptoms, and also for congestive oedema (swelling with fluid) and bronchitis. The liquid medicine in this prescription consisted of magnesium sulphate, a gum from the Manna Ash, and a tincture of senna, in an effusion of senna (*sulphatis magnesiae, manna, infus. foli. Sennae*). This is a very powerful laxative, described in modern pharmacopoeias as 'a coalheaver's medicine'.[24] The prescription on 30 May included the mercury pills, and a draught made from potassium carbonate, a camphor preparation, opium syrup, a sulphur compound (ether spirit), digitalis and fresh lemon juice. Potassium carbonate is an expectorant, and is used (usually as bicarbonate) with lemon juice as an antacid. Camphor is a stomach settler, often for flatulence, and is also used for colds, as an expectorant. Tincture of digitalis is a heart stimulant, sometimes used in cases of pneumonia, and necessary because of the stress put upon the heart by the other compounds. Opium syrup (*syr. papav. 1 drachm*) is used as a suppressant and sedative in cough mixtures. Compound ether spirit (*Sp. aetheris sulph. comp.*) stimulates the stomach and circulation, and reflexly excites the heart. This prescription is repeated later: three tablespoonsful to be taken during a spasm and one tablespoonful every half hour afterwards.

Two things are clear from this series of prescriptions. The first is that they were of a severity sufficient to render Mrs Radcliffe as weak and exhausted as Mary Russell Mitford's mother; the frequent use of mercury pills and draughts of senna or opium and digitalis is particularly dangerous for the heart. The second deduction is that today her illness would be diagnosed as recurrent bronchitis rather than asthma. This is borne out by the prescriptions for heart stimulants, which were often given for chest infections. Bronchial infections were incurable before the discovery of antibiotics, and even though Dr Scudamore's desperate remedies may have pushed his patient on her way several months before her time, in due course she would have died of this disease anyway.

She experienced mild relief during June and much of the following month, but there was a setback on 23 June, when she was foolhardy enough to set out across Green Park, intent on walking to her physician's house at No. 6, Wimpole Street.[25] This led to a collapse which prompted even more severe remedies:

A blister on the chest was directed by this prescription, and immediate bleeding. I had been much better for the last prescriptions but had this morning early a spasm. After breakfast I was so much better that I went to Dr. S. In going through the Park however I became worse, but reached a coach in St James street. When we Reached Dr S. I was almost speechless. Waited half an hour and little better when I saw him. He said I ought not to have come out. Ordered immediate bleeding and blistering, with the 7th Prescriptions. Said he w^d call tomorrow. I reached home wth great difficulty. Was soon bled by Mr [space left for a name], (Strand). Fainted and remained long helpless tho not senseless. Very weak all day; applied a blister to the stomach. My breathing relieved by bleeding before the blister rose. The next day felt so light and well that I ran down stairs. Doc^r Scudamore called; examined the blood with a spoon (it looked dark and heavy, and Mr [space left for name] had said it was very necessary to lose such). Doc^r S. said nothing; but desired [that] some water, of night and morning, might be saved, and he would call the day after the morrow. He left the eight prescriptions. He seemed to have some new view of my case, and asked particularly if I had had any pains on the right side. No. He pressed gently my sides and repeated the questions; still no. If I had ever pains, or stitch in the shoulder blade. I recollected that on the drawing-room day, when I had fainted in the G. Park [that is Green Park, during a royal view], after standing some hours, tho not in a crowd, the fit was preceded by cold shivering

and sharp pains about the right shoulder blade, which seemed to cause the
fainting. Advised me to remain at home, and quiet.

This sounds like pleurisy, though considering the duress of her current
regimen it is even possible that Mrs Radcliffe had had a mild heart attack,
which the doctor seems to have vaguely suspected. Nevertheless, as Rogers
points out, 'Since Scudamore's prescriptions merely increased the dosages
of the same medications he had already been prescribing, his ostensibly "new
view" of the case must not have differed dramatically from his initial
opinion.'[26] On 26 July there was some improvement, and she went for an
airing without experiencing difficulty in breathing. Dr Scudamore called,
and after examining her urine said the liver was slightly affected. 'He had
once before expressed a doubt of this, when I drew my hand athwart my
stomach to describe where the tightness of the spasm most affected me, and
had asked me the same questions he had done on the 24th. He said I was
much better, and he hoped he should soon make me well.' She followed his
ninth prescription until the beginning of September, when she felt well
enough to stop taking the pills, and took the mixture only irregularly. She
took frequent airings and little walks for exercise, and for nearly two months

> my diet has been chocolate (Han Sloan's) for break-fast, and one dish for tea;
> dinner a little meat, some pudding and rice, crust of bread or biscuits after tea.
> A very little porter now and then; half a glass of sherry mixt wth water after
> dinner, and grapes. Toast of water at dinner, and not half a pint of that or any
> hardly after two dishes of tea. I am convinced that but little liquid is best for
> my digestion.

Though she frequently experienced feverish nights and a parched mouth
on waking, and occasional pains in the right kidney, she felt no need to see
Dr Scudamore again until 24 September, when preparing to go on a holiday
to Ramsgate. But he was out of town, so she and her husband took the
journey without consulting him.

They set off for Dover on 3 October, and stayed in Ramsgate for four
weeks. Ramsgate had vied for the custom of the fashionable during the
closing years of the old century, and had largely succeeded in becoming a
higher class of resort, though there were those who felt that its increasing
fashionability threatened to lower its status. George Townsend in his satiric
poem on those who frequented it, *Ramsgate; or the Visitors of a Watering Place*
(1810), observed that the young ladies were as often seen reading novels as
strolling by the seaside, thinking of themselves as heroines of romance, and
meeting their ruin in the arms of villains.[27] The sea air inspired Mrs Radcliffe
to her old habits of describing the scenery, and a characteristic stormy

seascape was quoted in Talfourd's memoir for Saturday morning, 19 October 1822, with sailing ships, pilot boats and fishing boats pitching and dashing in the foam, as they sought the safety of the harbour.[28]

Experiencing no spasms or difficulty breathing except on some foggy mornings at Ramsgate, she walked a great deal during the holiday 'and grew stronger and in better spirits. I was on the Pier-head for hours together, in very high winds, and bore it well. Walked 5 miles to Broadstairs & back, hardly sitting down, but was much fatigued for want of resting.' Though she took no supper, she ate well at dinner, often having second helpings and half a pint of thin table-ale, finishing off with pears and swans' eggs.

She returned much strengthened, and took daily exercise in the park, but in the last entry in the commonplace book, dated 12 November, she noted: 'I have found my breathing lately affected by the fog and the north wind.' Although Mrs Radcliffe 'received considerable benefit' from this visit to Ramsgate, it was only temporary.[29] After but a short respite, her health succumbed to the severe cold of the ensuing winter:

> The last fatal attack commenced on the 9th of January, 1823. She had been out in the cold on that day, and at night she complained of a difficulty in breathing. In the first instance, her indisposition appeared less serious than most of her previous seizures. Unhappily, it increased. On the 11th of January, Dr Scudamore was called in; who did every thing for her that skill and tenderness could suggest; – but in vain. On the 6th of February, however, she did not appear in any immediate danger, although in a state of great weakness. At twelve o'clock at night, Mr Radcliffe assisted in giving her some nourishment, which she took with apparent satisfaction; her last words being, 'there is some substance in that'. She then fell into a slumber; but when Mr Radcliffe (who had been sitting up in the next room) re-entered her apartment, in the course of an hour or two, she was breathing rather hardly, and neither the nurse nor himself was able to awake her. Dr Scudamore was instantly sent for; but before his arrival she tranquilly expired, at between two and three o'clock in the morning of the 7th of February, 1823; being in the fifty-ninth year of her age. Her countenance after death was delightfully placid, and it continued so for several days.[30]

When the memoir was published in 1826, Dr Scudamore, in his own words, testified that his patient for 'several years' had been 'subject to severe catarrhal coughs, and also *occasionally* afflicted with asthma' (my emphasis), which suggests complicated bronchial disease rather than long-term asthma. He stated that in March 1822 she was 'ill with inflammation of the lungs' – though she did not begin recording her illness until mid-May 1822, and Dr Scudamore was not her physician until the end of May – and that this *inflammation* (not simply the asthmatic's difficulty in breathing) had recurred in early January 1823; that she had seemed to recover after several weeks, but then 'suddenly, in the very moment of seeming calm from the previous violence of disease, a new inflammation seized the membranes of the brain', leading to 'violent symptoms' and death.[31] Dr Scudamore's summary thus seems to confirm that Mrs Radcliffe died not from asthma, but from a bronchial infection, leading to pneumonia, high fever, delirium and death.

Ann Radcliffe's body was laid to rest in the church of the fashionable, Saint George's, Hanover Square. Contrary to the early obituaries, she was not buried in a vault inside the church, nor was she laid to rest in a separate grave in the churchyard, as some later biographers believe. She was in fact interred in the new vault in front of the Chapel of Ease in the burying ground, called the Front Centre Vault, on 15 February 1823; the inscription affixed to her coffin reads 'M 569 Mrs Ann Radcliffe died 7th Feby 1823 in her 59th Year.'[32] Clara Frances McIntyre believed that she was buried near the grave of Laurence Sterne: 'For information in regard to this I am indebted to Professor Wilbur L. Cross, of Yale University, who remembers seeing a stone to Mrs Radcliffe near the grave of Sterne.'[33] It is possible that a memorial stone was erected, but it is not cited in Westminster City Council's list of gravestones cleared away and stored on the site of the newly formed Mount Street Garden, compiled in 1931. During the First World War, S. M. Ellis

tried to identify her grave, but I found all the tombstones (except those to the memory of Laurence Sterne and a few other people) had been removed and piled up against the walls of the cemetery, the burial soil being used for the growing of vegetables. . . . The custodian of the Macabre Allotment had no knowledge as to the site of Mrs Radcliffe's grave amid the welter of cabbages and potatoes.[34]

After the announcement of Ann Radcliffe's death, several testimonies of esteem were passed to William Radcliffe, which he included in the subsequent obituary and memoir. The great dramatist Richard Brinsley Sheridan is said to have spoken of *The Mysteries of Udolpho* 'with great praise', and 'in terms of the highest eulogy'.[35] Probably Sheridan had contacted William Radcliffe to make this known, just as he and his wife were to contact the obituarist of Sophia Lee who died the year after Mrs Radcliffe, 'to bear witness to the delight which they have felt in reading "The Recess"'.[36] Sheridan probably read Mrs Radcliffe around 1798, when he returned to the stage after a lapse of twenty years to dramatize Kotzebue to appeal to the new highly coloured sensibility then fashionable.

William Radcliffe via Talfourd's memoir makes the point that his wife's romances appealed to both William Pitt and to Charles James Fox, that is, to the leaders of the opposing political parties. Radcliffe maintained that Fox praised *The Italian* soon after its publication in 1797 (when Fox retired from public life after many years defending Unitarian religious liberty) in a letter to an intimate friend (which I cannot trace), and that he entered into a detailed examination of the respective merits of *The Italian* and *The Mysteries of Udolpho*.[37] This friend might have been Ann Radcliffe's uncle Dr John Jebb (to whom Fox confided, for example, his love of power).[38] Or it might have been Fox's most intimate friend and companion John Bernard Trotter, who was an ardent admirer of 'that wild, yet captivating species of romance writing' of the Great Enchantress.[39] Had Mrs Radcliffe ever read Trotter's memoir of Fox, published in 1811, she would have been gratified to learn of Fox's tribute to her ancestors the De Witts, prompted by seeing the painting of their massacre at the Maison de Bois in The Hague during a trip in 1802: 'It was quite distressing to him to speak upon the catastrophe of the De Witts. His countenance was full of horror at sight of the memorable picture, and the soul of the sorrowing patriot spoke melancholy things, in his countenance, at the moment.'[40]

In November 1825 the *Monthly Review*, in its review of the tenth and last volume of Ballantyne's Novelist's Library covering Mrs Radcliffe's works, remarked that she died 'in a state of mental desolation not to be described'.[41] The reviewer had heard that a posthumous novel

> is about to be published by Mr Radcliffe. The well-known taste of that gentleman would hardly permit that a work unworthy of her name should see the light. At the same time, we much question whether, for several of the last years of her life, her mind was in a situation to produce a work comparable in any degree to the Mysteries of Udolpho.[42]

This reference to his wife's apparent insanity over a period of several years was most distressing to William Radcliffe, and he took pains to refute the remark in the forthcoming memoir. The full account of her last illness was prepared by Dr Scudamore at William Radcliffe's request in order to emphasize that his wife's difficulties were physical rather than mental. He acknowledged that 'a few days before her death, an account, which she had accidentally read, of a shocking murder recently perpetrated, pressed on her memory, and joined with the natural operation of the disease to produce a temporary delirium', though he insisted that she soon recovered, 'and remained sensible to the last'.[43] The crime she read about may have been that reported by *The Times* on 4 February, under the headline 'CHILD MURDER', describing the grisly details of a seventeen-year-old girl's murder of her newborn infant, in a misguided effort to avoid being dismissed from service.

This was the most sensational and, indeed, pathetic murder widely reported just prior to Mrs Radcliffe's death. Unfortunately her husband, by protesting too much, does not altogether convince us that the delirium was due solely to the final illness.

In July 1826 the *Monthly Review* pretended to be surprised by William Radcliffe's attack upon its probity, and its editors felt obliged to vindicate themselves.[44] They claimed that their information came from 'an authority upon which we had every reason to rely', and they did not feel that such literary history should be suppressed. Nevertheless, they professed that 'it was no part of our object to wound the feelings of any of her surviving friends, particularly not of Mr Radcliffe, for whom we entertain great respect'. They raised the matter again only because Mr Radcliffe, 'or some person by his authority', had charged them in public with impropriety, and had repeated the charge in the memoir. They then cleverly reproduced the whole of Dr Scudamore's report as if it were a justification of their previous assertion, though they pulled back from their broader implication about the last *several years* of her life:

> We did not speak generally of the latter part of Mrs R's life as clouded by "mental desolation", as Dr Scudamore has been taught to suppose; we distinctly said that she died in that unhappy state, and for this fact we need no further evidence than his own description of the melancholy close of her existence. We have been reluctantly drawn into this explanation, and we now quit the subject.[45]

As further evidence of his wife's sanity, William Radcliffe emphasized that 'she kept an exact account of daily disbursements, until a very short time before her death'.[46] Of course an obsessive concern with tallying accounts could just as easily be symptomatic of anxiety, a fact that was recognized in the tactfully worded judgement by Mrs Anne Katharine Elwood in 1843: 'She might possibly feel, in the mechanical management of her household affairs, the best repose for her perhaps somewhat overstrained mental powers.'[47] William Radcliffe also wanted to suggest that his wife was a dutiful housekeeper despite being a literary genius. Most nineteenth-century biographies of women authors tried to ensure that such women should appear to be domestic, and not to have stepped too far outside the sphere proper to their gender.

The editors of the *Monthly Review* were annoyed by the 'strain of unvarying eulogy' running throughout the memoir, and they quite correctly pointed out that 'Mr Radcliffe provided the materials, and, from motives of delicacy, which are perfectly excusable, he, of course, exhibited only those general traits which might lead posterity to form the most favourable opinion of her character.' They acknowledged that her life was spotless in every essential, but recognized that 'some of her peculiarities are very slightly glanced at'. The memoir made it appear that Mrs Radcliffe was independent from society because she was contented with refined mental pleasures, but the reviewer felt that her failure to interest herself in the community at large was linked to her lack of offspring. The reviewer rejected William Radcliffe's insistence upon his wife's disdain for literary fame, and found it inconsistent with his acknowledgement that unsolicited praise gave her pleasure. As far as the editors of the *Monthly Review* were concerned, 'it is not difficult to see that after she won the proud steeps of fame, it became her principal study to preserve herself from the most remote admission of rivalship'. This is a fair summing up of Mrs Radcliffe's motivation, and I think the editors are correct in their suggestion that she

> exacted a greater degree of homage than she could expect to find in the every-day intercourse of the world, and that she found it only in fame which reached her from a distance. She wrapped herself up in that mystery of authorship which, in her early days, was much more feared and respected than in these intelligent and bustling times.

Like the Honourable Stephen Tennant in V. S. Naipaul's *The Enigma of Arrival* (1987), Ann Radcliffe may have possessed 'the shyness that went at the same time with a great vanity, the shyness that wasn't so much a wish not to be seen as a wish to be applauded on sight, to be recognized on sight as someone stupendous and of great interest.'

Blackwood's, which reported in March 1822 the rumour that Ann Radcliffe was preparing a new romance, was the first journal to announce the publication of *Gaston de Blondeville* and the *Memoir*, in May 1826.[48] The *Monthly Review* in July 1826 understood that the Memoir of Mrs Radcliffe was written 'by a barrister of great promise in his profession'.[49] The unidentified barrister, Thomas Noon Talfourd (1795–1854), was the ideal candidate for writing an appreciation of the life and works of Ann Radcliffe. His romantic qualifications were unassailable. He prized romantic fiction specifically because of its escapist value for the masses. He felt that such novels reached an audience who had never heard of Milton and Shakespeare, and deserved praise for broadening the taste of the masses. He was grateful for Ann Radcliffe's 'wild and wondrous tales. When we read them, the world seems shut out, and we breathe only in an enchanted region'. As far as Talfourd was concerned, the world was not in danger of becoming too romantic, and 'of all romance writers Mrs Radcliffe is the most romantic'.[50]

Ann Radcliffe may have been gratified by this generous tribute, which appeared in Colburn's *New Monthly Magazine* in 1820.

Talfourd also possessed solid Unitarian credentials – for example, he was a subscriber to the Unitarian Association for the Protection of the Civil Rights of Unitarians in 1819.[51] This may have contributed to William Radcliffe's trust in him as his wife's biographer, and brings to a full circle Ann Radcliffe's connection with Dissenting, Unitarian culture. It is worth noting that Talfourd, a friend of Wordsworth, Coleridge and Charles and Mary Lamb, was a member of Leigh Hunt's Radical Dissenting circle, and Talfourd might even have had his attention first drawn to Ann Radcliffe by Hunt, whose favourite authors included Fielding, Smollett, Charlotte Smith and Mrs Radcliffe. Hunt subscribed to the circulating library in Leadenhall Street and was a glutton for novels: 'I can read their three-volume enormities to this day without skipping a syllable.'[52] In the 1840s Hunt gathered material to include in an anthology about country houses, quiet thoughts and 'pleasing terrors'.[53] It was published as *A Book for a Corner*, but its working title had always been 'our *Sequestered Book*';[54] the ideal novel for a sequestered corner is of course *The Mysteries of Udolpho*, and inevitably the collection excerpted 'Ludovico in the Haunted Chamber', for Hunt concurred with Hazlitt, who called this scene 'the chief treat' of the novel.

The 1824 obituary of Mrs Radcliffe had noted that she had left 'several manuscripts, some of them in a fit state for the press' – an invitation for an editor or publisher to come forward that was not taken up quickly.[55] Talfourd had written to his friend Henry Colburn on 9 September 1825 to suggest that he be commissioned to edit a collection of contemporary poetry. Nothing came of this project, but Colburn wrote back with the counter-proposal that he write a memoir of the life and writings of Mrs Radcliffe. Talfourd enthusiastically replied to Colburn on 29 November:

> *My Dear Sir,*
>
> *There is no literary work which I should like better to undertake than that which you propose to me when you suggest that I may have the honour of associating something of my own with the posthumous Romance of the most Romantic of Novelists. I can engage that you shall have the whole M.S. by 1 Jany; – probably the greater part earlier – but situated as I am at present, it would be a great comfort to me to have the Xmas Holidays to complete a work in. I shall be glad, however, to have the paper which Mr R. will supply as soon as convenient; and I should be glad to have directly if you can procure them for me all Mrs Radcliffe's Published Works . . . that I may prepare myself for doing what I should be very anxious to do well. As to Remuneration, even if you had not mentioned a very handsome sum, I am always more than safe in your hands. . . .*

P.S. I have opened the letter again to say that, for professional reasons, I should not wish my name to be announced in connexion with the work – tho' Heaven knows I should be proud enough of such a connexion if it would not frighten my Clients as much as the skeleton behind the Veil in the Mysteries of Udolpho![56]

Few things provide greater proof of the notoriety attached to the name of the Great Enchantress than this shameful postscript. Talfourd's sudden rush of enthusiasm was dampened by the reflection upon how his reputation might be damaged rather than enhanced by the very association he wished to establish. He was thirty-one years old, at the start of both his legal and literary careers. Though called to the bar in 1821, his position was still one of great promise rather than established security. The conflict between his desire to be a romantic critic and his need to get on in the legal profession must have presented a dilemma. Reason triumphed over imagination and the memoir was published anonymously, though his hand was recognized within a short time and revealed by a fellow journalist, perhaps an enemy, who accused the 'young barrister' of himself supplying 'mysteries of the most perplexing and inexplicable kind' in the memoir.[57]

Talfourd was well paid for his many contributions to Colburn's *New Monthly Magazine*; Mary Russell Mitford enviously recorded in December 1820 that 'Colburn is making magnificent offers. . . . he will give Talfourd his weight in gold rather than part with him.'[58] Talfourd was an excellent choice for editing Ann Radcliffe's posthumous works, and much of his perceptive criticism of her techniques and effects has not been superseded. No doubt he handled her personal life with too fastidious a sensitivity, but he was under certain constraints: the great impediment to a genuinely penetrating biography was the widower. Talfourd told Mary Russell Mitford 'that the trouble of drawing up this life, under the jealous supervision of Mr Radcliffe, exceeds anything that can be imagined; to use his own illustration, it is worse than drawing an affidavit, from the fidgetty scrupulousness he shows about things of no manner of consequence'.[59] Talfourd was a skilful user of words and nevertheless managed to convey intimations of the truth, allowing the reader to infer that his subject was in some respects eccentric and neurotic. The real problem is the difficulty of differentiating between Ann Radcliffe's own *amour propre* and her husband's overprotectiveness.

As a final gesture of his own commercial disinterestedness, William Radcliffe arranged for the royalty received for the copyright on *Gaston de Blondeville* and the *Posthumous Works* to be donated to a public charitable institution in England, the accounts of the distribution to be audited by the Lord Bishop of Bath and Wells and Sir Walter Stirling, Bart.[60]

Mary Russell Mitford, in a letter relaying Talfourd's report, said that 'Mr Radcliffe is an old gentleman, quite of the old school; who – notwithstanding he has since her decease married his housekeeper – retains the fondest affection for his more illustrious wife – calls her the dear deceased, and cries whenever she is mentioned.'[61] Biographers and scholars have been content to end the story there, and have failed to discover that the remaining years of William Radcliffe's life have their own unexplained mystery. His name appears in the rate books until 1823, but in the rates assessed on 29 March 1824 the house on Stamford Row was now occupied by a Mr Thwaites. William Radcliffe had moved to Park Place, Paddington, where his name reappears in the rate books compiled on 17 February 1824.[62] His name has been inserted between the lines allocated for other names, indicating that it was a last-minute entry.

We do not know how soon it was after his wife's death, but it was certainly before 1826, that William Radcliffe married their housekeeper. William and the new Mrs Radcliffe, named Elizabeth, continued to reside in Park Place (renamed St Mary's Terrace in 1914) until 1829. The last appearance of his name occurs in the rate books compiled on 7 July 1829; his name does not appear in the books for 1830, compiled on 5 January 1830. This is because late in 1829 or early in 1830, for reasons unknown, William Radcliffe sailed to France, where he died shortly afterwards, in the town of Versailles. Perhaps his wife/housekeeper was originally French, and she wished him to retire near her family. On 16 April 1830, the administration of 'the Goods, Chattels and Credits of William Radcliffe formerly of Park Place Paddington in the County of Middlesex but late at Versailles in France Esquire deceased was granted to Elizabeth Radcliffe Widow the Relict of the said Deceased'; his estate was worth the comfortable sum of £8,000.[63] The complete disappearance of Ann Radcliffe's papers is probably due to the circumstances of her husband's remarriage and his death abroad. They may have been destroyed just prior to the removal to France, but if any of her journals or manuscripts still exist, they may survive in an archive in France, unsigned and unattributed, provenance unknown.

Mother Radcliffe

———— • ————

There cannot be many writers of terror literature who have not been influenced by the novels of Ann Radcliffe. The first vision of the castle of Udolpho, the veiled picture and the gaunt appearance of Schedoni – all became icons for the literature of the next half-century, and beyond. Her images shaped experiences and perceptions, and governed the way people viewed ruins on their travels, or felt enchanted by moonlight or disturbed by low hollow sounds. And yet the pedestal of Romance upon which she stood was inexorably dismantled and replaced first by the pedestal of the male Romantic poet, and then by that of the male novelist.

The Romantic poets seem to have had a hidden agenda to purloin Ann Radcliffe's material for masculine poetry, and were so successful that today many images that are otherwise identical are ascribed to 'Fancy' in the poetry of women but to 'Imagination' in the poetry of men. Many 'serious' male poets borrowed the poetic phrases and techniques of her novels, while doing their best to cover the traces of her influence. Wordsworth in his Preface to *Lyrical Ballads* in 1800 consigned to oblivion nearly all of the poetry written by women in the eighteenth century:[1]

> The invaluable works of our elder writers, I had almost said the works of Shakespeare and Milton, are driven into neglect by frantic novels, sickly and stupid German Tragedies, and deluges of idle and extravagant stories in verse. – When I think upon this degrading thirst after outrageous stimulation, I am almost ashamed to have spoken of the feeble endeavour made in these volumes to counteract it.

But in his early work, such as his tragedy *The Borderers*, written in 1796–7, Mary Moorman feels that 'Wordsworth owes as much to Mrs Radcliffe and Schiller as he does to Godwin. Indeed *The Romance of the Forest* seems to have been lying beside him as he wrote.'[2] Ann Radcliffe's own view of how the creative act is consequent upon contemplative reverie helped to mould Wordsworth's perception of the romantic imagination. In both *The Romance of the Forest* and *The Mysteries of Udolpho* she characterizes intense emotion succeeded by tranquillity as the mainspring of creativity. The very phrasing in which she expresses her understanding of the workings of the imagination – 'The scenes of Château-le-Blanc often came to his remembrance, heightened by the touches, which a warm imagination gives to the recollection of early pleasures' (465) – are echoed in Wordsworth's most famous remarks on the subject: 'poetry is the spontaneous overflow of powerful feelings: it takes its origin from emotion recollected in tranquillity'. And as Frederick Beaty notes, Ann Radcliffe planted the seeds of the nature myth harvested by Wordsworth and Coleridge.[3]

Coleridge was the most authoritarian, patriarchal and masculinist (even misogynist) of the Romantic poets and critics. He saw himself as the fountainhead of a new male literary tradition, under threat by the feminine literary tradition of the novel and romance. Though he incorporated many Gothic stage properties from Ann Radcliffe's work into his own, he was probably vexed by the full title given by an editor to his poem 'Mad Monk' (1800) when it was first published: 'The Voice from the Side of Etna; or, The Mad Monk. An Ode; in Mrs Ratcliff's [*sic*] manner.'[4] Two years later the Aeolian music that sounded through 'Dejection, An Ode' came from *The Mysteries of Udolpho*: the 'Mad Lutanist' in Coleridge's poem is a direct and important allusion to Signora Laurentini (mad Sister Agnes), whose mysterious music in the grounds of the Château-le-Blanc persuades everyone that it is haunted. Whether or not Coleridge's poem is psychologically more complex than Ann Radcliffe's poem 'To the Winds', there seems little doubt that he is indebted to his predecessor's development of the imagery of grief and the sighing of the wind. Many parallels are suggested by Julia Di Stefano Pappageorge, though she takes the wrong-headed view of Ann Radcliffe as a Romantic *manquée*, and refuses to give her her due by maintaining that in every instance *without exception* Coleridge successfully 'transformed' all of her 'mere literary devices'.[5] Many close similarities between *Christabel* and *The Mysteries of Udolpho* have also been established.[6]

Many of Lord Byron's earlier works were indebted to Ann Radcliffe, notably the Schedoniac 'Byronic Heros' in *Giaour*, *The Bride of Abydos*, *The Corsair*, *Lara*, *Manfred* and *Childe Harold's Pilgrimage*. As early as 1818 Alexander Dyce publicly accused Byron of plagiarizing passages from *The Mysteries of Udolpho* for *Lara*.[7] A friend of the poet countered that similitude is no proof of imitation.[8] But Byron's description of the magical city of Venice in *Childe Harold* –

I stood in Venice, on the Bridge of Sighs;
A palace and a prison on each hand:
I saw from out the wave her structures rise
As from the stroke of the enchanter's wand:
. . .
She looks a sea Cybele, fresh from ocean,
Rising with her tiara of proud towers
At airy distance, with majestic motion,
A ruler of the waters and their powers:
(IV. i and ii)

– is manifestly appropriated from *The Mysteries of Udolpho*:

Nothing could exceed Emily's admiration on her first view of Venice, with its
islets, palaces, and towers rising out of the sea, whose clear surface reflected
the tremulous picture in all its colours. . . . its terraces, crowned with airy yet
majestic fabrics touched, as they now were, with the splendour of the setting
sun, appeared as if they had been called up from the ocean by the wand of an
enchanter. (174–5).[9]

The mighty magician's spirit also hovers over much of Percy Bysshe
Shelley's youthful work. The revolutionary, unorthodox and even destructive
possibilities of Gothic fiction in general helped to form the young poet's
sensibilities and led in due course to his humanitarian and political
preoccupations.[10] Again the influence extends to plagiarism, as in *Alastor, or,
The Spirit of Solitude*, composed late in 1815, where Shelley reuses the line
that Ann Radcliffe had picked up and improved from Avison via Gilpin: 'It
was a silent spot, that seemed to smile/Even in the lap of horror' (ll. 577–8).
Shelley was especially fond of Ann Radcliffe's novels,[11] and the copy of *The
Mysteries of Udolpho* which belonged to his mother is now in the Sadleir–Black
Gothic collection at the University of Virginia Library. Shelley shamelessly
exploited her popularity in his own Gothic novels; in *Zastrozzi* he borrowed
names from *Udolpho*, such as Verezzi, Ugo and La Contessa (and Castella)
di Laurentini; in *St Irvyne, or The Rosicrucian* he appropriated the name
Cavigni, and the scene in which Montoni is prevented from drinking from
the poisoned goblet by the breaking of the glass inspired the similar scene
in which Cavigni is saved from such a death.[12]

John Keats was annoyed to learn that most of his readers were women.
Aware that his works were linked with the Radcliffe school, he tried to
discount this, pretending that any similarities with *The Eve of St Agnes* (1820)
were superficial: 'In my next Packet as this is one by the way, I shall send
you the Pot of Basil, St Agnes eve, and if I should have finished it a little

thing call'd the "eve of St Mark" you see what fine mother Radcliff [*sic*] names I have.'[13] Martha Hale Shackford has persuasively demonstrated the influence of phrasing and images upon Keats through the citation of many parallel quotations from *The Mysteries of Udolpho*.[14] The evocative 'casements' which occur throughout *Udolpho* and *The Italian* seem to have suggested passages in Keats's *Ode to a Nightingale*, notably the lines epitomizing romantic creativity:

> Charm'd magic casements, opening on the foam
> Of perilous seas, in faery lands forlorn.[15]

David Jarrett has quite rightly re-evaluated Ann Radcliffe's creation of a powerful symbol of renewal, subsequently exploited, rather than 'transformed', by Keats.[16]

Mrs Radcliffe has been ejected from her rightful position among the Romantic poets, but that she no longer figures largely in the history of the English novel is less forgivable. Considering that she virtually invented a whole new class of fiction, 'the supernatural romance' or what we today call the Gothic novel;[17] considering that she originated at least two major features of the mainstream English novel, integrated description of scenery and a suspenseful and genuine plot in the modern sense; and considering that she was more influential than any other woman novelist – it is astonishing that she has been relegated to merely a footnote in literary history. Until about 1860 Ann Radcliffe was accorded a prominent position in the lists of the great novelists in the critical histories of fiction. She was usually ranked just below Richardson, Fielding, Smollett and Defoe, but at the head of all the women novelists, including Fanny Burney and Jane Austen, and above all other male novelists. Echoes of her work are nearly as pervasive as those of Richardson or Rousseau. Miles remarks: 'She was far and away the best-selling English novelist of the 1790s; the most read, the most imitated, and the most translated.'[18] As I suggested in Chapter 12, the history of Ann Radcliffe's reputation merits more study in conjunction with the modern feminist critique of how masculine fiction achieved its dominance.

Sydney Owensen (later Lady Morgan) was encouraged by one of her literary acquaintances to study the techniques employed by Ann Radcliffe in *The Mysteries of Udolpho* while she was writing *The Wild Irish Girl* (1806).[19] Lady Morgan's friend and fellow Irishman Charles Robert Maturin loved 'the twilight shade' of Mrs Radcliffe's romances, which he found 'irresistibly and dangerously delightful; fitted to inspire a mind devoted to them with a species of melancholy madness'.[20] In his play *The Fatal Revenge* (1807) the castle of Muralto is derived from *A Sicilian Romance* and *The Italian*, and the character of Schemoli owes much to Schedoni. In his preface to *Melmoth the*

Wanderer (dated 31 August 1820), Maturin reported that 'The "Spaniard's Tale" has been censured by a friend [probably either Lady Morgan or Godwin] to whom I read it, as containing too much attempt at the revivification of the horrors of Radcliffe-Romance, of the persecutions of convents, and the terrors of the Inquisition.'

Ann Radcliffe's most important fictional influence was upon Sir Walter Scott, and through him, Dickens and Thackeray – and through them, the mainstream of the novel in both England and France. Marilyn Butler makes the point that although it was Scott who established the charge that her fictional world consisted of mere fearful imaginings, 'yet all the while the full sweep of the *Waverley* series, with its fictional motif of pursuit and imprisonment, of the hero's neurotic depression, inner division, frustration, fear, and helplessness, is nothing if it is not Radcliffean'.[21] Henry Crabb Robinson felt that Scott's *Rokeby* was quite simply 'a romance *à la* Radcliffe turned into verse'.[22] Coleridge felt that Scott's *The Pirate* was partly in imitation of Mrs Radcliffe: 'Was it *auri sacra fames*? Or is it to be classed among the instances of self-nescience [*sic*] that Sir Walter Scott enters in competition with Mrs Radcliffe? Alas! This Norna . . . has not even the ordinary merit of failures in the horrible line – to be laughable.'[23]

Scott was galled by the knowledge that his work would be compared to that of Mrs Radcliffe. In his diary he recorded that his publishing partner James Ballantyne was

> severely critical on what he calls imitations of Mrs Radcliffe in Woodstock. Many will think with him – yet I am of opinion he is quite wrong, or as friend J. F. says *vrong*. In the first place, am I to look on the mere fact of another author having treated a subject happily, as a bird looks on a potato-bogle which scares it away from a field, otherwise as free to its depredations as any where else?[24]

Scott rationalized, weakly, that he did not wish to excite fear of the supernatural in his readers, but to show the effect of such fear upon his characters – hardly an altogether different matter, and in any case one in which Ann Radcliffe herself excelled.

Several attempts were made to revive romance in the second quarter of the nineteenth century. William Harrison Ainsworth acknowledged that in *Rookwood* (1834) 'I resolved to attempt a story in the by-gone style of Mrs Radcliffe (which had always inexpressible charms for me)'.[25] Ainsworth's formula was very successful, and sales were good. It was left to Edward Bulwer-Lytton, Ainsworth's competitor, to renovate the full-blooded supernatural, in *Falkland* (1827), *Zanoni* (1842) and 'The Haunted and the Haunters' (1859). Michael Sadleir feels that Bulwer-Lytton 'showed himself the true inheritor of the mantle of [Ann Radcliffe. . . . He was] her ordained successor on the throne of a kingdom still lurid and romantic, but now into the bargain modernised and metropolitan.'[26]

Ann Radcliffe fascinated even the creators of modern realism. William Makepeace Thackeray admired both Ann Radcliffe and Mary Ann Radcliffe, and obtained both *Manfrone* and *The Italian* from 'the old library on the Pantiles' in Tunbridge Wells.[27] Forty years after the event he reminisced about his schoolboy holidays in the summer of 1823, and was struck by the contrast with modern youth:

> Yonder comes a footman with a bundle of novels from the library. Are they as good as *our* novels? Oh! how delightful they were! Shades of Valancour [*sic*], awful ghost of Manfroni, how I shudder at your appearance! . . . – ah! I trouble you to find such novels in the present day![28]

He and his friend Briggs drew pictures to illustrate *The Mysteries of Udolpho*, and schoolmates begged him to draw Vivaldi tortured during the Inquisition. Allusions to Ann Radcliffe's characters are scattered throughout Thackeray's works. Thackeray knew he ought not to acknowledge the power of such a low, popular taste, yet he valued the power of such works to stimulate the imagination: 'Had Caroline read of Valancourt and Emily for nothing . . . ? the only instruction she had ever received was from these tender, kind-hearted, silly books: the only happiness which Fate had allowed her was in this little silent world of fancy.'[29]

The influence of Ann Radcliffe's literary skill, as well as her romantic atmosphere, has been discerned in the novels of Charles Dickens, particularly *The Old Curiosity Shop*, *Barnaby Rudge*, *Oliver Twist* and *Nicholas Nickleby*.[30] Like Lady Morgan, Dickens conscientiously studied her novels, especially *The Italian*, in order to master the techniques of arousing suspense by small degrees, and ending chapters with 'curtains' and 'cliffhangers' – which he put to such good use for the breaks between instalments in his serializations.

Scott's picturesque regionalism was more amenable to the American experience, but Ann Radcliffe's Gothic had a considerable impact upon American Romantic fiction. An American critic in 1845 expressed disgust at Charles Brockden Brown's use of 'make-shifts from the property-room of Mrs Radcliffe and Company' in his novel *Wieland*.[31] Nathaniel Hawthorne was influenced by Godwin, Maturin and Brockden Brown, all of whom were influenced by Ann Radcliffe. The interview between the dying Sister Agnes and Emily had a powerful influence upon the way Hawthorne depicted the relationship between Miriam and Hilda in *The Marble Faun*; the veiled picture in Udolpho can be clearly glimpsed in the chapter on 'The Silvery Veil' in *The Blithedale Romance*, and in the story 'Edward Randolph's Portrait'; the ghostly music of Alice Pyncheon's harpsichord in *The House of the Seven Gables* is inspired by the mysterious music heard in the forest around Château-le-Blanc; and the old portrait of Alice has exactly the same relevance as the waxwork effigy built into the walls of Udolpho, removal of which would forfeit part of the domain to the church: 'This picture, it must be understood, was supposed to be so intimately connected with the fate of the house, and so magically built into its walls, that, if once it would be removed, that very instant the whole edifice would come thundering down in a heap of dusty ruin.'[32]

Herman Melville acknowledged his debt to Ann Radcliffe in several of his works.[33] In *Billy Budd* the narrator observes that Claggart's hatred of Billy was 'as much charged with that prime element of Radcliffean romance, *the mysterious*, as any that the ingenuity of the author of the *Mysteries of Udolpho* could devise'. Readers of Melville's poem 'Clarel' were expected in the 1870s still to recognize the allusion to 'Ludovico . . . Within the haunted chamber'. Melville knew of the rumours surrounding Mrs Radcliffe: 'As the sight of haunted Haddon Hall suggested to Mrs Radcliffe her curdling romances, so I have little doubt, the diabolical landscape of Judea must have suggested to the Jewish Prophets, their ghastly theology.' Edgar Allan Poe describes the château in his story 'The Oval Portrait' (1842) as being 'one of those piles of commingled gloom and grandeur which have so long frowned among the Apennines, not less in fact than in the fancy of Mrs Radcliffe'. Although Poe's tales of the macabre contain a sickening clarity and overwrought intensity wholly antipathetic to the tranquillizing obscurity of Ann Radcliffe's works, the fantasy of the mother of the Gothic novel can be detected in his stories 'William Wilson', 'Ligeia', 'The Masque of the Red Death', 'The Fall of the House of Usher' and abundantly in 'The Assignation'.[34]

Ann Radcliffe's influence on French literature was immense. All of her novels were immediately translated into French, frequently reprinted, and most were adapted for very popular dramas.[35] Pixerécourt's melodramas, heavily influenced by Ann Radcliffe, were enormously successful.[36] French biographical encyclopedias provide more information about her than any similar English works.[37] Mary Russell Mitford, studying French literature in 1849 in preparation for a trip to Paris, was astonished that

> The only [English writer] whom they appear really to appreciate is Mrs Radcliffe. . . . It is quite amusing to see how much a writer, wellnigh forgotten in England, is admired in France. I dare say, now, you never read a page of her novels, and yet such critics as Ste.–Beauve, such poets as Victor Hugo, such novelists as Balzac and George Sand, to say nothing of a thousand inferior writers, talk of her in raptures. I will venture to say that she is quoted fifty times where Scott is quoted once.[38]

Balzac, Gautier and George Sand read Ann Radcliffe's *Le Château des Pyrénées* with delicious terror, and she had a tremendous influence upon popular writers such as Ducray-Duminil and Charles Nodier. The latter's *Inès de las Sierras* (1837) was so 'terrifiant' that it prompted Gautier to write the following:

Un vrai château d'Anne Radcliffe,
Aux plafonds que le temps ploya,
Aux vitraux rayés par la griffe
Des chauves-souris de Goya.[39]

There are dozens of references to Mrs Radcliffe's talent in Stendhal's journals, and ample evidence of the influence of the French editions of her works upon his novels, particularly *Le Rouge et le noir* and *La Chartreuse de Parme*.[40] On 12 August 1837, Stendhal summarized the essence of Ann Radcliffe's work very beautifully: 'J'ai remarqué que les belles decriptions de Mme Radcliffe ne décrivent rien; c'est le chant d'un matelot qui fait rêver.'

The French have always been more generous to Ann Radcliffe than have the English, and their praise has continued to modern times. For example, Julian Gracq in his surrealist novel *Château d'Argol* took pride in paying tribute, 'deliberately explicit', to Mrs Radcliffe, Horace Walpole and Edgar Allen Poe 'for the spell they have always inexhaustibly cast over him'. He felt that their familiar repertoire of Gothic trappings

> could not possibly, it seemed, be neglected without committing a glaring fault of taste. . . . And so, let there be mobilized here the potent marvels of the *Mysteries of Udolpho*, of the *Castle of Otranto*, and of the *House of Usher* to impart to these feeble pages a little of the power of enchantment which their chains, their phantoms, and their coffins still retail.[41]

But within England the traditions of the Gothic novel remained intact for little more than a single generation. Supernatural fiction fell into disrepute due to the unskilfulness of its practitioners and 'the unsparing manner in which their resources were employed'.[42] The mainstream of The English Novel, the novel of realism and domestic manners, reasserted itself, and the Horrid Novels fell from their position of dominance in the market. Mrs Oliphant, writing in 1882, felt that *The Mysteries of Udolpho*, though still beautiful, was nevertheless distinctly old-fashioned.[43]

In the first generation after Mrs Radcliffe's death, romances were superseded by novels of the fashionable world. The changing taste was observed by Thomas Haynes Bayly in his 1829 poem 'Lord Harry Has Written a Novel':

Oh, Radcliffe! thou once wert the charmer
    Of girls who sat reading all night;
Thy Heroes were striplings in armour!
    Thy Heroines damsels in white!
But past are thy terrible touches,
    Our lips in derision we curl,
Unless we are told how a Duchess
    Conversed with her cousin, the Earl![44]

The small talk of the *haut ton* replaced the frantic passions of romance. D'Israeli's smart country houses became more popular than ruinous Gothic castles. Upper-class novelists such as Lord Lytton overtook the lady novelists of the merely polite social class. A reviewer of Maturin's *Melmoth the Wanderer* observed that 'Radcliffe-romance' and horror novels were now fashionable only in the provincial circulating library, where 'they cast a vain retrospect on their brighter days; when the boudoir of the lady, instead of the closet of the housekeeper, enshrined their volumes'.[45] In other words, they had travelled down the social scale.

The most severe judgement always comes from the first generation after the death of an artist. By the 1850s it was the fashion to speak of Mrs Radcliffe's works with contempt and to point to them 'as the best possible representatives of stupidity'. Ironically, this scorn is due to the fact that she was so successful that she was still remembered while her imitators lay forgotten in a kind of oblivion.[46] By the end of the nineteenth century even her female rivals in the novel genre as a whole were largely forgotten, and only Fanny Burney and Jane Austen survived the passing of time.

Some feeble attempts were made to transform Mrs Radcliffe into an Angel of the House, so important to the ideology of the Victorians, and it is difficult even today to speak of 'Ann Radcliffe' instead of 'Mrs Radcliffe'. But the domestic devotion she and her husband displayed and her conscientious housekeeping could not offset the knowledge that she had 'dipped up to the elbows in horrors'.[47] Ann Radcliffe was more of a Sibyl or Magician than an Angel. Because she had firmly placed herself in the masculine company of Shakespeare, Ariosto, Salvator Rosa and Prospero, she could never be trivialized as was 'our dear Jane'. This was the real reason for her undoing.

Ann Radcliffe came to be perceived as the head of the German/Lewisian school of physically repulsive horror.[48] Jerom Murch, former Mayor of Bath, admitted serious reservations about his eminent Bath resident, 'inasmuch as with great literary skill and dramatic power, she lowered rather than elevated the public taste'.[49] Her reputation fared especially badly during the early Victorian period, when criticism made an unholy alliance with Christian evangelical morality:

The truth is, that such works were only calculated to excite the imagination and corrupt the sentiments. . . . Sir Walter Scott's philosophy might perceive the respectable qualities in Mrs Radcliffe's novels which he refers to, but perhaps the philosophy of many a piratical adventure, and highway murder, and mysterious seduction, is to be traced to these very pages. . . . In all criticism there should be suspended, before the eyes of the critic, the beams of Christian morality and utility, and if a work, when weighed in these scales, is found wanting, it is Christian truth and not intolerance that condemns it.[50]

This Scottish misogynist exults in the fact that by 1849 Mrs Radcliffe's name was allegedly almost unknown except to literary historians or devotees of antiquarian book auctions, where her romances, in reddish mottled boards, fetched no more than a penny per volume. A critic in 1871 dismissed in one sentence the unreal 'shadowy horrors' of 'The Radcliffe School', and devoted four pages to praising *Northanger Abbey* – a ratio of appreciation that has remained constant ever since.[51] Anthony Trollope promoted the view of the male literary establishment in *Barchester Towers* (1857): 'When we have once learnt what was that picture before which was hung Mrs Ratcliffe's [*sic*] solemn curtain, we feel no further interest about either the frame or the veil. They are to us, merely a receptacle for old bones, an inappropriate coffin, which we would wish to have decently buried out of our sight' (Chapter 15). This denigration is of course lifted straight from the memoir in which Sir Walter Scott had cleverly planted the seeds of his rival's downfall.

Notes

Preface

1. Pierre Arnaud, *Ann Radcliffe et le fantastique: essai de psychobiographie* (1976), p. 97. There are other near-misses: Arnaud suggests that the imprisonment of Louisa corresponds to the number of years that Elizabeth Oates acted as Bentley's housekeeper (p. 84), but Louisa was in prison for fifteen years, while Elizabeth's housekeeping lasted twelve or thirteen years.
2. Robert Miles, *Ann Radcliffe: The Great Enchantress* (1995), p. 4.
3. Jacqueline Howard, *Reading Gothic Fiction* (1994); Robert Miles, *Gothic Writing 1750–1820* (1993).
4. Rictor Norton, *The Myth of the Modern Homosexual* (1997).
5. Eugenia C. DeLamotte, *Perils of the Night: A Feminist Study of Nineteenth-Century Gothic* (1990), pp. 10–12.
6. See especially 'Speaking "I" and the Gothic nightmare: boundaries of the self as a woman's theme', in *Perils of the Night*, pp. 149–92.
7. Syndy M. Conger, 'Sensibility restored: Radcliffe's answer to Lewis's *The Monk*', in *Gothic Fictions: Prohibition/Transgression*, edited by Kenneth W. Graham (1989), pp. 137, 138–9.
8. Deborah Ross, *The Excellence of Falsehood: Romance, Realism, and Women's Contribution to the Novel* (1992).
9. Mrs Barbauld in 1810 said that Mrs Radcliffe's novels 'stand at the head of a class' (Anna Laetitia Barbauld, 'Mrs Radcliffe', biographical preface to *The Romance of the Forest*, in *The British Novelists* (1810) vol. 43, p. i); and Sir Walter Scott in 1824 declared that Mrs Radcliffe was among the favoured few 'distinguished as the founders of a class, or school' (Scott, 'Prefatory memoir to Mrs Ann Radcliffe', in *The Novels of Mrs Ann Radcliffe* (1824), vol. 10, p. xvii). She was described as being 'near the head of a school' in the 'unofficial' obituary in the *Gentleman's Magazine* (93, part 2 (July 1823), 87; reprinted in the *Annual Register for 1823* (1824), Chronicle entry for 7 February 1823, 338) and as having 'founded a new school of fiction' in 'Memoirs of Mrs Ann Radcliffe' Preface to *The Mysteries of Udolpho*, Limbird's British Novelists (1824), vol. 13, p. vi.

Throughout this present biography I have preferred the traditional phrase 'Radcliffean Gothic' (recognized as a class of novel during Ann Radcliffe's lifetime and soon after her death) rather than 'the female Gothic' (introduced by Ellen Moers in 1974 in two essays reprinted in *Literary Women* (1976) and consolidated by contributors to Julian Fleenor's collection *Female Gothic* in 1983), which I do not find to be a very helpful category, though it currently dominates Gothic feminist criticism. Theorization of its supposed opposite category 'the male Gothic' has been based almost entirely upon analysis of only Lewis and Maturin, and much of the theorization of 'the female Gothic' easily applies to the Gothic as a whole; for example, enclosed spaces are a salient feature of all Gothic novels, by men as well as by women. Robert Miles in *Gothic Writing* (1993) follows the consensus by characterizing 'the male Gothic' as primarily visual – despite the predominantly visual aesthetic of Ann Radcliffe's work (Miles himself analyses 'the male gaze' in her work) – and 'the female Gothic' as focusing upon a masculine image of the sublime, ignoring the fact that for her Terror, Mystery, Fate and Solitude are all specifically female allegories of the sublime. Once the genre is categorized by gender, a host of cross-overs rise up between female writers of 'male Gothic' and male writers of 'female Gothic', and the distinctions between classifiable types breaks down. Isaac Crookenden wrote 'the male Gothic' by the simple expedient of plagiarizing Ann Radcliffe's novels and reversing the gender of the characters. Jacqueline Howard in *Reading Gothic Fiction* (1994), while remaining sensitive to the feminist reading of the Gothic, rejects use of 'the female Gothic' because of the rigidity of its theorization, and because the overarching framework of female oppression in which it is placed has not been sensitive to historical discourses specific to the 1790s.

10. For example, every reference to Ann Radcliffe in *The Madwoman in the Attic: The Woman Writer and the Nineteenth-Century Literary Imagination* (1979) by Sandra M. Gilbert and Susan Gubar is at one remove, via Jane Austen's satire in *Northanger Abbey*. She is, however, accorded a significant 'proto-feminist' position in a number of studies, ranging from Joyce M. Horner, 'The English women novelists and their connection with the feminist movement (1688–1797)', *Smith College Studies in Modern Languages*, 11, (1–3) (October 1929; January and April 1930), 1–152; to Anne K. Mellor, *Romanticism & Gender* (1993).

11. E. J. Clery, 'The politics of the Gothic heroine in the 1790s', in *Reviewing Romanticism*, edited by Philip W. Martin and Robin Jarvis (1992), p. 70.

12. *Ibid.*, p. 81.

13. Miles, *Gothic Writing*, p. 83.

14. Eleanor Ty, *Unsex'd Revolutionaries* (1993), pp. 23–30.

1 The Great Enchantress

1. William Makepeace Thackeray, 'On a peal of bells', Roundabout Paper No XXIV, *Cornhill*, September 1862), *Roundabout Papers* (1925), p. 255.

2. J. Cordy Jeaffreson, *Novels and Novelists, from Elizabeth to Victoria* (1858), vol. 2, pp. 3–4.

3. Mary Poovey, *The Proper Lady and the Woman Writer* (1984).

4. Janet Todd, *The Sign of Angellica: Women, Writing and Fiction, 1660–1800* (1989), p. 126.

5. Jane Spencer, *The Rise of the Woman Novelist: from Aphra Behn to Jane Austen* (1986), p. 11.

6. Julia Kavanagh, *English Women of Letters* (1862), p. 118.

7. Sir Walter Scott, 'Prefatory memoir to Mrs Ann Radcliffe', *The Novels of Mrs Ann Radcliffe*, Ballantyne's Novelist's Library (1824), vol. 10, p. xv.

8. *Literary Gazette*, 3 June 1826, p. 346.

9. Kazlitt Arvine, *The Cyclopaedia of Anecdotes of Literature and the Fine Arts* (1852), p. 268.

10. H. T. Mackenzie Bell, *Christina Rossetti* (1898), pp. 88–90.

11. *Ibid.*, p. 14.

12. *Ibid.*, p. 91.

13. *Ibid.*, p. 92.

14. Letter to William Rossetti, 29 June 1883, *The Family Letters of Christina Georgina Rossetti* (1908), pp. 126–7.

15. 'A memoir of Mrs Radcliffe', letter dated 2 July 1883, in *The Athenaeum*, No. 2906 (7 July 1883), p. 15.

16. Bell, *Rossetti*, p. 92.

17. The advertisement appeared in *The Courier, and Evening Gazette* on 10 May 1794; the advertisements in all the other newspapers also cited £1 for its four large duodecimo volumes; the cost is cited as £1 in the review in the *British Critic*, 4 (August 1794), 110; but as 20 shillings in the review in the *Analytical Review*, 19 (II) (June 1794), 140. The reference to a year's savings is in David Punter, *The Literature of Terror: A History of Gothic Fictions from 1765 to the Present Day* (1980), pp. 24–5.

18. *The Scots Magazine*, 53 (August 1791), 396.

19. Advertisement in the back pages of vol. 1 of [Laetitia-Matilda Hawkins], *Letters on the Female Mind* (1793).

20. George Colman, the Younger, *My Night-Gown and Slippers; or Tales in Verse* (1797), pp. 7–8. Long excerpts from this satire appeared in the reviews: e.g. *Analytical Review*, 25 (May 1797), p. 524.

21. For a study of circulating libraries see Montague Summers, *The Gothic Quest* (1938), pp. 60–105.

22. Amy Cruse, *The Englishman and His Books in the Early Nineteenth Century* (1930), p. 93.

23. George William Frederick, 7th Earl of Carlisle, *Poems* (1869), pp. 89–91.

24. Scott, 'Prefatory memoir', p. vii.

25. Letter to M D'Arblay, 1 August 1797, *The Journals and Letters of Fanny Burney (Madame D'Arblay)* (1972–84), vol. 3, p. 337.

26. Allan Cunningham, *Biographical and Critical History of British Literature of the Last Fifty Years* (1834), p. 124.

27. Originally published in 1822, while Mrs Radcliffe was still living; *The Collected Writings of Thomas De Quincey* (1889–90), vol. 3, p. 282.

28. *Hogg's Instructor*, 3 (1849), 39.

29. Coral Ann Howells, *Love, Mystery and Misery: Feeling in Gothic Fiction* (1978), pp. 5–7.

30. *Ibid.*, pp. 49–50.

31. Wylie Sypher, 'Social ambiguity in the Gothic novel', *Partisan Review*, 12 (1) (1945), 50–60.

32. David Punter, 'Social relations of Gothic fiction', in *Romanticism and Ideology*, edited by David Aers, Jonathan Cook and David Punter (1981), pp. 103–17.

33. Ann Radcliffe, *The Romance of the Forest*, edited by Chloe Chard (1986), p. 281.

34. J. M. S. Tompkins, *The Popular Novel in England 1770–1800* (1932); Mary Poovey,

The Proper Lady and the Woman Writer (1984).

35. Mary Wollstonecraft, *A Vindication of the Rights of Woman* (1792), pp. 178–9.

36. Robert Miles, *Ann Radcliffe: The Great Enchantress* (1995), p. 32.

37. John Garrett, *Gothic Strains and Bourgeois Sentiments in the Novels of Mrs Ann Radcliffe and Her Imitators* (1980).

38. Malcolm Ware, *Sublimity in the Novels of Ann Radcliffe* (1963); Samuel H. Monk, *The Sublime: A Study of Critical Theories in XVIII–Century England* (1935).

39. Daniel Cottom, *The Civilized Imagination* (1985), p. 27.

40. Cited in William Doyle, *The Oxford History of the French Revolution* (1989), p. 161.

41. Letter dated 20 April 1794, Hester Lynch (Thrale) Piozzi, *The Intimate Letters of Hester Piozzi and Penelope Pennington 1788–1821* (1914), p. 109.

2 Dissent versus Decorum

1. *The Register Book of Christnings Belonging to the Parish of Saint Andrew Holborn*, Guildhall Library, London, MS 6667/11.

2. *Annual Biography and Obituary, for the Year 1824*, 8, 89, 98.

3. Thomas Noon Talfourd, 'Memoir of the life and writings of Mrs Radcliffe', (1826), vol. 1, p. 5.

4. Thomas Faulkner, *An Historical and Topographical Description of Chelsea and Its Environs* (1810), pp. 188–90.

5. *Annual Biography*, 8, 98.

6. *Ibid.*, 98–9.

7. *Ibid.*, 99.

8. The Jebb family history is outlined by John Nichols, *Literary Anecdotes of the Eighteenth Century; Comprising Biographical Memoirs of William Bowyer*, vol. 8 (1813), pp. 366–7. The Oates family can be traced back to the 1580s: various mayors, merchants, one surgeon, mainly in Leeds and Hull, Yorkshire, according to R. Gordon Smith, 'The Oates family of Pontefract' (and 'Horncastle family'), *Notes & Queries*, Series 13 (1) (29 September 1923), 247–8, 387–9, 428.

9. He died in 1782; Nichols incorrectly gives his name as Edward Buston of Chesterfield. She married, second, Revd George Bosley, Vicar of Chesterfield. Another sister married, first, Mr Villa-Real whose daughter married Sir Thomas Gooch, Bt., second, Mr Hutchinson and third, Henry Rooke, Esq., brother to Major Hayman Rooke. Nichols, *Literary Anecdotes*, pp. 366–7.

10. See [Georges Hall], *The History of Chesterfield* (1823; 1839), p. 97. (Much of the interior of the church was damaged by fire in 1961.)

11. John Pendleton and William Jacques, *Modern Chesterfield* (1903), p. 120.

12. John Jebb, *The Works . . . of John Jebb* (1787), vol. 1, pp. 10, 19, 25.

13. *Ibid.*, pp. 20–1, 27–8.

14. *Ibid.*, pp. 31–4.

15. Donald Davie, *Essays in Dissent* (1995), pp. 109, 116.

16. David Bogue and James Bennett, *History of Dissenters*, vol. 4 (1812), pp. 187, 212.

17. Priestley first met Jebb in 1772, as indicated in his letter to Revd T. Lindsey, 20 April 1772, in John Towill Rutt, *Life and Correspondence of Joseph Priestley* (1831), vol. 1, p. 165.

18. Jebb, *The Works*, pp. 167–8.

19. *Ibid.*, p. 244.

20. Letter to a friend dated 23 June 1784, *ibid.*, p. 201.

21. *Ibid.*, p. xxxi.

22. Michael R. Watts, *The Dissenters*, vol. 1 (1978), pp. 478–9.

23. *Ibid.*, vol. 2 (1995), p. 83.

24. *Ibid.*, p. 345.

25. R. K. Webb, 'The emergence of Rational Dissent', in *Enlightenment and Religion: Rational Dissent in Eighteenth-Century Britain*, edited by Knud Haakonssen (1996), p. 39.

26. Robert Miles, *Ann Radcliffe: The Great Enchantress* (1995), pp. 76–7.

27. *Ibid.*, p. 77.

28. Talfourd, 'Memoir', p. 105.

29. James Boardman, *Memoir of Thomas Bentley, Sometime of Liverpool, with Extracts from His Correspondence* (1851), p. 23; Boardman reproduces the entire sermon.

30. Pointed out by Robert Kiely, *The Romantic Novel in England* (1972), p. 72.

31. In *The Romance of the Forest*, edited by Chloe Chard (1986) (all quotations are from this edition): 'I trust in a merciful God that we shall meet in a state where sorrow never comes; *where the Son of Righteousness shall come with healing in his wings!*' (327) Cf. Malachi iv. 2: 'But unto you that fear my name shall the Son of righteousness arise with healing in his wings.'

32. P. O'Brien, *Warrington Academy 1757–86* (1989), p. 59.

33. Davie, *Essays in Dissent*, p. 247.

34. Miles, *Ann Radcliffe*, p. 114.

35. Victor Sage, *Horror Fiction in the Protestant Tradition* (1988), p. 30.

36. *Memoirs of Mrs Jebb*, signed G. W. M. and dated 20 August 1812.

37. Obituary of Ann Jebb, *Monthly Repository*, 7 (February 1812), 131.

38. John Gascoigne, 'Anglican latitudinarianism, Rational Dissent and political radicalism in the late eighteenth

century', in *Enlightenment and Religion*, edited by Knud Haakonssen (1996), p. 233.

39. Laetitia-Matilda Hawkins, *Anecdotes, Biographical Sketches and Memoirs* (1822), vol. 1, pp. 191–2.
40. Hester Lynch (Thrale) Piozzi, *Autobiography, Letters and Literary Remains of Mrs Piozzi (Thrale)* (1861), vol. 1, pp. 302–4.
41. Diary entry for 17 April 1779, Hester Lynch (Thrale) Piozzi, *Thraliana. The Diary of Mrs Hester Lynch Thrale (Later Mrs Piozzi) 1776–1809* (1942), vol. 1, p. 379.
42. George Hall, *The History of Chesterfield* (1823; 1839).
43. *Ibid.*, pp. 33–4. In 1831 the manor of Tapton had 171 inhabitants, p. 344.
44. *Annual Biography*, 8, 99.
45. Poor Rate Ledger, Second Division, St Andrew Parish, Holborn, London, Guildhall Library MS 9975/27; no assessment is given. The ledgers for the Second Division during 1750 are missing. During 1749 the site is occupied by George Bull, and there are no entries for either Purnell or Ward, then or earlier.
46. He can probably be identified as William Ward, son of William Ward and Elizabeth, christened on 16 September 1737 in St Andrew, Holborn, the same church in which Ann Ward would be christened.
47. Guildhall Library MSS 9975/31, 32, 34, 36, 37, 38, 39.
48. *Ibid.*, MS 9975/40.
49. *Kent's Directory* (1759), p. 120; (1763), p. 127; (1766), p. 139.
50. *Ibid.* (1768), p. 174; (1771), p. 186; *Baldwin's New Complete Guide* (1768), p. 170; (1770), 182; *The London Directory* (1768), p. 81; *The London Directory* (1772) (no page numbers).
51. Guildhall Library MS 9975/97, Second Division, p. 7.
52. *Ibid.*, MS 9975/98.
53. *The London Directory* (1773) (no page numbers); *The New Complete Guide* (R. Baldwin, 1774), p. 289. The directories were usually published in January.
54. *Kent's Directory* (1774), p. 25.
55. Letter to John Wedgwood, 16 February 1765, Josiah Wedgwood, *Letters of Josiah Wedgwood 1762 to 1772, 1772 to 1780* (1903), vol. 1, p. 28.
56. R. B., *Thomas Bentley 1730–1780 of Liverpool, Etruria, and London* (1927), p. 46.

3 Taste versus Trade

1. Llewellynn Jewitt, *The Wedgwoods* (1865), p. 268; Julia Wedgwood, *The Personal Life of Josiah Wedgwood*, revised and edited by C. H. Herford (1915), p. 25; R. B., *Thomas Bentley 1730–1780 of Liverpool, Etruria, and London* (1927), 15–16.
2. Eliza Meteyard, *The Life of Josiah Wedgwood* (1865), vol. 1, p. 305.
3. James Boardman, *A Memoir of Thomas Bentley, Sometime of Liverpool, with Extracts from His Correspondence* (1851), pp. 7–8.
4. *Ibid.*, 9.
5. Donald Davie, *Essays in Dissent: Church, Chapel, and the Unitarian Conspiracy* (1995), p. 98.
6. David L. Wykes, 'The contribution of the Dissenting academy to the emergence of Rational Dissent', in *Enlightenment and Religion: Rational Dissent in Eighteenth-Century Britain*, edited by Knud Haakonssen (1996), p. 132.
7. *Ibid.*, p. 134.
8. John Towill Rutt, *Life and Correspondence of Priestley* (1830), vol. 1, p. 60. Frequent visits by Priestley are also noted by Boardman, *Memoir of Thomas Bentley*, p. 8.
9. Boardman, *Memoir of Thomas Bentley*, p. 10.
10. Wedgwood, *Personal Life of Josiah Wedgwood*, p. 30.
11. Letter to Samuel Boardman, 15 December 1770, in Boardman, *Memoir of Thomas Bentley*, p. 18; see also Jewitt, *The Wedgwoods*.
12. Eliza Meteyard, *A Group of Englishmen* (1871), p. 187.
13. Meteyard, *Life of Josiah Wedgwood*, vol. 2, p. 175.
14. Letter from Wedgwood to Bentley, regarding the advertisement for the opening, 15 February 1769, Josiah Wedgwood, *Letters of Josiah Wedgwood* (1903), vol. 1, p. 246.
15. Meteyard, *Life of Josiah Wedgwood*, vol. 2, pp. 418–19; R. B., *Thomas Bentley*, pp. 37–9.
16. R. B., *Thomas Bentley*, pp. 47, 53.
17. Letter to Bentley, 26 December 1768, Wedgwood, *Letters of Josiah Wedgwood*, vol. 1, pp. 238–9.
18. R. B., *Thomas Bentley*, p. 40.
19. Meteyard, *Life of Josiah Wedgwood*, vol. 2, pp. 172–3.
20. Wedgwood, *Personal Life of Josiah Wedgwood*, p. 55.
21. *Annual Biography and Obituary, for the Year 1824*, 8, 99.
22. Letter to Bentley dated March 1772 (exact day not known), Wedgwood, *Letters of Josiah Wedgwood*, vol. 1, pp. 449–50; the negotiation is discussed on 17 February 1772, p. 446.
23. 'How shockingly bad the weather has been for traveling since we parted', letter from Wedgwood to Bentley, 2 February 1772, *ibid.*, p. 444; Bentley's visit to Etruria is mentioned on 13 October 1771, p. 433.

24. Jewitt, *The Wedgwoods*, pp. 212–13.
25. Letter from Wedgwood to Bentley, 21 December 1770, Wedgwood, *Letters of Josiah Wedgwood*, vol. 1, p. 381.
26. Meteyard, *Life of Josiah Wedgwood*, vol. 2, p. 257 (referring to a letter from Wedgwood to Bentley dated 22 March 1772).
27. R. B., *Thomas Bentley*, pp. 47, 82
28. PRO, PROB 11/1295. The will was signed on 27 July 1796, and proved on 4 August 1797.
29. Looseleaf letter inserted into Ann Ward Radcliffe's manuscript commonplace book, Boston Public Library, MS Ch.K.1.10.
30. R. B., *Thomas Bentley*, p. 48.
31. He was admitted into full possession of the house at a special court held on 11 and 13 July 1778 according to his statement in his will, PRO, PROB 11/1073.
32. R. B., *Thomas Bentley*, pp. 48–9.
33. *Ibid.*, p. 49.
34. PRO, PROB 11/1073. The will was made on 23 July 1778, and proved on 2 January 1781.
35. The monument is illustrated in Meteyard, *Life of Josiah Wedgwood*, vol. 2, p. 460.
36. Wedgwood, *Personal Life of Josiah Wedgwood*, p. 27.
37. See, for example, Wedgwood, *Letters of Josiah Wedgwood*, vol. 2: 30 July 1773, p. 44; 11 December 1775, p. 140; 27 January 1776, p. 147.
38. Jewitt, *The Wedgwoods*, p. 268; R. B., *Thomas Bentley*, p. 80.
39. *Annual Biography*, 8, 99–100.
40. Wedgwood, *Personal Life of Josiah Wedgwood*, p. 27.
41. Talfourd and the early biographers maintained this confusion. Clara Frances McIntyre was the first biographer to point out that Hannah died eight years before Ann was born (*Ann Radcliffe in Relation to Her Time*, 1920, p. 8), but she then goes on to say that her elder sister was 'loosely regarded' as her aunt, whereas in fact she was of course literally her aunt as much as was Hannah; it would be more appropriate to say that Mary Stamford loosely regarded as her aunt.
42. *Annual Biography*, 8, 100.
43. Bentley's friend Dr Ralph Griffiths, editor of the *Monthly Review*, lived at Linden House. The Turnham Green rates books show that eight properties separated their villas on what is now the High Street, Turnham Green, and that Bentley's property was one building west of Miss Johnstone's property, later called Annandale House. This means that Bentley lived in what was subsequently called Sulhamstead House, a five-bay two-storey chaste classical villa, photographed before being demolished around 1800. (*Chiswick As It Was*, compiled by London Borough of Hounslow, Department of Arts and Recreation, Libraries Division and the Brentford and Chiswick Local History Society, 1986; photograph no. 18). I am grateful to Carolyn Hammond, Local Studies Librarian, Chiswick Library, for her research towards identifying Bentley's property.
44. *Annual Biography*, 8, 100. Her name is misspelt 'Montague'.
45. Letter from Wedgwood to Bentley, 19 January 1776, Wedgwood, *Letters of Josiah Wedgwood*, vol. 2, pp. 88, 178; Wedgwood, *Personal Life of Josiah Wedgwood*, p. 30.
46. Walter S. Scott, *The Bluestocking Ladies* (1947), p. 69.
47. Letter from Wedgwood to Bentley, 24 December 1770, Wedgwood, *Letters of Josiah Wedgwood*, vol. 1, pp. 385–8.
48. The fullest account is by Charlotte Barrett (friend of both Ord and Fanny Burney), 'Memoirs and character of the late Mrs Ord', *Gentleman's Magazine*, 78 (July 1808), 581–3.
49. Journal letter dated 31 August 1791, Fanny Burney, *The Journals and Letters of Fanny Burney (Madame D'Arblay)* (1972–84), vol. 1, p. 49.
50. *The Poems of Anna Letitia Barbauld*, edited by William McCarthy and Elizabeth Kraft (1994), vol. 29, p. 224.
51. R. B., *Thomas Bentley*, p. 48.
52. *Ibid.*, p. 25.
53. *Ibid.*, pp. 61, 83.
54. Letter from Wedgwood to Bentley, 3 January 1768, Wedgwood, *Letters of Josiah Wedgwood*, vol. 1, p. 201.
55. Cited by George C. Williamson, *The Imperial Russian Dinner Service* (1909), p. 61.
56. Letter from Wedgwood to Bentley, 18 April 1771, Wedgwood, *Letters of Josiah Wedgwood*, vol. 1, p. 381.
57. This is described in the antiquarian notes to *Gaston de Blondeville* (1826; vol. 3, p. 85); the ultimate source is Thomas Warton's *History of English Poetry* (vol. 2, 1778, p. 215), a book which Ann Radcliffe had read certainly before writing *The Mysteries of Udolpho*.
58. R. B., *Thomas Bentley*, p. 69.
59. Letter from Wedgwood to Bentley, 2 August 1770, Wedgwood, *Letters of Josiah Wedgwood*, vol. 1, p. 356.
60. *Ibid.*, 18 April 1771, p. 411.
61. See, for example, *ibid.*, 21 February 1776, vol. 2, p. 159.
62. *Ibid.*, 25 March 1776, p. 167.
63. *Ibid.*, 12 September 1776, p. 196.
64. *Ibid.*, 17 December 1777, p. 285.
65. *Ibid.*, 4 April 1778, p. 305.
66. *Ibid.*, March 1772, vol. 1, p. 446.

67. *Ibid.*, 26 March 1778, vol. 2, p. 301.
68. *Ibid.*, 26 October 1762, vol. 1, p. 5.
69. Wedgwood, *Personal Life of Josiah Wedgwood*, p. 74.
70. Letter from Wedgwood to Bentley, 26 October 1762, Wedgwood, *Letters of Josiah Wedgwood*, vol. 1, p. 28.
71. Chloe Chard, in her Notes to the Oxford University Press edition of this novel in 1986, establishes numerous parallels between the last section of *The Romance of the Forest* and *Émile*, many of which are too close to be merely coincidental.
72. Letter to Samuel Boardman, 16 January 1770, in Boardman, *Memoir of Thomas Bentley*, p. 16; R. B., *Thomas Bentley*, pp. 44–5, 63.
73. R. B., *Thomas Bentley*, p. 48.
74. She was christened on 26 December 1726 in Chesterfield Nonconformist Chapel.
75. Talfourd, 'Memoir of the life and writings of Mrs Radcliffe', (1826), vol. 1, pp. 6–7.
76. Lucy Aikin, *Memoirs, Miscellanies and Letters of the Late Lucy Aikin* (1864), p. 16.
77. Talfourd, 'Memoir', p. 13.
78. *Ibid.*, pp. 120–1.
79. Looseleaf page inserted into Ann Ward Radcliffe's manuscript commonplace book, Boston Public Library, MS Ch.K.1.10.

4 Miss Nancy

1. Cyrus Redding, *Fifty Years' Recollections* (1858), vol. 1, p. 17.
2. Assessment dated 25 December 1771, *City of Bath Rate Books*, 1, 15.
3. Letter from Wedgwood to Bentley, 22 March 1772, Josiah Wedgwood, *Letters of Josiah Wedgwood* (1903), vol. 1, p. 453.
4. Eliza Meteyard, *The Life of Josiah Wedgwood* (1865), vol. 2, p. 259.
5. Letter from Wedgwood to Bentley from Bath, 6 June 1772, *Letters of Josiah Wedgwood*, vol. 1, pp. 464–5.
6. Meteyard, *Life of Josiah Wedgwood*, vol. 2, pp. 242–8.
7. Letter from Wedgwood to Bentley, 26 December 1772, Josiah Wedgwood, *The Selected Letters of Josiah Wedgwood* (1965), p. 142.
8. Letter from Wedgwood to Bentley, 11 April 1772, Wedgwood, *Letters of Josiah Wedgwood*, vol. 1, pp. 457–8.
9. *Ibid.*, 7 December 1772, vol. 2, p. 8.
10. Letter from Wedgwood to Bentley, 23 March 1773, Wedgwood, *Selected Letters of Josiah Wedgwood*, p. 146.
11. *City of Bath Rate Books*, 1, 15.
12. *Ibid.*, 2, 50. The Savoy Tailors' Guild currently occupies the premises.
13. *The New Bath Guide; or, Useful Pocket Companion* (1782), p. 69 (for the reference to Mr Ward's lodging or boarding house on Milsom Street) and p. 71 (for the prices). Ward is listed in editions of this guide up to at least 1787, when his daughter got married.
14. Ann Radcliffe, *The Italian*, edited by Frederick Garber (1968, 1981). All quotations are from this edition.
15. Seon Manley and Gogo Lewis, *Ladies of the Gothics* (1975), p. 217.
16. *Annual Biography and Obituary, for the Year 1824*, 8, 99.
17. 'Memoirs of Mrs Ann Radcliffe', Preface to *The Mysteries of Udolpho*, Limbird's British Novelists (1824), p. v.
18. Thomas Noon Talfourd, 'Memoir of the life and writings of Mrs Radcliffe' (1826), vol. 1, pp. 6–7.
19. *Annual Biography*, 8, 99.
20. Clara Frances McIntyre, *Ann Radcliffe in Relation to Her Time* (1920), pp. 10–11. We may recall that the earnest Count De Villefort whiles away the weary hours in the haunted chamber by 'reading a volume of Tacitus' (*The Mysteries of Udolpho*, p. 572).
21. Ann Radcliffe, *A Journey Made in the Summer of 1794* (1795), p. 423; Lucretius, *De Rerum Natura* (vol. 2, p. 1), translated (surely by William) as 'be my retreat/Between the groaning forest and the shore,/Beat by the boundless multitude of waves!' Tacitus *Hist.* 4.58 regarding the antiquity of the forests of Cleves is referred to in the *Journey* (p. 339). Tacitus is quoted a second time – *Ubi manu agitur, modestia et probitas nomina superioris sunt* (*Journey*, p. 434).
22. L. F. Thompson, 'Ann Radcliffe's knowledge of German', *Modern Language Review*, 20 (1925), 190–1.
23. Maurice Lévy, 'Une nouvelle source d'Anne Radcliffe: les mémoires du Comte de Comminge', *Caliban*, 1 (1964), 153.
24. For example, Stanley J. Kunitz and Howard Haycraft, *British Authors of the Nineteenth Century* (1936), p. 511; Bridget G. MacCarthy, *The Female Pen: The Later Women Novelists 1744–1818* (1947), p. 142; and many more recent literary biographical dictionaries.
25. *Gentleman's Magazine*, 94, part 2 (July 1824), 88; reprinted verbatim in the *Annual Register . . . of the Year 1824* (edition of Baldwin, Cradock and Joy, 1825), Appendix to the Chronicle, 217.
26. *Annual Biography and Obituary, for the Year 1825*, 9 (7), 127–35. Sophia Lee died at Clifton on 13 March 1824.
27. James Boaden, *Memoirs of Mrs Siddons* (1827), vol. 1, p. 212.
28. Susan Sibbald, *The Memoirs of Susan Sibbald (1783–1812)* (1926), p. xiii.
29. *Ibid.*, p. 34.

30. Boaden, *Mrs Siddons*, p. 211.
31. *Susan Sibbald*, pp. 42–5.
32. *Ibid.*, p. 60.
33. Mary Russell Mitford, *Recollections of a Literary Life* (1852), vol. 2, p. 194.
34. Jerom Murch, *Mrs Barbauld and Her Contemporaries; Sketches of Some Eminent Literary and Scientific English Women* (1877), p. 135.
35. MacCarthy, *The Female Pen*, p. 168.
36. Julia Kavanagh, *English Women of Letters* (1862), p. 123.
37. MacCarthy, *The Female Pen*, p. 169.
38. Cited by Montague Summers, *The Gothic Quest* (1938), pp. 66–7.
39. Warren Hunting Smith, *Architecture in English Fiction* (1934), pp. 53–60.
40. Hannah More in *The Mysteries of Udolpho*, vol. 3, chapter 10, epigraph; Mrs Barbauld in *A Journey Made in the Summer of 1794*, p. 393; Anna Seward in *The Romance of the Forest*, chapter 20, epigraph; Frank Sayers in *The Mysteries of Udolpho*, epigraphs to vol. 2, chapters 10 and 11; Charlotte Smith in *The Mysteries of Udolpho*, vol. 1, chapter 16.
41. See F. W. Price, 'Ann Radcliffe, Mrs Siddons and the character of Hamlet', *Notes and Queries*, NS 23 (4) (April 1976), 164–7; Price cites an advertisement in *Felix Farley's Bristol Journal* for 23 June 1781, saying the performance will be on 27 June for one night only, 'by Mrs Siddons, Her first appearance here in that Character, but the Sixth Time of her performing it', and a brief notice on 30 June praising the performance.
42. Ann Radcliffe, 'On the supernatural in poetry', *New Monthly Magazine*, 16 (1826), 147.
43. A contemporary watercolour drawing of Mrs Siddons in the costume of the melancholy prince is discussed by Price, 'Radcliffe, Siddons and Hamlet', p. 167.
44. Radcliffe, 'Supernatural in poetry', p. 147.
45. William Gilpin, *Observations on the River Wye* (1782; 1973), p. 93.
46. John Francis Meehan, *The Famous Houses of Bath and District* (1901), pp. 4–6.
47. Aline Grant, *Ann Radcliffe: A Biography* (1951), p. 35.
48. J. Hassell, Ibbetson and Laporte, *A Picturesque Guide to Bath, Bristol Hot-Wells, the River Avon, and the Adjacent Country* (1793), pp. 112ff.
49. *Ibid.*, pp. 120–2.
50. Samuel and Nathaniel Buck, *Buck's Antiquities; or Venerable Remains of above Four Hundred Castles, Monasteries, Palaces, &c. &c. in England and Wales* (1774).
51. Talfourd, 'Memoir', p. 7.
52. 'Mrs Ann Radcliffe', *Hogg's Instructor*, 3 (1849), 39.
53. Looseleaf letter inserted into Ann Radcliffe's manuscript commonplace book, Boston Public Library, MS Ch.K.1.10.
54. Letter from Wedgwood to Bentley, 26 October 1775, Wedgwood, *Letters of Josiah Wedgwood*, vol. 2, pp. 127–9.
55. *Ibid.*, 1, 10, 15 and 28 September, pp. 331–41; also R. B., *Thomas Bentley, 1730–1780, of Liverpool, Etruria, and London* (1927), p. 75.
56. Ann Radcliffe, *The Romance of the Forest*, edited by Chloe Chard (1986), p. 288.

5 A Literary Establishment

1. *Annual Biography and Obituary, for the year 1824*, 8, 89.
2. Thomas Noon Talfourd, 'Memoir of the life and writings of Mrs Radcliffe' (1826), p. 7.
3. *Alumni Cantabrigienses*, compiled by J. A. Venn, Part II, vol. 5 (1953), p. 231.; *Registrum Orielense*, collected by Charles Lancelot Shadwell (1902), vol. 2, pp. 218–19; *Alumni Oxonienses*, edited by Joseph Foster (1968), vol. 3, p. 1170; *A Catalogue of All Graduates in . . . the University of Oxford* (1851), p. 549.
4. Pierre Arnaud, 'William Radcliffe journaliste', *Etudes Anglaises*, 22 (3) (1969), 234–7; Pierre Arnaud, *Ann Radcliffe et le fantastique: essai de psychobiographie* (1976), pp. 61–2.
5. R. B., *Thomas Bentley, 1730–1780, of Liverpool, Etruria, and London* (1927), pp. 70–1.
6. *Annual Biography*, 8, 99.
7. See letter from Wedgwood to Bentley, 30 December 1773, Josiah Wedgwood, *Letters of Josiah Wedgwood* (1903), vol. 2, pp. 60–1; and 19 December 1773, *The Selected Letters of Josiah Wedgwood* (1965), pp. 157–8.
8. The following biography of Ebenezer Radcliffe is based upon the *Monthly Repository*, 4 (1809), Supplement, 707–11, 'Memoir of Ebenezer Radcliffe, Esq.'; E. Cogan, *A Sermon Delivered at the Old Meeting-House, Walthamstow, October 29 1809, on Occasion of the Death of Ebenezer Radcliffe, Esq.* (1809); *The Theological and Miscellaneous Works of Joseph Priestley* (1817–31), vol. 1, p. 495; John Towill Rutt, *Life and Correspondence of Joseph Priestley* (1831), vol. 1, pp. 215, 334.
9. R. K. Webb, 'The emergence of Rational Dissent', in *Enlightenment and Religion*, edited by Knud Haakonssen (1996), p. 36.
10. Ebenezer Radcliffe, *Two Letters, Addressed to the Right Rev Prelates, Who a Second Time Rejected the Dissenters' Bill* (1773), pp. 1–4.
11. 'I am very glad to hear of your & Miss Oats' [*sic*] health by your very agreeable

neighbour Mrs Forbes', letter from Wedgwood to Bentley, 28 May 1764, *Letters of Josiah Wedgwood*, vol. 1, p. 17.

12. *An Introduction to University History.* Translated from the Latin of Baron Holberg; with Notes, Historical, Chronological, and Critical. By Gregory Sharpe. A New Edition, Revised, Corrected, and Improved, By William Radcliffe, A.B. of Oriel College, Oxford (London: Printed for L. Davis, J. Johnson, and R. Baldwin, 1787). Radcliffe's prefatory advertisement is signed 1 January 1787.

13. *The Natural History of East Tartary . . .* Rendered into English from the French Translation. By William Radcliffe, A.B. of Oriel College, Oxford (London: Printed by M. Vint; for W. Richardson, 1789).

14. *A Journey through Sweden*, Written in French by a Dutch Officer, and Translated into English by William Radcliffe, A.B. of Oriel College, Oxford (London: G. Kearsley [1790]; and Dublin: P. Byrne, J. Moore, J. Jones, Grueber & M'Allister, and W. Jones, 1790).

15. It is listed in the 'Catalogue of Books . . . published during the first six months of 1789' in the *Analytical Review*, 4 (August 1789), 506.

16. *Critical Review*, 68 (November 1789), 251.

17. *Monthly Review*, 81 (December 1789), 563; repeated verbatim in *The Scots Magazine*, Appendix, 51 (1789), 645.

18. Robert Miles, *Ann Radcliffe: The Great Enchantress* (1995), p. 78.

19. For its bibliographical history and translations see *The New Cambridge Bibliography of English Literature*, edited by George Watson, vol. 3: 1800–1900 (1969), pp. 758–9.

20. This explains the discrepancy about whether the two-volume novel cost 5 or 6 shillings according to the details given at the heads of the first reviews.

21. *Critical Review*, N. Ar., 1 (March 1791), 350.

22. *Monthly Review*, 3 (September 1790), 91. These words are repeated in *The Scots Magazine*, 52 (September 1790), 438.

23. *Monthly Magazine*, 55 (March 1823), 182–3; reprinted in *New Monthly Magazine and Literary Journal*, Historical Register, NS 9 (May 1823), 232.

24. Sir Walter Scott, 'Prefatory memoir to Mrs Ann Radcliffe', *The Novels of Mrs Ann Radcliffe*, Ballantyne's Novelist's Library (1824), vol. 10, p. iv.

25. Diary entry for 13 January 1817, Henry Crabb Robinson, *Henry Crabb Robinson on Books and Their Writers* (1938), p. 202.

26. See Mario Praz, *The Romantic Agony*, translated by Angus Davidson (1933; 1956), p. 164.

27. Robert Princeton Reno, *The Gothic Visions of Ann Radcliffe and Matthew G. Lewis* (1980), pp. 26–7.

28. Alexander Andrews, *The History of British Journalism* (1859), vol. 1, pp. 195–6.

29. Thomas Rees, *Reminiscences of Literary London from 1779 to 1853* (1896; 1853), pp. 133–4.

30. Robert L. Haig, 'The last years of the *Gazetteer*', *Library*, 5th series, 7 (4) (December 1952), 242; Arnaud, 'William Radcliffe journaliste', 239ff.

31. His engagement ceased on 27 November 1790 according to the minutes of the management committee meeting on 3 December (PRO, C 104/68, Book C, p. 18 verso).

32. Andrews, *History of British Journalism*, pp. 230–1.

33. Haig, 'Last years of the *Gazetteer*', 243.

34. Andrews, *History of British Journalism*, pp. 232, 224.

35. David Bogue and James Bennett, *History of Dissenters*, vol. 4 (1812), p. 196.

36. *Ibid.*, pp. 201–2.

37. PRO, C 104/68, Book C, p. 20.

38. James Boaden, *Memoirs of the Life of John Philip Kemble, Esq.* (1825). Season of 1784–5 (all from vol. 1): *The Orphan* (pp. 250–1), *Hamlet* (pp. 250–1), *The Tempest* (p. 268); 1785–6: *Hamlet* and *Comus* (pp. 328–30); 1786–7: *Richard Coeur de Lion* (p. 340), *Cymbeline* (p. 343), *Count of Narbonne and Julia* (pp. 346–9); 1787–8: *Macbeth* (pp. 415–19).

39. Talfourd, 'Memoir', pp. 99–100.

40. Ann Radcliffe, *A Journey Made in the Summer of 1794* (1795), p. 233.

41. *Annual Biography*, 8, 95–6.

42. Talfourd, 'Memoir', pp. 7–8.

43. *Ibid.*, p. 7.

44. *Monthly Review*, 3 (September 1790), 89, 91.

45. *English Review*, 15 (February 1790), 137–44. The review consists mostly of excerpts.

6 The Aesthetics of Terror

1. Donald Davie, *Essays in Dissent: Church, Chapel, and the Unitarian Conspiracy*, (1995), p. 11.

2. *Ibid.*, p. 55.

3. Michael R. Watts, *The Dissenters*, vol. 2 (1995), pp. 385–7.

4. An 1830s letter from Lucy Aikin, quoted by P. O'Brien, *Warrington Academy 1757–86: Its Predecessors and Successors* (1989), pp. 52–3.

5. John and Anna Laetitia Aikin, 'Sir Bertrand', *Miscellaneous Pieces, in Prose* (1773). The reviewer of Nathan Drake's *Literary Hours* corrects Drake to say that

Sir Bertrand was written by Dr Aikin, not
Mrs Barbauld (*Analytical Review*, 28
(December 1798), 605). This fragmentary
tale continues to be wrongly attributed to
Anna Laetitia Aikin (later Barbauld),
though as Montague Summers points out
in *The Gothic Quest* (1938, p. 48) Lucy Aikin
in the memoir prefixed to *The Works of
Anna Laetitia Barbauld*, (1825) specifically
assigns the tale to John Aikin and the
essay on terror to Anna Laetitia Aikin.

6. John and Anna Laetitia Aikin, 'On the
pleasure derived from objects of terror',
Miscellaneous Pieces, pp. 119–27.

7. William Enfield, *The Speaker: or
Miscellaneous Pieces, Selected from the Best
English Writers* (1774), p. iv (her entire
poem is printed on pp. 268–72).

8. Thomas Noon Talfourd, 'Memoir of the
life and writings of Mrs Radcliffe' (1826)
vol. 1, p. 8.

9. Ann Radcliffe, *The Italian*, edited by
Frederick Garber (1968, 1981), pp. 397–8.

10. Victor Sage, *Horror Fiction in the Protestant
Tradition* (1988), p. 397.

11. Watts, *The Dissenters*, vol. 2, p. 92.

12. Ann Radcliffe, *Gaston de Blondeville* (1826),
vol. 1, p. 6.

13. Ann Radcliffe, 'On the Supernatural in
poetry', *New Monthly Magazine*, 16 (1826),
145.

14. *Ibid.*, pp. 148–9.

15. Patrick Brydone, *A Tour through Sicily and
Malta* (1773), vol. 2, pp. 11, 160, 254.

16. *Ibid.*, vol. 1, pp. 68–9.

17. Marie-Joseph De Chénier, *Tableau
historique de l'état et des progrès de la
littérature française, depuis 1798* (1816),
p. 229.

18. Nathan Drake, *Literary Hours: or Sketches
Critical, Narrative, and Poetical*, 3rd edn.
(1804), vol. 1, p. 361.

19. Scores of Shakespearian influences upon
her work have been noted by Eino Railo,
The Haunted Castle (1927), pp. 17, 18, 47–8,
51–2.

20. See a review of the Catalogue of the
Shakespeare Gallery, *Analytical Review*, 3
(May 1789), 111–12. At least thirty-four
paintings covered Shakespearian subjects.

21. J. M. S. Tompkins, 'Ramond de
Carbonnières, Grosley and Mrs Radcliffe',
Review of English Studies, 5 (July 1929),
294–301. Tompkins also suggests a source
in Henry Swinburne's *Journey from
Bayonne to Marseilles* (published with the
second edition of *Travels through Spain*,
1787), but this does not seem likely to me.

22. Ann Radcliffe, *Gaston de Blondeville . . .
Posthumous Works* (1826), vol. 4, p. 217;
Henry Swinburne, *Travels in the Two
Sicilies* (1783), vol. 1, pp. 365–6.

23. Tompkins, 'Ramond de Carbonnières'.

24. Mary Robinson, *Hubert de Sevrac, a
Romance, of the Eighteenth Century* (1796),
vol. 1, p. 30.

25. William Coxe, *Travels in Switzerland*
(1789), vol. 1, pp. 2, 25; vol. 2, p. 9.

26. *Ibid.*, vol. 1, pp. 135–6.

27. *Ibid.*, p. 143. Coxe also discusses
Rousseau's island of La Motte (vol. 2,
pp. 135ff), which may have suggested the
name of La Motte in *The Romance of the
Forest*.

28. Many similarities between the two works
are demonstrated by Clara Frances
McIntyre, *Ann Radcliffe in Relation to Her
Time* (1920), pp. 59–61. Other picturesque
influences might be William Beckford's
*Dreams, Waking Thoughts, and Incidents; in a
Series of Letters, from Various Parts of Europe*
(1783), Lady Anne (Riggs) Miller's *Letters
from Italy* (1776), John Smith's *Select Views
of Italy* (1792–6), Sir William Young's
Journal of a Summer's Excursion (c. 1773)
and Brian Hill's *Observations and Remarks
on a Journey through Sicily and Calabria*
(1792), but the evidence is weak;
Roderick Marshall, *Italy in English
Literature 1755–1815* (1934), pp. 108,
167–8, 197–9.

29. Hester Lynch Piozzi, *Observations and
Reflections Made in the Course of a Journey
through France, Italy and Germany* (1789),
vol. 1, pp. 151, 160, 167.

30. *Ibid.*, pp. 174–5.

31. This entry comes from the continuation of
Thomas Green's *Extracts from the Diary of
a Lover of Literature*, from MSS held by his
son, published in the *Gentleman's
Magazine*, NS, 1 (January 1834), 10.

32. Piozzi, *Observations*, p. 39.

33. In *Gaston de Blondeville . . . Posthumous
Works*, vol. 4, pp. 223–4.

34. Warren Hunting Smith, *Architecture in
English Fiction* (1934), p. 20.

35. George Keate, *Netley Abbey. An Elegy*, 2nd
edn., rev. (1769), p. 20. (First published in
1764 as *The Ruins of Netley Abbey*.)

36. Ford Harris Swigart, jun., *A Study of the
Imagery in the Gothic Romances of Ann
Radcliffe* (1980).

37. For an interesting psychological
interpretation of ink on paper being
analogous to blood on flesh, see Eve
Kosofsky Sedgwick, 'The character in the
veil: imagery of the surface in the Gothic
novel', *PMLA*, 96 (2) (March 1981),
255–70. Swigart also notices this image
group, but wrongly relates it to images of
conflict (Swigart, *Imagery in the Gothic
Romances of Ann Radcliffe*, pp. 59ff).

38. Edward Dayes, *A Picturesque Tour in
Yorkshire and Derbyshire* (1825), p. 2.

39. From *The Romance of the Forest*: by William
Hodges, 1794, No. 180. From *The Mysteries
of Udolpho*: by J. C. Denham, 1796, No.

751; by Henry Singleton, 1796, No. 217; by Mary Lloyd, 1798, No. 428; by S. Drummond, 1799, No. 59. From *The Italian*: by James Nixon, 1798, Nos. 540 and 570; by P. Ninsey, 1801, No. 657; by H. P. Bone, 1805, Nos. 57 and 155. Some, but not all, of these were listed by Maurice Lévy, *Le Roman 'gothique' anglais 1764–1824* (1968) and Samuel H. Monk, *The Sublime: A Study of Critical Theories in XVIII-Century England* (1935). My list is based upon a review of the annual catalogues of *The Exhibition of the Royal Academy* for the years 1789 to 1809 inclusive.

40. William Gilpin, *Observations on the River Wye* (1782), p. 16.
41. Anna Laetitia Barbauld, 'Mrs Radcliffe', biographical preface to *The Romance of the Forest*, in *The British Novelists* (1810), vol. 43, p. vi.
42. William Gilpin, *Remarks on Forest Scenery* (1791), vol. 1, p. 252.
43. William Gilpin, *Observations . . . on Several Parts of England; Particularly the Mountains, and Lakes of Cumberland, and Westmorland* (1786), vol. 1, pp. 13–16, vol. 2, p. 119.
44. *Ibid.*, vol. 1, p. 163.
45. *Ibid.*, pp. 100, 126, 164.
46. *Ibid.*, p. 171.
47. *Ibid.*, p. 183.
48. Charles Avison, *An Essay on Musical Expression* (1752), pp. 3–4, 6–7.
49. Rictor Norton, 'Aesthetic Gothic horror', *Yearbook of Comparative and General Literature*, 21 (1972), 31–40.
50. James Beattie, 'An essay on laughter and ludicrous composition', in *Essays* (1776), pp. 581–705.
51. James Beattie, *The Minstrel, in Two Books: with Some Other Poems* (1779), p. 11. This is Beattie's own first collected edition, the latest and fullest edition of his works which Mrs Radcliffe could have read.
52. James Beattie, *Dissertations Moral and Critical* (1783), pp. 92–4.
53. William Duff, *An Essay on Original Genius* (1767), pp. 170–1.
54. Noted by Jacqueline Howard in relation to Duff, *Reading Gothic Fiction* (1994), p. 93.

7 Portrait of the Artist

1. *Gazetteer*, 28 January 1791.
2. *Ibid.*, 14 April 1791.
3. *Ibid.*, 15 June 1794.
4. *Critical Review*, N. Ar., 4 (April 1792), 458–60.
5. Ann Radcliffe, *Romance of the Forest*, edited by Chloe Card (1986), p. 1. All quotations are from this edition.
6. Charlotte Smith, *The Romance of Real Life* (1787), vol. 3, pp. 128–62; C. F. McIntyre in *Ann Radcliffe in Relation to Her Time* (1920), pp. 57–8; Chloe Chard, notes to *The Romance of the Forest*, p. 367.
7. Robert D. Mayo, 'Ann Radcliffe and Ducray-Duminil', *Modern Language Review*, 36 (1941), 501–5.
8. 'Alexis; or, The Cottage in the Woods', part 1, chapter 4, *Lady's Magazine*, 22 (June 1791), 289–95.
9. *Ibid.*, part 2, chapter 4 (November 1791), 574–9.
10. Adeline's father, holding a mirror before her face in which she sees herself wounded and bleeding profusely, is interpreted as an image of rape and loss of virginity by Raymond W. Mise, *The Gothic Heroine and the Nature of the Gothic Novel* (1980), p. 71. Mise pushes his interpretation too far when he says that her fainting suggests compliance.
11. John Dunlop, *The History of Fiction* (1814), vol. 3, p. 387.
12. Jacqueline Howard, *Reading Gothic Fiction* (1994), pp. 92–3.
13. James Beattie, *Dissertations Moral and Critical* (1783), pp. 615–16.
14. *English Review*, 20 (November 1792), 352–3.
15. Sir Walter Scott, 'Prefatory memoir to Mrs Ann Radcliffe', *The Novels of Mrs Ann Radcliffe*, Ballantyne's Novelist's Library (1824), vol. 10, p. vi.
16. *Monthly Review*, 15 (November 1794), 278.
17. Maria Edgeworth, *Chosen Letters* (1931), p. 58; she also thought of Ann Radcliffe's tapestried apartments during a visit to Bruges, letter to Miss Sophy Ruxton, 15 October 1802, p. 99.
18. *Critical Review*, N. Ar., 10 (May 1794), 349.
19. *Ibid.*, (March 1794), 347.
20. For full details, and translations, see *The New Cambridge Bibliography of English Literature*, edited by George Watson, vol. 3: 1800–1900 (1969), pp. 758-9.
21. Dunlop, *History of Fiction*, p. 394.
22. Anna Laetitia Barbauld, 'Mrs Radcliffe', biographical preface to *The Romance of the Forest*, in *The British Novelists* (1810) vol. 43, p. iii.
23. James Boaden, *Memoirs of the Life of John Philip Kemble, Esq.* (1825), vol. 2, pp. 97–102, 116–19.
24. *Ibid.*, pp. 120, 126; *Critical Review*, S. 2, 13 (March 1795), 338.
25. Entry for 20 August 1794, Hester Lynch (Thrale) Piozzi, *Thraliana. The Diary of Mrs Hester Lynch Thrale (Later Mrs Piozzi) 1776–1809* (1942), vol. 2, p. 886.
26. See entry for April 1794, no day given, *ibid.*, p. 881.
27. See, for example, *Monthly Review*, NS 16 (March 1795), 344–51; (April 1795), 467–9.
28. M. Aikin, *Memoirs of Religious Imposters* (1821), *passim*.

29. The following comments are derived from Eugene P. Wright, 'A divine analysis of *The Romance of the Forest*', *Discourse*, 13 (3) (Summer 1970), 379–87.

8 Unrivalled Genius

1. Minutes of the committee meeting on 10 January 1792, PRO, C 104/68, Book C, p. 26. The ledger confirms the payments to William Radcliffe of £16 16s in February 1792, £21 in March, £16 16s in April and May, £21 in June, and so on (PRO, C 104/67, Book F, pp. 9–24).
2. Minutes of the committee meeting on 15 February 1792, PRO, C 104/68, Book C, p. 27.
3. *Ibid.*
4. For example, the ledger (PRO, C 104/67, Book F) records payments of £1 6s in June 1792 (p. 9), August (p. 17) and October (p. 17). See also Robert L. Haig, 'The last years of the *Gazetteer*', *The Library*, 5th series, 7 (4) (December 1952), 249.
5. Minutes of the management committee meeting on 19 December 1792, PRO, C 104/68, Book C, p. 35.
6. PRO, C 104/68, Book C, p. 36 verso, p. 37. The ledger confirms the increase for October when he was paid £17 17s (PRO, C 104/67, Book F, p. 17); and records that in January he was paid only £10 10s (Book F, p. 23). The new acting editor Mr McDonald, alias McDonnel, receives the old rate in February 1793, £16 16s (Book F, p. 25).
7. Minutes of the committee meeting on 10 January 1973, PRO, C 104/68, Book C, p. 37 verso.
8. Letter to his mother, 18 May 1794, Louis F. Peck, *A Life of Matthew G. Lewis* (1961), p. 208.
9. PRO, C 104/67, Book K, p. 265; Book L, p. 250.
10. Robert K. Black, *The Sadleir-Black Gothic Collection: An Address before the Bibliographical Society of the University of Virginia* (1949), p. 13.
11. Nor are they listed in the poor rates books for Brownlow Street in the Parish of St Giles in the Fields, near Drury Lane Theatre and Covent Garden Opera House (modern Betterton Street). Pierre Arnaud mistakenly identifies this Brownlow Street as their residence, but this would not have been considered part of Holborn in 1794.
12. The contract is reproduced by Pierre Arnaud, 'Un document inédit: le contrât des *Mysteries of Udolpho*', *Etudes Anglaises*, 20 (1) (January–March 1967), 55–7.
13. *New Monthly Magazine and Literary Journal*, Historical Register, 9 (May 1823), 232.
14. Thomas Rees, *Reminiscences of Literary London from 1779 to 1853* (1896), p. 87.
15. Letter to Edward Fergus Graham, 1 April 1810, Percy Bysshe Shelley, *The Letters of Percy Bysshe Shelley* (1964), vol. 1, p. 6.
16. James Boaden, *Memoirs of Mrs Inchbald* (1833), vol. 1, p. 273, vol. 2, pp. 3, 259.
17. Sydney Owenson, *Lady Morgan's Memoirs: Autobiography, Diaries and Correspondence* (1862), vol. 2, p. 153.
18. *Gentleman's Magazine*, 91, part 2 (November 1821), 451.
19. *Biographie Universelle, Ancienne et Moderne* (1823), vol. 36, pp. 525–6; A. V. Arnault *et al.*, *Nouvelle des Contemporains* (1824), vol. 17, pp. 204–5. The exaggerated figures are mentioned in the *New Monthly Magazine*, 9 (May 1823), 232; the *Gentleman's Magazine*, 93, part 2 (July 1823), 87–8; the *Annual Register for 1823* (1824), Chronicle entry for 7 February 1823, 337–8.
20. *Annual Biography and Obituary, for the Year 1824*, 8 (1824), p. 96.
21. Elizabeth Mavor, *The Ladies of Llangollen* (1971), p. 73.
22. *Ibid.*, p. 56.
23. Letter to Mr Walker, 8 March 1794, *The Letters of Joseph Ritson* (1833), vol. 2, pp. 49–50.
24. Godwin's *Things As They Are; or, The Adventures of Caleb Williams* was published in 1794 by B. Crosby, and the first three volumes of Thomas Holcroft's *The Adventures of Hugh Trevor* were published by Shepperson and Reynolds. The Robinsons published the second edition of *Caleb Williams* in 1796.
25. Letter to Dr Charles Burney, beginning 9 May 1794, Fanny Burney, *The Journals and Letters of Fanny Burney (Madame D'Arblay)* (1972–84), vol. 3, p. 63.
26. *Ibid.*, 18 June 1795, p. 117.
27. *Athlin and Dunbayne* comprises 40,000 words, *Sicilian Romance* 67,000, *Romance of the Forest* 133,000, *Udolpho* 292,000, *Italian* 181,000 and *Gaston* 106,000, according to Ford Harris Swigart, jun., *A Study of the Imagery in the Gothic Romances of Ann Radcliffe* (1980), pp. 147–8.
28. Letters to Dr Charles Burney, 5 and 15 July 1795, *Journals and Letters of Fanny Burney*, vol. 3, pp. 126, 136-7.
29. Ann Radcliffe, *The Mysteries of Udolpho*, edited by Bonamy Dobrée (1966, 1970), p. 224. All quotations are from this edition.
30. Letter to Samuel Boardman, 3 October 1776, in James Boardman, *A Memoir of Thomas Bentley* (1851), p. 20.
31. Thomas Warton, *The History of English Poetry*, vol. 1 (1774), pp. 111–18, 147–8.
32. *The Progress of Romance*, 'by C. R., Author of The English Baron' (1785), vol. 1, p. iv.

33. Warton, *History of English Poetry*, vol. 1 (1778), Dissertation I, H2 recto. Warton frequently digresses upon necromancy, and gives full excerpts from the romance of Richard Coeur de Lyon in which Richard confronts Saladin and his 'mayster nygromansoure' at the siege of Babylon (pp. 150–61).

34. Lodovico Ariosto, *Orlando Furioso*, translated by John Hoole (1783). Editions appeared in 1783, 1785, 1791 and later.

35. Adolpho is the father of two sisters in 'The Trial of Female Friendship', *Lady's Magazine*, 23, Supplement (1792), 718–22. Ann Radcliffe's poem 'Song of a Spirit' from *Romance of the Forest* had been printed in the November issue, so her interest may have been called to the November issue, and if she also read the December issue (with its Supplement) she might have noted the name 'Adolpho'.

36. Jacqueline Howard, *Reading Gothic Fiction* (1994), p. 138.

37. Ellen Moers, *Literary Women* (1976), pp. 136–7.

38. Sir Walter Scott, 'Prefatory memoir to Mrs Ann Radcliffe', *The Novels of Mrs Ann Radcliffe*, Ballantyne's Novelist's Library (1824), vol. 10, p. vii.

39. William Hazlitt, *Lectures on the English Comic Writers* (1819), p. 251.

40. Thomas Moore, *Memoirs, Journal and Correspondence of Thomas Moore* (1853), vol. 1, p. 24.

41. *Annual Biography*, 8, 95; Thomas Noon Talfourd, 'Memoir of the life and writings of Mrs Radcliffe' (1826), vol. 1, p. 11.

42. Jules Le Fevre-Deumier, *Célébrités anglaises* (1895), p. 203.

43. Horace Walpole, *The Letters of Horace Walpole* (1905), vol. 15, p. 301.

44. Letter dated 4 August 1794, Hester Lynch (Thrale) Piozzi, *The Intimate Letters of Hester Piozzi and Penelope Pennington 1788–1821* (1914), p. 113.

45. Sold at the auction of her library in 1816, facsimile *Sale Catalogues of Libraries of Eminent Persons*, edited by Stephen Parks (1972), vol. 5, p. 491.

46. Letter dated 11 September 1794, Piozzi, *Letters of Hester Piozzi and Penelope Pennington*, p. 116. This *bon mot* was recorded in her diary for 20 August 1794, Hester Lynch (Thrale) Piozzi, *Thraliana. The Diary of Mrs Hester Lynch Thrale (Later Mrs Piozzi) 1776–1809* (1942), vol. 2, p. 886.

47. *Monthly Magazine*, 55 (March 1823), 182–3; and *New Monthly Magazine and Literary Journal*, 9 (May 1823), 232.

48. Clara Reeve, *The Progress of Romance* (1785), vol. 2, p. 47.

49. *Critical Review*, 11 (August 1794), 361.

50. 'Correspondence. Mysteries of Udolpho', *Critical Review*, 12 (November 1794), 359–60.

51. Letter to William Lisle Bowles, 16 March 1797, Samuel Taylor Coleridge, *Collected Letters of Samuel Taylor Coleridge*, vol. 1: 1785–1800 (1956), p. 183. On the basis of this letter, and because the author of the review of *The Italian* that appeared in the *Critical Review* in June 1798 acknowledged that he also wrote the review of *The Mysteries of Udolpho* that appeared in August 1794, four reviews from the *Critical Review* were attributed to Coleridge and reprinted in *A Wiltshire Parson and His Friend: The Correspondence of William Lisle Bowles*, edited by Garland Greever (1926); and reprinted in *Coleridge's Miscellaneous Criticism*, edited by Thomas Middleton Rayslor (1936): *The Mysteries of Udolpho*, 2 (August 1794), 361–72; *The Monk*, 19 (February 1797), 194–200; *The Italian*, 23 (June 1798), 166–9; and *Hubert de Sevrac*, 23 (August 1798), 472. The evidence against Coleridge's authorship of three of the reviews was presented by Charles L. Patterson, 'The authenticity of Coleridge's reviews of Gothic romances' *Journal of English and Germanic Philology*, 50 (4) (October 1951), 517–21.

David Erdman in 'Immoral acts of a library cormorant. The extent of Coleridge's contributions to the *Critical Review*', (*Bulletin of the New York Public Library*, 63 (September–November 1959), 433–54, 515–30, 575–87) maintains the attribution to Coleridge on the basis that he is supposed to have dashed off a 2-guinea review for Charles Dyer (who wrote for the *Critical Review*) with whom he breakfasted in the week of 7 August, and the review of *Udolpho* appeared in the last week of August and therefore cannot be excluded. However, the review copies of this massive novel must have been sent to their regular reviewer a month or two before this, and it is hardly likely that they would suddenly put the lead review in the hands of an untested newcomer. Erdman attributes the reviews of *Sevrac* and *The Italian* to Coleridge merely because their style, though crude, is 'not unColeridgean'; he suggests that the original reviews were burned but then rewritten and submitted much later in obligation of having received reading copies – a slight and unconvincing argument. Derek Roper, 'Coleridge, Dyer, and The Mysteries of Udolpho', *Notes and Queries*, NS, 19 (August 1972), 287–9, notes that 'It has always seemed unlikely that the editors of the *Critical* would have left this popular romance to be reviewed by an undergraduate who happened to be visiting London' – especially as one of the proprietors was George Robinson, who had paid £500 for the novel and was not likely to risk his investment at the hands of an amateur. Roper has established that Coleridge was with Southey in Bristol until 3 September, and could not have written such a review until 10 September, nearly two weeks after it appeared.

None of the proponents of the Coleridge attribution mentions the subsequent reply to the criticism, published in November 1794, which is obviously by the same author as the original review, and which clearly is by a regular and non-Coleridgean contributor who accepts responsibility for the *Critical Review*'s reputation. Since Coleridge did not write the review of *The Mysteries of Udolpho*, it therefore follows that he did not write the review of *The Italian* (whose author acknowledged writing the former); Roper suggests that the author was George Dyer himself.

52. Letter to the editor of the *Quarterly Review* (J. G. Lockhart), sometime during 1828, Samuel Taylor Coleridge, *Unpublished Letters of Samuel Taylor Coleridge* (1932), vol. 2, p. 407.
53. In another, less trustworthy, version of the anecdote it is a poet's volume of verse that was being unjustly ridiculed, reported by Professor J. Anster of Dublin in 1835, as having occurred around 1800, in A. A. Watts, *Alaric Watts*, vol. 1, p. 247, cited by David Erdman, 'Coleridge's contributions to the *Critical Review*', p. 439: 'Coleridge described himself as so affected that he never afterwards wrote a review, and he appeared to me to have even a morbid feeling on the subject.'
54. According to Robinson, diary entry for 20 March 1813, Henry Crabb Robinson, *Henry Crabb Robinson on Books and Their Writers*, (1938) vol. 1, p. 124.
55. Letter to William Wordsworth, mid-October 1810, Coleridge, *Collected Letters of Samuel Taylor Coleridge*, vol. 3: 1807–14 (1959), p. 294.
56. Obituary of William Enfield (1741–97), *Monthly Magazine*, 4 (November 1797), 400–2, by J. A. (i.e. John Aikin).
57. *Monthly Review*, NS, 15 (November 1798), 279–80.
58. *Analytical Review*, 19 (2) (June 1794), 140.
59. *Monthly Review*, 108 (November 1825), 269.
60. Scott, 'Prefatory memoir', p. xxvii. Scott also criticized the improbability of her rational explanations, in his Introduction to Horace Walpole, *The Castle of Otranto* (1811), p. xxv.
61. Letter to William Pattisson dated 22 April 1798, and entries in his travel journal for

23 and 27 June 1829, in Robinson, *Books and Their Writers*, pp. 843, 366.
62. William Hazlitt, *Lectures on the English Comic Writers* (1819), p. 250.
63. Charles Bucke, *On the Beauties, Harmonies, and Sublimities of Nature* (1837), vol. 2, p. 123.

9 Picturesque Tours

1. *The Lady's Magazine*, 26 (1795): July, 320–4; August, 359–63; September, 417–18; November, 505–9. *Scots Magazine*, 57 (October 1795), 636–9.
2. Ann Radcliffe, *A Journey Made in the Summer of 1794* (1795), p. v. All quotations are from this edition.
3. *English Review*, 26 (July 1795), 2.
4. The obelisk and its inscription ('SACRED TO LIBERTY') are described in Thomas West's *A Guide to the Lakes in Cumberland, Westmorland, and Lancashire* (1802), p. 183.
5. Charlotte Smith, note to *The Emigrants, A Poem* (1793), p. 36.
6. R. K. Webb, 'The emergence of Rational Dissent', in *Enlightenment and Religion*, edited by Knud Haakonssen (1996), p. 40.
7. David Bogue and James Bennett, *History of Dissenters*, vol. 4 (1812), p. 199.
8. Robert Miles, *Ann Radcliffe: The Great Enchantress* (1995), pp. 61–2, 63–4.
9. Michael R. Watts, *The Dissenters*, vol. 2 (1995), p. 353.
10. *Ibid.*
11. *Ibid.*, p. 354.
12. Stanley J. Kunitz and Howard Haycraft, *British Authors of the Nineteenth Century* (1936), p. 511.
13. *Monthly Review*, NS, 18 (November 1795), 245.
14. *British Critic*, 6 (Preface, July 1795), viii.
15. *Ibid.*, (October 1795), 363–4.
16. *Analytical Review*, 22 (4) (October 1795), 350.
17. *English Review*, 26 (1795), July, 1–5; August, 89–90; September, 173–8.
18. *British Critic*, 4 (August 1794), 110.
19. James Boaden, *Memoirs of Mrs Inchbald* (1833), vol. 1, p. 308.
20. *Ibid.*, p. 342.
21. Thomas Noon Talfourd, 'Memoir of the life and writings of Mrs Radcliffe' (1826), vol. 1, p. 13.
22. Boaden, *Memoirs of Mrs Inchbald*, vol. 2, pp. 53–4.
23. PRO, C 104/68, Book C, p. 55.
24. *Ibid.*, p. 56 verso.
25. *Ibid.*, item 63.
26. *Ibid.*, item 65.
27. William Ward's will dated 22 April 1793 describes him as 'late of the City of Bath but now of Chesterfield', PRO, PROB 11/1312.

28. Thomas Percy, *Reliques of Ancient English Poetry* (1765), vol. 1, p. 310–13.
29. For example, the archaeological description of the 'caul and scuplary' Cistercian choir dress (pp. 493–4) is found in Thomas West, *The Antiquities of Furness* (1774), p. 51.
30. Ann Seward, *Letters of Anna Seward: Written between the Years 1784 and 1807* (1811), vol. 4, p. 150.
31. Entry for 26 May 1800, Thomas Green, *Extracts from the Diary of a Lover of Literature* (1810), p. 225.
32. 'Article xi. Mrs Radcliffe' Description of the Scenery in a ride over Skiddaw', *A Guide to the Lakes in Cumberland, Westmorland, and Lancashire*, By the Author of The Antiquities of Furness, 8th edn., edited by William Cockin (1802), pp. 306–11.
33. Thomas De Quincey, *The Collected Writings of Thomas De Quincey* (1889–90), vol. 3, p. 282.
34. Joseph Farington, *Britannia Depicta; A Series of Views of the Most Interesting and Picturesque Objects in Great Britain* . . . engraved from drawings made by Joseph Farington. *Part V. Cumberland* (1816). No page numbering. The quotation and paraphrase are from Ann Radcliffe's *Journey*, pp. 451, 466.
35. Ebenezer Rhodes, *Peak Scenery, or Excursions in Derbyshire: Made Chiefly for the Purpose of Picturesque Obsevation*, part 4 (1823), p. 112.
36. *Ibid.*, part 2 (1819), p. 84.
37. William Maton, 'A sketch of a tour from London to the Lakes made in the summer of the year 1799', cited by Malcolm Andrews, *The Search for the Picturesque* (1989), p. 77.
38. Henry Matthews, *The Diary of an Invalid* (1820), p. 268.
39. Cited by Maurice Lévy, *Le Roman 'gothique' anglais* (1968), p. 302.
40. See letter to Lady Clarke, May 1819, Sydney Owensen, *Lady Morgan's Memoirs: Autobiography, Diaries and Correspondence* (1862), vol. 2, pp. 89–90; editorial comment, p. 94.
41. John Sheppard, *Letters, Descriptive of a Tour through Some Parts of France, Italy, Switzerland, and Germany, in 1816* (1817), vol. 2, p. 438.
42. [Jane Waldie] *Sketches Descriptive of Italy in the Years 1816 and 1817* (1820), vol. 4, pp. 163–4.
43. Letter to J. H. Reynolds, 14 March 1818, in John Keats, *The Letters of John Keats 1814–1821* (1958), vol. 1, p. 245.
44. Talfourd, 'Memoir', p. 14.
45. *New Monthly Magazine and Literary Journal*, Historical Register NS, 9 (May 1823), 232.
46. For example, the first obituary, *ibid.*; and J. Cordy Jeaffreson, *Novels and Novelists* (1858), vol. 2, p. 2.
47. Sir Walter Scott, 'Prefatory memoir to Mrs Ann Radcliffe', *The Novels of Mrs Ann Radcliffe*, p. vi. Jerome Murch repeats this suggestion in *Mrs Barbauld and Her Contemporaries* (1877), p. 142.
48. *Edinburgh Review*, 38 (May 1823), 360.
49. *Annual Biography and Obituary*, 8, 96.

10 The Mighty Magician

1. PRO, C 104/68, Book C, p. 58 verso.
2. Robert L. Haig, 'The last years of the *Gazetteer*', *The Library*, 5th series, 7 (4) (December 1952), 241; PRO, C 104/68, Book C, p. 59.
3. PRO, C 104/68, item 59.
4. Haig, 'The *Gazetteer*', pp. 252–60.
5. Charles Henry Timperley, *Encyclopaedia of Literary and Typographical Anecdote*, 2nd edn. (1842), p. 959.
6. *Edinburgh Review*, 38 (76) (May 1823), 360.
7. William B. Todd (compiler), *A Directory of Printers* (1972), p. 155.
8. The name 'Wm Radcliff' first appears in the quarterly rate assessment made on 3 June 1795, Poor Rate, Parish of St George the Martyr, Borough of Southwark, Southwark Local Studies Library. The number of the house is given in the assessment made on 5 April 1799.
9. The site of Melina Place today is the north side of Westminster Bridge Road, between Morley Street and Waterloo Street. See the map in R. Horwood, *Plan of the Cities of London and Westminster, the Borough of Southwark and Parts Adjoining, Shewing Every House* (1799).
10. Theodore Besterman, Preface to Thomas Cadell, *The Publishing Firm of Cadell & Davies* (1938), p. xiii.
11. *New Monthly Magazine and Literary Journal*, Historical Register, NS, 9 (May 1823), 232.
12. Philip a Limborch, *The History of the Inquisition*, translated by Samuel Chandler (1731).
13. The resemblances are overstated by John Thomson, 'Ann Radcliffe's use of Philippus van Limborch's *The History of the Inquisition*', *English Language Notes*, 18 (September 1980), 31–3.
14. Eino Railo, *The Haunted Castle* (1927), pp. 174, 177.
15. Louis F. Peck, *A Life of Matthew G. Lewis* (1961), p. 208.
16. Syndy M. Conger analyses *The Italian* as an 'answer' to *The Monk*, 'Sensibility restored: Radcliffe's answer to Lewis's *The Monk*', in *Gothic Fictions: Prohibition/Transgression*, edited by Kenneth W.

Graham (1989), pp. 113–49. Robert Miles, *Ann Radcliffe: The Great Enchantress* (1995, p. 170) feels that the opening paragraphs of *The Italian* are a 'direct response' to the opening paragraphs of *The Monk* (An 'old lady' in church is accompanied by Antonia whose 'words were pronounced in a tone of unexampled sweetness. . . . The voice came from a female, the delicacy and elegance of whose figure inspired the youths with the most lively curiosity to view the face to which it belonged. . . . Her features were hidden by a thick veil.' – 'The sweetness and fine expression of [Ellena's] voice attracted [Vivaldi's] attention to her figure, which had a distinguished air of delicacy and grace; but her face was concealed in her veil. . . . [he was] fascinated by the voice . . . he observed her leave the church with an aged lady'). I do not myself feel that this is justly called a 'reprise' of Lewis.

17. Robert Princeton Reno, *The Gothic Visions of Ann Radcliffe and Matthew G. Lewis* (1980), esp. pp. 99ff, 158, 168, 184–8, 206.

18. Charles Bucke, *On the Beauties, Harmonies, and Sublimities of Nature* (1837), vol. 2, p. 123.

19. Frederick Schiller, *The Robbers. A Tragedy* [translated by Lord Woodhouselee] (1792).

20. Clara Frances McIntyre, *Ann Radcliffe in Relation to Her Time* (1920), p. 62.

21. Cited by J. M. S. Tompkins, *The Popular Novel in England 1770–1800* (1932), p. 376.

22. Geoffrey Buyers, 'The influence of Schiller's drama and fiction upon English Literature in the period 1780–1830', *Englische Studien*, 48 (1914–15), 349–93.

23. Sarah Josepha Hale, *Woman's Record* (1853), p. 482.

24. Archibald C. Coolidge, jun., 'Charles Dickens and Mrs Radcliffe: a farewell to Wilkie Collins', *The Dickensian*, 58 (May 1962), 113; Joyce M. Horner, 'The English women novelists and their connection with the feminist movement (1688–1797)', *Smith College Studies in Modern Languages*, 11 (1–3) (October 1929; January and April 1930), 72.

25. Sir Walter Scott, 'Prefatory memoir to Mrs Ann Radcliffe', *The Novels of Mrs Ann Radcliffe*, Ballantyne's Novelist's Library (1824), vol. 10, pp. xi–xii.

26. Nathan Drake, *Literary Hours*, 3rd edn. (1804), vol. 1, pp. 361–2.

27. Mathew Gregory Lewis, *The Life and Correspondence of M. G. Lewis* (1839), vol. 1, p. 173.

28. Miles, *Ann Radcliffe*, pp. 70–1.

29. Montague Summers, 'A great mistress of romance: Ann Radcliffe, 1764–1823', in *Essays in Petto* [1928], p. 18.

30. *English Review*, 28 (December 1796), 574–9; *British Critic*, 10 (September 1797), 266–70; *Monthly Review*, NS, 22 (March 1797), 282–4; *Monthly Mirror*, 3 (March 1797), 155–8.

31. *New Monthly Magazine and Literary Journal*, 9 (May 1823), 232.

32. *Analytical Review*, 25 (May 1797), 516. This review has been tentatively (I think mistakenly) attributed to Mary Wollstonecraft by Deborah D. Rogers in *The Critical Response to Ann Radcliffe*, p. xl.

33. [Thomas James Mathias], *The Pursuits of Literature, or What You Will: A Satirical Poem in Dialogue*. Part the First. The Third Edition Revised (1797), p. 14. The date August 1797 is mentioned in a note on p. 21, and the book was reviewed in October in the *Analytical Review*, so we may deduce that publication was in late August or September 1797.

34. Lodovico Ariosto, *Orlando Furioso*, translated by John Hoole (1783), vol. 5, pp. 259–60. The correct quotation is: 'e la notrita/Damigella Trivulzia al sacro speco' (*Orlando Furioso*, C. XLVI. 4. 3–4).

35. M. H. (i.e. Mary Hays), 'On novel-writing', letter to the editor, *Monthly Magazine*, 4 (September 1797), 180–1.

36. Cited by Alice M. Killen, *Le Roman terrifiant ou roman noir de Walpole à Ann Radcliffe et son influence sur la littérature française jusqu'en 1840* (1923), p. 123.

37. Mary Robinson, *Hubert de Sevrac, a Romance, of the Eighteenth Century* (1796), vol. 1, pp. 50–1.

38. *Annual Biography and Obituary, for the Year 1824*, 8, 95.

39. Nathan Drake, *Literary Hours*, 3rd edn. (1804), vol. 2, pp. 180–1.

40. [David Rivers], *Literary Memoirs of Living Authors of Great Britain* (1798), vol. 2, p. 31.

41. Scott, 'Prefatory memoir', p. xxii.

42. For example, in the Macmillan Casebook *The Gothick Novel*, edited by Victor Sage (1990), pp. 58, 63.

43. *Monthly Mirror*, 3 (March 1797), 155–8.

44. The last entry in his literary journal for the period 15 May to 3 June 1797, in Henry Cary, *Memoir of the Rev Henry Francis Cary* (1847), vol. 1, p. 112.

45. Entry for 25 March 1800, Thomas Green, *Extracts from the Diary of a Lover of Literature* (1810), p. 209.

46. William Weller Pepys, *A Later Pepys. The Correspondence of Sir William Weller Pepys, Bart.* (1904), vol. 2, p. 133.

47. *Hogg's Instructor*, 3 (1849), 39.

48. *Critical Review*, 21 (November 1797), 285–9; *Monthly Mirror*, 4 (August 1797), 100–3; Summers, 'Mistress of romance', p. 19.

49. James Boaden, *Memoirs of the Life of John Philip Kemble, Esq.* (1825), vol. 2, pp. 219–20, 225.
50. Joseph Farington, *Memoirs of the Life of Sir Joshua Reynolds* (1819), pp. 32, 125.
51. Joseph Farington, *The Farington Diary*, vol. 1 [1922], p. 214.
52. See Poor Rate, St George the Martyr, assessment made 5 April 1799.
53. Rivers, *Living Authors of Great Britain*, p. 181.
54. Anna Laetitia Barbauld, Preface to *The British Novelists* (1810) vol. 43, p. viii.

11 Behind the Veil

1. William Hazlitt, *Sketches and Essays by William Hazlitt, Now First Collected by His Son* (1839), p. 267.
2. The reader believes Agnes, who says that Emily is the daughter of the Marchioness de Villeroi, and that her father St Aubert was the Marchioness's secret lover – despite being her brother. Clues have been deliberately planted to lead us to the discovery that the Marchioness gave birth to Emily just before she died. As Sister Frances explains, the convent of St Clair has been Sister Agnes's place of refuge 'for nearly as many years as make your age', and Emily, a clever detective, remarks that 'it was about that same period that the Marchioness de Villeroi expired' (578). St Aubert's obsession with prudence is seen to stem from guilt over a passionate affair with the Marchioness. It is wholly unbelievable that St Aubert totally suppressed all knowledge of the existence of the Marchioness because he wished to spare his daughter the pain of learning merely that an aunt had died in mysterious circumstances. Emily, far from resembling St Aubert's wife, is on the contrary identical to the portrait of the Marchioness. At the end of the novel the significance of these clues is simply dismissed.
3. Eugenia C. DeLamotte, *Perils of the Night* (1990), pp. 158–9.
4. [Radcliffe, Ann] *A Sicilian Romance*, 2 vols. (1790), vol. 1, p. 6. All quotations are from this edition.
5. [Ann Radcliffe] *The Castles of Athlin and Dunbayne. A Highland Story* (1789), pp. 4–5. All references are from this first edition.
6. Thomas Noon Talfourd, 'Memoir of the life and writings of Mrs Radcliffe', (1826), vol. 1, p. 9.
7. David Punter, *The Romantic Unconscious: A Study in Narcissism and Patriarchy* (1989), p. 121.
8. Ann Radcliffe, *The Mysteries of Udolpho*, edited by Bonamy Dobrée (1966, 1970). All quotations are from this edition.
9. Daniel Cottom, *The Civilized Imagination. A Study of Ann Radcliffe, Jane Austen and Sir Walter Scott* (1985), pp. 49–50; Punter, *The Romantic Unconscious*, pp. 121, 134–5.
10. Robert Princeton Reno, *The Gothic Visions of Ann Radcliffe and Matthew G. Lewis* (1980), pp. 76–8.
11. Kenneth W. Graham, 'Emily's demon-lover: the Gothic revolution and *The Mysteries of Udolpho*', in *Gothic Fictions: Prohibition/Transgression*, edited by Kenneth W. Graham (1989), pp. 163–71.
12. Janet Todd, *The Sign of Angellica* (1989), p. 263.
13. Patrick Brydone, *A Tour through Sicily and Malta* (1773), vol. 1, pp. 142–3.
14. For a discussion of the womb-tomb of the female body in *The Mysteries of Udolpho* and other Gothic novels see Claire Kahane, 'Gothic mirrors and feminine identity', *Centennial Review*, 24 (1) (Winter 1980), 43–64. DeLamotte calls attention to the series of boundaries or thresholds through which the Self (Emily) travels into the Other (Udolpho), in *Perils of the Night*, p. 19.
15. Kahane, 'Gothic mirrors', pp. 47–8.
16. Terry Castle, *The Apparitional Lesbian: Female Homosexuality and Modern Culture* (1993), esp. pp. 28–65.
17. Terry Castle, 'The spectralization of the other in *The Mysteries of Udolpho*', in *The New Eighteenth Century*, edited by Felicity Nussbaum and Laura Brown (1987), pp. 231–53.
18. Kahane, 'Gothic mirrors', pp. 54–60.
19. Camille Paglia, *Sexual Personae* (1990), p. 157.
20. An anomaly emphasized by Reno, *Gothic Visions of Ann Radcliffe and Matthew G. Lewis*, p. 96.
21. Coral Ann Howells, 'The pleasure of the woman's text: Ann Radcliffe's subtle transgressions', in Graham, *Gothic Fictions*, pp. 153, 155.
22. Preface to *The Poems of Mrs Ann Radcliffe* (1815).
23. No. 687, by R. Westall, *The Exhibition of the Royal Academy* (1790), p. 20.
24. Rictor Norton, 'The fallacy of "anachronism"', in *The Myth of the Modern Homosexual* (1997), pp. 142–7.
25. Emma Donoghue, *Passions between Women: British Lesbian Culture 1668–1801* (1993), p. 109.
26. *Ibid.*, pp. 149–50.
27. Anne Lister, *I Know My Own Heart: The Diaries [1817–1824] of Anne Lister (1791–1840)*, edited by Helena Whitbread (1988), p. 210.

28. Donoghue, *Passions between Women*, pp. 109–11, 149–50.
29. Lillian Faderman (ed.), *Chloe Plus Olivia* (1994), p. 34.
30. For its various sexual meanings, see Eve Kosofsky Sedgwick, 'The character in the veil: imagery of the surface in the Gothic novel', *PMLA*, 46 (2) (March 1981), 256.
31. The lesbian interpretation of the veil is emphasized by Susan C. Greenfield, 'Veiled desire: mother-daughter love and sexual imagery in Ann Radcliffe's *The Italian*', *The Eighteenth Century: Theory and Interpretation*, 33 (1992), 73–89, as revised and reprinted in *The Critical Response to Ann Radcliffe*, edited by Deborah D. Rogers (1994), pp. 57–70.
32. Janet Todd describes this as 'very much a male love affair excluding any woman' and argues that 'As the novel proceeds, Paolo grows into his most flamboyant role, that of lover, making of his master a much feted and caressed beloved'; the guards of the Inquisition have to part the two men as if from the embrace of lovers; at the end Paulo spurns marriage and freedom for himself in order to remain in Vivaldi's service; the servant's delirious affection for his master at the conclusion of the novel suggests that it is Paulo and Vivaldi who are getting married rather than Ellena and Vivaldi. Janet Todd, 'Posture and imposture: the Gothic manservant in Ann Radcliffe's *The Italian*', *Women & Literature*, 2 (1982), 25–38; Todd, *Sign of Angellica*, pp. 260–1.
33. Jane Spencer, *The Rise of the Woman Novelist: From Aphra Behn to Jane Austen* (1986), p. 207.
34. George E. Haggerty, 'Sensibility and sexuality in *The Romance of the Forest*', in Rogers, *Critical Response to Ann Radcliffe*, p. 14.

12 Horrid Mysteries

1. *Annual Biography and Obituary, for the Year 1824*, 8, 100.
2. Letter to Revd Joseph Cooper Walker (undated, but presumed to be 1802 on the basis of internal evidence and related dated letters), cited by Alan Dugald McKillop, 'Charlotte Smith's letters', *Huntington Library Quarterly*, 15 (1951–2), 255.
3. *New Monthly Magazine and Literary Journal*, Historical Register, NS, 9 (May 1823), 232.
4. *Annual Biography*, 8, 104.
5. Sir Walter Scott, 'Prefatory memoir to Mrs Ann Radcliffe', *The Novels of Mrs Ann Radcliffe*, Ballantyne's Novelist's Library (1824), vol. 10, p. xx.
6. *Quarterly Review*, 3 (May 1810), 345.
7. Thomas Noon Talfourd, 'Memoir of the life and writings of Mrs Radcliffe' (1826), vol. 1, p. 99.
8. Sir Walter Scott, *Waverley; or, 'Tis Sixty Years Since* (1814), vol. 1, p. 5.
9. Letter to R. P. Gillies, March or April 1815, cited by Deborah D. Rogers, *Ann Radcliffe: A Bio-Bibliography* (1996), pp. 54–5.
10. *Monthly Mirror*, 4 (1797), 38.
11. For the publishing history see R. W. Chapman, 'Introductory note', in Jane Austen, *The Novels of Jane Austen* (1923; 1965), vol. 5, pp. xi–xiii.
12. Charlotte Smith, *The Banished Man. A Novel* (1794), vol. 2, pp. iii–v.
13. Anna Maria Mackenzie, *Mysteries Elucidated, a Novel* (1795), vol. 1, pp. x–xii.
14. *Critical Review*, 16 (March 1796), 359.
15. Mary Wollstonecraft, *The Wrongs of Woman, or Maria*, in *Posthumous Works* (1798), vol. 1, pp. 1–2.
16. Robert Miles, *Ann Radcliffe: The Great Enchantress* (1995), pp. 24–5, similarly focuses specifically upon reviews of *The Italian*, noting that 'there was one purely hostile review', which was in 1801, rather too late to have been responsible for silencing her.
17. *Monthly Magazine*, 4 (August 1797), pp. 102–4. Reprinted in *Spirit of the Public Journals* (1797), pp. 227–8.
18. 'On the titles of modern novels', *Monthly Magazine*, 4 (November 1797), pp. 347–9.
19. Entry for 8 September 1797, Thomas Green, *Extracts from the Diary of a Lover of Literature* (1810), p. 44.
20. *Edinburgh Review*, 59 (July 1834), 328.
21. *Monthly Magazine*, 4 (August 1797), 120–1.
22. *Monthly Review*, NS, 23 (August 1797), 451.
23. *Analytical Review*, 28 (August 1798), 183.
24. [Thomas James Mathias], *The Pursuits of Literature, or What You Will: A Satirical Poem in Dialogue*, Part the Fourth and Last (1797), pp. ii–iv.
25. *Critical Review*, 20 (May 1797), 118.
26. *Ibid.*, 16 (February 1796), 222.
27. *Ibid.*, 20 (August 1797), 469.
28. *Ibid.*, 21 (December 1797), 472.
29. *Ibid.*, 24 (September 1798), 77.
30. Cited by Montague Summers, *The Gothic Quest* (1938), p. 89.
31. *British Critic*, 10 (October 1797), 433.
32. Review of *The Italian* in *The Anti-Jacobin Review and Magazine*, 7 (September 1800), 27–30.
33. *Analytical Review*, 28 (August 1798), 180.
34. 'On the absurdities of the modern stage', *Monthly Mirror*, 10 (September 1800), 180–2.
35. 'Novels and romances', by Rimelli, in *Monthly Mirror*, 14 (August 1802), 81–2.

36. William Barrow, *An Essay on Education* (1802), vol. 2, p. 68; cited by F. Blagdon and F. Prevost, *Flowers of Literature; for 1801 & 1802* (1803), p. 425.

37. *Ibid.,* . . . *for 1803* (1804), p. xlix, p. 442.

38. *Ibid.,* . . . *for 1801 & 1802,* p. 393.

39. Ibid., . . . *for 1806* (1807), p. lxxv.

40. For a systematic comparison of the main imitators see John Garrett, *Gothic Strains and Bourgeois Sentiments in the Novels of Mrs Ann Radcliffe and Her Imitators* (1980).

41. Eliza Parsons, *Lucy: A Novel* (1794): e.g. vol. 1, pp. 29–30, 71.

42. Letter to Earl Harcourt, 5 August 1783, Horace Walpole, *The Letters of Horace Walpole,* vol. 13 (1905), p. 42.

43. Anne Ker, *Adeline St Julian; or, The Midnight Hour. A Novel* (1800), vol. 1, pp. v–vii. For the Radcliffean forest scenes see especially pp. 1–9, and for the Radcliffean Inquisition scenes see pp. 146–8.

44. *Athenaeum,* 2 (7) (1 July 1807), 50–1. Lady Bedingfeld frequently wrote to Matilda Betham from 'the East turret of my Old Castle', Oxburgh Hall, Norfolk; see *A House of Letters,* edited by Ernest Betham [1905].

45. Betham, *A House of Letters,* p. 77.

46. She was also seen at 'Smith the sculptors . . . with a lady', letter from Southey, 30 May 1814, in *ibid.,* p. 147. Her translation of the *Lay of Marie de France* was published in 1816, probably too late to have influenced Ann Radcliffe's *Gaston.*

47. *Analytical Review,* 23 (January 1796), 55.

48. *English Review,* 26 (December 1795), 468; and *Critical Review,* S. 2, 15 (December 1795), 480.

49. *Critical Review,* S. 2, 14 (May 1795), 101.

50. *Ibid.,* (July 1795), 349.

51. *Ibid.,* 24 (October 1798), 236.

52. *Ibid.,* (November 1798), 356.

53. *Ibid.,* 23 (August 1798), 472. (Wrongly attributed to Coleridge.)

54. Donald K. Adams, 'The second Mrs Radcliffe', in *The Mystery & Detection Annual* (1972), p. 49.

55. [Cassandra Cooke], *Battleridge: An Historical Tale* (1799), vol. 1, p. viii.

56. Robert D. Mayo, *The English Novel in the Magazines 1740–1815* (1962), pp. 349ff.

57. Many examples are discussed in William W. Watt's *Shilling Shockers of the Gothic School* (1932).

58. The story is reprinted in *The Oxford Book of Gothic Tales,* edited by Chris Baldick (1992), pp. 51-9.

59. Clara F. McIntyre, *Ann Radcliffe in Relation to Her Time* (1920), p. 14.

60. *Critical Review,* 22 (February 1798), 238–9.

61. Royall Tyler, *The Algerine Captive; or, The Life and Adventures of Doctor Updike Underhill: Six Years a Prisoner among the Algerines* (1797), vol. 1, pp. viii–ix.

62. Hugh Murray, *Morality of Fiction; or, An Inquiry into the Tendency of Fictitious Narratives* (1805), pp. 113–19, 126–7.

63. George Gregory, *Letters on Literature, Taste, and Composition* (1808), vol. 2, pp. 74–5.

64. *Critical Review,* 19 (February 1797), 194–5.

65. Cited by Warren Hunting Smith, *Architecture in English Fiction* (1934), p. 164.

66. So she is styled in *Biographical Dictionary of Living Authors* (1816).

67. [William Beckford], *Azemia, a Novel,* 2nd edn. (1798); vol. 2, p. 248.

68. *Ibid.,* pp. 237–8.

69. *Monthly Mirror,* 4 (August 1797), 96–7. It was also attributed to Robert Merry in the *Critical Review,* 20 (August 1797), 470.

70. Entry for 11 October 1804, Hester Lynch (Thrale) Piozzi, *Thraliana. The Diary of Mrs Hester Lynch Thrale (later Mrs Piozzi) 1776–1809,* vol. 2, p. 1061.

71. Letter to Cassandra, 2 March 1814, Jane Austen, *Jane Austen's Letters to her Sister Cassandra and Others* (1932), vol. 2, p. 377.

72. Eaton Stannard Barrett, *The Heroine, or Adventures of Cherubina,* 2nd edn. (1814), vol. 3, p. 190. All quotations are from this edition, which has various additions and alterations to the first edition.

73. *Ibid.,* p. 168.

74. *Idée sur les Romans* (1800), *Selected Writings of De Sade* (1954), p. 287. He criticized her French imitators: a character in *Zolaé* (July 1800) laughs at 'all that bombastic twaddle and . . . those mysteries and tortures which have never existed save in the sickly imagination of the novelists themselves', cited by Montague Summers, 'A great mistress of romance', in *Essays in Petto* [1928], p. 27.

75. William Hazlitt, *Lectures on the English Comic Writers* (1819), p. 244.

76. For a suggestive socio-economic analysis (along the lines of Plekhanov's dialectical materialism) of Ann Radcliffe's ambivalence and oblique negation of bourgeois standards, see Wilie Sypher, 'Social ambiguity in a Gothic novel', *Partisan Review,* 12 (1945), 50–60.

77. Marilyn Butler, *Romantics, Rebels and Reactionaries* (1981), p. 15.

78. *Ibid.,* p. 95.

79. Janet Todd, *The Sign of Angellica* (1989), p. 197.

80. Donald Davie, *Essays in Dissent* (1995), p. 106.

81. Miles, *Ann Radcliffe: The Great Enchantress,* stresses her Dissenting background, though he does not make it clear that it was significantly Unitarian rather than Methodist.

82. Todd, *Sign of Angellica*, pp. 21, 196.
83. Michael R. Watts, *The Dissenters*, vol. 1 (1978), p. 487.
84. *Ibid*.
85. *The Poems of Anna Letitia Barbauld*, edited by William McCarthy and Elizabeth Kraft (1994), p. 125.
86. *Orpheus, Priest of Nature, and Prophet of Infidelity; or, The Eleusinian Mysteries Revived* (1781), pp. 28, 33–4.
87. Priestley to his brother-in-law Mr Wilkinson, from Clapton, 19 March 1793, Joseph Priestley, *Collection of Letters* (typescript), edited by John F. March (1915).
88. For example, Richard Martin, *Reasons for Renouncing Unitarianism; Containing Scriptural and Historical Arguments for the Divinity of Jesus Christ, and against the Reasonings of Dr Priestley* (1822). Contemporary debates over Priestley's book – 'Viewed as a historial [*sic*] defence of socinianism, or rather as a death stroke to the deity and atonement of Christ' – are reviewed by David Bogue and James Bennett, *History of Dissenters*, vol. 4 (1812), pp. 249–54.
89. Watts, *Dissenters*, vol. 1 (1978), pp. 487–9; vol. 2 (1995), pp. 91–2.
90. Mary Hays, *Memoirs of Emma Courtney* (1796), vol. 1, pp. 5–6.
91. A 'This day is published . . .' advertisement appeared in the *London Chronicle* for 3–5 June 1794.
92. Allan Cunningham, *Biographical and Critical History of British Literature of the Last Fifty Years* (1834), p. 126.
93. Miles, *Ann Radcliffe*, p. 50.
94. *Ibid*.
95. For the conflicting commitments to feminine sensibility in Wollstonecraft and Hays, see Todd, *Sign of Angellica*, pp. 236–52.
96. Mary Wollstonecraft, *A Vindication of the Rights of Women* (1792), cited by Jacqueline Howard, *Reading Gothic Fiction* (1994), p. 133.
97. Cited by Todd, *Sign of Angellica*, p. 199.
98. [Thomas James Mathias] *The Shade of Alexander Pope on the Banks of the Thames* (1799), Preface dated November 1798, pp. 51–2.
99. Richard Polwhele, 'The unsex'd females', *Poems* (1810), vol. 2, pp. 36–44.
100. *Public Characters of 1803–1804* (London: Richard Phillips, 1804), p. 553; Polwhele was himself the subject of a fulsome biography the previous year, *Public Characters of 1802–1803*, pp. 254–67.
101. Letter from Whitaker to Polwhele, 7 May 1799, in Richard Polwhele, *Traditions and Recollections* (1826), vol. 2, p. 502.
102. *Ibid*., p. 366.

103. For their otherwise traditional 'feminine' concerns see Anne K. Mellor, *Romanticism & Gender* (1993), p. 3.
104. 'Modern literature', *Aberdeen Magazine*, 3 (1798), 338; cited by Elizabeth R. Napier, *The Failure of Gothic: Problems of Disjunction in an Eighteenth-Century Literary Form* (1987), p. vii.
105. Charles Caleb Colton, *Hypocrisy; A Satire* (1812), pp. 10–11; also quoted in a review in *Gentleman's Magazine*, 86, part 2 (October 1816), 334.
106. Howard, *Gothic Fiction*, pp. 96–7.
107. 'Memoirs of Mrs Ann Radcliffe', Preface to *The Mysteries of Udolpho*, Limbird's British Novelists (1824), vols. 13–17, p. v.
108. *Ibid*., p. vi.
109. T. J. Horsley Curties, *Ancient Records, or, The Abbey of Saint Oswythe. A Romance* (1801), vol. 1, p. vi.
110. *Ibid*., Preface, pp. vii–viii.

13 The Gothic Tourist

1. The 'English Chronicle Office' was listed in Holden's Directory until 1802; Ian Maxted, *The London Book Trades 1775–1800* (1977), p. 183.
2. *The Waterloo Directory of Victorian Periodicals*, p. 347.
3. *Gentleman's Magazine*, 81, part 2 (October 1811), 345; Henry Crabb Robinson, *Diary, Reminiscences, and Correspondence of Henry Crabb Robinson* (1869), vol. 1, pp. 75–6.
4. Alexander Andrews, *History of British Journalism* (1859), vol. 2, pp. 195–6.
5. Lucy Aikin, *Memoirs, Miscellanies and Letters of the Late Lucy Aikin* (1864), pp. 16–18.
6. The letter is in the Robert H. Taylor Collection, Princeton University Library; it is published as Facsimile III by Margaret M. Smith and Alexander Lindsay, *Index of English Literary Manuscripts*, vol. 3: 1700–1800, part 3 (1992), where it is dated 'c. 1800'. Mark R. Farrell, Curator of the Robert H. Taylor Collection, tells me that this date cannot be relied upon, because it 'appears only on the catalogue card for the letter, without reference to any authority', and that there are no records concerning the provenance of the letter.
7. Thomas Noon Talfourd, 'Memoir of the life and writings of Mrs Radcliffe' (1826), vol. 1, p. 14.
8. *Ibid*., p. 43.
9. Letter to Revd William Harness, 4 March 1826, Mary Russell Mitford, *The Life of Mary Russell Mitford* (1870), vol. 2, p. 221.
10. Talfourd, 'Memoir', pp. 16–23.

11. PRO, PROB 11/1312. The will was signed on 22 April 1793, and proved on 3 August 1798.
12. Deborah D. Rogers, *Ann Radcliffe: A Bio-Bibliography* (1996), pp. 11, 12.
13. Talfourd, 'Memoir', pp. 24–33.
14. William Gilpin, *Observations on the Western Parts of England* (1798), pp. 49–50.
15. J. Hassell, *Tour of the Isle of Wight* (1790), vol. 2, p. 102.
16. Remarked upon by Gilpin, *Observations on the Western Parts*, p. 318.
17. Hassell, *Tour of the Isle of Wight*, illustration facing vol. 2, p. 101. See also *The Ancient Castles of England and Wales*, engraved by William Woolnoth, historical descriptions by E. W. Brayley, jun. (1825).
18. See letters to Mrs Vesey, 11 September and 1 October 1781, in Elizabeth Carter, *A Series of Letters between Mrs Elizabeth Carter and Miss Catherine Talbot . . . [and] to Mrs Vesey* (1808), vol. 2, pp. 388–9.
19. Elizabeth Carter, *Letters from Mrs Elizabeth Carter to Mrs Montague* (1817), vol. 1, p. 69 (note).
20. Letter to Mrs Montagu, 15 December 1790, *Letters . . . to Mrs Montagu*, vol. 3, pp. 323–4.
21. Entry for 15 September 1794, in Joseph Farington, *The Farington Diary* (1922), vol. 1, p. 71.
22. Montagu Pennington, *Memoirs of the Life of Mrs Elizabeth Carter* (1807), p. 300.
23. *Annual Biography and Obituary, for the Year 1824*, 8, 103–4.
24. Elizabeth Mavor, *The Ladies of Llangollen* (1971), p. 162.
25. Mary Pilkington, *Memoirs of Celebrated Female Characters* (1804), p. 59.
26. *Annual Biography*, 8, 103.
27. Pennington, *Memoirs of the Life of Mrs Carter*, p. 300.
28. *Annual Biography*, 8, 103.
29. Talfourd, 'Memoir', p. 94.
30. Joanna Baillie, *De Monfort; A Tragedy* [1807], pp. 4–5.
31. Letter to Revd T. S. Whalley, 7 June 1799, in Anna Seward, *Letters of Anna Seward: Written between the Years 1784 and 1807* (1811), vol. 5, p. 244.
32. Letter to Miss Ponsonby, 21 May 1799, *ibid.*, p. 226.
33. Letter to Revd T. W. Whalley, 7 October 1799, *ibid.*, p. 253.
34. Letter to Mrs M. Powys, 17 October 1799, *ibid.*, pp. 256–7.
35. Entry for 11 March 1799, in Hester Lynch (Thrale) Piozzi, *Thraliana. The Diary of Mrs Hester Lynch Thrale (Later Mrs Piozzi) 1776–1809* (1942), vol. 2, p. 991.
36. Noted in her commonplace book; Hester Lynch (Thrale) Piozzi, *The Intimate Letters of Hester Piozzi and Penelope Pennington 1788–1821* (1914), p. 173.

37. *Ibid.*, 5 April 1799, p. 171.
38. *Ibid.*, 29 May 1799, p. 175.
39. Hester Lynch (Thrale) Piozzi, *The Piozzi Letters*, edited by Edward A. Bloom and Lillian D. Bloom (1989), vol. 1, p. 347, note.
40. Diary entry for 20 April 1791, *Thraliana*, vol. 2, p. 808.
41. *Ibid.*
42. Entry for 14 December 1791, *ibid.*, p. 830.
43. Mary Alcock, *Poems* (1799), pp. 173–7.
44. Poor Rate, St George the Martyr, Southwark Local Studies Library.
45. Lambeth Archives Department, Minet Library, Parish of Lambeth, Poor Rate, 28 February 1800, p. 33; 11 December 1799, p. 33.
46. *Particulars and Conditions of Sale, of Sundry Valuable Leasehold Estates . . . Which Will Be Sold by Auction . . . On Friday the 29th December, 1820 . . . By Order of the Executor of the late Horatio Goodbehere, Esq.*, Lambeth Archives Department, Class 1, 12,905. See also the Will of Horatio Goodbehere, witnessed 13 September 1820, Class 1, Calendar of Surrey Deeds, Deed No. 6016. The Goodbehere house was No. 1; the houses are unnumbered in the rate books, but a comparison of the order of occupants with the same tenants still occupying their property at the auction establishes that the Radcliffes lived at No. 2.
47. *Annual Biography*, 8, 97.
48. PRO, PROB 11/1341.
49. *Ibid.* The will was signed on 4 April 1799, and proved on 19 April 1800.
50. John Timpane, 'Ann Ward Radcliffe', in *An Encyclopedia of British Women Writers*, edited by Paul Schlueter and June Schlueter (1988), p. 373.
51. Talfourd, 'Memoir', pp. 33–43.
52. *Ibid.*, pp. 43–4.
53. *Ibid.*, pp. 45–56.
54. Letter from David Hartley to Pepys, 26 September 1801, in William Weller Pepys, *A Later Pepys, The Correspondence of Sir William Weller Pepys* (1904), vol. 2, p. 173.
55. Compare Gilpin, *Observations on the Western Parts*, p. 55: 'no spire can be so pleasing an object as an elegant Gothic tower'.
56. Compare Gilpin, *ibid.*, p. 54: the cathedral 'marks the period when Saxon heaviness began first to give way'.

14 Olden Times

1. Thomas Noon Talfourd, 'Memoir of the life and writings of Mrs Radcliffe' (1826), vol. 1, pp. 56–64.
2. *Ibid.*, p. 60.
3. *Ibid.*, p. 90.

4. *Port Folio*, 3 (47) (19 November 1803), 375.
5. Sir Walter Scott, 'Prefatory memoir to Mrs Ann Radcliffe', *The Novels of Mrs Ann Radcliffe*, Ballantyne's Novelist's Library (1824), vol. 10, p. xvi.
6. *Museum of Foreign Literature and Science* (Philadelphia and New York), NSI, 8 (January 1826), 94. Cited by Clara Frances McIntyre, *Ann Radcliffe in Relation to Her Time* (1920), pp. 49–50.
7. *Literary Gazette* (London), 27 May 1826, p. 321. The full review appears in the issues for 27 May (pp. 321–3) and 3 June (pp. 346–7).
8. Talfourd, 'Memoir', p. 90.
9. Montague Summers, 'A great mistress of romance', in *Essays in Petto* [1928], p. 20.
10. *Leland's Collectanea in Six Volumes*, being the half title of *Joannis Lelandi Antiquarii de Rebus Britannicis Collectanea* (1770 and other editions); *A Collection of Ordinances and Regulations for the Government of the Royal Household, Made in Divers Reigns. From King Edward III to King William and Queen Mary. Also Receipts in Ancient Cookery* (1790); Sir George Buck's *The History of the Life and Reign of Richard the Third* (1646, but later editions in *A Complete History of England*); Thomas Madox's *The History and Antiquities of the Exchequer of the Kings of England* (1769, and earlier editions from 1711); Samuel Pegge's *A Series of Dissertations on Some Elegant and Very Valuable Anglo-Saxon Remains* (1756, and other editions); Sir John Fenn's collection of *Original Letters Written during the Reigns of Henry VI, Edward IV, and Richard III* (1787; better known to us as the Paston Letters); George Ellis's *Specimens of the Early English Poets* (1790); *The Life of Benvenuto Cellini* (translated by Thomas Nugent, 1771); Thomas Warton's *History of English Poetry* (3 vols., 1774–81); the Abbé de la Rue's 'Dissertation on the life and writings of Marie de France' in *Archaeologia*, the journal of the Society of Antiquaries (vol. 13, 1800); Bishop Percy's *Reliques of Ancient English Poetry* (1765); and a reprint of the 1592 edition of Stowe's *Survey of London*. From references to Hanmer and Warburton in a discussion of a scene between Hamlet and Horatio, it is fairly clear that she used *The Plays of Shakespeare, from the Text of Dr S. Johnson*, with the prefaces notes, &c. of Rowe, Pope, Theobald, Hanmer, Warburton, Johnson, and select notes from many other critics (7 vols., Dublin, 1771). All of these sources were published before the winter of 1802–3, the date ascribed to the novel.
11. For example, the reviewer in *The London Magazine*, 6 (1 September 1826), 34–40.
12. *Monthly Review*, S. 2, 2 (July 1826), 281.
13. Talfourd, 'Memoir', pp. 97–8. The lines are spoken by Bernardo to Horatio, and broken off by the appearance of the ghost of Hamlet's father, *Hamlet*, I. i. 35–9.
14. This comes from that part of the Introduction which was printed separately, as noted below: Ann Radcliffe, 'On the supernatural in poetry', *New Monthly Magazine*, 16 (1826), 151–2.
15. *Ibid.*, pp. 145–52.
16. [Elizabeth Montagu], *An Essay on the Writings and Genius of Shakespeare* (1778), pp. 116–17.
17. Joseph Priestley, *A Course of Lectures on Oratory and Criticism* (1777), p. 106.
18. Unfortunately Jacqueline Howard's lengthy analysis (*Reading Gothic Fiction*, 1994, pp. 113–20) of 'Radcliffe's intervention in the landscaping debate' in *The Mysteries of Udolpho* is based upon the assumption that Ann Radcliffe had already read Knight's long poem *The Landscape*, and implies that she was familiar with Price's *An Essay on the Picturesque*, all three books having been published in 1794. However, Price's *Essay* was published after *Udolpho*, and Knight's poem seems to have been published in March (the first reviews were in April) – barely two months before *Udolpho*. The contract for *Udolpho* is dated 11 March and suggests that the book had already been written; in any case she would hardly have had time to absorb many ideas from Knight before writing a novel of nearly 300,000 words and handing it in to the publisher for printing by 8 May.
19. William Radcliffe, writing in 1826, said it was 'about twenty years since'; his notes to *St Alban's Abbey* in *Gaston de Blondeville . . . Posthumous Works*, vol. 4, pp. 81–2.
20. Talfourd, 'Memoir', pp. 69–70.
21. Victor Sage, *Horror Fiction in the Protestant Tradition* (1988), pp. 31–2.
22. Talfourd, 'Memoir', p. 96.
23. Radcliffe, notes to *St Alban's Abbey*, p. 94.
24. Particular reference is made to an illustration of the north side of the nave showing Saxon architecture, which matches Plate XIV, F, p. 15.
25. Talfourd, 'Memoir', pp. 82–6.
26. *Ibid.*, p. 83.
27. Charlotte Smith, *Elegiac Sonnets*, 6th edn. (1792; first published in 1784), p. 46.
28. Talfourd, 'Memoir', p. 84.

15 Construction of the Legend

1. Julia Kavanagh, *English Women of Letters: Biographical Sketches* (1862), p. 121.
2. *Annual Biography and Obituary, for the Year 1824*, 8, 97

3. Thomas Noon Talfourd, 'Memoir of the life and writings of Mrs Radcliffe' (1826), vol. 1, p. 100.

4. *Edinburgh Review*, 38 (76) (May 1823), 360.

5. *Biographie Moderne, ou Dictionnaire Biographique*, 2nd edn. (1806), vol. 4, p. 119. This work also ascribes *l'Avocat des Femmes* (by Mary Ann Radcliffe) to her.

6. *Gentleman's Magazine*, 79, part 1 (28 February 1809), 188.

7. Antoine-Alexandre Barbier, *Dictionnaire des Ouvrages Anonymes et Pseudonymes* [1809], vol. 4, p. 345.

8. M. Barbier, *Dictionnaire des Ouvrages Anonymes et Pseudonymes* [1809], vol. 4, p. 345; 2nd edn. (1822–7), vol. 4, p. 426; *Biographie Universelle, Ancienne et Moderne* (1823), vol. 36, p. 526.

9. *Biographie Universelle* (n.d.), vol. 35, p. 56; *Biographie Universelle, Ancienne et Moderne*, vol. 36, p. 526; *Biographie Nouvelle des Contemporains*, edited by A. V. Arnault *et al.* (1824), vol. 17, p. 203.

10. A.-A. Barbier and N. L. M. Desessarts, *Nouvelle Bibliothèque d'un Homme de Goût* (1810), vol. 5, p. 161.

11. *Biographie Étrangère, ou Galerie Universelle* (1819), vol. 2, pp. 75–6.

12. *New Monthly Magazine and Literary Journal*, Historical Register, NS, 9 (May 1823), 232.

13. Arnault *et al.*, *Biographie Nouvelle des Contemporains*, vol. 17, p. 205.

14. *Biographie Universelle, Ancienne et Moderne*, vol. 36, p. 527.

15. Richard Switzer, *Etienne-Léon de Lamothe-Langon et le roman populaire français de 1800 à 1830* (1962), p. 45.

16. I. viii, cited by Switzer, *Etienne-Léon de Lamothe-Langon*, p. 102.

17. For the foreign novels falsely attributed to Ann Radcliffe – including a dozen German works I have not even alluded to – see the valuable Appendix in Alida Alberdina Sibbellina Wieten, *Mrs Radcliffe – Her Relation towards Romanticism* (1926). For detailed bibliographical notes on the major French false attributions see J.–M. Quérard, *Les Supercheries littéraires dévoilées* (1870), vol. 3, pp. 310–11.

18. Kazlitt Arvine, *The Cyclopaedia of Anecdotes of Literature and the Fine Arts* (1852), pp. 268–70.

19. Montague Summers, *A Gothic Bibliography* (1941; 1964), pp. 434, 503.

20. Elizabeth Isabella Spence, *Summer Excursions through Parts of Oxfordshire, Gloucestershire, Warwickshire, Staffordshire, Herefordshire, Derbyshire, and South Wales*, 2nd edn. (1809), pp. 161, 162–3.

21. *Ibid.*, pp. 164–5.

22. Michael R. Watts, *The Dissenters*, vol. 2 (1995), pp. 379–80.

23. Elizabeth Isabella Spence, *A Traveller's Tale of the Last Century* (1819), vol. 1, p. x.

24. *Gentleman's Magazine*, 80 (May 1810), 452–4.

25. *Annual Biography*, 8. 97.

26. For example, *The Ancient Castles of England and Wales*, by William Woolnoth and E. W. Brayley, jun. (1825).

27. Ann Radcliffe, *Gaston de Blondeville, or The Court of Henry III . . . St Alban's Abbey . . . Posthumous Works . . . Memoir* (1826), vol. 4, pp. 236–9.

28. Looseleaf letter inserted into Ann Ward Radcliffe's manuscript commonplace book, Boston Public Library, MS Ch.K.1.10.

29. Ebenezer Rhodes, *Peak Scenery, or Excursions in Derbyshire: Made Chiefly for the Purpose of Picturesque Observation*, part 2 (1819), pp. 92–3.

30. Entry for 6 August 1824, Anne Lister, *No Priest but Love: Excerpts from the Diaries of Anne Lister, 1824–1826* (1992), p. 113.

31. [Elizabeth Selwyn] *Journal of Excursions through the Most Interesting Parts of England, Wales and Scotland, during the Summers and Autumns of 1819, 1820, 1821, 1822, & 1823* [1824], pp. 87–8.

32. Nathaniel H. Carter, *Letters from Europe* (1827), vol. 1, p. 83.

33. Sir Walter Scott, 'Prefatory memoir to Mrs Ann Radcliffe', *The Novels of Mrs Ann Radcliffe*, Ballantyne's Novelist's Library (1824), vol. 10, p. xxxv.

34. Mary Sterndale, *Vignettes of Derbyshire* (1824), pp. 69–70.

35. Talfourd, 'Memoir', p. 95.

36. Charles Apthorp Wheelwright, *Poems, Original and Translated; Including Versions of the Medea and Octavio of Seneca* (1810), pp. 274–5.

37. *Ibid.*, p. 275.

38. *Alumni Cantabrigienses*, compiled by J. A. Venn, Part II, vol. 2 (1953), p. 424.

39. Scott, 'Prefatory memoir', p. xvii.

40. Arnault *et al.*, *Biographie Nouvelle des Contemporains*, p. 204.

41. Mary Russell Mitford, *The Life of Mary Russell Mitford, Related in a Selection from Her Letters to Her Friends* (1870), vol. 1, pp. 143–4.

42. *Ibid.*, p. 227.

43. Thomas Rees, *Reminiscences of Literary London from 1779 to 1853* (1896), p. 117.

44. *A Biographical Dictionary of Living Authors* (1816), p. 382.

45. *Monthly Review*, 44 (March 1811), 313; cited by Montague Summers, *The Gothic Quest* (1938; 1964), p. 135.

46. *Velina* was attributed to Ann Radcliffe in the catalogues of 1802 and 1814, and *Radzivil* was attributed to her in the catalogue of 1814; Dorothy Blakey, *The*

Minerva Press 1790–1820 (1939), pp. 150–1.

47. Donald K. Adams, 'The second Mrs Radcliffe', *The Mystery & Detection Annual* (1972), pp. 53–4.

48. For example, '*Manfrone; or, The One-Handed Monk. A Romance*. By Mary Anne Radcliffe, Author of "The Romance of the Forest", "The Italian", &c., &c.' (n.d.). Janet Todd in the *Dictionary of British Women Writers* (1989/1991) has scrupulously listed two separate entries, one for Mary Ann Radcliffe the author of the memoirs and the *Female Advocate*, and one for Mary Anne Radcliffe the author of *Manfroné*, 'about whom no biography is known'. We know from the memoirs that she lived in Edinburgh for a while as a governess and spent her last years there, which seems to account for the publication of *Radclife's New Novelist's Pocket Magazine* in Edinburgh, which would identify her as the novelist. But it is not certain that she wrote *Manfroné*: Louisa Belinda Ker listed this title among her novels in several letters applying for assistance to the Royal Literary Fund in 1822 and later (Case 400) (British Library, Department of Manuscripts, Loan No. 96).

49. *L'Avocat des Femmes*, attributed to Mrs Ann Ward Radcliffe in works such as *Biographie Etrangère*, vol. 2, p. 75.

50. Mary Ann Radcliffe, *The Memoirs of Mrs Mary Ann Radcliffe; in Familiar Letters to Her Female Friend* (1810), p. 387.

51. *British Critic*, 40 (August 1812), 189.

52. Radcliffe, *Memoirs of Mrs Mary Ann Radcliffe*, pp. 63–4.

53. Robert Macnish, *The Philosophy of Sleep* (1830), p. 57.

54. Quoted by Richmond Croom Beatty, *Bayard Taylor* (1936), p. 151.

55. Elizabeth R. Napier, 'Ann Radcliffe', *Dictionary of Literary Biography, Vol. 39: British Novelists, 1660–1800* (1985), part 2, p. 365.

56. Talfourd, 'Memoir', p. 96.

57. *Ibid.*, pp. 74–5.

58. *Ibid.*, pp. 75–6.

59. *Ibid.*, p. 75.

60. *Ibid.*, pp. 77–9. Reference to *The Tempest*, I. ii. 400–1.

61. *Ibid.*, p. 81. Reference to *Hamlet*, I. i. 42.

62. *Ibid.*, pp. 81–2.

16 Sequestered at Windsor

1. Thomas Noon Talfourd, 'Memoir of the life and writings of Mrs Radcliffe' (1826), vol. 1, p. 95.

2. For example, see Anonymous, *Poems Written by Somebody* (1818), pp. 35–6.

3. *Sketches in Bedlam; or Characteristic Traits of Insanity*, 2nd edn. (1824), *passim*.

4. Samuel Egerton Brydges, *The Autobiography . . . of Sir Egerton Brydges* (1834), vol. 1, p. 59.

5. John Haslam, *Observations on Madness and Melancholy* (1809), p. v.

6. *Annual Biography and Obituary, for the Year 1824*, 8, 97.

7. *New Monthly Magazine and Literary Journal* (1823), Historical Register, NS, 9 (May 1823), 232. The short obituary was reprinted in Boston in *The Athenaeum; or, Spirit of the English Magazines*, 13 (1 July 1823), 275–6.

8. Robert Kiely, *The Romantic Novel in England* (1972), p. 69.

9. G. W. M., *Memoirs of Mrs Jebb* [1812].

10. Letter to Mr Savile, 19 September 1796, in Anna Seward, *Letters of Anna Seward: Written between the Years 1784 and 1807* (1811), vol. 4, pp. 255–9.

11. Letter to Court Dewes, 30 March 1786, *Ibid.*, vol. 1, p. 148.

12. Letter to C. Smyth, 3 August 1794, *ibid.*, vol. 3, pp. 389–90; to Mrs Childers, 16 August 1797, *ibid.*, vol. 4, pp. 382–3.

13. Letter to Miss Ponsonby, 21 May 1799, *ibid.*, vol. 5, pp. 226–7.

14. Letter to Mrs M. Powys, 17 October 1799, *ibid.*, pp. 256–7; to Thomas Park, 25 September 1800, *ibid.*, p. 324.

15. *Annual Biography*, 8, 101.

16. *Ibid.*, 101–2.

17. Robert Miles, *Ann Radcliffe: The Great Enchantress* (1995), p. 30.

18. *Ibid.*, p. 28.

19. *Annual Biography*, 100, 102.

20. Talfourd, 'Memoir', 93.

21. *Ibid.*, p. 90.

22. Sir Walter Scott, 'Prefatory memoir to Mrs Ann Radcliffe', *The Novels of Mrs Ann Radcliffe*, Ballantyne's Novelist's Library (1824), vol. 10, p. xvii.

23. *Annual Biography*, 103.

24. Talfourd, 'Memoir', pp. 168–9.

25. *Ibid.*, p. 96.

26. *New Monthly Magazine*, 9 (May 1823), 232.

27. Parish of Lambeth, Poor Rate, 25 August 1815, p. 146, Lambeth Archives Department, Minet Library. Radcliffe's name disappears at the next assessment, 17 November 1815, p. 274. See following chapter for their move to Pimlico.

28. John Thomas Smith, *Nollekens and His Times* (1828), vol. 1, p. 169.

29. Register of Poor Rates for New Windsor Parish, Berkshire Record Office, D/P 149 11/5. I have examined all of the records for 1811–13, and a sample for each year until 1818.

30. Charles Knight, *Passages of a Working Life* (1864), vol. 1, p. 41.

31. Smith, *Nollekens*, p. 109. Smith incorrectly ascribes the acquisition of Fanny to the period when Mrs Radcliffe lived in Stafford Row, but the following anecdote shows that she possessed Fanny earlier, in Windsor.

32. *Ibid.*, p. 169.

33. Letters to Dr Burney, 10 July 1796 and 18 June 1795, in Fanny Burney, *Diary and Letters of Madame D'Arblay* (1846), vol. 6, pp. 65–7, 71, 47.

34. Ann Radcliffe, *The Romance of the Forest*, The Fourth Edition (London: T. Hookham and J. Carpenter, M,DCC,XCIV), I, pp. iii–v. Although the title page is dated 1794, it is generally believed the book was printed in 1795.

35. Advertisement in back of volume one of [Laetitia-Maria Hawkins], *Letters on the Female Mind* (1793). H. Colbert's 1794 Dublin edition of *The Castles of Athlin and Dunbayne* was inscribed to the Honourable Lady Viscountess Headfort, but it is made clear that this was provided by the publisher rather than the author.

36. Ellis Cornelia Knight, *Autobiography of Miss Cornelia Knight, Lady Companion to the Princess Charlotte of Wales* (1861), vol. 1, p. 203; *Annual Register*, 41 (Chronicle entry for 31 May 1799), 55.

37. Letter from Fanny Burney to Dr Burney, 30 January 1813, in Fanny Burney, *The Journals and Letters of Fanny Burney (Madame D'Arblay)* (1972–84), vol. 7, p. 390. Fanny Burney met her in 1787, and again in July 1814 and subsequent years; note, p. 390.

38. G. E. C., *Complete Peerage*, vol. 7 (1929), 515–16.

39. *Windsor and Eton Express*, 10 to 17 January 1813.

40. Knight, *Autobiography of Miss Cornelia Knight*, vol. 1, p. 203; though Lady Charlotte Bury believed she had been 'placed by the recommendation of Mrs Nugent, through the Duke of C[umberland]' (*Diary Illustrative of the Times of George the Fourth* (1838; 1839), vol. 1, p. 194).

41. Bury, *Diary of the Times of George the Fourth*, p. 194.

42. Letter dated 20 February 1813, Charlotte Augusta, *Letters of the Princess Charlotte 1811–1817* (1949), pp. 57–8.

43. Knight, *Autobiography of Miss Cornelia Knight*, vol. 1, pp. 233–4.

44. Letter dated 14 August 1813, Charlotte Augusta, *Letters of the Princess Charlotte*, p. 63.

45. Bury, *Diary of the Times of George the Fourth*, p. 189.

46. Jerom Murch, *Mrs Barbauld and Her Contemporaries* (1877), p. 45.

47. For contemporary references to Mrs Damer's lesbianism see Rictor Norton, *Mother Clap's Molly House: The Gay Subculture in England 1700–1830* (1992), pp. 234–6; Emma Donoghue, *Passions between Women: British Lesbian Culture 1668–1801* (1993), pp. 145–8, 262–5.

48. Mary Berry, *Extracts of the Journals and Correspondence of Miss Berry* (1865), vol. 2, p. 476. Agnes Berry refers to 'Mr Nolkin' in a letter to her sister Mary on 1 January 1812: *The Berry Papers* (1914), p. 303.

49. Berry, *Extracts of the Journals . . . of Mary Berry*: see especially 31 May 1809 (vol. 2, p. 380); 7 August 1809 (vol. 2, pp. 388ff); 7 January 1810 (vol. 2, p. 409); 19 June 1811 (vol. 2, pp. 479ff); 15 January 1814 (vol. 3, p. 1).

50. *Ibid.*, August 1807 (vol. 2, pp. 319ff); they visited Knole on 3 October 1812 (vol. 2, p. 506).

51. *Windsor and Eton Express*, 3 October 1812.

52. Ann Radcliffe, *Gaston de Blondeville, or The Court of Henry II . . . St Alban's Abbey . . . Posthumous Works . . . Memoir* (1826), vol. 4, pp. 259–328.

53. *Ibid.*, pp. 261, 270, 280.

54. *Ibid.*, p. 279.

55. Ann Radcliffe, *The Poems of Mrs Ann Radcliffe* (London: Printed by Schulze and Dean, 13, Poland Street; For J. Bounden, 19, Mortimer Street, Cavendish Square, 1815).

56. The copy of the 1815 edition in the British Library is defective, and lacks the preface and table of contents. I am quoting from the preface to the second edition: *The Poems of Mrs Ann Radcliffe* (London: Printed by and for J. Smith, Princes Street, 1816), pp. 5–6. The impression of these two editions is absolutely identical between pages 9 and 114, and I assume the preface would have been identical. The 1816 edition is really a reimpression of the 1815 edition; during the course of printing the last leaf of gathering K (K6) was cut off, leaving a half-inch strip for stitching, and two leaves were added from a new gathering, L 1 & 2 (pp. 115–18), to accommodate the addition of two more poems by the editor: 'Sonnet: When Midnight Robes the World' and 'Fragment: Dark Is the Night, and through the Forest Drear'. Presumably nothing was printed on K6 except the name of the printer of the first edition, and it was removed so that two blank pages would not awkwardly divide the poems of the first edition from the poems added to the second. Another collection of *The Poetical Works of Anne Radcliffe* appeared in 1834, but this was merely a reprint of the two volumes of poetry from the *Posthumous Works*.

57. The poems are reprinted in the same order in which they appear in the novels, with the exception that the first poem in *The Mysteries of Udolpho*, 'Sonnet – Go, Pencil! Faithful to Thy Master's Sight!', is omitted, and 'Stanzas – O'er Ilion's Plains' appears after 'The Butter-fly to His Love' instead of after 'Rondeau – Soft as Yon Silver Ray'.

58. Radcliffe, *The Poems of Mrs Ann Radcliffe* (1816), p. 116.

59. Michael Sadleir, 'Poems by Ann Radcliffe', *Times Literary Supplement*, 29 March 1928, p. 242. Sadleir did not recognize that the poems were gathered from her novels.

17 The Final Years

1. *New Monthly Magazine and Literary Journal*, Historical Register, NS, 9 (May 1823), 232 (it was really fewer than 'ten years').

2. Rate Book for 1816, Parish of Saint George, Hanover Square, City of Westminster, p. 54. A William Radcliffe is cited in the addenda to the rate book for 1815, but as being responsible for the rates on an empty house in Chapel Street Mews – perhaps he originally planned to move there, or perhaps this is a different William Radcliffe.

3. John Thomas Smith, *Nollekens and His Times* (1828), vol. 1, pp. 169–70. Ann Radcliffe also refers to her dog in her posthumous poem 'December's Eve, At Home', *Gaston de Blondeville, or The Court of Henry III . . . St Alban's Abbey . . . Posthumous Works . . . Memoir* (1826), vol. 4, pp. 213-14.

4. Thomas Noon Talfourd, 'Memoir of the life and writings of Mrs Radcliffe' (1826), vol. 1, p. 96.

5. He is described as 'late proprietor and editor of the English Chronicle' in *Gentleman's Magazine*, 93, part 2 (July 1823), 87; reprinted in *Annual Register for 1823* (1824), Chronicle entry for 7 February 1823, 337.

6. Charles Bucke, *The Philosophy of Nature; or, The Influence of Scenery on the Mind and Heart* (1813), vol. 1, p. 149.

7. Charles Bucke, *On the Beauties, Harmonies, and Sublimities of Nature* (1821), vol. 2, pp. 316–17.

8. Charles Bucke, *On the Beauties, Harmonies, and Sublimities of Nature* (1837), vol. 2, p. 123.

9. Charles Bucke, *Amusements in Retirement* (1816), pp. 215–16.

10. *Gazetteer*, 8 March 1793; *Monthly Mirror*, 3 (March 1797), 179.

11. *Blackwood's Edinburgh Magazine*, 11 (62) (March 1822), 331. The account was reprinted in Boston in *The Athenaeum; or, Spirit of the English Magazines*, 11 (April 1822), 196.

12. *Annual Biography and Obituary for the Year 1824*, 8, 97.

13. Letter to Sir William Elford, 18 January 1824, in Mary Russell Mitford, *The Life of Mary Russell Mitford, Related in a Selection from Her Letters to Her Friends* (1870), vol. 2, p. 171.

14. Robert Bree, *A Practical Inquiry on Disordered Respiration*, 2nd edn. (1800), p. 183.

15. *Ibid.*, pp. 196–200, 235.

16. Letter to the editor, *Gentleman's Magazine*, vol. 69, (February 1811), 132–3. John Theobald, *Every Man His Own Physician* (1764), p. 5.

17. Thomas Beddoes, *Letters from Dr Wittering . . . Dr Ewart . . . Dr Thornton . . . and Dr Biggs . . . on Asthma, Consumption, Fever* [1794], p. 7.

18. Michael Ryan, *Observations on the History and Cure of Asthma* (1793).

19. Bree, *A Practical Inquiry*, p. 40.

20. Manuscript commonplace book, forty-two leaves, quarto, bound in marbled boards, with original prescriptions and some letters inserted. Boston Public Library, MS Ch.K.1.10. Deborah D. Rogers quotes extensively from this manuscript in *Ann Radcliffe: A Bio-Bibliography* (1996), pp. 14–20, though her reading of the handwriting frequently differs from mine in minor details (e.g. she reads 'half a glass of sherry mint wth water' where I read 'half a glass of sherry mixt wth water'; she reads 'to Broad-stairs and back' where I read 'to Broadstairs & back'; she reads 'Mrs Norris' where I read 'Mrs Morris'); all my quotations are from my reading of the manuscript.

21. Anne Lister went to Paris in 1824 to find a cure for a venereal infection resulting in chronic vaginal discharge passed to her by her lover Marianna Lawton in 1821 who, Anne believed, had caught it from her husband Charles Lawton (and which Anne had subsequently passed on to a Scottish woman she met in York). The famous Parisian surgeon Guillaume Dupuytren prescribed various douches, baths and mercury, but failed to cure her. She told Dr Scudamore 'about what Dupuytren had done for me, etc., only saying I had caught it from an unclean cabinet at an Inn'; he also failed to cure her. Anne Lister, *No Priest but Love* (1992), diary entries for 26–29 November 1824, pp. 57–60; 21 August 1825, p. 117; and 1 September 1825, p. 123. Lister described

her sexual behaviour in great detail, in a secret cypher.

22. Rogers, *Ann Radcliffe*, p. 14, believes, on the basis of handwriting in an extant letter from William Radcliffe, that the 'prescriptions appear to have been painstakingly copied, almost certainly, by her husband'; but in my view although these prescriptions are more carefully composed and in larger letters than the commentary, the handwriting itself is identical, with common characteristics such as the same sharp slant to the right, an identical capital 'T', the identical crossing of the lower-case 't', the downward-sloping dot to the letter 'i'. This is clearly seen in the copy of Dr Scudamore's seventh prescription, for July 23, followed by Mrs Radcliffe's commentary in handwriting indistinguishable from the prescription for several lines ('A blister on the chest was directed by this prescription'), which then gets smaller and less angular towards the end of the page ('and immediate bleeding. I had been much better for the last prescription') as she runs out of space. At the end of the commonplace book is an inserted page in Mrs Radcliffe's hand listing the ingredients for a medicine which 'relieved me, under the blessing of Providence, from the most violent bowel complaint I ever had'. The Latin prescription (which is clearly in her hand) is followed by the statement: 'Though this appears to be a prescription for *one* draft to be taken, at bed time, I find in my copy the following addition, in my hand writing "Two drafts for Mrs Radcliffe".' This clearly demonstrates that she herself made the copies of the prescriptions.

23. *Ibid.*

24. R. H. Micks, *Essentials of Materia Medica Pharmacology and Therapaeutics* (1950).

25. Dr Scudamore's residence is established in *Boyle's Court and Country Guide*: e.g. the issue for April 1823, p. 454.

26. Rogers, *Ann Radcliffe*, p. 16.

27. George Townsend, *Poems* (1810), p. 135.

28. Talfourd, 'Memoir', pp. 100–1.

29. *Annual Biography*, p. 97.

30. *Ibid.*, pp. 97–8.

31. Talfourd, 'Memoir', pp. 103–4.

32. Index to Interments, Saint George's, Hanover Square, p. 435; Index to Inscriptions, no page number. The funeral ceremony was performed by J. Glen on 15 February according to the Register of the Burials in the Parish of St George's, Hanover Square, p. 171.

33. Clara Frances McIntyre, *Ann Radcliffe in Relation to Her Time* (1920), p. 21 and note.

34. Stewart M. Ellis, 'Ann Radcliffe and her literary influence', *The Contemporary Review*, 123 (February 1923), 197.

35. *Annual Biography*, p. 95; Talfourd, 'Memoir', p. 11.

36. *Annual Biography and Obituary, for the year 1825*, 9, p. 130.

37. Talfourd, 'Memoir', pp. 11–12. Fox's admiration for her works was first mentioned in the *Annual Biography*, p. 95.

38. *Gentleman's Magazine*, vol. 69 (November 1799), 174.

39. John Bernard Trotter, *Memoirs of the Latter Years of the Right Honourable Charles James Fox* (1811), p. 75.

40. *Ibid.*, p. 123.

41. *Monthly Review, or Literary Journal*, 108 (November 1825), 269.

42. *Ibid.*, 269–70.

43. Talfourd, 'Memoir', p. 102.

44. *Monthly Review*, S. 2, 2 (July 1826), 280–93.

45. *Ibid.*, 283.

46. Talfourd, 'Memoir', p. 99.

47. Large portions of the memoir in Anne Katharine Elwood's *Memoirs of the Literary Ladies of England* (1843), vol. 2, pp. 155–73 consist of unacknowledged quotations from Talfourd's memoir, the 1823 obituary and critical commentary by Mrs Barbauld and Scott.

48. *Blackwood's*, 19 (May 1826), 609.

49. *Monthly Review*, S. 2, 2 (July 1826), 281.

50. Thomas Noon Talfourd, 'On the British novels and romances', *New Monthly Magazine*, 13 (February 1820), 205–9. Also reprinted in *Critical and Miscellaneous Writings of T. Noon Talfourd* (1850), pp. 5–8.

51. *Monthly Repository*, Appendix, 14 (1819), 8.

52. Leigh Hunt, *The Autobiography of Leigh Hunt* (1850), vol. 1, pp. 259–60.

53. Letter to J. F. dated 3 August 1846, in Leigh Hunt, *The Correspondence of Leigh Hunt* (1862), vol. 2, p. 83.

54. Leigh Hunt, Introduction to *A Book for a Corner* (1849), vol. 1, p. 9.

55. *Annual Biography*, 8, 105.

56. Robert S. Newdick, *The First 'Life and Letters' of Charles Lamb: A Study of Thomas Noon Talfourd as Editor and Biographer* (1935), pp. 2–3.

57. *The London Magazine*, 6 (1 September 1826), 35, 39.

58. Mitford, *Life of Mary Russell Mitford*, p. 119.

59. Letter to Revd William Harness, 4 March 1826, *ibid.*, p. 221.

60. Talfourd, 'Memoir', p. 132.

61. Letter to Revd William Harness, 4 March 1826, Mitford, *Life of Mary Russell Mitford*, p. 221.

62. Rate Book for 1824, Parish of Paddington, p. 31.

63. PRO, PROB 6/206. A note in the margin says that it was re-sworn at the Stamp Office on 11 August 1838, and was now under £1,500.

18 Mother Radcliffe

1. Introduction to *Eighteenth-Century Women Poets*, edited by Roger Lonsdale (1990), p. xl.
2. Mary Moorman, *William Wordsworth: A Biography* (1957, 1965), vol. 1, pp. 307–8.
3. Frederick L. Beaty, 'Mrs Radcliffe's fading gleam', *Philological Quarterly*, 42 (January 1963), 126–9.
4. *The Morning Post and Gazetteer*, 13 October 1800.
5. Julia Di Stefano Pappageorge, 'Coleridge's "Mad Lutanist": a romantic response to Ann Radcliffe', *Bulletin of Research in the Humanities*, 82 (Summer 1979), 222–5.
6. Donald Renel Tuttle, '*Christabel* sources in Percy's *Reliques* and the Gothic romance', *Publications of the Modern Language Association*, 53 (June 1938), 445–74.
7. Alexander Dyce, 'Plagiarisms of Lord Byron', *Gentleman's Magazine*, 88 (February 1818), 121–2.
8. C. C., 'Lord Byron vindicated from alleged plagiarism', *Gentleman's Magazine*, 88, part 1 (May 1818), 390–1.
9. Margaret L. Farrand, '*Udolpho* and *Childe Harold*', *Modern Language Notes*, 45 (April 1930), 220–1, claims to be the first one to have noted the obvious similarity between the two descriptions of Venice. Other critics have noted that Harold's trip down the Brenta (stanzas xxviii–xxix) closely resembles Emily's similar trip (208–9).
10. John V. Murphy, *The Dark Angel: Gothic Elements in Shelley's Works* (1975).
11. Thomas Medwin, *The Life of Percy Bysshe Shelley* (Oxford University Press, 1913 edition, which contains additional author's notes not used in the original 1847 edition), p. 25.
12. Walter E. Peck, 'Keats, Shelley, and Mrs Radcliffe', *Modern Language Notes*, 39 (April 1924), 251–2. A. M. D. Hughes points out some parallels between *St Irvyne* and *The Mysteries of Udolpho*, and also some borrowings from Godwin's *St Leon*, in *The Nascent Mind of Shelley* (1947), pp. 35–6.
13. Letter to George and Georgiana Keats, 14 February 1819, in John Keats, *The Letters of John Keats 1814–1821* (1958), vol. 2, p. 62.
14. Martha Hale Shackford, '*The Eve of St Agnes* and *The Mysteries of Udolpho*', *PMLA*, 36 (March 1921), 104–18.
15. Peck, 'Keats, Shelley, and Mrs Radcliffe', pp. 251–2.
16. David Jarrett, 'A source for Keats's magic casements', *Notes and Queries*, NS, 26 (June 1979), 232–5.
17. Henry F. Chorley, *The Authors of England* (1838), p. 79.
18. Robert Miles, *Ann Radcliffe: The Great Enchantress* (1995), p. 8.
19. See letter from J. C. Walker to Sydney Owenson, 4 February 1806, in Sydney Owensen, *Lady Morgan's Memoirs: Autobiography, Diaries and Correspondence* (1862), vol. 1, p. 262.
20. Unsigned article 'Harrington and Ormond, tales by Maria Edgeworth', *British Review and London Journal*, 11 (1818), 37–61; cited by Coral Ann Howells, *Love, Mystery, and Misery: Feeling in Gothic Fiction* (1978), p. 31.
21. Marilyn Butler, 'The woman at the window: Ann Radcliffe in the novels of Mary Wollstonecraft and Jane Austen', *Women and Literature*, NS, 1 (1980), p. 128.
22. Diary entry for 2 August 1813, in Henry Crabb Robinson, *Henry Crabb Robinson on Books and Their Writers* (1938), vol. 1, p. 130.
23. Note written in the margin of his copy, in chapter xix containing the narrative of Norna, cited in Samuel Taylor Coleridge, *Coleridge's Miscellaneous Criticism* (1936), p. 333.
24. Diary entry for 3 February 1826, in [John Gibson Lockhart], *Memoirs of the Life of Sir Walter Scott, Bart.* (1837), vol. 6, pp. 206–7.
25. William Harrison Ainsworth, Preface to *Rookwood: A Romance*, 5th edn. (1837), p. xiii. (The 1834 first edition had no preface; Mrs Radcliffe is first referred to in the preface to the fourth edition of 1836, and then at greater length in this fifth edition.) Rookwood Hall is based on Château-le-Blanc in *The Mysteries of Udolpho*. Montague Summers believes that *Sir John Chiverton* (1826), co-written with John Partington Aston, was 'obviously modelled upon *Gaston de Blondeville*': *The Gothic Quest* (1938), p. 31.
26. Michael Sadleir, *Bulwer and His Wife: A Panorama 1803–1836*, (1931), pp. 314–15.
27. Letter to Mrs Carmichael-Smyth, 11 June 1842, *The Letters and Private Papers of William Makepeace Thackeray* (1946), vol. 2, p. 55.
28. Essays on 'Tunbridge toys' (Roundabout Paper No. VII, *Cornhill*, September 1860), and 'De Juventute' (Roundabout Papers Nos. VIII and IX, *Cornhill*, October 1860), in William Makepeace Thackeray, *Roundabout Papers* (1925), pp. 69, 80–1.
29. William Makepeace Thackeray, *A Shabby Genteel Story* (1840, 1879; 1971), p. 49.

30. Archibald C. Coolidge, jun., 'Charles Dickens and Mrs Radcliffe: a farewell to Wilkie Collins', *The Dickensian*, 58 (May 1962), 112–16.

31. William H. Prescott, *Biographical and Critical Miscellanies* (1845), p. 21.

32. Although this specific borrowing is not noted, a host of general resemblances is listed by Jane Lundblad, *Nathaniel Hawthorne and the Tradition of Gothic Romance. Studio Neophilologica*, 19 (1946–7), 1–92.

33. Newton Arvin, 'Melville and the Gothic novel', *New England Quarterly*, 22 (1949), 33–48.

34. Celia Whitt, 'Poe and *The Mysteries of Udolpho*', *University of Texas Studies in English*, 17 (July 1937), 124–31; Barton Levi St Armand, 'The "mysteries" of Edgar Poe: the quest for a monomyth in Gothic literature', in *The Gothic Imagination: Essays in Dark Romanticism*, edited by G. R. Thompson (1974), pp. 65–93.

35. For the list of translations see 'Radcliffe', *Biographie Nouvelle des Contemporains*, edited by Antoine Vincent Arnault *et al.* (1824), vol. 17; for a survey of translations and adaptations see Clara Frances McIntyre, *Ann Radcliffe in Relation to Her Time* (1920), pp. 68–76.

36. Alida Alberdina Sibbellina Wieten, *Mrs Radcliffe – Her Relation towards Romanticism* (1926), p. 60.

37. See, for example, *Biographie Universelle, Ancienne et Moderne* (1823), vol. 36, pp. 525–7, nouvelle edition (1843), vol. 35, p. 56; Arnault *et al.*, *Biographie Nouvelle des Contemporains*, pp. 203–5); M. Barbier, *Dictionnaire des Ouvrages Anonymes et Pseudonymes*, 2nd edn. (1824); *Revue Britannique*, vol. 7 (1838), pp. 21–2, cited by Richard Switzer, *Etienne-Léon de*

Lamothe-Langon et le roman populaire français de 1800 à 1830 (1962), p. 99.

38. Letter to Charles Boner, 6 May 1849, Mary Russell Mitford, *Correspondence with Charles Boner & John Ruskin* (1914), pp. 134–5.

39. For an exhaustive survey of French translations and dramatic adaptations, and her influence, see Alice M. Killen, *Le Roman terrifant ou roman noir de Walpole à Ann Radcliffe et son influence sur la littérature française jusqu'en 1840* (1923).

40. See Simon Jeune, 'Autour de *L'Abbesse de Castro*', *Travaux de Linguistique et de Littérature*, 10 (2) (1972), 99–111; and Philippe Berthier, 'Stendhal, Mme Radcliffe et l'art du paysage', *Stendhal-Club*, 17 (1975), 305–7.

41. Julian Gracq, 'Notice to the reader', *The Castle of Argol*, translated by Louise Varèse (1951), pp. 145–6.

42. 'Some remarks on the use of the preternatural in works of fiction', *Blackwood's Edinburgh Magazine*, 3 (18) (September 1818), 648–50.

43. Margaret Oliphant, *The Literary History of England in the End of the Eighteenth and Beginning of the Nineteenth Century* (1882), vol. 2, pp. 277–82.

44. Thomas Haynes Bayly, *Fifty Lyrical Ballads* (1829), p. 57.

45. *Monthly Review*, NS, 94 (January 1821), 81.

46. J. Cordy Jeaffreson, *Novels and Novelists, from Elizabeth to Victoria* (1858), vol. 2, p. 4.

47. William H. Prescott, *Biographical and Critical Miscellanies* (1845), p. 175.

48. Allan Cunningham, *Biographical and Critical History of British Literature of the Last Fifty Years* (1834), p. 122.

49. Jerom Murch, *Mrs Barbauld and Her Contemporaries* (1877), p. 139.

50. *Hogg's Instructor*, 3 (1849), 39.

51. William Forsyth, *The Novels and Novelists of the Eighteenth Century* (1871), pp. 313–17.

Bibliography

(London is the place of publication unless noted otherwise.)

Primary Works

Aikin, Anna Laetitia [Barbauld], *Poems*. J. Johnson, 1773.

Aikin, John and Anna Laetitia [Barbauld], *Miscellaneous Pieces, in Prose*. J. Johnson, 1773.

Aikin, Lucy, *Memoirs, Miscellanies and Letters of the Late Lucy Aikin*, edited by Philip Hemery Le Breton. Longman, Green, Longman, Roberts and Green, 1864.

Aikin, M., *Memoirs of Religious Imposters*. Jones, 1821.

Ainsworth, William Harrison, *Rookwood: A Romance*. Standard Novels No. 60. Richard Bentley, 1837.

Alcock, Mary, *Poems*. C. Dilly, 1799.

Alison, Archibald, *Essay on the Nature and Principles of Taste*. London: J. J. G. and G. Robinson; Edinburgh: Bell and Bradfute, 1790.

[Alison, Archibald], 'The historical romance', *Blackwood's Edinburgh Magazine*, 58 (September 1845), 341–56.

Andrews, Miles Peter, *The Mysteries of the Castle: A Dramatic Tale, in Three Acts*. T. N. Longman, 1795.

The Annual Biography and Obituary, for the Year 1824, 8 (1824).

The Annual Biography and Obituary, for the Year 1825, 9 (1825).

Annual Register . . . of the Year 1823. Baldwin, Cradock and Joy, 1824. Obituary of Ann Radcliffe, *Chronicle* entry for February 7, 1823, 337.

Annual Register . . . of the Year 1824. Baldwin, Cradock and Joy, 1825. Obituary of Sophia Lee, Appendix to the Chronicle, 216–17.

Ariosto, Lodovico, *Orlando Furioso*, translated by John Hoole, 5 vols. C. Bathurst, J. Dodsley, T. Cadell and others, 1783.

Arvine, Kazlitt, *The Cyclopaedia of Anecdotes of Literature and the Fine Arts*. Boston, 1852.

[d'Aufdiener, Caroline], *Le Couvent de Sainte Catherine, ou les moeurs du XIIIe siècle*, Roman Historique d'Anne Radclife [*sic*], Traduit par Mme. la baronne Caroline A**********, née W*** de M*******, 2 vols. Paris: Chez Renard, 1810.

Austen, Jane, *Jane Austen's Letters to her Sister Cassandra and Others*, edited by R. W. Chapman, 2 vols. Oxford: Clarendon Press, 1932.

Austen, Jane, *Northanger Abbey*, in *The Novels of Jane Austen*, edited by R. W. Chapman, vol. 5. Oxford University Press, 1923, rev. 1965.

Avison, Charles, *An Essay on Musical Expression*. C. Davis, 1752.

Baillie, Joanna, *De Monfort; A Tragedy*, with remarks by Mrs Inchbald. Longman, Hurst, Rees and Orme [1807].

Baldick, Chris (ed.), *The Oxford Book of Gothic Tales*. Oxford and New York: Oxford University Press, 1992.

Baldwin's New Complete Guide to All Persons Who Have Any Trade or Concern with The City of London, continued as *The New Complete Guide to . . . The City of London*, edns. for 1768, 1770, 1774, 1777.

Barbauld, Anna Laetitia, 'Mrs Radcliffe', biographical preface to *The Romance of the Forest*, vol. 43 of *The British Novelists*. Rivington, 1810.

Barbauld, Anna Laetitia, 'On the origin and progress of novel writing', *The British Novelists* (Rivington, 1810), vol. 1, 1–62.

Barbauld, Anna Laetitia, *The Poems of Anna Letitia Barbauld*, edited by William McCarthy and Elizabeth Kraft. Athens and London: University of Georgia Press, 1994.

Barbauld, Anna Laetitia (Aikin), *The Works of Anna Laetitia Barbauld*, 2 vols. Longman, 1825. With a memoir by Lucy Aikin.

Barbier, A.-A., *Dictionnaire des Ouvrages Anonymes et Pseudonymes*, 4 vols. (1st edn) Paris: Imprimerie Bibliographique, 1806–9.

Barbier, A.-A. and N. L. M. Desessarts, *Nouvelle Bibliothèque d'un Homme de Goût*, 5 vols. Paris: Duminil-Lesueur, 1808–10.

Barbier, M., *Dictionnaire des Ouvrages Anonymes et Pseudonymes*, 4 vols., 2nd edn., Paris, 1822–7.

Barrett, Eaton Stannard, *The Heroine, or Adventures of Cherubina*, 3 vols., 2nd edn., Henry Colburn, 1814.

Barrow, William, *An Essay on Education*, 2 vols. F. and C. Rivington, 1802.

Bayly, Thomas Haynes, *Fifty Lyrical Ballads*. Bath: Mary Meyler, 1829.

Beattie, James, *Dissertations Moral and Critical*. London: W. Strahan and T. Cadell; Edinburgh: W. Creech, 1783.

Beattie, James, *Essays*. Edinburgh: William Creech, 1776.

Beattie, James, *The Minstrel, in Two Books: with Some Other Poems*. London: Edward and Charles Dilly; Edinburgh: W. Creech, 1779.

[Beckford, William], *Azemia, a Novel: Containing Imitations of the Manner, Both in Prose and Verse, of Many of the Authors of the Present Day*. By J. A. M. Jenks, 2 vols, 2nd edn. Sampson Low, 1798.

Beckford, William, *Dreams, Waking Thoughts, and Incidents; in a Series of Letters, from Various Parts of Europe*. J. Johnson and P. Elmsly, 1783.

[Beckford, William], *Modern Novel Writing, or The Elegant Enthusiast; and Interesting Emotions of Arabella Bloomville. A Rhapsodical Romance; Interspersed with Poetry*. By Lady Harriet Marlow, 2 vols. G. G. and J. Robinson, 1796.

Beddoes, Thomas, *Letters from Dr Withering . . . Dr Ewart . . . Dr Thornton . . . and Dr Biggs . . . on Asthma, Consumption, Fever . . .* Bristol: Bulgin and Rosser [1794].

Berry, Mary, *The Berry Papers*, edited by Lewis Melville. London and New York: John Lane; Toronto: Bell and Cockburn, 1914.

Berry, Mary, *Extracts of the Journals and Correspondence of Miss Berry*, edited by Lady Theresa Lewis, 3 vols. Longmans, Green, 1865.

Betham, Ernest (ed.), *A House of Letters: Being Excerpts from the Correspondence of Miss Charlotte Jerningham (the Honbl. Lady Bedingfeld), Lady Jerningham, Coleridge, Lamb, Southey, Bernard and Lucy Barton, and others, with Matilda Betham*. Jarrold and Sons [1905].

Betham, Matilda, *Poems*. J. Hatchard, 1808.

A Biographical Dictionary of Living Authors. Henry Colburn, 1816.

Biographie Étrangère, ou Galerie Universelle. Paris: Alexis Eymery, 1819.

Biographie Moderne, ou Dictionnaire Biographique, 2nd edn. Leipzig: Paul-Jacques Besson, 1806.

Biographie Nouvelle des Contemporains, edited by Antoine Vincent Arnault, A. Jay, E. Jouy and J. Norvins, vol. 17. Paris: La Libraire Historique, 1824.

Biographie Universelle. Paris: L. G. Michaud, n.d.

Biographie Universelle, Ancienne et Moderne. Paris: L. G. Michaud, 1823.

Biographie Universelle Ancienne et Moderne, Nouvelle Édition. Paris: C. Desplaces; Leipzig: F. A. Brockhaus, 1843–66.

Blagdon, Francis William (and F. Prevost for the first two volumes), *Flowers of Literature*, 7 vols. B. Crosby, 1803–10.

Boaden, James, *Memoirs of the Life of John Philip Kemble, Esq.*, 2 vols. Longman, Hurst, Rees, Orme, Brown and Green, 1825.

Boaden, James, *Memoirs of Mrs Inchbald*, 2 vols. Richard Bentley, 1833.

Boaden, James, *Memoirs of Mrs Siddons*, 2 vols. Henry Colburn, 1827.

Boaden, James, *Memoirs of Mrs Siddons. Interspersed with Anecdotes of Authors and Actors*. Philadelphia, 1827.

Boardman, James, *A Memoir of Thomas Bentley, Sometime of Liverpool, with Extracts from His Correspondence*. Liverpool: Wareing Webb, 1851.

Bogue, David and James Bennett, *The History of Dissenters from the Revolution in 1688, to the Year 1808*, 4 vols. London, 1808–12.

Bonhote, Elizabeth, *Bungay Castle*, 2 vols. Vol. 1: Bungay, 1797; vol. 2: William Lane, Minerva Press, 1796.

Boyle's Court and Country Guide, edns. for 1812–23.

Brain, John A., *An Evening with Thomas Noon Talfourd*. 1888.

Brayley, E. W., *Views of Ancient Castles in England and Wales. c.* 1823.

[Brayley, James], *London and Its Environs*. London, 1820.

Bree, Robert, *A Practical Inquiry on Disordered Respiration*, 2nd edn. London: G. G. and J. Robinson; Edinburgh: W. Creech, 1800.

[Brontë, Charlotte], *Shirley. A Tale*, 3 vols. Smith, Elder, 1849.

[Brown, Charles Brockden], 'On a taste for the picturesque', *The Literary Magazine, and American Register*, 2 (9) (June 1804), 163–5.

Brulart de Genlis, Madame, *Adelaide and Theodore; or Letters on Education*, 2 vols. C. Bathurst and T. Cadell, 1783.

Brydges, Samuel Egerton, *The Autobiography . . . of Sir Egerton Brydges*, 2 vols. Cochrane and M'Crane, 1834.

Brydges, Samuel Egerton, *Censura Literaria*, 10 vols. London, 1805–9.

Brydone, Patrick, *A Tour through Sicily and Malta*. T. Cadell, 1773.

Buck, Nathaniel and Samuel Buck, *Buck's Antiquities; or Venerable Remains of Above Four Hundred Castles, Monasteries, Palaces, &c. &c. in England and Wales*, 3 vols. D. Bond, 1774.

Bucke, Charles, *Amusements in Retirement*. Henry Colburn, 1816.

Bucke, Charles, *The Fall of the Leaf; and Other Poems*. G. and W. B. Whittaker, 1819.

Bucke, Charles, *On the Beauties, Harmonies, and Sublimities of Nature*, 4 vols. G. and W. B. Whittaker, 1821.

Bucke, Charles, *On the Beauties, Harmonies, and Sublimities of Nature*, 3 vols. A New Edition, Greatly Enlarged. Thomas Tegg and Son, 1837.

Bucke, Charles, *The Philosophy of Nature; or, The Influence of Scenery on the Mind and Heart*, 2 vols. John Murray, 1813.

Burney, Fanny, *Diary and Letters of Madame D'Arblay*, 7 vols. Henry Colburn, 1842, 1846.

Burney, Fanny, *The Journals and Letters of Fanny Burney (Madame D'Arblay)*, edited by Joyce Hemlow with Curtis D. Cecil and Althea Douglas, 12 vols. Oxford: Clarendon Press, 1972–84.

Bury, Lady Charlotte, *Diary Illustrative of the Times of George the Fourth*, 4 vols. Henry Colburn, 1838, 1839.

Bury, Lady Charlotte, *The Diary of a Lady-in-Waiting*, edited by A. Francis Steuart, 2 vols. London and New York: John Lane, 1908.

C. C., 'Lord Byron vindicated from alleged plagiarism', *Gentleman's Magazine*, 88, part 1 (May 1818), 390–1.

Carter, Elizabeth, *Letters from Mrs Elizabeth Carter to Mrs Montagu*, edited by Revd Montague Pennington, 3 vols. London, 1817.

Carter, Elizabeth, *A Series of Letters between Mrs Elizabeth Carter and Miss Catherine Talbot . . . [and] to Mrs Vesey*, edited by Revd Montague Pennington, 2 vols. 1808.

Carter, Nathaniel H., *Letters from Europe*. New York: G. and C. Carvill, 1827.

Cary, Henry, *Memoir of the Rev Henry Francis Cary*, 2 vols. Edward Moxon, 1847.

Cawthorn, James, *The Poems of Mr Cawthorn*, in *The Works of the English Poets*, vol. 65. T. Wright, 1790.

Charlotte Augusta, *Letters of the Princess Charlotte 1811–1817*, edited by A. Aspinall. Home and Van Thal, 1949.

Chénier, Marie-Joseph de, *Tableau historique de l'état et des progrès de la littérature française, depuis 1789*. Paris: Maradan, 1816.

Chorley, Henry F., *The Authors of England*. Charles Tilt, 1838.

Coleridge, Samuel Taylor, *Coleridge's Miscellaneous Criticism*, edited by Thomas Middleton Raysor. Constable, 1936.

Coleridge, Samuel Taylor, *Collected Letters of Samuel Taylor Coleridge*, edited by Earl Leslie Griggs, 4 vols. Oxford: Clarendon Press, 1956, 1959.

Coleridge, Samuel Taylor, *Unpublished Letters of Samuel Taylor Coleridge*, edited by Earl Leslie Griggs, 2 vols. Constable, 1932.

Collins, William, *The Poems of Gray and Collins*, edited by Austin Lane Poole, 3rd edn. Oxford University Press, 1937.

Colman, George, the Younger, *My Night-Gown and Slippers; or, Tales in Verse*. T. Cadell, jun. and W. Davies, 1797.

[Cooke, Cassandra], *Battleridge: An Historical Tale*, 2 vols. G. Cawthorn, 1799.

Colton, Charles Caleb, *Hypocrisy. A Satire*. Tiverton, Devon: T. Smith, 1812.

Coxe, William, *Travels in Switzerland*, 3 vols. T. Cadell, 1789.

Cunningham, Allan, *Biographical and Critical History of British Literature of the Last Fifty Years*. Paris: Baudry's Foreign Library, 1834.

Curties, T. J. Horsley, *Ancient Records, or, The Abbey of Saint Oswythe. A Romance*, 4 vols. William Lane, 1801, Minerva Press.

Dayes, Edward, *A Picturesque Tour in Yorkshire and Derbyshire*. John Nichols, 1825.

De Quincey, Thomas, *The Collected Writings of Thomas De Quincey*, edited by David Masson, 14 vols. Edinburgh: Adam and Charles Black, 1889–90.

Dibdin, Thomas Frognall, *Reminiscences of a Literary Life*, 2 vols. John Major, 1836.

Drake, Nathan, *The Gleaner: A Series of Periodical Essays . . . from Scarce or Neglected Volumes*, 4 vols. W. Davies, 1811.

Drake, Nathan, *Literary Hours: or Sketches Critical, Narrative, and Poetical*, 3 vols, 3rd edn. T. Cadell and W. Davies, 1804. (First published in 1798).

Duff, William, *An Essay on Original Genius*. Edward and Charles Dilly, 1767.

Dunlop, John, *The History of Fiction*, 3 vols. Longman, Hurst, Rees, Orme and Brown, 1814.

Dyce, Alexander, 'Plagiarisms of Lord Byron', *Gentleman's Magazine*, 88 (February 1818), 121–2.

Edgeworth, Maria, *Chosen Letters*, edited by F. V. Barry. Jonathan Cape, 1931.
Elwood, Anne Katharine, *Memoirs of the Literary Ladies of England*, 2 vols. Henry Colburn, 1843.
Enfield, William, *The Speaker: or, Miscellaneous Pieces, Selected from the Best English Writers*. J. Johnson, 1774.
Farington, Joseph (illustrator), *Britannia Depicta; A Series of Views of the Most Interesting and Picturesque Objects in Great Britain*. T. Cadell and W. Davies, 1816.
Farington, Joseph, *The Farington Diary*, edited by James Greig, 8 vols. Hutchinson [1922–8].
Farington, Joseph, *Memoirs of the Life of Sir Joshua Reynolds*. T. Cadell and W. Davies, 1819.
Fate of Velina De Guidova, The. A Novel, 3 vols. W. Lane, 1790.
Faulkner, Thomas, *An Historical and Topographical Description of Chelsea and Its Environs*. 1810.
Gilpin, William, *Observations on the River Wye*. 1782 facsimile edn, introduction by Sutherland Lyall. Richmond Publishing, 1973.
Gilpin, William, *Observations on the Western Parts of England, Relative Chiefly to Picturesque Beauty . . . to Which Are Added, a Few Remarks on the Picturesque Beauties of the Isle of Wight*. T. Cadell, jun. and W. Davies, 1798.
Gilpin, William, *Observations, Relative Chiefly to Picturesque Beauty, Made in the Year 1772, on Several Parts of England; Particularly the Mountains, and Lakes of Cumberland, and Westmorland*, 2 vols. R. Blamire, 1786.
Gilpin, William, *Remarks on Forest Scenery*, 2 vols. R. Blamire, 1791.
Godey's Magazine and Lady's Book, 45 (September 1852), 225–7. 'Anecdote of Mrs Radcliffe'.
Gray, Thomas, *The Poems of Gray and Collins*, edited by Austin Lane Poole, 3rd edn., Oxford University Press, 1937.
Green, Thomas, *Extracts from the Diary of a Lover of Literature*. Ipswich: Longman, Hurst, Rees and Orme, 1810. A continuation was published in *Gentleman's Magazine*, NS, 1 (January 1834), 5–16.
Gregory, George, *Letters on Literature, Taste, and Composition*, 2 vols. Richard Phillips, 1808.
Hale, Sarah Josepha, *Woman's Record; or, Sketches of All Distinguished Women, from 'The Beginning' till A.D. 1850*. New York: Harper and Brothers, 1853.
[Hall, George], *The History of Chesterfield*. Chesterfield: John Ford, 1823. Enlarged edn., Chesterfield: T. Ford; London: Whittaker, 1839.
Haslam, John, *Observations on Madness and Melancholy*. J. Callow, 1809.
Hassell, J., *Picturesque Rides and Walks, with Excursions by Water, Thirty Miles round the British Metropolis*, 2 vols. J. Hassell, 1817.
Hassell, J., *Tour of the Isle of Wight*, 2 vols. T. Hookham, 1790.
Hassell, J., Ibbetson and Laporte. *A Picturesque Guide to Bath, Bristol Hot-Wells, the River Avon, and the Adjacent Country*. Hookham and Carpenter, 1793.
Hawkins, Laetitia-Matilda, *Anecdotes, Biographical Sketches and Memoirs*, 2 vols. F. C. and J. Rivington, 1822.
[Hawkins, Laetitia-Matilda], *Letters on the Female Mind*, 2 vols. T. Hookham and J. Carpenter, 1793.
Hays, Mary, *Memoirs of Emma Courtney*, 2 vols. G. G. and J. Robinson, 1796.
Hazlitt, William, *Lectures on the English Comic Writers*. Printed for Taylor and Hessey, 1819.
Hazlitt, William, *Sketches and Essays by William Hazlitt*. John Templeman, 1839.
Hill, Brian, *Observations and Remarks on a Journey through Sicily and Calabria, in the Year 1791*. John Stockdale, 1792.
Holberg, Baron, *An Introduction to Universal History*. Translated from the Latin of Baron Holberg; with Notes . . . By Gregory Sharpe. A New Edition, Revised, Corrected, and Improved, By William Radcliffe, A.B. of Oriel College, Oxford. L. Davis, J. Johnson and R. Baldwin, 1787.
Holcroft, Thomas, *Memoirs of the Late Thomas Holcroft*, 3 vols. Longman, Hurst, Rees, Orme and Brown, 1816.
Horwood, R., *Plan of the Cities of London and Westminster, the Borough of Southwark and Parts Adjoining, Shewing Every House*. R. Horwood, 1799.
Howard, George William Frederick, 7th Earl of Carlisle, *Poems*. E. Moxon, 1869.
Hume, David, *The History of England*, 8 vols, new edn. T. Cadell, 1790–1.
Hunt, Leigh, *The Autobiography of Leigh Hunt*, 3 vols. Smith, Elder, 1850.
Hunt, Leigh (ed.), *A Book for a Corner*, 2 vols. Chapman and Hall, 1849.
Hunt, Leigh, *The Correspondence of Leigh Hunt*, 2 vols. Smith, Elder, 1862.
Hurd, Richard, *Letters on Chivalry and Romance*. A. Millar, W. Thurlbourn and J. Woodyer, 1762.
Impartial Strictures on the Poem Called 'The Pursuits of Literature': and Particularly a Vindication of the Romance of 'The Monk'. J. Bell, 1798.
Jackson, E. E. (Mrs John), *Dialogues on the Doctrines and Duties of Christianity: Intended for the Instruction of the Young*, 2 vols. London: Rivingtons, J. Hookham, S. Hatchard; Sloane Square, Chelsea: Mrs Pollard; Edinburgh: Manners and Miller, Stewart Cheyne, John Anderson, 1806.
Jebb, John, *The Works . . . of John Jebb, M.D. F.R.S. with Memoirs of the Life of the Author* by John Disney, 2 vols. London: T. Cadell, J. Johnson, J. Stockdale; Cambridge: J. and J. Merrill, 1787.
A Journey through Sweden, Written in French by a Dutch Officer, and Translated into English, by William Radcliffe, A.B. of Oriel College, Oxford. Printed for G. Kearsley [1790].

A Journey through Sweden, Written in French by a Dutch Officer, and Translated into English, by William Radcliffe, A.B. of Oriel College, Oxford. Dublin: P. Byrne, J. Moore, J. Jones, Grueber & M'Allister, and W. Jones, 1790.

Keate, George, *Netley Abbey. An Elegy*, 2nd edn., rev. J. Dodsley, 1769. (First published in 1764 as *The Ruins of Netley Abbey*.)

Keats, John, *The Letters of John Keats 1814–1821*, edited by Hyder Edward Rollins, 2 vols. Cambridge, MA: Harvard University Press, 1958.

Kent's Directory, edns. for the years 1759, 1763, 1766, 1768, 1771, 1774, 1787–91.

Ker, Anne, *The Heiress di Montalde; or, The Castle of Bezanto*, 2 vols. Printed for the author, 1799.

Ker, Anne, *Adeline St Julian; or, The Midnight Hour. A Novel*, 2 vols. J. and E. Kerby, 1800.

Knight, Charles, *Passages of a Working Life*, 3 vols. London, 1864.

Knight, Ellis Cornelia, *Autobiography of Miss Cornelia Knight, Lady Companion to the Princess Charlotte of Wales*, 2 vols. W. H. Allen, 1861.

Lambert, B., *History and Survey of London and Its Environs*, 4 vols. T. Hughes, 1806.

[Lee, Sophia], *The Recess; or, A Tale of Other Times*, 3 vols. T. Cadell, 1785.

Lewis, Matthew Gregory, *The Life and Correspondence of M. G. Lewis* [edited by Margaret Baron-Wilson], 2 vols. Henry Colburn, 1839.

Lewis, Matthew Gregory, *The Monk*, edited by Louis F. Peck, introduction by John Berryman. New York: Grove Press, 1952; Evergreen edn., 1959.

Limborch, Philip a, *The History of the Inquisition*, translated by Samuel Chandler, 2 vols. J. Gray, 1731.

Lister, Anne, *I Know My Own Heart: The Diaries [1817–1824] of Anne Lister (1791–1840)*, edited by Helena Whitbread. Virago, 1988.

Lister, Anne, *No Priest but Love: Excerpts from the Diaries of Anne Lister, 1824–1826*, edited by Helena Whitbread. Otley, West Yorkshire: Smith Settle, 1992.

[Lockhart, John Gibson], *Memoirs of the Life of Sir Walter Scott, Bart.*, 7 vols. Edinburgh: Robert Cadell; London: John Murray and Whittaker and Co., 1837, 1838.

London Directory (T. Lowndes), edns. for the years 1768, 1772 – 1773.

MacKenzie, Anna Maria, *Mysteries Elucidated, a Novel*, 3 vols. William Lane, Minerva Press, 1795.

Macnish, Robert, *The Philosophy of Sleep*. Glasgow: W. R. M'Phun, 1830.

Macpherson, James, *The Poems of Ossian*, 2 vols., new edition. W. Straham and T. Cadell, 1784, 1785.

Mason, William, *Caractacus, a Dramatic Poem*. R. and J. Dodsley, 1759.

Mason, William, *Elfrida, a Dramatic Poem*. J. and P. Knapton, 1752. (First published in 1751.)

[Mathias, Thomas James], *The Pursuits of Literature, or What You Will: A Satirical Poem in Dialogue*. Part One, First Edition, J. Owen, 1794. Second Edition of Part One, and First Edition of Parts Two and Three, J. Owen, 1796. Part the Fourth and Last, T. Becket, 1797. Part the First, Third Edition Revised, T. Beckett, 1797. Sixteenth Edition (all four parts), Becket and Porter, 1812.

[Mathias, Thomas James], *The Shade of Alexander Pope on the Banks of the Thames. A Satirical Poem*. T. Becket, 1799.

Matthews, Henry, *The Diary of an Invalid; Being the Journal of a Tour in Pursuit of Health; in Portugal, Italy, Switzerland, and France, in the Years 1817, 1818, and 1819*. John Murray, 1820.

Maturin, Charles Robert, *Melmoth the Wanderer* (1820). Penguin Books, 1977.

'Memoirs of Mrs Ann Radcliffe', Preface to *The Mysteries of Udolpho*, Limbird's British Novelists (1824), vols. 13–17, pp. v–vii.

[Miller, Lady Anne], *Letters from Italy*, 3 vols. Edward and Charles Dilly, 1776.

Mitford, Mary Russell, *Correspondence with Charles Boner & John Ruskin*, edited by Elizabeth Lee. London and Leipzig: T. Fisher Unwin, 1914.

Mitford, Mary Russell, *The Dramatic Works of Mary Russell Mitford*, 2 vols. Hurst and Blackett, 1854.

Mitford, Mary Russell, *The Friendships of Mary Russell Mitford as Recorded in Letters from Her Literary Correspondents*, edited by Alfred Guy L'Estrange, 2 vols. Hurst and Blackett, 1882.

Mitford, Mary Russell, *Letters of Mary Russell Mitford*, 2nd series, edited by Henry Chorley, 2 vols. Richard Bentley, 1872.

Mitford, Mary Russell, *The Letters of Mary Russell Mitford*, edited by R. Brimley Johnson. John Lane, The Bodley Head, 1925.

Mitford, Mary Russell, *The Life of Mary Russell Mitford, Related in a Selection from Her Letters to Her Friends*, edited by Rev Alfred Guy L'Estrange, 3 vols. Richard Bentley, 1870.

Mitford, Mary Russell, *Recollections of a Literary Life*, 3 vols. Richard Bentley, 1852.

[Montagu, Elizabeth], *An Essay on the Writings and Genius of Shakespeare*. Dublin, 1778.

Moore, Henry, *Picturesque Excursions from Derby to Matlock Bath*. Derby: H. Moore, 1818.

Moore, Thomas, *Memoirs, Journal and Correspondence of Thomas Moore*, 8 vols. Longman, Brown, Green and Longmans, 1853–6.

More, Hannah, *Sacred Dramas . . . to Which Is Added, Sensibility, A Poem*. T. Cadell, 1782.

Murch, Jerom, *Mrs Barbauld and Her Contemporaries; Sketches of Some Eminent Literary and Scientific English Women*. Longmans, Green and Co., 1877.

Murray, Hugh, *Morality of Fiction; or, An Inquiry into the Tendency of Fictitious Narratives*. Edinburgh: A. Constable and J. Anderson; London: Longman, Hurst, Rees and Orme, 1805.

[Hablitz, Karl Ivanovich], *The Natural History of East Tartary* . . . rendered into English from the French Translation. By William Radcliffe, A.B. of Oriel College, Oxford. Printed by M. Vint; for W. Richardson, 1789.

The New Bath Guide; or, Useful Pocket Companion. Bath: R. Cruttwell, 1782.

New Monthly Magazine and Literary Journal (Henry Colburn), Historical Register, NS, 9 (May 1823), 232 (obituary of Mrs Radcliffe).

Nichols, John, *Literary Anecdotes of the Eighteenth Century; Comprising Biographical Memoirs of William Bowyer*, 9 vols. 1812–15.

Oliphant, Margaret, *The Literary History of England in the End of the Eighteenth and Beginning of the Nineteenth Century*, 3 vols. Macmillan, 1882.

Orpheus, Priest of Nature, and Prophet of Infidelity; or, The Eleusinian Mysteries Revived. J. Stockdale, 1781.

Owenson, Sydney (Lady Morgan), *Lady Morgan's Memoirs: Autobiography, Diaries and Correspondence*, edited by W. Hepworth Dixon, 2 vols. W. H. Allen, 1862.

Parsons, Eliza, *Lucy: A Novel*, 3 vols. William Lane, Minerva Press, 1794.

Pennington, Montagu, *Memoirs of the Life of Mrs Elizabeth Carter*, 1st edn. London, 1807.

Pennington, Montagu, *Memoirs of the Life of Mrs Elizabeth Carter*, 2 vols, 3rd edn. London, 1816.

Pepys, William Weller, *A Later Pepys. The Correspondence of Sir William Weller Pepys, Bart.*, edited by Alice C. C. Gaussen, 2 vols. London and New York: John Lane, The Bodley Head, 1904.

Percy, Thomas, *Reliques of Ancient English Poetry*, 3 vols. J. Dodsley, 1765.

Pilkington, Mary, *Memoirs of Celebrated Female Characters*. Albion Press, 1804.

Piozzi, Hester Lynch (Thrale), *Autobiography, Letters and Literary Remains of Mrs Piozzi (Thrale)*, edited by A. Hayward, 2 vols. Longman, Green, Longman and Roberts, 1861.

Piozzi, Hester Lynch (Thrale), *The Intimate Letters of Hester Piozzi and Penelope Pennington 1788–1821*, edited by Oswald G. Knapp. London: John Lane, The Bodley Head; New York: John Lane; Toronto: Bell and Cockburn, 1914.

Piozzi, Hester Lynch (Thrale), *Observations and Reflections Made in the Course of a Journey through France, Italy and Germany*, 2 vols. A. Strahan and T. Cadell, 1789.

Piozzi, Hester Lynch (Thrale), *The Piozzi Letters*, vol. 1, edited by Edward A. Bloom and Lillian D. Bloom. Newark, NJ: University of Delaware Press; London and Toronto: Associated University Presses, 1989.

Piozzi, Hester Lynch (Thrale), *Thraliana. The Diary of Mrs Hester Lynch Thrale (Later Mrs Piozzi) 1776–1809*, edited by Katharine C. Balderston, 2 vols. Oxford: Clarendon Press, 1942.

Polwhele, Richard, *Poems*, 5 vols. Truro and London: Rivingtons, 1810.

Polwhele, Richard, *Traditions and Recollections*, 2 vols. John Nichols, 1826.

Prescott, William H., *Biographical and Critical Miscellanies*. Richard Bentley, 1845.

[Prescott, William H.], 'Review of *English Literature of the Nineteenth Century*', *The North American Review* 35 (76) (Boston: Gray and Bowen, July 1832), 165–95.

Priestley, Joseph, *Collection of Letters* (typescript), edited by John F. March. 1915. British Library Shelf-mark 10902.i.8.

Joseph Priestley, *A Course of Lectures on Oratory and Criticism*. J. Johnson, 1777.

Public Characters, 10 vols. Richard Phillips, 1798–1809.

R. B., *Thomas Bentley, 1730–1780, of Liverpool, Etruria, and London*. Guildford, 1927.

[Radcliffe, Ann], *The Castles of Athlin and Dunbayne. A Highland Story*. T. Hookham, 1789.

[Radcliffe, Ann], *The Castles of Athlin and Dunbayne. A Highland Story*. 2nd edn. Hookham and Carpenter, 1793.

Radcliffe, Ann, *The Castles of Athlin and Dunbayne. A Highland Story*. 3rd edn. James Carpenter, 1799.

Radcliffe, Ann, *Gaston de Blondeville, or The Court of Henry III . . . St Alban's Abbey . . . Posthumous Works . . . Memoir*, 4 vols. Henry Colburn, 1826.

Radcliffe, Ann, *The Italian, or The Confessional of the Black Penitents*, 3 vols. T. Cadell and W. Davies, 1797.

Radcliffe, Ann, *The Italian*, edited by Frederick Garber. Oxford University Press, 1968, World's Classics paperback, 1981.

Radcliffe, Ann, *A Journey Made in the Summer of 1794, through Holland and the Western Frontier of Germany, with a Return Down the Rhine: To Which Are Added Observations during a Tour to the Lakes of Lancashire, Westmorland, and Cumberland*. G. G. and J. Robinson, 1795.

Radcliffe, Ann, *The Mysteries of Udolpho, A Romance*, 4 vols. G. G. and J. Robinson, 1794.

Radcliffe, Ann, *The Mysteries of Udolpho*, edited by Bonamy Dobrée. Oxford University Press (1966, 1970), World's Classics paperback, 1980.

Radcliffe, Ann, 'On the supernatural in poetry', *New Monthly Magazine*, 16 (1826), 145–52.

Radcliffe, Ann, *The Poems of Mrs Ann Radcliffe*. Schulze and Dean, J. Bounden, 1815.

Radcliffe, Ann, *The Poems of Mrs Ann Radcliffe*. J. Smith, 1816.

Radcliffe, Ann, *The Poetical Works of Reginald Heber, Lord Bishop of Calcutta. Poems and Lyrics, by Felicia Hemans. Poems, by Ann Radcliffe*. H. G. Bohn, 1852.

Radcliffe, Ann, *The Romance of the Forest*, 3 vols., 4th edn. T. Hookham and J. Carpenter, 1794.

Radcliffe, Ann, *The Romance of the Forest*, edited by Chloe Chard. Oxford University Press, 1986, World's Classics paperback, 1986.

[Radcliffe, Ann], *A Sicilian Romance*, 2 vols. T. Hookham, 1790.

Radcliffe, Ann, *A Sicilian Romance*, 2 vols., 4th edn. Longman, Hurst, Rees and Orme, 1809.

Radcliffe, Ann, *A Sicilian Romance*, edited by Alison Milbank. Oxford University Press, 1986, World's Classics, 1993.

Radcliffe, Ebenezer, *Two Letters, Addressed to the Right Rev Prelates, Who a Second Time Rejected the Dissenters' Bill*. J. Johnson, 1773.

Radcliffe, Mary Ann, *The Memoirs of Mrs Mary Ann Radcliffe; in Familiar Letters to Her Female Friend* (includes reprint of *The Female Advocate*). Edinburgh: printed for the author, 1810.

Radcliffe, Mary Anne, *Manfrone; or, The One-Handed Monk. A Romance*. Milner and Company, Paternoster Row, [1878]. (First published in 1809.)

Redding, Cyrus, *Fifty Years' Recollections*, 3 vols. Charles J. Skeet, 1858.

Rees, Thomas, *Reminiscences of Literary London from 1779 to 1853*, with additions by John Britton. Suckling and Galloway, 1896. Privately issued in 1853.

[Reeve, Clara], *Edwy and Edilda: A Gothic Tale*. Dublin: S. Colbert, 1783.

Reeve, Clara, *The Old English Baron* [1777], edited by James Trainer. Oxford University Press, 1977.

Reeve, Clara, *Plans of Education*. T. Hookham and J. Carpenter, 1792.

[Reeve, Clara] *The Progress of Romance*, 'by C. R., Author of The English Baron', 2 vols. Colchester: W. Keymer; London: G. G. J. and J. Robinson, 1785.

Rhodes, Ebenezer, *Peak Scenery, or Excursions in Derbyshire: Made Chiefly for the Purpose of Picturesque Observation*, 4 parts. Longman, Hurst, Rees, Orme and Brown, 1818–23.

Ritson, Joseph, *The Letters of Joseph Ritson, ed. chiefly from Originals in the Possession of his Nephew*, 2 vols. London: W. Pickering, 1833.

[Rivers, David], *Literary Memoirs of Living Authors of Great Britain*, 2 vols. R. Fauldner, T. Egerton, W. Richardson, 1798.

Robinson, Henry Crabb, *Diary, Reminiscences, and Correspondence of Henry Crabb Robinson, Barrister-at-Law*, edited by Thomas Sadler, 3 vols. Macmillan, 1869.

Robinson, Henry Crabb, *Henry Crabb Robinson on Books and Their Writers*, edited by Edith J. Morley, 3 vols. J. M. Dent, 1938.

Robinson, Mary, *Hubert de Sevrac, a Romance, of the Eighteenth Century*, 3 vols. T. Hookham and J. Carpenter, 1796.

Rossetti, Christina, 'A Memoir of Mrs Radcliffe', *The Athenaeum*, No. 2906 (7 July 1883), 15.

Royal Academy, *The Exhibition of the Royal Academy*. Catalogues for the annual exhibitions from 1789 to 1809.

Rutt, John Towill, *Life and Correspondence of Joseph Priestley*, 2 vols. R. Hunter, 1831.

Sade, Donatien Alphonse François, Comte de, *Selected Writings of De Sade*, translated by Leonard de Saint-Yves. New York: British Book Centre, 1954.

Saint Palaye, J. B. de Lacurne de, *The Literary History of the Troubadours*, translated by Susannah Dobson. T. Cadell, 1779.

Savage, James, *An Account of the London Daily Newspapers*. B. R. Howlett; Gale and Curtis [1811].

Sayers, Frank, *Poems*. Norfolk and London: J. Johnston, 1792. (Contains the *Dramatic Sketches of Ancient Northern Mythology* first published in 1789.)

Schiller, Frederick, *The Robbers. A Tragedy* [translated by Lord Woodhouselee]. G. G. J. and J. Robinsons [sic], 1792.

Scott, Sir Walter, 'Prefatory memoir to Mrs Ann Radcliffe', in *The Novels of Mrs Ann Radcliffe*, Ballantyne's Novelist's Library (Edinburgh: James Ballantyne; London: Hurst, Robinson, 1824), vol. 10, pp. i–xxxix.

[Scott, Sir Walter], *Waverley; or, 'Tis Sixty Years Since*, 3 vols. Edinburgh: James Ballantyne and Archibald Constable; London: Longman, Hurst, Rees, Orme and Brown, 1814.

[Selwyn, Elizabeth], *Journal of Excursions through the Most Interesting Parts of England, Wales and Scotland, during the Summers and Autumns of 1819, 1820, 1821, 1822, & 1823*. Plummer and Brewis [1824].

Seward, Anna, *Letters of Anna Seward: Written between the Years 1784 and 1807*, 6 vols. Edinburgh: George Ramsey, 1811.

Seward, Anna, *Monody on Major André*. Lichfield: J. Jackson; London: Robinson, Cadell and Evans, and others, 1781.

Shelley, Percy Bysshe, *The Letters of Percy Bysshe Shelley*, edited by Frederick L. Jones, 2 vols. Oxford: Clarendon Press, 1964.

Sheppard, John, *Letters, Descriptive of a Tour through Some Parts of France, Italy, Switzerland, and Germany, in 1816*, 2 vols. Edinburgh: Oliphant, Waugh and Innes, 1817.

Sibbald, Susan (Mein), *Memoirs of Susan Sibbald (1783–1812)*, edited by Francis Paget Hett. John Lane, The Bodley Head, 1926.

Sketches in Bedlam; or Characteristic Traits of Insanity, 2nd edn. By a Constant Observer. Sherwood, Jones, 1824.

Smith, Charlotte, *The Banished Man. A Novel*, 4 vols. T. Cadell, jun. and W. Davies, 1794.

Smith, Charlotte, *Elegiac Sonnets*, 6th edn. T. Cadell, 1792. (First published in 1784).

Smith, Charlotte, *Emmeline: The Orphan of the Castle* [1788], introduction by Zoë Fairbairns. Pandora, 1988.

Smith, Charlotte, *The Emigrants, A Poem*. T. Cadell, 1793.

Smith, Charlotte, *The Romance of Real Life*, 3 vols. T. Cadell, 1787. A translation of *Les Causes Célèbres* by Gayot de Pitaval.

Smith, John Thomas, *Nollekens and his Times*, 2 vols. Henry Colburn, 1828.

Smith, Margaret M. and Alexander Lindsay, *Index of English Literary Manuscripts*, vol. 3: 1700–1800, part 3. Mansel, 1992.

Spence, Elizabeth Isabella, *Letters from the North Highlands*. Longman, Hurst, Rees, Orme and Brown, 1817.

Spence, Elizabeth Isabella, *Summer Excursions through Parts of Oxfordshire, Gloucestershire, Warwickshire, Staffordshire, Herefordshire, Derbyshire, and South Wales*, 2 vols., 2nd edn. Longman, Hurst, Rees and Orme, 1809.

Spence, Elizabeth Isabella, *A Traveller's Tale of the Last Century*, 3 vols. Longman, Hurst, Rees, Orme and Brown, 1819.

Sterndale, Mary, *Vignettes of Derbyshire*. G. and W. B. Whittaker, 1824.

Swinburne, Henry, *Travels in the Two Sicilies*, 2 vols. P. Elmsly, 1783 (vol. 1); J. Davis, 1785 (vol. 2).

Swinburne, Henry, *Travels through Spain, in the Years 1775 and 1776*, 2nd edn., to which is added *A Journey from Bayonne to Marseilles*, 2 vols. J. Davis, P. Elmsly, 1787.

Talfourd, Thomas Noon, *Critical and Miscellaneous Writings of T. Noon Talfourd*. Philadelphia: A. Hart, 1850.

Talfourd, Thomas Noon, 'Memoir of the life and writings of Mrs Radcliffe', prefixed to Ann Radcliffe, *Gaston de Blondeville, or The Court of Henry III . . . St Alban's Abbey . . . Posthumous Works . . . Memoir*, 4 vols. Henry Colburn, 1826.

Tasso, Torquato, *Jerusalem Delivered*, translated by John Hoole, 2 vols. 6th edn. J. Dodsley, 1787. (First published in 1763.)

Thackeray, William Makepeace, *Roundabout Papers*, edited by John Edwin Wells. New York: Harcourt, Brace, 1925. (First published in 1860–2.)

Theobald, John, *Every Man His Own Physician*. W. Griffin, 1764.

Thomson, James, *The Poetical Works of James Thomson*, edited by J. Logie Robertson. Oxford University Press, 1908.

Timperley, Charles Henry, *Encyclopaedia of Literary and Typographical Anecdote*, 2nd edn. Henry G. Bohn, 1842.

Townsend, George, *Poems*. Longman, Hurst, Rees and Orme; Cambridge: Deighton, 1810.

Trotter, John Bernard, *Memoirs of the Latter Years of the Right Honourable Charles James Fox*. Richard Phillips, 1811.

[Tyler, Royall], *The Algerine Captive; or, The Life and Adventures of Doctor Updike Underhill: Six Years a Prisoner among the Algerines*, 2 vols. Walpole, NH: David Carlisle, jun., 1797.

Tyler, Royall, *The Algerine Captive*, 2 vols. London: G.G. and J. Robinson, 1802. Gainesville: Scholars' Facsimiles and Reprints, 1967. Introduction by Jack B. Moore.

Valpy's Literary Chronology, in *Chronology; or An Introduction and Index to Universal History, Biography, and Useful Knowledge*. New York: Jonathan Leavitt, 1833.

[Waldie, Jane], *Sketches Descriptive of Italy in the Years 1816 and 1817*, 4 vols. John Murray, 1820.

Walpole, Horace, *The Castle of Otranto*, introduction [by Sir Walter Scott]. Edinburgh: James Ballantyne; London: Longman, Hurst, Rees, Orme and Brown, 1811.

Walpole, Horace, *The Letters of Horace Walpole*, edited by Mrs Paget Toynbee, 16 vols. Oxford: Clarendon Press, 1905.

Warton, Thomas, *The History of English Poetry*, 3 vols. J. Dodsley, [. . .] G. Robinson and others, 1774–81.

Wedgwood, Josiah, *Letters of Josiah Wedgwood 1762 to 1772, 1772 to 1780*, edited by Katherine Eufemia Farrer, 2 vols. Printed by the Women's Printing Society, 1903.

Wedgwood, Josiah, *The Selected Letters of Josiah Wedgwood*, edited by Ann Finer and George Savage. Cory, Adams and Mackay, 1965.

West, Thomas, *The Antiquities of Furness*. 1774.

West, Thomas, *A Guide to the Lakes in Cumberland, Westmorland, and Lancashire*, edited by William Cockin, 8th edn. Kendal, Cumbria: William Pennington, 1802.

Wheelwright, Charles Apthorp, *Poems, Original and Translated; Including Versions of the Medea and Octavio of Seneca*. Longman, Hurst, Rees, Orme and Brown, 1810. Second edn., 2 vols, 1811.

Wollstonecraft, Mary, *Posthumous Works*, 4 vols. J. Johnson and G. G. and J. Robinson, 1798.

Wollstonecraft, Mary, *A Vindication of the Rights of Woman* (1792), edited by Miriam Brody. Penguin Books, 1992 bicentenary edition.

Woolf, Virginia, *Collected Essays*, 4 vols. Hogarth Press, 1966–7.

Woolnoth, William (engraver), *The Ancient Castles of England and Wales*. Historical Descriptions by E. W. Brayley, jun., 2 vols. Longman, Hurst, 1825.

Secondary Works

Adams, Donald K., 'The second Mrs Radcliffe', in Donald K. Adams (ed.), *The Mystery & Detection Annual*. Beverly Hills: Donald Adams, 1972, pp. 48–64.

Aers, David, Jonathan Cook and David Punter, *Romanticism and Ideology*. Routledge and Kegan Paul, 1981.

Allen, M. L., 'The Black Veil: three versions of a symbol', *English Studies*, 47 (4) (August 1966), 286–9.

Allibone, S. Austin, *A Critical Dictionary of English Literature*, 3 vols. Philadelphia: J. B. Lippincott, 1859–71.

Alumni Cantabrigienses, compiled by J. A. Venn. Part II, v. Cambridge: Cambridge University Press, 1953.

Andrews, Alexander, *The History of British Journalism*, 2 vols. Richard Bentley, 1859.

Andrews, Malcolm, *The Search for the Picturesque: Landscape Aesthetics and Tourism in Britain, 1760-1800*. Scolar Press, 1989.

Arnaud, Pierre, *Ann Radcliffe et le fantastique: essai de psychobiographie*. Paris: Aubier Montaigne, 1976.

Arnaud, Pierre, 'Un document inédit: le contrât des *Mysteries of Udolpho*', *Etudes Anglaises*, 20 (1) (1967), 55–7.

Arnaud, Pierre, 'William Radcliffe journaliste', *Études Anglaises*, 22 (3) (1969), 231–49.

Arvin, Newton, 'Melville and the Gothic Novel', *New England Quarterly*, 22 (1949), 33–48.

Baker, Ernest A., *The History of the English Novel*, 10 vols. New York: Barnes and Noble, 1967. (First published 1929.)

Beatty, Richmond Croom, *Bayard Taylor: Laureate of the Gilded Age*. Norman: University of Oklahoma Press, 1936.

Beaty, Frederick L., 'Mrs Radcliffe's fading gleam', *Philological Quarterly*, 42 (January 1963), 126–9.

Bell, H. T. Mackenzie, *Christina Rossetti: A Biographical and Critical Study*. Hurst and Blackett, 1898.

Benedict, Barbara M., 'Pictures of conformity: sentiment and structure in Ann Radcliffe's style', *Philological Quarterly*, 68 (3) (Summer 1989), 363–77.

Birkhead, Edith, *The Tale of Terror: A Study of the Gothic Romance*. Constable, 1921.

Black, Robert K., *The Sadleir–Black Gothic Collection*. Charlottesville: University of Virginia Library, 1949.

Blakey, Dorothy, *The Minerva Press 1790–1820*. Bibliographical Society, 1939.

Bowles, W. L., *A Wiltshire Parson and His Friends: The Correspondence of William Lisle Bowles, Together with Four Hitherto Unidentified Reviews by Coleridge*, edited by Garland Greever. Constable, 1926.

Breen, Jennifer (ed.), *Women Romantic Poets 1785–1832: An Anthology*. J. M. Dent, Everyman's Library, 1992.

Broadwell, Elizabeth P., 'The veil image in Ann Radcliffe's *The Italian*', *South Atlantic Bulletin*, 40 (4) (November 1975), 76–87.

Buck, Claire (ed.), *Bloomsbury Guide to Women's Literature*. Bloomsbury, 1992.

Butler, Marilyn, *Romantics, Rebels, and Reactionaries. English Literature and Its Background 1760–1830*. Oxford University Press, 1981.

Butler, Marilyn, 'The woman at the window: Ann Radcliffe in the novels of Mary Wollstonecraft and Jane Austen', *Women and Literature*, NS, 1 (1980), 128–48.

Buyers, Geoffrey, 'The influence of Schiller's drama and fiction upon English Literature in the period 1780–1830', *Englische Studien*, 48 (1914–15), 349–93.

Cadell, Thomas, *The Publishing Firm of Cadell & Davies: Select Correspondence and Accounts 1793–1836*, edited by Theodore Besterman. Humphrey Mitford; Oxford University Press, 1938.

Castle, Terry, *The Apparitional Lesbian: Female Homosexuality and Modern Culture*. New York: Columbia University Press, 1993.

Castle, Terry, 'The spectralization of the other in *The Mysteries of Udolpho*', in Felicity Nussbaum and Laura Brown (eds), *The New Eighteenth Century: Theory, Politics, English Literature*. New York: Methuen, 1987, pp. 231–53.

A Catalogue of All Graduates in . . . the University of Oxford. Oxford University Press, 1851.

Cates, William L. R., *A Dictionary of General Biography*. Longmans, Green, 1867.

Clery, E. J., 'The politics of the Gothic heroine in the 1790s', in Philip W. Martin and Robin Jarvis (eds), *Reviewing Romanticism*. Macmillan, 1992, 69–85.

Coolidge, Archibald C., jun., 'Charles Dickens and Mrs Radcliffe: a farewell to Wilkie Collins', *The Dickensian*, 58 (May 1962), 112–16.

Cottom, Daniel, *The Civilized Imagination. A Study of Ann Radcliffe, Jane Austen and Sir Walter Scott*. Cambridge: Cambridge University Press, 1985.

Cruse, Amy, *The Englishman and His Books in the Early Nineteenth Century*. George G. Harrap, 1930.

Davie, Donald, *Essays in Dissent: Church, Chapel, and the Unitarian Conspiracy*. Manchester: Carcanet, 1995.

DeLamotte, Eugenia C., *Perils of the Night: A Feminist Study of Nineteenth-Century Gothic*. New York and Oxford: Oxford University Press, 1990.

Dictionary of National Biography, edited by Sidney Lee. Smith, Elder, 1885–1900.

Donoghue, Emma, *Passions between Women: British Lesbian Culture 1668–1801*. Scarlet Press, 1993.

Doody, Margaret Anne, 'Deserts, ruins and troubled waters: female dreams in fiction and the development of the Gothic novel', *Genre*, 10 (Winter 1977), 529–72.

Doyle, William, *The Oxford History of the French Revolution*. Oxford: Clarendon Press, 1989.

Ellis, Stewart M., 'Ann Radcliffe and her literary influence', *Contemporary Review* (London) 123 (February 1923), 188–97.

Encyclopaedia Britannica. 11th edn., 1910–11. 'Ann Radcliffe', vol. 20, pp. 783–4.

Encyclopedia of Literature and Criticism. Routledge, 1990.

Erdman, David, 'Immoral acts of a library cormorant. The extent of Coleridge's contributions to the *Critical Review*', *Bulletin of the New York Public Library*, 63 (September–November 1959), 433–54, 515–30, 575–87.

Faderman, Lillian (ed.), *Chloe Plus Olivia: An Anthology of Lesbian Literature from the Seventeenth Century to the Present*. Viking Penguin, 1994.

Farrand, Margaret L., '*Udolpho* and *Childe Harold*', *Modern Language Notes*, 45 (April 1930), 220–1.

Fawcett, Mary Laughlin, '*Udolpho*'s primal mystery', *Studies in English Literature 1500–1900*, 23 (3) (Summer 1982), 481–94.

Fevre-Deumier, Jules Le, *Célébrités anglaises*. Paris: Librairie de Fermin-Didot, 1895.

Finley, Ruth E., *The Lady of Godey's: Sarah Josepha Hale*. Philadelphia and London: J. B. Lippincott, 1931.

Fleenor, Julian E. (ed.), *The Female Gothic*. Montreal: Eden Press, 1983.

Forsyth, William, *The Novels and Novelists of the Eighteenth Century: An Illustration of the Manners and Morals of the Age*. John Murray, 1871.

Foster, Joseph (ed.), *Alumni Oxonienses*. Nendeln, Liechtenstein: Kraus Reprint, 1968.

Foucault, Michel, *Madness and Civilization: A History of Insanity in the Age of Reason*, translated by Richard Howard. London, Sydney, Wellington: Tavistock, 1967.

Frank, Frederick S., *The First Gothics: A Critical Guide to the English Gothic Novel*. New York and London: Garland, 1987.

Frank, Frederick S., *Gothic Fiction: A Master List of Twentieth-Century Criticism and Research*. Westport, CT: Meckler, 1988.

Frank, Frederick S., *Guide to the Gothic: An Annotated Bibliography of Criticism*. Metuchen, NJ and London: Scarecrow Press, 1984.

G. E. C., *The Complete Peerage*, 13 vols. St Catherine Press, 1910–40.

G. W. M., *Memoirs of Mrs Jebb*. London, 1812.

Garner, Shirley Nelson, Claire Kahane and Madelon Sprengnether (eds), *The (M)other Tongue: Essays in Feminist Psychoanalytic Interpretation*. Ithaca, NY, and London: Cornell University Press, 1985.

Garnett, Richard, 'Ann Radcliffe', *Dictionary of National Biography*, edited by Sidney Lee, vol. 47 (1896), pp. 120–1.

Garrett, John, *Gothic Strains and Bourgeois Sentiments in the Novels of Mrs Ann Radcliffe and Her Imitators*. New York: Arno Press, 1980.

Garrow, David, *The History of Lymington and its Immediate Vicinity*. Simpkin and Marshall, 1825.

Gascoigne, John, 'Anglican latitudinarianism, Rational Dissent and political radicalism in the late eighteenth century', in Knud Haakonssen (ed.), *Enlightenment and Religion*. Cambridge: Cambridge University Press, 1996, 219–40.

Gilbert, Sandra M. and Susan Gubar, *The Madwoman in the Attic: The Woman Writer and the Nineteenth-Century Literary Imagination*. New Haven, CT, and London: Yale University Press, 1979.

Graham, Kenneth W. (ed.), *Gothic Fictions: Prohibition/Transgression*. New York: AMS Press, 1989.

Grant, Aline, *Ann Radcliffe: A Biography*. Denver, Colo.: Alan Swallow, 1951.

Greenfield, Susan C., 'Veiled desire: mother-daughter love and sexual imagery in Ann Radcliffe's *The Italian*', in Deborah D. Rogers (ed.), *The Critical Response to Ann Radcliffe*. Westport, CT, and London: Greenwood Press, 1994.

Grieder, Josephe, 'The prose fiction of Baculard D'Arnaud in late eighteenth-century England', *French Studies*, 24 (April 1970), 113–26.

Haakonssen, Knud (ed.), *Enlightenment and Religion: Rational Dissent in Eighteenth-Century Britain*. Cambridge: Cambridge University Press, 1996.

Haggerty, George E., 'Sensibility and sexuality in *The Romance of the Forest*', in Deborah D. Rogers (ed.), *The Critical Response to Ann Radcliffe*. Westport, CT, and London: Greenwood Press, 1994.

Haig, Robert L., 'The last years of the *Gazetteer*', *The Library*, 5th series, 7 (4) (December 1952), 242–61.

Havlice, Patricia Pate, *And So to Bed: A Bibliography of Diaries Published in English*. Metuchen and London: Scarecrow Press, 1987.

Hennessy, Brendan, *The Gothic Novel*. Writers and Their Work. Longman, 1978.

Hilbish, Florence May Anna, *Charlotte Smith, Poet and Novelist (1749–1806)*. Philadelphia: University of Pennsylvania, 1941.

Hipple, Walter John, jun., *The Beautiful, the Sublime, & the Picturesque in Eighteenth-Century British Aesthetic Theory*. Carbondale: Southern Illinois University Press, 1957.

Horner, Joyce M., 'The English women novelists and their connection with the feminist movement (1688–1797)', *Smith College Studies in Modern Languages*, 11 (1–3) (October 1929; January and April 1930), 1–152.

Howard, Jacqueline, *Reading Gothic Fiction: A Bakhtinian Approach*. Oxford: Clarendon Press, 1994.

Howells, Coral Ann, *Love, Mystery and Misery: Feeling in Gothic Fiction*. Athlone Press, 1978.

Hughes, A. M. D., *The Nascent Mind of Shelley*. Oxford: Clarendon Press, 1947.

Ingram, Allan, *The Madhouse of Language: Writing and Reading Madness in the Eighteenth Century*. London and New York: Routledge, 1991.

Jack, Ian, *English Literature 1815–1832*. Oxford History of English Literature. Oxford: Clarendon Press, 1963.

Jackson, J. R. de J., *Annals of English Verse 1770–1835*. New York and London: Garland Publishing, 1985.

Jarrett, David, 'A source for Keats's magic casements', *Notes and Queries*, NS, 26 (June 1979), 232–5.

Jeaffreson, J. Cordy, *Novels and Novelists, from Elizabeth to Victoria*, 2 vols. Hurst and Blackett, 1858.

Jeune, Simon, 'Autour de *L'Abbesse de Castro*', *Travaux de Linguistique et de Littérature* (Université de Strasbourg), 10 (2) (1972), 99–111.

Jewitt, Llewellynn, *The Wedgwoods*. 1865.

Kahane, Claire, 'Gothic mirrors and feminine identity', *Centennial Review*, 24 (1) (Winter 1980), 43–64.

Kavanagh, Julia, *English Women of Letters: Biographical Sketches*, vol. 622 in Tauchnitz British Authors. Bernhard Tauchnitz, 1862.

Kiely, Robert, *The Romantic Novel in England*. Cambridge, MA: Harvard University Press, 1972.

Killen, Alice M., *Le Roman terrifant ou roman noir de Walpole à Ann Radcliffe et son influence sur la littérature française jusqu'en 1840*. Paris: Librairie Ancienne Edouard Champion, 1923.

Kunitz, Stanley J. and Howard Haycraft, *British Authors of the Nineteenth Century*. New York: Wilson, 1936.

Lèvy, Maurice, *Le Roman 'gothique' anglais 1764–1824*. Toulouse: Association des publications de la faculté des lettres et sciences humaines de Toulouse [1968].

Lévy, Maurice, 'Une nouvelle source d'Anne Radcliffe: les mémoires du Comte de Comminge', *Caliban*, 1 (1964), 149–56.

Lonsdale, Roger (ed.), *Eighteenth-Century Women Poets: An Oxford Anthology*. Oxford and New York: Oxford University Press, 1990.

Low, Donald A., *That Sunny Dome: A Portrait of Regency Britain*. J. M. Dent and Sons, 1977.

Lundblad, Jane, *Nathaniel Hawthorne and the Tradition of Gothic Romance*. Studio Neophilologica, 19 (1946/47), 1–92.

MacAndrew, Elizabeth, *The Gothic Tradition in Fiction*. New York: Columbia University Press, 1979.

MacCarthy, Bridget G., *The Female Pen: The Later Women Novelists 1744–1818*. Cork: Cork University Press; Oxford: Blackwell, 1947.

McGann, Jerome J. (ed.), *The New Oxford Book of Romantic Period Verse*. Oxford and New York: Oxford University Press, 1994.

McIntyre, Clara Frances, *Ann Radcliffe in Relation to Her Time*. Yale Studies in English, No. 62. New Haven, CT: Yale University Press, 1920.

McIntyre, Clara F., 'Were the "Gothic Novels" Gothic?', *PMLA*, 36 (1921), 644–67.

McKillop, Alan Dugald, 'Charlotte Smith's letters', *Huntington Library Quarterly*, 15 (1951–2), 237–55.

McNutt, Dan J., *The Eighteenth-Century Gothic Novel: An Annotated Bibliography of Criticism and Selected Texts*, foreword by Devendra Varma and Maurice Lévy. New York: Garland; Folkestone, Kent: Dawson, 1975.

Manley, Seon, and Gogo Lewis (eds), *Ladies of the Gothics: Tales of Romance and Terror by the Gentle Sex*. New York: Lothrop, Lee and Shepard, a division of William Morrow, 1975.

Marshall, Roderick, *Italy in English Literature 1755–1815. Origins of the Romantic Interest in Italy*. New York: Columbia University Press, 1934.

Masson, David, *British Novelists and Their Styles*. Cambridge and London: Macmillan, 1859.

Matthews, William (compiler), *British Diaries: An Annotated Bibliography of British Diaries Written between 1442 and 1942*. Berkeley and Los Angeles: University of California Press; London: Cambridge University Press, 1950.

Maunder, Samuel, *The Biographical Treasury*, 13th edn. London, 1866.

Mavor, Elizabeth, *The Ladies of Llangollen*. Michael Joseph, 1971.

Maxted, Ian, *The London Book Trades 1775–1800*. Folkestone, Kent: Dawson, 1977.

Mayo, Robert D., 'Ann Radcliffe and Ducray-Duminil', *Modern Language Review*, 36 (October 1941), 501–5.

Mayo, Robert D., *The English Novel in the Magazines 1740–1815*. Evanston: Northwestern University Press; London: Oxford University Press, 1962.

Medwin, Thomas, *The Life of Percy Bysshe Shelley*. Oxford University Press, 1913.

Meehan, John Francis, *The Famous Houses of Bath and District*. Bath, Avon: B. and J. F. Meehan, 1901.

Meehan, John Francis, *Famous Houses of Bath and their Occupants*. Bath [1897].

Mellor, Anne K., *Romanticism & Gender*. New York and London: Routledge, 1993.

Meteyard, Eliza, *A Group of Englishmen*. Longmans, Green, 1871.

Meteyard, Eliza, *The Life of Josiah Wedgwood*, 2 vols. London, 1865.

Michaud, *Biographie Universelle*. Paris, n.d.

Micks, R. H., *Essentials of Materia Medica Pharmacology and Therapaeutics*. Churchill, 1950.

Miles, Robert, *Ann Radcliffe: The Great Enchantress*. Manchester and New York: Manchester University Press, 1995.

Miles, Robert, *Gothic Writing 1750–1820*. London and New York: Routledge, 1993.

Miller, Samuel, *A Brief Retrospect of the Eighteenth Century*, 2 vols. New York, 1803.

Mise, Raymond W., *The Gothic Heroine and the Nature of the Gothic Novel*. New York: Arno Press, 1980.

Moers, Ellen, *Literary Women*. New York: Doubleday, 1976.

Moir, David Macbeth, *Sketches of the Poetical Literature of the Past Half-Century*. Edinburgh and London: William Blackwood, 1851.

Moir, George, 'Romance', *Encyclopaedia Britannica*, 7th edn., vol. 19 (1842), pp. 318–59.

Monk, Samuel H., *The Sublime: A Study of Critical Theories in XVIII-Century England*. New York: Modern Language Association of America, 1935.

Moorman, Mary, *William Wordsworth: A Biography*, 2 vols. Oxford: Clarendon Press, 1957, 1965.

Murphy, John V., *The Dark Angel: Gothic Elements in Shelley's Works*. Lewisburg, PA: Bucknell University Press; London: Associated University Presses, 1975.

Murray, E. B., *Ann Radcliffe*. New York: Twayne, 1972.

Napier, Elizabeth R., 'Ann Radcliffe', *Dictionary of Literary Biography, Vol. 39: British Novelists, 1660–1800, Part 2: M-Z*, ed. Martin C. Battestin. Detroit: Gale Research, 1985, pp. 365–71.

Napier, Elizabeth R., *The Failure of Gothic: Problems of Disjunction in an Eighteenth-Century Literary Form*. Oxford: Clarendon Press, 1987.

The New Cambridge Bibliography of English Literature, ed. George Watson, 5 vols. Cambridge: Cambridge University Press, 1969–77.

Newdick, Robert S., *The First 'Life and Letters' of Charles Lamb: A Study of Thomas Noon Talfourd as Editor and Biographer*. Columbus: Ohio State University, 1935.

Norton, Rictor, 'Aesthetic Gothic horror', *Yearbook of Comparative and General Literature*, 21 (1972), 31–40.

Norton, Rictor, *Mother Clap's Molly House: The Gay Subculture in England 1700–1830*. GMP Publishers, 1992.

Norton, Rictor, *The Myth of the Modern Homosexual*. Cassell, 1997.

Noyes, Russell (ed.), *English Romantic Poetry and Prose*. New York: Oxford University Press, 1956.

O'Brien, P., *Warrington Academy 1757–86: Its Predecessors and Successors*. Wigan, Lancashire: Owl Books, 1989.

Paglia, Camille, *Sexual Personae*. New Haven, CT: Yale University Press, 1990.

Pappageorge, Julia Di Stefano, 'Coleridge's "Mad Lutanist": a Romantic response to Ann Radcliffe', *Bulletin of Research in the Humanities*, 82 (Summer 1979), 222–35.

Parks, Stephen (ed.), *Sale Catalogues of Libraries of Eminent Persons*, 12 vols. Mansell and Sotheby Parke Bernet, 1972.

Patterson, Charles L., 'The authenticity of Coleridge's reviews of Gothic romances', *Journal of English and Germanic Philology*, 50 (4) (October 1951), 517–21.

Peck, Louis F., *A Life of Matthew G. Lewis*. Cambridge, MA: Harvard University Press, 1961.

Peck, Walter E., 'Keats, Shelley, and Mrs Radcliffe', *Modern Language Notes*, 39 (4) (April 1924), 251–2.

Pendleton, John and William Jacques, *Modern Chesterfield*. Chesterfield: Derbyshire Courier, 1903.

Poovey, Mary, 'Ideology and "The Mysteries of Udolpho"', *Criticism*, 21 (4) (Autumn 1979), 307–30.

Poovey, Mary, *The Proper Lady and the Woman Writer: Ideology as Style in the Works of Mary Wollstonecraft, Mary Shelley, and Jane Austen*. Chicago and London: University of Chicago Press, 1984.

Praz, Mario, *The Romantic Agony*, translated by Angus Davidson. Oxford: Oxford University Press, 1933; Cleveland and New York: Meridian Books, 1956.

Price, F. W., 'Ann Radcliffe, Mrs Siddons and the character of Hamlet', *Notes and Queries*, NS, 23 (4) (April 1976), 164–7.

Punter, David, *The Literature of Terror: A History of Gothic Fictions from 1765 to the Present Day*. London and New York: Longman, 1980.

Punter, David, *The Romantic Unconscious: A Study in Narcissism and Patriarchy*. New York, London, etc.: Harvester Wheatsheaf, 1989.

Quérard, J.-M., *Les Supercheries littéraires dévoilées*, 3 vols. Paris: Paul Daffis, 1869–70.

Railo, Eino, *The Haunted Castle: A Study of the Elements of English Romanticism*. London: George Routledge and Sons; New York: E. P. Dutton, 1927.

Registrum Orielense; An Account of the Members of Oriel College, Oxford, 2 vols, collected by Charles Lancelot Shadwell. Henry Frowde, 1902.

Reno, Robert Princeton, *The Gothic Visions of Ann Radcliffe and Matthew G. Lewis*. New York: Arno Press, 1980.

Rogers, Deborah D., *Ann Radcliffe: A Bio-Bibliography*. Westport, CI, and London: Greenwood Press, 1996.

Rogers, Deborah D. (ed.), *The Critical Response to Ann Radcliffe*. Westport, CT, and London: Greenwood Press, 1994.

Ronald, Ann, *Functions of Setting in the Novel: From Mrs Radcliffe to Charles Dickens*. New York: Arno Press, 1980.

Roper, Derek, 'Coleridge, Dyer, and *The Mysteries of Udolpho*', *Notes and Queries*, NS, 19 (August 1972), 287–9.

Ross, Deborah, *The Excellence of Falsehood: Romance, Realism, and Women's Contribution to the Novel*. Lexington: University Press of Kentucky, 1992.

Rossetti, Christina, *The Family Letters of Christina Georgina Rossetti*, edited by William Michael Rossetti. Brown, Langham, 1908.

Rowton, Frederic, *The Female Poets of Great Britain*. Longman, Brown, Green and Longmans, 1848.

Ruff, William, 'Ann Radcliffe, or, the hand of taste', in *The Age of Johnson*, Essays Presented to Chauncey Brewster Tinker. New Haven and London: Yale University Press, 1949, pp. 183–93.

Sadleir, Michael, '"All horrid?" Jane Austen and the Gothic Romance', in *Things Past*. Constable, 1944, pp. 167–200.

Sadleir, Michael, *The Northanger Novels: A Footnote to Jane Austen*, English Association Pamphlet No. 68. (Oxford, 1927).

Sadleir, Michael, 'Poems by Ann Radcliffe', *Times Literary Supplement*, 29 March 1928, p. 242.

Sage, Victor (ed.), *The Gothick Novel*, Casebook Series. Macmillan Education, 1990.

Sage, Victor, *Horror Fiction in the Protestant Tradition*. Macmillan, 1988.

Schlueter, Paul and June Schlueter (eds), *An Encyclopedia of British Women Writers*. Chicago and London: St James's Press, 1988.

Scott, Walter S., *The Bluestocking Ladies*. John Green, 1947.

Sedgwick, Eve Kosofsky, 'The character in the veil: imagery of the surface in the Gothic novel', *PMLA*, 96 (2) (March 1981), 255–70.

Shackford, Martha Hale, '*The Eve of St Agnes* and *The Mysteries of Udolpho*', *PMLA*, 36 (March 1921), 104–18.

Showalter, Elaine, *The Female Malady: Women, Madness and English Culture, 1830–1980*. Virago, 1987.

Showalter, Elaine (ed.), *The New Feminist Criticism*. Virago, 1986.

Skarda, Patricia L. and Nora Crow Jaffe (eds), *The Evil Image: Two Centuries of Gothic Short Fiction and Poetry*. New York and London: New American Library, 1981.

Smith, R. Gordon, 'The Oates family of Pontefract' (and 'Horncastle family'), *Notes & Queries*, Series 13, 1 (29 September 1923), 247–8, 387–9, 428.

Smith, Warren Hunting, *Architecture in English Fiction*. New Haven, CT: Yale University Press; London: Humphrey Milford; Oxford University Press, 1934.

Spacks, Patricia Meyer, *Imagining a Self: Autobiography and Novel in Eighteenth-Century England*. Cambridge, MA, and London: Harvard University Press, 1976.

Spector, Robert Donald, *The English Gothic: A Bibliographic Guide to Writers from Horace Walpole to Mary Shelley*. Westport, CT, and London: Greenwood Press, 1984.

Spencer, Jane, *The Rise of the Woman Novelist: From Aphra Behn to Jane Austen*. Oxford and New York: Blackwell, 1986.

Spender, Dale, *Mothers of the Novel: 100 Good Women Writers before Jane Austen*. London and New York: Pandora, 1986.

Sullivan, Alvin (ed.), *British Literary Magazines. The Romantic Age, 1789–1836*. Westport, CT, and London: Greenwood Press, 1983.

Summers, Montague, 'A great mistress of romance: Ann Radcliffe, 1764–1823', in *Essays in Petto* (Fortune Press [1928]), 3–29.

Summers, Montague, *A Gothic Bibliography*. London: Fortune, 1941; New York: Russell and Russell, 1964.

Summers, Montague, *The Gothic Quest*. Fortune Press, 1938.

Swigart, Ford Harris jun., *A Study of the Imagery in the Gothic Romances of Ann Radcliffe*. New York: Arno Press, 1980.

Switzer, Richard, *Etienne-Léon de Lamothe-Langon et le roman populaire français de 1800 à 1830*. Toulouse: Edouard Privat, 1962.

Sypher, Wylie, 'Social ambiguity in the Gothic novel', *Partisan Review*, 12 (1) (1945), 50–60.

Thompson, G. R. (ed.), *The Gothic Imagination: Essays in Dark Romanticism*. Pullman: Washington State University Press, 1974.

Thompson, L. F., 'Ann Radcliffe's knowledge of German', *Modern Language Review*, 20 (April 1925), 190–1.

Thomson, John, 'Ann Radcliffe's use of Philippus van Limborch's *The History of the Inquisition*', *English Language Notes*, 18 (September 1980), 31–3.

Timpane, John, 'Ann Ward Radcliffe', in Paul Schlueter and June Schlueter (eds), *An Encyclopedia of British Women Writers*. Chicago and London: St James's Press, 1988, pp. 373–4.

Todd, Janet (ed.), *A Dictionary of British and American Women Writers 1660–1800*. Methuen, 1984.

Todd, Janet (ed.), *Dictionary of British Women Writers*. Routledge, 1991. (First published in 1989.)

Todd, Janet, 'Posture and imposture: the Gothic manservant in Ann Radcliffe's *The Italian*', *Women & Literature*, 2 (1982), 25–38.

Todd, Janet, *The Sign of Angellica: Women, Writing and Fiction, 1660–1800*. Virago, 1989.

Todd, William B. (compiler), *A Directory of Printers*. Printing Historical Society, 1972.

Tompkins, J. M. S., *The Popular Novel in England 1770–1800*. Constable, 1932.

Tompkins, J. M. S., 'Ramond de Carbonnières, Grosley and Mrs Radcliffe', *Review of English Studies*, 5 (July 1929), 294–301.

Tracy, Ann B., *The Gothic Novel 1790–1830. Plot Summaries and Index to Motifs*. Lexington: University of Kentucky Press, 1981.

Tuttle, Donald Renel, '*Christabel* sources in Percy's *Reliques* and the Gothic romance', *Publications of the Modern Language Association*, 53 (June 1938), 445–74.

Ty, Eleanor, *Unsex'd Revolutionaries: Five Women Novelists of the 1790s*. Toronto: University of Toronto Press, 1993.

Van Luchene, Stephen Robert, *Essays in Gothic Fiction: from Horace Walpole to Mary Shelley*. New York: Arno Press, 1980.

Varma, Devendra P., *The Gothic Flame*. Arthur Barker, 1957.

Vavlice, Patricia Pate, *Index to Literary Biography*, 2 vols. Metuchen: Scarecrow Press, 1975. Two-volume Supplement, 1983.

Ward, A. W. and A. R. Waller (eds), *The Cambridge History of English Literature*, 14 vols. Cambridge: Cambridge University Press, 1907–16.

Ware, Malcolm, *Sublimity in the Novels of Ann Radcliffe: a Study of the Influence upon Her Craft of Edmund Burke's 'Enquiry into the Origin of Our Ideas of the Sublime and Beautiful'*. Essays and Studies on English Language and Literature, No. 25. English Institute, Upsala University. Upsala: Lundequistska, 1963.

Watt, William W., *Shilling Shockers of the Gothic School: A Study of Chapbook Gothic Romances*. Cambridge, MA: Harvard University Press, 1932.

Watts, Michael R., *The Dissenters*, 2 vols. Oxford: Clarendon Press, 1978, 1995.

Webb, R. K., 'The emergence of Rational Dissent', in Knud Haakonssen (ed.), *Enlightenment and Religion*. Cambridge: Cambridge University Press, 1996, 12–41.

Wedgwood, Frances Julia, *The Personal Life of Josiah Wedgwood*, revised and edited by C. H. Herford. Macmillan, 1915.

Wieten, Alida Alberdina Sibbellina, *Mrs Radcliffe – Her Relation towards Romanticism*. Amsterdam: H. J. Paris, 1926.

Williamson, George C., *The Imperial Russian Dinner Service*. George Bell and Sons, 1909.

Wolff, Cynthia Griffin, 'The Radcliffean Gothic model: a form for feminine sexuality', *Modern Language Studies*, 9 (3) (Autumn 1979), 98–113.

Wolstenholme, Susan, *Gothic (Re)Visions: Writing Women as Readers*. Albany: State University of New York Press, 1993.

Wright, Eugene Patrick (compiler), *A Catalogue of the Joanna Southcott Collection at the University of Texas*. Austin: University of Texas at Austin, 1968.

Wright, Eugene P., 'A divine analysis of *The Romance of the Forest*', *Discourse*, 13 (3) (Summer 1970), 379–87.

Wykes, David L., 'The contribution of the Dissenting academy to the emergence of Rational Dissent', in Knud Haakonssen (ed.), *Enlightenment and Religion*. Cambridge: Cambridge University Press, 1996, pp. 99–139.

[Yonge, Charlotte M. (ed.)], *Biographies of Good Women*. J. and C. Mozley; Masters, 1862. 2nd series, 1865.

Index